After Engulfment

The Hippocampus Press Library of Criticism

S. T. Joshi, *Primal Sources: Essays on H. P. Lovecraft* (2003)
S. T. Joshi, *The Evolution of the Weird Tale* (2004)
Robert H. Waugh, *The Monster in the Mirror: Looking for H. P. Lovecraft* (2006)
Scott Connors, ed., *The Freedom of Fantastic Things: Selected Criticism on Clark Ashton Smith* (2006)
Ben Szumskyj, ed., *Two-Gun Bob: A Centennial Study of Robert E. Howard* (2006)
S. T. Joshi and Rosemary Pardoe, ed., *Warnings to the Curious: A Sheaf of Criticism on M. R. James* (2007)
S. T. Joshi, *Classics and Contemporaries: Some Notes on Horror Fiction* (2009)
Kenneth W. Faig, Jr., *The Unknown Lovecraft* (2009)
Massimo Berruti, *Dim-Remembered Stories: A Critical Study of R. H. Barlow* (2010)
Gary William Crawford, Jim Rockhill, and Brian J. Showers, ed., *Reflections in a Glass Darkly: Essays on J. Sheridan Le Fanu* (2011)
Robert H. Waugh, *A Monster of Voices: Speaking for H. P. Lovecraft* (2011)
Donald Sidney-Fryer, *The Golden State Phantasticks: The California Romantics and Related Subjects* (2012)
William F. Nolan, *Nolan on Bradbury: Sixty Years of Writing about the Master of Science Fiction* (2013)
Steven J. Mariconda, *H. P. Lovecraft: Art, Artifact, and Reality* (2013)
S. T. Joshi, *Unutterable Horror: A History of Supernatural Fiction* (2014)
Bobby Derie, *Sex and the Cthulhu Mythos* (2014)
S. T. Joshi, *Lovecraft and a World in Transition* (2014)
Massimo Berruti, S. T. Joshi, and Sam Gafford, ed., *William Hope Hodgson: Voices from the Borderland* (2014)
S. T. Joshi, *The Rise, Fall, and Rise of the Cthulhu Mythos* (2015)
Donald R. Burleson, *Lovecraft–An American Allegory* (2015)
Kenneth W. Faig, Jr., *Lovecraftian Voyages* (2017)
Robert H. Waugh, *The Tragic Thread in Science Fiction: Essays on David Lindsay, Olaf Stapledon, et al.* (2019)
Bobby Derie, *Weird Talers: Essays on Robert E. Howard and Others* (2019)
Charles Hoffman and Marc Cerasini, *Robert E. Howard: A Closer Look* (2020)
Robert H. Waugh, *A Monster for Many: Talking with H. P. Lovecraft* (2021)
Kenneth W. Faig, Jr., *Lovecraftian People and Places* (2022)
Arthur S. Koki, *H. P. Lovecraft: An Introduction to His Life and Writings* (2022)
Lovecraft Annual (2007–)
Dead Reckonings (2007–)

Ellen J. Greenham

After Engulfment

Cosmicism and Neocosmicism in
H. P. Lovecraft, Philip K. Dick,
Robert A. Heinlein, and Frank Herbert

Hippocampus Press

New York

After Engulfment copyright © 2022 by Ellen J. Greenham.
This edition copyright © 2022 by Hippocampus Press.

Published by Hippocampus Press
P.O. Box 641, New York, NY 10156.
www.hippocampuspress.com

All rights reserved.
No part of this work may be reproduced in any form or by any means without the written permission of the publisher.

Cover © 2022 by Dan Sauer, dansauerdesign.com
Hippocampus Press logo designed by Anastasia Damianakos.

First Edition
1 3 5 7 9 8 6 4 2
ISBN: 978-1-61498-377-4 (paperback)
ISBN: 978-1-61498-381-1 (ebook)

Contents

Introduction 7
Glossary of Terms.. 21
Abbreviations for Major Works 27
Part I: Universe... 29
   Chapter 1: Universe and Cosmos 31
   Chapter 2: Cosmologies 39
   Chapter 3: Fractured Universe 53
Part II: Cosmicism 67
   Chapter 4: Cosmicism Is 69
   Chapter 5: Schizophrenic Universe 79
   Chapter 6: Heimlich Universe 105
   Chapter 7: Frozen Universe.. 130
   Chapter 8: Perihelion 169
Part III: Neocosmicism... 193
   Chapter 9: Neocosmicism Is...................................... 195
   Chapter 10: Aphelion 210
   Chapter 11: Psychotic Universe 235
   Chapter 12: Chimeras and Cannibals 263
   Chapter 13: The Romance of the Universe............... 280
Bibliography 301
Index 325

Introduction

What does it mean to be human in the *universe*? When the cosmological *maps* that have been used in the past no longer fit the *territory* they are meant to describe, how does the human creature navigate that territory? How does it know where and what it is? In the early twentieth century, weird fiction writer and essayist H. P. Lovecraft offered the human creature a view of the universe—a view however, through the lens of Lovecraft's *cosmicism*, that leads to an isolated end of madness or death. The development of *neocosmicism* offered in this text is an outgrowth of Lovecraft's cosmic philosophy and a response to the limiting options that cosmicism extends to the human creature. In its simplest terms, neocosmicism offers the human an experience that leads to the revitalisation of its relationship with the universe.

There are four core aims that this book endeavours to achieve and selected works by Philip K. Dick (1928-1982), Robert A. Heinlein (1902-1988), Frank Herbert (1920-1986), and H. P. Lovecraft (1890-1937) are used to exemplify these aims. The first is to demonstrate how science fiction interrogates the experience of being human in the universe, and the ways in which the human creature responds to the universe in which it exists and of which it is a part. Second, this book offers a critique of Lovecraft's philosophy of cosmicism and in doing so demonstrates the failure of static, cosmological models for enabling a direct relationship between the human creature and the universe, and between the human creature and *others* within the universe. Third, this book seeks to demonstrate the validity of cosmicism as a lens through which to critically interrogate not only Lovecraft's corpus, but science fiction more generally. Finally, and most critically as a development of theory based upon the first three aims, what follows in this text intends to extend but not replace Lovecraft's philosophy of cosmicism with what is herein called neocosmicism.

The central concern of neocosmicism is to provide a theoretical framework that, by taking into account the significant shift in the human creature's understanding of the universe from a Cartesian view to a quantum view, allows for a sense of existence in the universe that reaches far beyond the limiting parameters allowed by the dominant occidental cosmologies and the philosophy of cosmicism.

It is important to note at this juncture that given the vast field of enquiry implicit in any one of the aims herein stated, this text is not proposed as a comprehensive development of neocosmicism, but rather an introduction. In addition, this book is offered as neither an exhaustive study of the works of the primary authors whose texts are herein used nor an exhaustive critical enquiry of cosmicism. There is already a significant body of knowledge that addresses in detail each author and his works; and while cosmicism remains largely only employed in the direct critical enquiry of Lovecraft's corpus, a significant body of knowledge does exist that addresses how his philosophy manifests itself within his creative works. Identifying the value of cosmicism as a tool for the critical interrogation of science fiction is central to this book, and the limitation to the authors and texts to which concern is addressed in no way diminishes the argument for cosmicism's wider application.

In addition, the primary authors herein discussed have been chosen on the basis of authors and works that I as a reader enjoy and are not, as could be suggested, continuing a historical trend that has seen both the authorship and critical examination of science fiction to be skewed through a male-oriented perspective. Addressing issues of gender would be a useful addition to this work, but a gendered reading or critical analysis of creative text is not the focus of the argument here. While the usefulness of such lenses for interpretation and their implied presence within this book is readily acknowledged in this introductory statement, the overall coherence of the core argument is not dependent upon the theoretical positioning of gender, ethnicity, religion, or political persuasion. Furthermore, while the choice of authors for focused engagement is recognised as diverse in both their socio-historic contexts and their contemporaneous reckoning, and while they present their readers with significantly different writing voices, it is also noted that an extensive body of critical work that addresses these issues is well established. To engage in such discussions here—as to the changing perception of authors' relevance over time, or the nature and accomplishment of their writing styles—would be to replicate work that is not itself our central concern. The aim here is to demonstrate the presence of a holistic textural voice across science fiction's diversity rather than highlighting stylistic and perceptual fragmentations.

Although science fiction has entered the twenty-first century as a significant generative ground of critical scholarship, it appears that, until quite recently, this scholarship has suffered from a lingering reluctance to acknowledge Lovecraft's corpus and its far-reaching influence as worthwhile. This view is changing, and the impetus for the change initially emerged largely from within Lovecraftian scholarship itself.

In 1963, the American science fiction author Fritz Leiber claims that the science fiction community relegates Lovecraft's work to a "superstitious interpretation of reality," and follows this statement with the claim that Lovecraft produced a body of text that is anything but such an interpretation (Leiber et al. 15). The prevailing historical view may be that Lovecraft has not written science fiction, thereby making it easy to exclude him from the canon; but as the parameters that define science fiction have been shifting in recent years, an increasingly substantial argument can be made that his work is indeed firmly located in the canon. With the groundswell initiated by Leiber, scholars followed his lead and began considering Lovecraft in terms of science fiction. In 1972, the American science fiction critic and author Lin Carter claimed for Lovecraft that "his essential themes are more closely akin to science fiction—so closely that it might well be said that he indeed wrote science fiction" (xv); a quarter-century later, S. T. Joshi proclaimed *At the Mountains of Madness* and "The Shadow out of Time" as being "considered classics of science fiction" (*Subtler Magick* 263). It is worth pointing out that these two stories were first published in the science fiction magazine *Astounding Stories*; and another of Lovecraft's stories, "The Colour out of Space," was first published in *Amazing Stories*. During his own lifetime, Lovecraft's work was at least in part recognised as science fiction, and yet criticism until recently has been reluctant to categorise it as such. What has happened during this time to have changed the view from one of an ambiguous claim for the genre, to a definite statement of inclusion among its classics?

In 1978, Darrell Schweitzer noted in his summing up that "[v]irtually every major science fiction writer of the next generation was aware of [Lovecraft], and acknowledges his influence" (*Dream Quest* 61). S. T. Joshi iterates this perspective when he writes that "Lovecraft emphatically influenced such later writers of science fiction as John W. Campbell, Fritz Leiber, Philip K. Dick, Gene Wolfe, and many others" (*Subtler Magick* 265), and that "[i]t is only a seeming paradox that Lovecraft's influence on weird fiction is actually less significant that his influence on science fiction" (267).

The seeds of why this shift in perspective has gained momentum and established itself are clearly stated by the historian and critic of modern and contemporary literature, Roger Luckhurst, in chapter 3 of his cultural history text *Science Fiction* (2005). Luckhurst discusses not only the inherent hybridity of science fiction, but also the cultural and political circumstances from which it emerges and into which the pulp fiction phenomena of the United States establishes itself (64–65). With its evolution firmly, though by no means exclusively, rooted in the pulp magazine phenomena of the early twentieth century, science fiction developed prior to this time as a genre "interweaving with strands of Gothic, Realist, fantasy and utopian writing" (Luckhurst 11). Prior to Luckhurst, both Lin Carter (xv) and S. T. Joshi have also noted the hybridity that "link[s] the weird to science, and hence to science fiction" (*Subtler Magick* 49). In recognition of the shared cultural origins of the genres of science fiction and horror, the American author and editor Jason Colavito claims that "[e]ven science fiction concealed a quiet undercurrent of horror, often disguised under the name 'fantastic literature,' or later, 'the weird tale'" (13). What this all suggests is that criticism is better positioned now to retrospectively view and assess the development and emergent characteristics of science fiction. It has had, quite simply, time enough to evolve.

The history of science fiction can be read through a lens that reveals a sense of itself and its canon as something far more comprehensive than older definitions often place upon it; confines that are readily symbolised by the period of science fiction development that is marked by the progression from an exclusively pulp platform to a broader reach of varying media. This development is signified by what in the genre is often referred to as the Golden Age of science fiction (James and Mendlesohn

37, 50, 52, 65), a term that some critics and scholars parallel with the notion of "Campbellian science fiction" (99) and characterised, though not exclusively, by what is also termed "hard science fiction" (186-89).

By 2008, it was clearly and succinctly stated that Lovecraft wrote what can be described as "dark science-fiction" (Colavito 186), and his philosophical stance, herein called *cosmicism*, pervaded not only his own work, but also a significant portion of texts and ideas that are enshrined within the wider canon. However, *cosmicism* as a philosophy and theoretical tool for access into text remains somewhat elusive, leading to the question of why it is that *cosmicism* as a formalised philosophical lens persists with inhabiting a subterranean theoretical quietude.

In the case of what until recent years has been the general academic and critical reception of Lovecraft—that is, a predisposition for framing literature within the parameters of a particular standard of formal education and format of publication—the influence of a culturally driven elitism cannot be overstated. Like an echo of George Orwell's observation that "art is not the same thing as cerebration" (39), and Terry Eagleton's similar recognition of the shifting ground of ideologies that can inform "[w]hat counts as Literature," and that it is "the ideologies which constitute our very ability to recognise a text as a certain kind of text in the first place" ("Literature and Politics Now" 66), Michel Houellebecq arrives some sixty and thirty years after Orwell and Eagleton respectively to the same point of issue regarding critical value judgements and literary elitism when he notes:

> [R. E.] Howard, Lovecraft and Tolkien—three radically different universes. Three pillars of dream literature, as despised by critics as they are loved by the public. Who cares? In the end critics always recognise their mistakes; or, to be more exact, in the end critics die and are replaced by others. So, after thirty years of scornful silence, "intellectuals" decided to take an interest in Lovecraft. They concluded that as an individual he was endowed with a truly astonishing imagination (they did after all have to attribute his success to something) but that his style was abominable.
>
> That's a joke. If Lovecraft's style is deplorable, one might as well conclude style is inconsequential in literature; and then move on to some other subject. (87)

As Houellebecq identifies, Lovecraft's body of fiction is "loved by the public," or at least loved by a public that enjoys stories of a weird or speculative nature. The drivers behind the lack of critical recognition that has until the past two or so decades of scholarship been applied to Lovecraft's fiction can also be applied to the scope of his philosophy of *cosmicism*; and this is identifiably located within a wider cultural context that has also had a direct relationship with the development of the science fiction genre.

During his lifetime Lovecraft published exclusively in the pulp magazines, and this is perhaps the single biggest reason why it has taken so long for his works to gain broad acceptance as more than literary trash, and for him to be approached as a theorist toward whom serious attention should be given. Roger Luckhurst establishes the cultural circumstances in which the pulp magazines and the new forms of writing they engendered emerged, citing one of the first and highly influential drivers behind this as "the 1870 Education Act" in England "and the subsequent laws tightening the enforcement of compulsory education" (*Science Fiction* 17-18). Enmeshed within the growing commercial and industrial environment of mechanisation, this shift to enforced literacy through a government's legislation stimulates an emerging market that is hungry for an inexpensive and accessible resource of reading material. Luckhurst delivers his survey with a convincing argument for the importance of the rise of the pulp fiction market during the late nineteenth and early twentieth centuries and for the rationale as to why, even with an increasingly literate population, the literature of this market does not, and most probably cannot, penetrate the more lofty realm of the literary canon.

This is the cultural and critical environment in which Lovecraft has historically been located and, by consequence, so too has his philosophy. Such a perspective has, perhaps, made it easier for his ideas to be dismissed as not worth consideration, and this is, I believe, the single biggest reason why cosmicism has continued to operate very much below the metaphoric radar. Cosmicism, as a lens through which to view the universe, is not only clearly developed and expressed by Lovecraft, it resonates throughout the twentieth and most certainly into the twenty-first century in all its nuance and manifestations to influence a significant sector of the literary and creative arts; indeed, popular culture more broadly. As a formalised theory of influence and enquiry, cosmicism can be applied to a far greater body of work than the canon of Lovecraft alone, and it is an excellent tool for the analysis of science fiction texts in general.

It is perhaps fitting, then, to iterate Jason Colavito's statement that, while directed toward Lovecraft's positioning within the horror genre, also speaks to the contemporary view of his work and philosophy as fundamentally grounded within science fiction:

> H. P. Lovecraft was something of a prophet for modern horror. In 1996, the scholar S. T. Joshi published a new biography of Lovecraft, and in 2005 Lovecraft entered the Library of America, steadily growing in stature and in academic respectability. His bleak vision of amoral cosmic indifference fit perfectly with the tenor of the times. The events of the years surrounding the millennium have brought Lovecraft's vision to fruition; Cthulhu pointed the way toward the godless cosmos of science. (365)

The shift in formal recognition of Lovecraft's creative work and philosophical contribution has emerged in parallel with a postmodernist framework in which the primacy of "high" or "elite" culture has been irrevocably disrupted.

With Lovecraft as our foundation, we come to our other primary authors in this text, Philip K. Dick, Robert A. Heinlein, and Frank Herbert. All three of these authors are considered pioneers of science fiction in the twentieth century and reach into the twenty-first with enduring, if sometimes less than obvious, influence. Developing their creative ideologies and speculative visions in parallel with significant frontier developments in hard sciences such as physics and evolutionary biology and social sciences such as psychology and philosophy, there is a unity of sorts disseminated across the creative works of all three, even though the superficialities of those works may offer to us as readers an appearance of difference. In their extrapolative discourses on the nature of the universe and the human creature within it, these writers interrogate the precariousness and paradox that exist between the human's internal landscapes and the external realities in which they are enmeshed. While this may seem a perspective perhaps not so extraordinary to the twenty-first-century reader, for their time these writers were pioneers within the rise of modern science fiction over what constitutes little more than the past one hundred years.

While the roots of science fiction can arguably be traced back through recorded history to images of stars painted in caves and stories in mythic traditions, it is no accident that the modern genre has risen in parallel with significant changes wrought upon Western culture and Christian mythology during the twentieth century. Modernity's energising of philosophical enquiry into the state and purpose of being, coupled with new scientific theory and subsequent discovery, significantly in physics, has shattered much of what was long presumed of the world and the universe. The world we live in and the way we support it as a reality cannot now always be substantiated by 'fact' inasmuch as we can now explore space and time, past presumptions of how the universe was created and then held together no longer appear to always seem true.

The authors on whom this book turns its focus all say something fundamental about the human creature, about what it is that creature seeks, and what the possibilities for that creature as a sentient being may very well be in a universe of infinite possibility. The questions our authors of focus ask, through the process of redrawing the landscape upon which human consciousness operates, openly challenge many aspects of cultural assumption, human morality, and what it means to exist at all. Dick, Heinlein, and Herbert all disrupt implicit assumptions of our human and Western way of thinking about our place in the universe, indeed our behaviour in the universe, and they all dare in some way to rewrite our understanding of ourselves. While the landscapes in which this is done may vary, the driving questions for our authors remain nonetheless fundamentally the same. Deceptively simple, infinitely complex, these authors offer to us a unified signal beneath the noise. For them all, it is the question that asks how the *experience* of being human relates to the *consciousness* of being human in the post-quantum, indeed post-deity world.

Historically and largely, the selected authors have been reviewed, analysed, and criticised in isolation of one another. There appears, for example, to be a general sense that what has been written by Heinlein has no similarity to Dick, or that Dick's continual exploration of sanity, madness, and the intersection of parallel realities bears no reflection in the prescience of Herbert's characters Paul Atreides and Leto II. There appears to be no deep analysis of the similarities of Herbert's characters with Heinlein's character Lazarus Long, and certainly no exploration of how any of these ideas or characters may be comparable with the unreliable and often dangerous simulacras and mechanical ambiguities of Dick's worlds or Lovecraft's pantheon.

While the question of what it means to be human in the universe may seem obvious as a central concern for science fiction, I draw attention to this often unarticulated assumption as our authors' styles and storytelling are, in many respects, unique each to themselves as 'firsts' in the genre, and more than a cursory glance at their work might lead the reader to feel there is little in common at all between them.

During his lifetime Philip K. Dick remained an outlier; generally disregarded by the reading mainstream and literary scholarship but embraced by the counterculture and appreciated by the science fiction-reading audience as a brilliant if sometimes eccentric writer. In a manner similar to Lovecraft, Dick found a loyal reading audience attached to a consistently low-paying publishing machine. In the later years of his life and well into this century, ironically, significant praise, profit, and audience have taken a cultural ownership, so to speak, of Dick's work within reinterpretations of his corpus in the media of film and television. Dick's novel *Do Androids Dream of Electric Sheep?*, as it is offered in Ridley Scott's 1982 direction of *Blade Runner*, remains a seminal film in the science fiction genre, despite the ongoing spectrum of criticism for the film that runs from nearly-not-at-all what we find in Dick's text through to subtly and well done. The Emmy Award-winning Amazon Prime series of *The Man in the High Castle* (2015-19) mirrors the previous Hugo Award-winning success of Dick's novel of the same title, but is again 'loosely' based. What remains as a curious issue in translation of Dick's novels and short stories to the screen is a seeming ongoing need to 'loosely' translate stories that in and of themselves are complex, fascinating, and deft in their orations. A significantly good example of how far such translations ignore the really great elements of Dick's writings to create a film with the right kind of box-office appeal is the crossing from print to film of the short story "We Can Remember It for You Wholesale" to Arnold Schwarzenegger's high-impact box-office hit *Total Recall* (1990)—a film with a place in its own right in the science fiction genre, to be sure, but also a film that could have capitalised further if it remained true to some of the story's more salient details. Bringing the subtleties of Dick's view of the universe to the screen is more authentically evident in the lesser known *Screamers* (1995), an adaptation of the short story "Second Variety" that under the direction of Christian Duguay remains, to my mind, one of the best adaptations to screen of Dick's work.

As with Dick, so too has Robert A. Heinlein had his work translated for a film-going audience; the best-known perhaps being Paul Verhoeven's direction of *Starship Troopers* (1997), and perhaps the least-known being that of Michael Spierig's direction in 2014 of *Predestination*, an utterly underacknowledged and well-rendered adaptation of the short story "All You Zombies." Once dubbed the Dean of Science Fiction, an idea that has persisted with the whole spectrum of possible implications of this title for Heinlein and the genre more broadly, Heinlein writes from an often right-wing, colonial frontier mentality, and is now in the twenty-first century more frequently dismissed on the basis of promoting right-wing militarism and varying degrees of misogyny; the latter being problematic and far too simplistic in my view given the significantly complex, strong, and independent female characters who populate his works. Best known as the author of *Starship Troopers* (1959) and *Stranger in a Strange Land* (1961), Heinlein's corpus contains publications spanning six decades and dozens of novels, short stories, and essays. Like the frontier grandeur of his settings, Heinlein asks big questions and tackles the idea of eternity; confronting us with uncomfortable considerations of meaning and purpose for the human creature, if indeed eternity or immortality are achievable, and forcing the reader to ask along with his characters if it is possible to become bored with it all. Central to Heinlein's work are speculations around the operation of time and around how it is that humanity actually uses its time. Heinlein offers to readers explorations of personal responsibility and taking charge of one's own self and future; of being at the metaphoric helm, though not necessarily in control. Often solipsistic in their philosophical underpinnings, his narratives present human creatures engaged with trying to make sense of the discrepancies and differences they encounter in themselves, one another, and more pointedly in the way the universe works, all the while trying to strike some kind of balance between paradoxes.

While Heinlein has been, perhaps wrongly, easy to dismiss as a historical curiosity of sorts, a founding father of twentieth-century science fiction in all its glory and its dubious political incorrectness, Frank Herbert seems to have been relegated to history and resurrected more than once as the author of a single and great novel called *Dune,* an epic that deals with planetary ecology and human politics. This view has a tendency to emerge in exclusion of considering the even greater depths and harder lessons explored in his subsequent five novels of the *Dune* universe, which offer a sustained and challenging discussion of the human creature in a universe unbound by time.

Just as J. R. R. Tolkien is often cited as the first world-builder in the realm of fantasy, so it is with Herbert in the realm of science fiction. But the *Dune* series is far more than brilliant world-building or a thoughtful ecological first in the genre of the novel. The *Dune* series explores the question of being human in the universe with an eye to examining where we may be led as consequence of the ways we manipulate what we are, what strengthens and what destroys. Herbert asks vital questions about human purpose, exploring the creation of not only the idea of the martyr but of the god himself. While the idea of the sacrificed god for the atonement of others is readily identified in one form or other in the narratives of all the writers under examination here, in Herbert's work we are discomfited by difficult questions in the troublesome territory of deliberate interference in genetic lines, cloning, and manipulations to create non-human humans. What are the ramifications of bringing back the dead and where does memory reside? Herbert holds the mirror up to humanity's propensity for perpetuating cycles of behaviour and the reasons why this in itself may be enough to be hold humanity back from evolving to what it could become. Stepping beyond all this, Herbert asks his reader to re-examine the idea of a necessity for tyrants and societal control as part of a larger human interaction with itself, and he questions constantly the moralities of the way the human universe operates. In Herbert, we find a constant push to expand and explore human consciousness in its endeavour to locate that which is transcendent. Interestingly, in this new century we are poised to see a resurgence of interest in Herbert's work with Denis Villeneuve's new cinematic vision of *Dune,* released in 2021. The question begs to be asked, however: what of the other five books that expand the discourse?

The discussion that follows this introduction, then, can be located broadly within the remit of postmodernity, and therefore seeks to provide a framework that opens a critical space for exploring alternatives to some of modernity's more vexing human questions rather than just reactions or polarising oppositions. The hope embedded within the development of neocosmicism is for the provision of a theoretical apparatus that is complementary to the array of tools already available for the critical interrogation of texts, science fiction specifically, but also other forms of expression that explore the human creature's experience of the universe in which it exists.

The methodology here employed is eclectic in that it draws upon a theoretically diverse body of knowledge and is literary through its focus on the use of primary fictional text to support its argument. The central line across which argument is carried is the trajectory of development from cosmicism to neocosmicism, rather than presenting how an examination of cosmicism and neocosmicism might be evidenced within discrete categories of authors' texts. The works of each author are used to discuss, exemplify, and support the development of cosmicism and to highlight the textural evidence that, in being present within their works, also foreshadows the outgrowth of neocosmicism. The authors and texts in use here operate as points of exemplification rather than as subjects of argument, in order to evidence how cosmicism and neocosmicism might also be traced through the wider science fiction corpus. This book is divided into three parts, and each part is further divided into a series of chapters with sub-sections.

Part I deals with the idea of the universe, and sets out the distinction between the terms *cosmos* and universe, the alignment of these terms with the concepts of the map and the territory respectively, and the distinction within this overarching framework of what can be classified as the visible and familiar, from the invisible and unfamiliar aspects of the universe. Following this is a general overview of two dominant Occidental cosmological models—the *Genesis cosmology* and the *universe as machine*—and how these models are interpreted. With these models established, the presence of other sentient beings in the universe and their relationship with the human creature are introduced, followed by a discussion of the disruption between the cosmos and the universe that, in becoming problematic for the human creature, affects that creature's sense of relationship with the universe as adversarial and divisive.

In order to use cosmicism as the underlying philosophical principle of Part II, an examination of its tenets is first established. After this, the principles of cosmicism are applied to an enquiry of the human creature's position in and response to the universe, culminating in the arguably untenable conclusion that cosmicism draws; that in the knowledge of what the universe is, as distinct from what a cosmos suggests it might be, the human creature is afforded no option other than madness or death in response. It is from this point that consideration is made for the significant body of evidence within science fiction that suggests that while the basic tenets of cosmicism are viable, that philosophy's summation of human options when the universe is revealed are limiting and unreflective of other possible outcomes. As a consequence, cosmicism is opened up in a manner that retains many of its defining characteristics, while also drawing on a view of the universe that is more inclusive of twenty-first-century scientific and cultural theory and thinking.

Part III then, in beginning with the human creature's arrival at cosmicism's ultimate and life-negating end, develops neocosmicism. Rather than negate cosmicism by offering an alternative, neocosmicism offers a complement. Neocosmicism is presented as a philosophical extension of cosmicism that builds upon cosmicism's existing and viable *foundation*. An alternate path for the human creature is offered, and rather than succumb to a shattering observation of the universe, neocosmicism explores the possibility for the human creature to choose the *engulfment* that cosmicism warns against as destructive, in order that it might enter an experience of the universe that is affirmative. By choosing to be engulfed by the universe, rather than simply observe it from a distance, the human creature in neocosmicism can move beyond what stops and destroys it, to enter a vitalised engagement with the universe and with others.

Glossary of Terms

amnesia of the cosmos
The loss of the memory of the universe that arises from the human creature's mistaking of the ordered and static cosmos as the universe, and that creature's subsequent loss of a sense of embodied relationship with the universe.

chaos
The condition that precedes and underpins all else, chaos is the underlying state or condition of the universe. Furthermore, chaos is also a fundamental component of the universe's overlying, visible landscape of experience.

cold equations
Derived from Tom Godwin's short story "The Cold Equations," and for the purpose of this book, the cold equations are the "fixed rules" of the universe that operate beyond the sphere of human morals and ethics.

cosmicism
Cosmicism is drawn from the philosophy of H. P. Lovecraft as it is exemplified in his fiction and explicated in his nonfiction texts. The principal tenets of cosmicism are that the universe operates as an indifferent mechanism, without purpose or direction, and the human creature is not only insignificant but exists as a biological mutation or accident of elemental and chemical stellar processes. The mechanism of the universe operates without emotions or ethics of human parameters and understanding, thereby rendering any ethical effort as pointless, for morality has influence and meaning only at an insignificant and localised level.

The universe is also characterised by the absence of a moral deity that cares for the human creature.

cosmos
A cosmos has logic and order and is one version or one way of thinking about and making sense of the universe. As one version, indeed as one vision, a cosmos is like a snapshot, a single ordered view, or even an illusion of some part, but not the entirety, of the universe.

NOTE: in both fiction and nonfiction, Lovecraft often uses the terms cosmos and universe interchangeably, and in any material quoted in this book from Lovecraft the term cosmos is to be read as meaning universe.

engulfment
Engulfment refers to a submersion or overwhelming of the physical, mental, emotional, or sensory aspects of the human creature. It is not only precipitated by a force greater in some way than the creature being engulfed, but also involves some form of conflict or pull between opposing forces which, through a total immersion or plunging into the experience, threatens the survival of that being. Should the engulfed survive the experience, some form of change occurs that renders it incapable of returning to the same state of being or understanding as it was in prior to the engulfment.

foundation
A foundation is that fundamental structure supporting a more visible and tangible formation. It not only refers to a physical object, such as a building or biological body, but it also refers to ideological, geographical, and sociological grouping—as evident in modern Western culture. Furthermore, a foundation continues to support and inform any new structure in which it remains embedded.

Genesis cosmology
The cosmological view of creation and the Noachian Deluge that has been a substantial part of the foundation of Western culture is written in the book of Genesis in the Christian Bible, and will hereafter be called the Genesis cosmology. This can be referred to as a religious cosmological model.

heimlich
Within its Germanic origin, heimlich is most commonly used to mean homely, but also equally represents its own opposite to connote a distinct meaning of unheimlich. This is to say that the term heimlich can be used to mean either the familiar or the unfamiliar. More specifically, and the meaning more pertinent to this book, what has been familiar and homely becomes hidden and unfamiliar. The heimlich, in both its "homely" and its "secretive" manifestations, are two sides of the same coin.

heimlich conundrum
A heimlich conundrum is the sense of damnation that the human creature feels, irrespective of the direction that creature chooses to move toward, when faced with the revelation of the universe; the outcome of this will only ever be one of madness or death.

landscape
A landscape is a view that is taken from one aspect within either a cosmos or the universe. Both cosmos and universe contain a multiplicity of varying landscapes that encircle the human creature like the layers of an onion, and at any point in time all these differing landscapes contribute to the reality perceived by that creature and are variously interpreted depending upon which map or part of the territory that creature is operating from. A landscape can be a part of the territory, in the same manner as a foot is a part of the body; or a landscape can be a map, in the same manner as a photograph of a foot is a representation of that foot, but not the foot itself.

map
A map is an ordered view or representation of a territory. The term *map* can be considered synonymous with cosmos, in the same way that territory is synonymous with universe.

neocosmicism
Neocosmicism realigns the human creature's relationship with the universe and others in such a way as to make it possible for that creature to move beyond the incarcerating confines of a cosmos. Though it remains insignificant, the human creature's reinscription by engulfment allows it

to engage with the universe and in doing so, affords possibilities for existence other than cosmicism's madness or death.

proving ground
Derived from military terminology; a testing ground.

psychotic universe
The psychotic universe is a proving ground wherein the gap between illusion and reality, map and territory, cosmos and universe simply does not exist. The human creature is neither outside of nor incarcerated within the psychotic universe, and through emotional investment in the cold equations, that creature's participation influences and is influenced by the universe.

romance of the universe
The participatory and at times symbiotic relationship between the human creature and the universe in neocosmicism.

schizophrenic universe
The schizophrenic universe of cosmicism is no longer one stable thing or another; it is neither machine nor the creation of deity. It is split from itself and the human creature is also split from it and adrift within it.

tele-objectivity
A restriction in the field of view that is unnoticed by an individual or framework, and which renders all that exists outside the field of view as invisible to that individual or framework. (Adapted from Virilio, Grey Ecology.)

territory
A territory is the substance or reality; what is represented by a map. The term territory can be considered synonymous with universe, in the same way that map is synonymous with cosmos. Implicit within this, although not necessarily visible, is the idea that the territory, like the universe, is chaos.

threshold
A threshold is that liminal space between one state and another, where varying degrees of transformative experience are encountered, where

conflicting opposites merge into one and the same moment of experience. The threshold is where the potential of engulfment manifests itself, and where the capacity of the human creature either to cross or to resist the threshold is greatly tested. Once crossed, there is no return to the previous state, and the human creature will be irrevocably changed by the experience.

universe
The universe is, quite simply, everything. The underlying foundation of the universe is chaos, distinguishing the universe as different from the cosmos where chaos is put into order. There is no requirement for the universe to be ordered, although order may be found within the chaos.

universe as machine
The universe as machine is a metaphorical image of putting order into chaos, and provides an overlying schematic map for, but not the reality of, the universe. As a machine, the universe is without emotion or human morality, and continues to function through the impersonal and perpetual motion of components in the mechanism. The cold equations are inherent within the universe as machine and this can be referred to as a scientific cosmological model.

vitalised materialism
Neocosmicism's psychotic universe unveils the heimlich attribute of cause and purpose. What cosmicism refers to as the "outside" is simply the territory beyond the parameters of the map; in neocosmicism, everything is universe. Everything will end because there is no outside, there is no external cause, and the psychotic universe is materialist by virtue of this. However, because neocosmicism's universe is also a proving ground in which the human creature can be vitalised, the universe has purpose, and in having purpose implies cause. Neocosmicism's universe is a universe of vitalised materialism.

void
As an ultimate indeterminacy the void has no borders or boundaries; it is an emptiness that is nowhere and everywhere, a ubiquitous merging of oppositions that cancel one from another, a littoral space where shore and ocean merge.

Abbreviations for Major Works

Philip K. Dick
CS   *The Collected Stories* (5 volumes)
DAD   *Do Androids Dream of Electric Sheep?*
SD   *A Scanner Darkly*
TSPE *The Three Stigmata of Palmer Eldritch*

Robert A. Heinlein
MC   *Methuselah's Children*
TEL   *Time Enough for Love*

Frank Herbert
CD   *Children of Dune*
D   *Dune*
DM   *Dune Messiah*
GED *God Emperor of Dune*

H. P. Lovecraft
CF   *Collected Fiction: A Variorum Edition* (4 volumes)
SHL   *The Annotated Supernatural Horror in Literature*
SL   *Selected Letters* (5 volumes)

Others
OED Simpson and Weiner, *Oxford English Dictionary*

Part I: Universe

Chapter 1: Universe and Cosmos

> Deep in the human unconscious is a pervasive need for a logical universe that makes sense. But the real universe is always one step beyond logic.— From "The Sayings of Muad'Dib" by the Princess Irulan.
>
> —Frank Herbert, *Dune*

In 1922, Albert Einstein claimed that "[t]he only justification for our concepts and system of concepts is that they serve to represent the complex of our experiences; beyond this they have no legitimacy' (*Meaning of Relativity* 2), and this may readily be claimed for what we call the universe. The immediate question that emerges from this, then, is not so much one of concept but of actuality, asking: what is the universe? The *Oxford English Dictionary* (OED) defines the universe as "the whole of created or existing things regarded collectively; all things (including the Earth, the heavens, and all the phenomena of space)" (OED 19.86), and although the OED continues by saying that the universe is a "systematic whole," it requires neither the inclusion nor exclusion of order within this whole.

Additionally, the modern word universe comes from the French *univers* and from the Latin "*universum* the whole world . . . of *universus* all taken together, lit[erally] 'turned into one'" (Onions 961), and is a combination of *uni* (meaning one) and *versus* (meaning "turn of the plough, furrow, line, row, line of writing" [Onions 976]). The point being made by means of this etymology is that it renders an image of one mechanical act or simple machine creating separable portions from a greater whole. Such a view opens up not only the possibility for interpreting the universe as machine because the idea of a machine is embedded in the term universe; but also the idea that this particular image of what the *OED* defines as the universe is in fact more like a limited view, and in the terms of this text is more readily aligned with the concept of cosmos.

A cosmos has logic and order and is one version or one way of thinking about and making sense of the universe. As one version, indeed as one vision, a cosmos is like a snapshot, a single ordered view or even an illusion of some part, but not the entirety, of the universe. Frank

Herbert writes in *Children of Dune* that "anything which we can identify as our universe is merely part of a larger phenomena" (210), and this promotes the idea that what the human creature has commonly called the universe is in fact a view or perspective that may well be concealing what lies beneath. Indeed, it is worth noting here also the framework that urbanist Paul Virilio installs around the term "human" in *Grey Ecology* when he writes that "[h]uman comes from the word humus. Humus speaks of humility" (40); a term that itself is not inconceivably far removed from that of insignificance, a concept we shall later see is in and of itself significant. Of course, the term humus also speaks of the Earth or of soil, and while the connection between these variants of term and related images does not bear directly upon the immediate argument here, there is an ongoing albeit inferred discussion throughout the whole of this text that traces the intimate connections between Earth, blade—as signified in this chapter by the plough—and machine, tracing from this starting point and into the heart of neocosmicism.

So what, then, is cosmos? The *OED* frames cosmos as "the world or universe [considered] as an ordered and harmonious system," and as such, it is "the opposite of chaos" (*OED* 3.986). The second point here is critical to the argument to be developed in subsequent chapters, for the suggestion of the cosmos as "ordered" is disturbed by a quantum physics view of the universe as *chaos*. Furthermore, to define the cosmos as an "ordered system" is to imply that the cosmos is a mechanism inasmuch as it is "a system of mutually adapted parts working together" (*OED* 9.536).

It might initially be considered that the terms cosmos and universe are readily interchangeable, as they appear to speak of the same idea. I suggest, however, that such is not the case, but rather that cosmos is only one version or one way of thinking about and making sense of the universe. As one version, the cosmos is like a picture taken of a single moment, a representation or convincing illusion of what it attempts to describe. In *The Book: On the Taboo against Knowing Who You Are* (hereafter referred to as *The Book*), the London-born Zen Buddhist philosopher and theologian Alan Watts describes the difference between the universe and the cosmos by metaphorically re-imaging these concepts as "wiggly" lines and a "net" respectively to illustrate how the disordered lines of the universe are captured and sectioned into more manageable portions by the ordered net of the cosmos. As Watts says, "[o]rder has been imposed on chaos" and "the net has thus become one of the presiding images of human thought" (59); an image that will later be demonstrated as significant in cosmicism with respect to the idea of a carceral universe.[1] The significant difference between cosmos and universe is located in the idea that cosmos is the capture of a single ordered view of some part only of the universe and not the whole. To say that the universe underlies the cosmos is synonymous with saying that the territory underlies the map and also reaches beyond the limits of that map.

Additionally, the human creature may identify varying landscapes within either the universe or a cosmos, and each landscape may be considered as a view that is taken from a single position. Both the universe and cosmoses contain a multiplicity of varying landscapes encircling the human creature, and at any point in time all these differing landscapes contribute to the reality perceived by that creature and are variously interpreted depending upon which map or part of the territory that creature is operating from.

Similar to though not synonymous with cosmos, a landscape as "a view taken from one aspect" does not present the human creature with a complete view. This may be likened to a concept framed by Watts in terms of the "on" and the "off," and his parallel example of the binary language of computers that deal in zeroes and ones. In both cases Watts notes that the two positions can be arranged into such a complexity of patterning that these two apparently opposing positions can produce an infinite array of pictures, sounds, sensations, and views. The significant point Watts makes is that even in the instance of an apparently uninterrupted sound or sensation, it is not only both the "on" and "off" that are operating, it is also the silence between these poles that defines the sound (Watts 25–28). Similarly, it is what lies hidden in the landscape, what is not charted on the map between points, that is in direct relationship with the visible features of the landscape.

Like Watts's relationships between the "on" and the "off" and "between bodies" (28), the American author Gary Zukav notes that "as a complete theory even though it gives no explanation of what the world is 'really like'... quantum mechanics correctly correlates experience" (110). Zukav later claims that "[t]he distinction between a transient, virtual (noth-

---

1. The idea of the carceral universe is discussed in chapter 8.

ing-something-nothing) state," which is equivalent to Watts's "on" and "off," or a computer's binary language, "is similar to the Buddhist distinction between reality as it actually is and the way we usually see it" (262). While I acknowledge this is a very simplistic reading of the states of "on" and "off," it is sufficient for the purpose here of demonstrating that the idea of a territory overlain by a map that is an approximation or single view of a larger whole is reflected in fields of investigation that are diverse not only in their perspective or discipline, but also the historical timeframe in which they have arisen.

Watts's image of the net of the map (59) is perhaps nowhere more visible than in a network of streets that intersect each other on any map of an urbanised landscape. But as Lovecraft's character Richard Upton Pickman says: "What do maps, and records and guidebooks really tell ... At a guess I'll guarantee to lead you to thirty or forty alleys and networks of alleys north of Prince Street that aren't suspected by ten living beings outside of the foreigners that swarm them" ("Pickman's Model," CF 2.61). Maps do not speak of the territory that lies beyond their reach. Pickman assures the story's young narrator, Thurber, that "there are things that won't do for Newbury Street," on "artificial streets on made land" (CF 2.59), and parts of this town are not made but grown. At the North End the map fails to represent the territory, Thurber does not keep track of the streets through which he is led, and the map is only re-engaged via streets that Thurber knows of *after* his experience of the territory beneath those streets—a territory for which no map exists (CF 2.62–63). The territory, it seems, can only be engaged when the map either fails or is discarded.

Chapter 7 of Michel de Certeau's text *The Practice of Everyday Life* (1984)—"Walking in the City"—presents a useful analysis of the relationship between the map and territory through its discussion of the city in which the human creature walks. The city is presented as a map in which the territory hides, and "reading such a cosmos" is offered in terms of "the two-fold projection of an opaque past and an uncertain future onto a surface that can be dealt with." Furthermore, Certeau aligns the relationship between the human creature that walks within the city to a tracing of something only recorded as an "absence of what has passed by." The city, like the map, is representative of the concept of synecdoche inasmuch as it only names or represents a part of the whole in which it resides; and the concept of asyndeton wherein the map "skips over links," "omits" or "disconnects" varying elements of what it apparently contains within its representation, and in doing so creates unknown and potentially unreadable spaces. The city, like the map, renders the potentially infinite as a legible, bordered, ordered, and regulated space wherein the act of movement itself is not mapped and "[t]he trace left behind is substituted for the practice" (92-101).

The decaying, crumbling landscape that Pickman and Thurber enter when the map is forsaken is a landscape steeped in water from the "burying ground, and the sea" and follows a subterranean network of tunnels, basements and "brick well[s]." Beyond the net of the map there is a "worm-eaten" and water-threatened landscape of "antediluvian" proportions where the streets above are both mirrored and disrupted by the subterranean matrix of tunnels and wells (CF 2.60-62, 63).

Similarly, in Lovecraft's story "The Music of Erich Zann," no maps, neither new nor old, show where the narrator has been; no map accurately reflects the territory of his experience (CF 1.279-81). The territory is encountered beyond the reach of the map, across a dark river in a street and rooms that are unlike those from anywhere else. This street, these buildings, and their inhabitants, like the towns and inhabitants of "The Dunwich Horror" (CF 2.414-17) and "The Shadow over Innsmouth" (CF 3.158-59), are "incredibly old ... all very old" ("The Music of Erich Zann," CF 1.280); they are antediluvian landscapes caught within crumbling decay. The maps fail to reflect the territory accurately. Furthermore, it is the human creature's reliance on the map to define the territory—the reliance on a cosmos to describe the universe—that prevents that creature from engaging directly with the universe in which it exists. American anthropologist and folklorist Timothy Evans refers to Lovecraft's work as a "postmodern fusion of the real and the virtual" ("Last Defense" 123), a blurring of boundaries that later chapters of this book will argue necessitates a significant shift in that creature's perspective if it is to survive in the universe.

The point to be made is that differentiating the cosmos from the universe is not always straightforward, and in Lovecraft's story "The Outsider" this task is made all the more problematic as a consequence of Lovecraft's subverting the customary practice of first presenting the cosmos as a map from under which the territory is later exposed. "The Outsider" begins from within the territory and for some considerable time the moonlit, crumbling castle in which the narrator lives is presented as being the human creature's familiar, albeit dark and mouldy, landscape. This landscape is pervaded by a sense of immanent revelation, of something as yet unseen beyond the border of the dark forest. When the revelation comes, the reader discovers that the unfamiliar is not beneath the narrator, as it is for Thurber in "Pickman's Model," but lies above the narrator, in the world of bright light. In the disclosure that the landscape into which the narrator emerges is the familiar landscape of the human world, what should be familiar becomes uncomfortably unfamiliar. When the narrator sees himself in the mirror, he understands that he does not belong in the bright light of the human creature's cosmos.

"The Outsider" presents an excellent example of what the Austrian neurologist and founding psychoanalyst Sigmund Freud discusses in his essay "The Uncanny" with respect to the mirror meaning of heimlich. The importance of Freud's distinctive use of the word heimlich cannot be overstressed, and although the word is most commonly used for one meaning, that is, the homely, it also represents and can be used for its own opposite to connote a distinct meaning of unheimlich, or unhomely. The familiar becomes unfamiliar. More specifically, and the meaning more pertinent to this text, what has been familiar becomes hidden and unfamiliar. The heimlich, in both its "homely" and its "secretive" manifestations are two sides of the same metaphorical coin.

What the heimlich points towards is the idea of a particular view or map overlying something else beneath it. What first appears to be the true nature of the landscape is in fact only an approximation or partial view; and in the definitions for the term that Freud examines in "The Uncanny," he writes that the heimlich is *"like a buried spring or a dried-up pond. One cannot walk over it without always having the feeling that water might come up there again"* (419). He then goes on to say that "on the one hand, it means that which is familiar and congenial, and on the other, that which is concealed and kept out of sight" (420). When the heimlich is viewed as only what is comfortable, its other aspect is taken off the map. Furthermore, when this other aspect is negatively connoted as the unheimlich, and banished from view, the map no longer fits the territory.

It might be said that the single biggest mistake that the human creature appears to make in the universe is when it mistakes the map for the territory. In *The Three Stigmata of Palmer Eldritch*, Philip K. Dick not only draws out this idea, but then reveals the motivation behind why the human creature makes such an error. Setting the rules and conditions of the map and how it will be used prior to engaging with it, then pretending that it is a legitimate landscape, is a tactic for self-preservation from the hidden dangers that exist in the territory. During a discussion with the titular character Palmer Eldritch, Leo Bulero understands that "[a]t least with the Perky Pat layouts, one was limited to what one had provided in advance . . . [a]nd—there was a certain safety in this" (95). What the Perky Pat layouts fail to accommodate, however, in both this novel and Dick's story "The Days of Perky Pat" is the fact that no human creature can stay in the illusion of the layouts indefinitely, and when this creature emerges back into the dust of the planet it inhabits, it is ill-equipped for living (CS 4.303-5, 308-9; *TSPE* 139-40). The illusion it understands and feels comfortable living within is not the reality that it ultimately inhabits.

The map alone is insufficient and reliance on the map remains viable only to a certain point. Every time the territory represented by the map changes in some way, the context in which the human creature is participating within that territory is also changed. As Watts says: "Blood in a test-tube is not the same thing as blood in the veins because it is not behaving in the same way. Its behavior has changed because its environment or context has changed" (68). A stagnant map can lead the human creature to feeling as if it is straddling some inexplicable space into which it might fall, with at best the dissatisfaction of a metaphoric foot on either side and more probably a profound sense of no longer belonging anywhere in a universe that appears to be sectioned into landscapes of difference.

Within science fiction, one of the most frequent shifts faced by the human creature that requires a rewriting of the map, or even a completely new map, is the shift between the terrestrial landscape and the landscape of space. In Dick's novel *Do Androids Dream of Electric Sheep?*, Rachael Rosen fails the Voigt-Kampff empathy test simply because she was not raised on Earth, but in space. As her uncle explains to the bounty hunter Rick Deckard: "'I can explain why she scored as an android might. Rachael grew up aboard the *Salander 3*. She was born on it; she spent fourteen years of her eighteen years living off its tape library and what the nine other crew members, all adults, knew about Earth'" (45). The map given to Rachael growing up in space was not sufficient for her to navigate the human creature's landscape on Earth. The map provides only symbols and abstractions, not experiences. It is also important to note that the V-K test applied by Deckard is designed to test for levels of empathy, and Rachael's failure on this point is not to be interpreted as an indication that she is an android—even though this fact is revealed later in the novel—but rather as an indication that space is unsuited to fostering empathy. This lies at the heart of what the British cultural historian of popular literature Farah Mendlesohn refers to in *The Cambridge Companion to Science Fiction* as the "cold equations" (James and Mendlesohn 10) of the universe, and these equations operate beyond the sphere of human morals and ethics. The phrase, and the idea of these equations as "those fixed rules that decide whether we live or die, irrespective of whether we love" (10), is a reference to the story "The Cold Equations" by Tom Godwin, first published in the August 1954 issue of *Astounding Science Fiction*.

The degrees of difference between the map and the territory, between the cosmos and the universe, strike directly to the question of what happens to the human creature when its map no longer fits the territory it is trying to describe. For Lovecraft's narrator in "The Outsider" before his ascent of the "black tower" to the world of the human creature, without knowing what it is that exists beyond his field of vision, he knows that there is something more than what his cosmos of existence has revealed, and "through the endless twilights [he] dreamed and waited, though [he] knew not what [he] waited for" (CF 1.266).

So too has the human creature looked upon its cosmos, knowing that there is something more that it cannot see. In chapters 2 and 3, I will present two cosmological models that have dominated an Occidental perception of the universe; maps that in being mistaken for the territory have transformed the human creature's view of the universe as a dark and dangerous place in which it is caught.

Chapter 2: Cosmologies

> Slumber, watcher, till the spheres,
> Six and twenty thousand years
> Have revolv'd, and I return
> To the spot where now I burn.
> —H. P. Lovecraft, "Polaris"

The Universe as Machine

In an attempt to describe and thereby understand the universe, the human creature has developed numerous cosmological models, one of which is the model hereafter referred to as the universe as machine. The universe as machine is a metaphorical image of putting order into chaos, and it provides an overlying schematic for, but not the reality of, the universe. As a machine, the universe is without emotion or human morality, and continues to function through the impersonal and perpetual motion of its components.

According to American comparative mythologist Joseph Campbell, one of the earliest accounts of the development of a mechanistic view of the universe can be linked directly to the Babylonian ziggurats—large terraced temples—that were built in ancient Sumer during the fourth millennium B.C.E. (*Masks of God* 1.143-44). The use of mathematics and numeric patterning, coupled with early geometric principles and orderings, were the foundations upon which the ziggurats were built as expressions of not only the "world order," but of the relationship between the terrestrial human landscape and the universe. As the Swiss-American surrealist and historian of magic Kurt Seligmann writes: "For the first time in history numbers expressed the world order [and s]uch speculations became frequent among later philosophers" (33). As symbols that "represent graphically an arithmetical total" (*OED* 10.590), numbers underpin the universe as machine and represent that machine's inherent equations.

The presence of numeric patterning as a part of the foundation of an assumed mechanism strengthens the idea of the universe as machine.

Any machine that uses the most basic of computing power operates by the language of mathematics and the numeric symbols of that language. Widely called "machine language" or machine code (Nisan and Schocken 57-60), this language consists of a series of ones and zeros, or as Watts describes it in *The Book*, a simple system of "on" and "off" (25-26). Something is one thing or the other, and the machine computes according to the information—that is, the combination of ones and zeros—it is given.

Having considered the presence of numeric patterning within ancient cosmological expressions, it is perhaps appropriate to examine briefly the cultural environment in which such thinking developed. By 3500-2500 B.C.E. Mesopotamia was undergoing a significant cultural change wherein the symbiosis of the scientific and spiritual considerations of the human creature was transformed through the establishment of "the professional, full-time, initiated, strictly regimented temple priest" (Campbell, *Masks of God* 1.146). With this division of specialisation among human creatures—the kind of "specialisation" that Heinlein refers to in *Time Enough for Love* as the behaviour of "insects" (248)—explanations of how the universe is structured and what place that creature holds in the universe became the "professional" domain of a select group and necessitated, at least in their view, the need for constructing a readable map.

The priests of Sumer recorded, revised, and confirmed what they observed in the night skies until they could identify "visible or barely visible heavenly spheres ... which moved in established courses, according to established laws, along the ways followed by the sun and moon, among the fixed stars" (Campbell, *Masks of God* 1.146). What Campbell identifies is an image of the ordered grid of a map; an ordered system of stellar parts within the mechanism of the continuing cycles of the universe.

By the sixth century B.C.E. the Greek philosopher Anaximander (618-546)[1] developed what historians consider as being the first mechanical model of the universe. Anaximander's model includes the idea

---

1. Anaximander is recognised as one of the first Greek philosophers located within a school of thought known as the Milesians, because of their geographical location in Miletus, the eastern part of the Greek world, known today as Turkey. The Milesians are regarded in the West as the first formalised group who considered the nature of the universe from a philosophical viewpoint and tried to discover its "underlying order" (Smith, Allhoff, and Vaidya 13).

of vast cycles of time (Santillana 27-29), and in this is similar to the Sumerian model. The strength in the case for Anaximander's model as the first is perhaps not so much that he developed it, but that he was being very specific about it as a model.

Using the circle as his foundation and devising a system of interconnecting and dependent parts, Anaximander advanced the idea of the universe as machine by claiming that the world remained where it was through its sheer indifference, as "there was no reason why it should go this way or that, since all directions around the centre are the same" (Santillana 34). Furthermore, Anaximander also proposed that the universe was made from a pre-existing substance which could not be any of the known elements nominated by alchemy as fire, earth, water, and air (Abraham 68-69) but rather—and conveniently, it might be said—some other substance that was "infinite, eternal and ageless" (Russell, *History* 46). Anaximander's model conjures an image of unassembled parts that, once put together and set in motion, have continued to operate. While it appears he does not deny the existence of a deity, what Anaximander proposes is neither moralistic nor participatory within the universe. It is this lack of deific participation that strengthens the coherency of the idea of the universe as machine; for a machine is invariably taken to be "a combination of parts moving mechanically, as contrasted with a being having life, consciousness and will" (*OED* 9.157).

While the Sumerians observed the movement of stellar bodies on fixed paths across the night skies, and Anaximander specifically developed a model to explain this movement, it was the Greek philosopher Pythagoras[2] and his followers who, in approximately the sixth century B.C.E., determined numbers to be the foundation of the universe. Seligmann writes that "according to Pythagoras," numbers were "older than

---

2. Most of what is written about Pythagoras can be regarded as either questionable or in the order of mythic metaphor. Some commentators claim that he obtained a deified status during his life and was thereby attributed a mythic status understood to be just that (Santillana 53-57). Other commentators note that many of the ideas attributed to Pythagoras are most likely, and in some cases almost unquestionably, the ideas of his followers, the Pythagoreans (Smith et al. 25). But without question he is viewed as one of the most significant figures in early philosophy, scientific development, and mathematics (Russell, *History* 49-56).

bodies and hence more powerful . . . In the size, weight and intervals of the stars lurk mystic numbers" (79).

From a Pythagorean perspective, numbers calculate and form the universe in measured shapes and distances, fitting these components together like cogs in a machine, with each one having a place and a function. Just as the cogs of a machine are circular and interlocking, so too are the components of the universe as machine made of circles and spheres that move within cycles of time like the motions of clockwork. The machine of the universe is measurable in space-time as if it were a great cosmic clock of perpetual motion. It is worth noting here that while it remains commonplace for space and time to be thought of in Newtonian terms as separate phenomena, "[a]ccording to relativity theory . . . Both are intimately connected and form a four-dimensional continuum" (Capra 167).

In being a machine, the Greek idea of the universe is similar to Lovecraft's imaging of the universe in cosmicism, wherein the perpetual motion of the mechanism is clearly visible inasmuch as "there is no such thing as a final result, since all cosmic existence is but an endless and purposeless chain beginning and leading nowhere" (SL 1.132). This is the universe as it will be more fully explored in Part II.

While the idea of the universe as machine had been proposed millennia beforehand, it was the emergence of astronomy as a specific science and the employ of the scientific method that offered more concrete support for a mechanistic cosmological model. As it is with Lovecraft's "piecing together of dissociated knowledge [that] will open up such terrifying vistas of reality, and of our frightful position therein" in "The Call of Cthulhu" (CF 2.22), so too it might be argued that one of the largest crises faced by the religious cosmological doctrine of the West came with the publication of *De Revolutionibus Orbium Coelestium* in 1543 by the Polish astronomer Copernicus (1473–1543), in which he proposes a heliocentric model of the universe. Due to a fear of persecution, however, this seminal work was not published until near the end of Copernicus's life, and then dismissed as a serious work within Andreas Osiander's preface when he writes of Copernicus's text as a hypothesis rather than a "revolutionary truth." When the Italian astronomer and mathematician Giordano Bruno (1549–1600) used Copernicus's text as a basis for his own work, however, the Church officially denounced it as "expressly contrary to Holy Scripture ... and opposed to the true faith" (Ergang 358-61).

It was the Italian astronomer, mathematician, and physicist Galileo Galilei (1564-1642) who, having observed through his telescope four satellites orbiting Jupiter, produced evidence in support of the Copernican model and published as much in his *Dialogue concerning the Two Chief World Systems* (1632). After Galileo, the English astronomer, mathematician, and physicist Sir Isaac Newton (1642-1727), in publishing his *Philosophiae Naturalis Principia Mathematica* in 1687, set out the universal laws of motion and the law of universal gravitation, and in doing so provided what might be considered substantial evidence in support of the idea of the universe as machine. It might be said that since Newton, the human creature, in becoming increasingly exposed to machines in the landscape, has also become more open to the idea of the universe as machine as a cogent metaphor that appears to fits its observation of the universe in which it exists.

The Genesis Cosmology

An alternate and in many ways opposing view to the universe as machine is found in the biblical book of Genesis, and referred to hereafter as the Genesis cosmology. It is important to note at this point also that the use of the term God throughout this text refers specifically to the God of the Genesis cosmology on which the Christian tradition is based. According to this model: "In the beginning God created the heavens and the Earth," and "the Spirit of God was hovering over the waters" (Genesis 1:1-2). On this first day, God also creates the light and then "separate[s] light from darkness" (Genesis 1:3-5). On the second day, God creates the sky to separate "the water under the expanse from the water above it" (Genesis 1:7), and it is significant that nowhere in these first two days of creation does Genesis mention the creation of water. I suggest that this is an image that locates water as co-existent with God in the darkness before the ordering of the Genesis cosmology's landscapes.

The German Old Testament scholar Klaus Westermann writes in *Genesis 1-11: A Commentary* that two separate questions relating to creation are identifiable across varying world religions and relate to the distinct ideas of "the creation or origin of the whole and ... the creation or origin of the one (i.e. of a particular thing)" (23). Considering this, and bearing in mind the point that historically for the human creature "[t]he question of what was created, precedes the question, how did creation take place" (22), the Genesis cosmology's specific accounting of the idea of "the creator and creation," as opposed to the idea of "origin" (25), is significant. Westermann points out that the idea of God as "creator" of objects—of the world and the human creature—dominates Genesis. It is the idea of "the one," however, rather than the idea of "the whole" that is the older idea (23). The point to be drawn from this is that before ever God created "the whole" of the world and the human creature, there is the "origin" of the One; that which is undivided from or within itself and of which God is an indivisible and unequivocal part, rather than a creator that is in some way above or separate from it. The sense of separation of what is created from what has created it—that is, a separation of what comes forth from the foundation of its origin—is, according to Westermann, unique to Genesis:

> Before Israel and outside Israel people spoke of the creation [or origin] of the gods in the same way as they spoke of the creation [or origin] of the world or of humanity. But this is not possible in Israel. Creation, therefore, be it simple creation or making or forming, has different overtones. The object of creation is without exception something outside the divine. The action of God as creator is directed exclusively to the world. God is outside creation; to be created means to be not-god. Creation completely dominates origin in the Old Testament. (25-26)

The heavens and the Earth are located in a dark and silent fluid universe—an image subtly evocative of an embryo in a womb. The silence is shattered when God speaks, and it is the voice of God that initiates the division of the universe as if it were Watts's capture of wiggly lines in the grid that I have discussed in chapter 1. The effect of the first breath of God's creative utterance is a contraction of space, a limiting of the possible view. The first breath and the first words of God occur at the same time, and they occur *after* the creation of the heavens and the Earth. After this first breath, and its corresponding creation of light (Genesis 1:3), the boundaries that separate one thing from another are established in ever decreasing and encircling landscapes. The voice that divides the heavens from the Earth and the light from the darkness is the voice that initiates the temporal cosmos and transforms the universe into a series of binary opposites pitted one against the other. What is interesting about what God creates prior to his first utterance is that the heavens and the Earth are created together within the same ubiquitous ocean and only divided by the creation of the sky on the second day. Before it became an object in the ordered cosmos, without form and its depths without light, the Earth was inseparable from the universe as if it were an embryo in a womb.

The undivided waters of the Genesis cosmology are echoed in Heinlein's novel *Methuselah's Children*, where, travelling through space onboard the *New Frontiers*, Andrew Jackson Libby "continued to sleep, the luxurious return-to-the womb sleep of those who have learned to enjoy free fall" (377). Libby is enfolded within the metaphorical womb of heaven. This is a metaphor *founded* within the figure of the Sumerian goddess Tiamat, in whose body the first gods were birthed and dwelt, and whose body after being slain became the heavens and the Earth within which the human creature was created (Coleman 1016; Dalley 233, 236, 255-57). Similarly, in Herbert's *Dune* chronicles, the character Alia Atreides in her elevation to the status of goddess is also given the title of the womb of heaven (*DM* 166; McNelly 44-45).

From the coexisting water of the Genesis cosmology and Sumerian *Epic of Creation* at one end of the historical spectrum, to the work of a twentieth-century quantum physicist at the other, the metaphorical womb of heaven that Heinlein's Libby traverses and Herbert's Alia Atreides represents is described by David Bohm as a vast ocean, wherein

> An interesting image is obtained by considering that in the middle of the actual ocean (i.e. on the surface of the Earth) myriads of small waves occasionally come together fortuitously with such phase relationships that they end up in certain small regions of space, suddenly to produce a very high wave which just appears as if from nowhere and out of nothing. Perhaps something like this could happen in the immense ocean of cosmic energy, creating a sudden wave pulse, from which our "universe" would be born. (244)

Texts thousands of years old and a twentieth-century quantum physicist both describe the universe using similar imagery, and in the context of a territory that is both unified and saturated. When God divides the waters, the landscape of the Earth is ever after below the sky and beneath that God. The "formless and empty" Earth created in the womb of heaven is separated from those heavenly waters, and the cosmos is ever after imprinted with the imperative of division and splitting—a splitting that the Bene Gesserit Anteac refers to in *God Emperor of Dune* as "'a principle of conflict which originated with the single cell and has never deteriorated'" (180). Separation from deity and from the universe does not occur in the Genesis cosmology's Garden of Eden. The Garden of Eden was "a terrestrial garden created by God" (Collins 151) where He put "the idealized first man and woman [to] live in a state of grace and innocence" (Collins 39). It is said that when Adam and Eve ate the fruit of the tree of knowledge of good and evil that God has planted in the Garden, they "fell" from their "state of grace." But it is proposed here that this "fall of man," as it is commonly referred to, is not the first moment of separation from God, and that by the time Adam and Eve have eaten the fruit God was already in hiding. God's accusatory question to Adam when asking why he was hiding is an accusation against a *secondary* act of hiding. It could even be said that as a good son, Adam was simply emulating the Father—that is, hiding from what the universe is rather that what the cosmos has constructed it to be (Genesis 3:8-10). Separation from deity, then, occurs before the human creature is formed, and the positing of this event acts as a seemingly impenetrable barrier between the sunlit landscape of Earth and the dark universe above that Earth.

The demarcation of the sky as separating everything upon the Earth from the rest of the universe above is the *founding* principle of the cosmological division between one state and another. This separation from the ubiquitous ocean of the universe, coupled with an apparent impossibility of reconciling the conflict between pairs of opposites, hereafter characterise the terrestrial landscape. This could be paralleled with the Buddhist idea that life is suffering, and the physicist Fritjof Capra claims in relation to this idea that suffering arises as a consequence of "the futile grasping of life based on a wrong point of view . . . we divide the perceived world into individual and separate things and thus attempt to confine the fluid forms of reality" (107).

The subsequent days of creation further separate landscapes and objects, such as plants and animals; the fixed lights of sun, moon, and stars in the sky; the "great creatures of the sea," birds of the air, creatures of the dry land; and eventually the human creature (Genesis 1:9-31). From the perspective of all terrestrially bound creatures, the placement of the fixed heavenly bodies of light not only accentuates the difference between the night and day, it further demarcates the barrier between the waters above and the waters below. The direct light of the sun or its reflected light on the moon ensures that the landscapes of both day and night are lit and the darkness of space beyond the limits of the sky recedes into the background. The light of the sun fortifies what is above and beyond the horizon as being beyond the reach of life. As Heinlein writes in MC:

> The Sun is not a large star, nor is it very hot. But it is hot with reference to men, hot enough to strike them down dead if they are careless about tropic noonday ninety-two million miles away from it, hot enough that we who are reared under its rays nevertheless dare not look directly at it.
>
> At a distance of two and a half million miles the Sun beats out with a glare fourteen hundred times as bright as the worst ever endured in Death Valley, the Sahara, or Aden. Such radiance would not be perceived as heat or light; it would be death more sudden than the full power of a blaster. (378–79)

As a burning fire of nuclear reaction (Gribbin 216) the sun dominates the Earth, and its heat or lack thereof separates the habitable from the uninhabitable. Its proximity in the daytime sky obliterates the universe beyond the reach of its light.

The moon, however, as the body that "lights" the night sky of Earth, reflects rather than generates light and gives off no tangible heat. Without the direct light of the sun to frame and direct the human creature's view, the moon's reflected light of the nearest star creates shadows in the landscape that imply a break in the sunlit cosmos which the universe might seep through. In order to secure the attention of the human creature away from this possibility, the Genesis cosmology's successive demarcation of boundaries between polarities estranges that creature from the dark and fluid universe by enclosing that creature in an ordered cosmos where the light and warmth of the sun are equivalent to God's sanctioned goodness and safety.

When life is created by God on the sixth day, it is created not for the waters or the air but for the dry land. As Part II will elaborate, it is the estranging nature of this divide, coupled with the human creature's inability to survive in watery environments without some sort of assistance, that plays a significant role in driving that creature's fear of others in cosmicism.

The dust of dry land, deserts, fire, and the ash of nuclear aftermath are signatures of the human landscape, and notable examples include, but are not limited to, Dick's Earth in stories such as *DAD*, "Second Variety" (CS 2.15-52), "Jon's World" (CS 2.53-81), and "To Serve the Master" (CS 3.145-54); and Dick's Mars in *TSPE*, "Martians Come in Clouds" (CS 2.119-27), and "The Days of Perky Pat" (CS 4.301-21); the sands of Herbert's planet Dune pervade the first three *Dune* novels, and that planet's influence resonates through the Dune universe in all six novels, culminating in the re-establishment of the desert on the planet Chapterhouse (1985); and Lovecraft deals with deserts in "Under the Pyramids"[3] (CF 1.417-49) and "The Shadow out of Time" (CF 3.363-452). Unlike the watery domain of the first creatures, the landscape inhabited by the human creature has, from the beginning, been one of dust and ash.

It takes a different kind of creature to survive on dry land, a different kind of body. That creature may be a stranger to the water but it nonetheless requires an embodied maintenance of a particular level of water, without which its body will fail. It could be said that from the first moment of creation in the Genesis cosmology, the human creature is destined for conflict inasmuch as the prevailing separation of landscapes is further exacerbated by the parameters of a body that is made for the dry land but utterly dependent on water for its survival. The point to be made here is that by the time God creates the human creature, the days of creation have by several degrees of separation estranged that creature from the universe in which its God and the waters exist.

The encircling nature of the Genesis cosmology contracted to the individual body encloses the human creature so that it identifies itself as *something* separate from *everything*. It is cut off from the universe and views itself as an object that is separate from all other objects in the cosmos. As a consequence of this, the universe that the human creature's cosmos represents has become an alien and dangerous place. The cos-

---

3. Lovecraft ghostwrote the story for Harry Houdini in 1924.

mos frames the universe as an unchanging vista of individual objects, rather than a unified territory in perpetual and fluid motion, and the human creature begins to suffer what is referred to in this text as the *amnesia of the cosmos*. This is to say that the human creature loses its memory of the universe as a consequence of its mistaking the ordered and static cosmos for the universe, leading to that creature's subsequent loss of a sense of embodied relationship with the universe.

The once all-pervasive waters of the foundation are divided and corralled within increasingly smaller portions, and the estrangement of the human creature from the universe is infused with the threat of these submerged waters and all that they contain re-emerging. Water surrounds the tower of the body like a moat around a fortress, and in doing so subdues the human creature; an act that reflects an utter reversal of the purpose of the Babylonian ziggurat—also discussed in chapter 2— from where that creature looked outward and opened itself up to the great vista of the dark, night sky.

This contracting focus of view in the universe from that of the infinite territory to that of the isolated body is an image inferred by the physicist George FitzGerald when in 1892 he proposed an idea that essentially claims "that *everything* contracts," and while at the time this was considered a questionable hypothesis, it was also at that time "impossible to disprove" (Zukav 148). By the following year, the Dutch physicist Hendrik Lorentz arrived at the same conclusion as FitzGerald and "expressed his discovery in rigorous mathematical terms," that indeed everything does contract, the terms forming what has become known as the Lorentz transformations (Zukav 148-49).

In estranging the human creature from the universe, the Genesis cosmology renders the expansive view of the universe as beyond human capability and presents such a diminished scale of position that the universe can only be perceived as a threat against that creature's solitary body. This installation of fear is a fear that has been taught, culturally embraced and embedded within the cosmos.

Cartography and Cryptography—The Language of Cosmoses

The Genesis cosmology claims that light enters the universe and that the waters are separated when God speaks (Genesis 1:3-6). The sky that separates the waters and the words of God carried within the air of the breeze that moves in the new-formed sky stir the still waters to move. The description of any state of being when it is uttered by words, however, is not the state or object itself. The words of description are symbols, that is all (Zukav 284), and when God speaks during creation, what he summons by his word is something other than the word itself. Watts also makes the point that the human creature thinks in terms of language and images that are not its own, or more precisely, that creature confuses names with nature and in doing so "come[s] to believe that having a separate names makes you a separate being" (69-70).

Like the view of the map and the experience of the territory, the symbols of words and the experience of what they attempt to describe *"do not follow the same rules"* (Zukav 285, 290). If the map that fails to represent the perpetually moving territory is problematic, the failure of language in its attempt to describe the human experience of that territory is nothing short of major trauma. As Zukav claims:

> The difference between experience and symbol is the difference between mythos and logos. Logos imitates, but can never replace, experience. It is a *substitute* for experience. Logos is the artificial construction of dead symbols which mimics experience on a one-to-one basis ... From any point of view, logos (literally) is a dead letter. (290-91)

The way the human creature asks its questions limits the array of available response, and in a system where "everything is a symbol" this limitation can often lead to the "illusory limits" of an "either/or" response (Zukav 301), a view where everything is black and white, an echo of Watts's "on" and "off." These limits are initiated when God utters his first words and commences dividing the territory by means of the sharp instrument of language.

The cosmos begins with the advent of symbolic representation encapsulated as language, and linguistic mapping of the universe is an attempt to use abstracted symbols to represent concrete experience—illusions held up and mistaken for reality. This approximation of reality may be read in terms of positing God as the architect of a simulation, but more significantly what arises from the establishment of the signified cosmos is its resulting capacity to then eradicate from view what lies beyond its parameters by simply remaining silent.

Zukav's observation that a symbol and the reality it represents can never be the same (284)[4] highlights the idea that even when objects in the cosmos are signified by language, with its inherent capacity for the slippage of meaning, language not only prevents alignment between the map and the territory, it can also block relationships between human creatures because any cosmos remains only a partial view of the universe. It is said of Heinlein's Lazarus Long in *TEL*, a man described by another human creature in *MC* as "an atavism" (334-35), that it is

> "doubt[ful] if anyone can understand him, in depth. He's a primitive, dear—a living fossil."
> "I would certainly like to try to understand him. This language he uses—is it difficult?"
> "Very. Irrational, complicated syntax, and so loaded with idioms and multivalues that I trip even on words I think I know." (*TEL* 46)

Similarly, Dick's novel *DAD* provides numerous examples of such difficulties between human creatures, but perhaps the most specific, as literary academic and critic Jill Galvan points out, is when the bounty hunter Rick Deckard attempts to test Luba Luft using the Voigt-Kampff test (88-90). As Galvan states, "I think it's worth noting that Luba's subversion involves, principally, a deliberate equivocation on points of the linguistic code—a code that in and of itself has the power to condemn her" (420). This is similar to Zukav's example of an American in Lebanon, who, when asked if he were Christian or Muslim, replied by saying he was a tourist (301). In such circumstances, individuals feel the pressure of the limiting nature of the language about them and the very real threat to their lives if they cannot find a way to circumvent these limitations.

Like many maps, language and its system of signification are often encountered prior to the territory they are attempting to describe. In

---

4. The French postmodern cultural theorist and philosopher Jean Baudrillard writes extensively on this idea with respect to the notions of simulacra and hyperreality. While an examination of Baudrillard is beyond the scope of this current discussion, further illumination from his work as it relates to the argument here may be best sourced from the text *Simulations* (1983), an English translation that combines the texts *Simulacre et simulations* (1981) and *L'Échange symbolique et la mort* (1977).

Lovecraft's story "The Whisperer in Darkness," Henry Wentworth Akeley's letters, wire cable, and photographs signpost the landscape for Albert N. Wilmarth in significant detail some time before Wilmarth actually travels to the remote location in Vermont (CF 2.471–75, 476–80, 488–89, 491–500, 502). Similarly in "Pickman's Model," the artist's pictures map a progressive journey through the territory of bodies and faces. The first works viewed by Thurber arouse curiosity, then others arouse suspicion, until having moved through the building in which these pictures are housed, they become disturbing enough to sicken; the succession of images culminating in a photograph of the *actual body* of some other creature (CF 2.63–69, 72).

The words that make up any language, as symbols, encode the maps of the territory they represent. The symbols of cryptography and conventions of cartography, as representations but not realities, transpose the view in such a manner as to allow the removal of the requirement for participation. The human creature can operate from the safe and ordered distance of the cosmos. However, that creature must know what the symbols mean, or it will become lost.

Chapter 3: Fractured Universe

> St Thomas was preserved in the Orange Catholic Bible and the Azhar Book, but Canterbury was gone from the memories of men, as was the planet which had known it.
> —Frank Herbert, *Children of Dune*

Mapping the Unmappable Ocean

As we have seen, a cosmological model, like a map, is only one particular view and not the territory itself. The "real universe" that Paul Atreides says "is always one step beyond logic" (*D* 354) is like the universe perceived in "[t]he world view of particle physics [that] is a picture of *chaos beneath order*" (Zukav 216).

The territory of chaos that the human creature calls the universe is the underlying foundation supporting the ordered cosmological map. As "the first state of the universe . . . The 'formless void' of primordial matter, the 'great deep' or 'abyss' out of which the cosmos or order of the universe evolved" (*OED* 3.22), chaos in this discussion is to be read as the condition that precedes and underpins all else. Furthermore, when chaos is also taken as an "[e]lement; environment; [or] space" (3.23) it becomes not only an underlying state or condition of the universe, but is also a fundamental component of the visible landscape.

The pursuit of a cosmological model that imposes order upon chaos is credited as first attempted by the Greek philosopher Thales, who claims water as the pre-existing material from which the universe is formed (Smith, Allhoff, and Vaidya 15–16). Similarly, Anaximander also suggests that life began from or within the water (Russell, *History* 47). This idea of water being a substance that in some form pre-exists the ordered cosmos is supported by both the Greek philosophers and their universe as machine, and by the Genesis cosmology.[1] If water is to be taken as the per-

---

1. It is also worth noting that older than either the universe as machine or the Genesis cosmology as models of the universe is the Sumerian cosmological model presented in *The Epic of Creation* and later embedded in some part into

vasive element of the universe that cosmological models suggest, beyond the biological requirement for survival then, what is the significance for the human creature of water in the universe? In beginning to answer this question, the human creature comes to realise that the universe looks very different from the cosmos to which it has become accustomed.

The Deluge

The *OED* defines deluge as "[a] great flood or overflowing of water, a destructive inundation" and as a term referring specifically to"[t]he great Flood in the time of Noah (also called *the general* or *universal deluge*)" (*OED* 4.427). In the Genesis cosmology, the Deluge is clearly presented as the consequence of God's displeasure with the human creature and other land-dwelling creatures. It is important to highlight that in this text, capitalisation of the term designates the specific use of Deluge as referring to the Noachian Deluge in the Genesis cosmology, whereas a lower-case usage designates a generic, though nonetheless specific, use of the term.

The event is motivated by a moral assessment, and what is interesting here is that while God casts judgement upon "men and animals, and creatures that moved along the ground, and birds of the air" (Genesis 6:7), water-dwelling creatures are exempt. Of course, it can be said that in a deluge it is logical that water-borne creatures will not be threatened, but God being God, he could determine to wipe them out one way or the other if they were unfavourable to him. The point is that this was not the case.

As an act of God motivated by a moral judgement, it is difficult to consider that the human creature did not take the Deluge personally. To reinforce the displeasure of God toward his own creation, the Genesis cosmology reiterates that

> Every living thing that moved on the Earth perished–birds, livestock, wild animals, all the creatures that swarm over the Earth, and all man-

---

the Genesis cosmology. In this model, the god Apsu, who is correlated with the "domain of sweet, fresh water beneath the Earth" (Dalley 318) and the goddess Tiamat, who is correlated with the "'[s]ea,' salt water personified" (329), "mixed their waters together" (233).

kind. Everything on dry land that had the breath of life in its nostrils died. Every living thing on the face of the Earth was wiped out; men and animals and the creatures that move along the ground and the birds of the air were wiped from the Earth. (Genesis 7:21-23)

Indeed, the evaluation of such a large-scale extinction into very personal terms has resonated within the human creature's landscape ever since, evidenced in no small part by that creature's preoccupation with sin, moralities of good and evil, its separation from deity, and an obsessive drive to evaluate everything in terms of binary opposites with one of the poles being the right, best, and favourable at the significant expense of the other. As Watts sums it up, rather than the game of black-and-white, the human creature plays "White-versus-Black," and in this circumstance black becomes negative, and then "[w]hite *must* win is no longer a game. It is a fight" (35).

The Deluge of the Genesis cosmology is a critical *threshold*[2] event within the human creature's cosmos, and it acts as a warning of what lengths God will go to if that creature steps too far out of line. Furthermore, the Deluge iterates just how far removed from its source the human creature has become. The only positive aspect of this event is that God also promises not to unleash another one and seals that promise with the appearance of the rainbow (Genesis 9:11-17).

Rather than another Deluge, God decides to save up judgement for an undisclosed point in future history, an event to be accompanied by an ultimate and irrevocable possibility at the end of qualifying for either life or for the "lake of fire" (Revelation 20:11-15), and qualifying for eternity. The sum total of this unknown event—to be held at an unknown time with, until that day for any human creature, an unknown outcome—is

---

2. A threshold is that liminal space between one state and another, where varying degrees of transformative experience are encountered, where conflicting opposites merge into one and the same moment of experience. For further expansion on various issues related to the idea of the threshold, the work of British anthropologist Victor Turner related to the "liminal," and "liminoid" in general, and the text *From Ritual to Theatre: The Human Seriousness of Play* (1982) specifically, are an excellent starting point. Further to this, a substantial portion of Joseph Campbell's corpus also deals comprehensively with ways to read and interpret threshold and liminal experiences and transformations.

the generation of crippling fear that will stop that creature in its tracks and keep it confined to the cosmos. This fear is informed under the pretext of a cosmological model that is presented to that creature as the divine truth of a loving and just anthropomorphic God, and the threshold that the Deluge signposts opens up like some unfathomable gulf that the human creature has been continually taught it cannot reach beyond.

The waters of the Deluge are an important component of the threshold between the antediluvian landscape of the "great creatures of the sea," and the dust-dry, postdiluvian landscape of the human creature. It is important here to draw the distinction between the antediluvian and the postdiluvian, for like much else related to the Genesis cosmology, this distinction is important within cosmicism and neocosmicism. The landscape of the first eight chapters of Genesis is antediluvian, as it is, "[o]f or belonging to the world before the Noachian deluge; [the landscape] existing before the Flood" (OED 1.505).[3]

As chapter 2 acknowledges, the Genesis cosmology refers to the "great creatures of the sea" as favoured by God, but these others and their landscape are hidden by the engulfing waters of the Deluge; submerged and forgotten in the same manner as Lovecraft's Old Ones in a landscape where

> In the elder times chosen men had talked with the entombed Old Ones in dreams, but then something had happened. The great stone city R'lyeh, with its monoliths and sepulchres, had sunk beneath the waves; and the deep waters, full of the one primal mystery through which not even thought can pass, had cut off the spectral intercourse. But memory never died, and high priests said that the city would rise again when the stars were right. Then came out of the Earth the black spirits of Earth, mouldy and shadowy, and full of dim rumours picked up in caverns beneath forgotten sea-bottoms. ("The Call of Cthulhu," CF 2.40)

The "something" that happens is the Deluge, and this event is the pivotal moment where the human creature's view of the universe is altered, resulting in a radical shift that Part II of this text will explore in some detail. What is of interest here is Lovecraft's use of the phrase "the one

---

3. The root word *diluvium* means "flood, DELUGE" (Onions 39, 268), and the prefix *ante-* designates a thing or event as coming "before in place or time" (39).

primal mystery" and the location of this "mystery" in the "deep waters." I suggest that this image supports the idea that the threshold signified by the Deluge appears to the human creature as an impassable one. Of considerable interest also is the implication that the human creature's endeavour to reach for what lies on the other side of the threshold might indeed reveal the "primal mystery."

The Great Creatures of the Sea

On the sixth day of creation in the Genesis cosmology, the human creature enters a landscape that interacts directly with the "great creatures of the sea." However, as a creature of dry land the human cohabits a cosmos in which it is not only estranged from these "great creatures," it is also estranged from the water in which those others live; and its sense of embodied safety on the dry land is constantly under threat from the pervasiveness of water, for "streams came up from the Earth and watered the whole surface of the ground" (Genesis 2:6). It is perhaps no coincidence that this image resonates with Freud's idea of the heimlich in "The Uncanny"—previously discussed in chapter 1 with respect to the ideas of the map and the territory—and the importance of this cannot be overstated.

The waters are a threat because they are the substance of the universe that lies beyond the human creature's ordered cosmos and for which that creature's body is not designed. The pervasive imminence of water invading the landscape is a disturbing reminder of a universe in which many things exist that the cosmos has hidden away from the human creature. As Lovecraft's character Albert N. Wilmarth is only too well aware in "The Whisperer in Darkness," "the only thing that reached my ears was the gurgling, insidious trickle of strange waters from numberless hidden fountains in the shadowy woods" (CF 2.507).

With Lovecraft's image in mind then, and returning to the Genesis cosmology's "great creatures," it is worth pausing to consider the notes provided in *The NIV Study Bible* stating that:

> The Hebrew word underlying this phrase was used in Canaanite mythology to name a dreaded sea monster. He is often referred to figuratively in O[ld] T[estament] poetry as one of God's most powerful opponents ... In Genesis however, the creatures of the sea are portrayed not as enemies

to be feared but as part of God's good creation to be appreciated. (Barker 7)

As the human creature establishes itself in the landscape, evidence from numerous ancient texts, including various books within the Bible, supports the idea of the "great creatures" "as part of God's good creation," and indicates that communion between these others and the human creature exists.[4] This relationship, however, undergoes a shift that utterly reverses the relative positions of human creature and others, and the postdiluvian cosmos re-inscribes the "great creatures" as others to be feared. Significantly, the "great creatures" that the Deluge hides beneath its waters are also those that God does not bring to the human creature for naming and consequent linguistic capture within the cosmological map (Genesis 2:19-20). There is an interesting parallel between this event and what American literary critic and scholar Bradley Will writes of as Immanuel Kant's distinction between the phenomenal and the noumenal.[5] In his essay "H. P. Lovecraft and the Semiotic Kantian Sublime," Will writes that without a distinct form, "we cannot hypothesize a universal rule to apply to it . . . We cannot grasp the formless object" (9-10); and without a distinct name, I suggest, the human creature is similarly unable to "grasp" the nameless object, indeed, the nameless other.

While the Genesis cosmology's God neither allows these others to

---

4. Such others include, but are not limited to, giants, leviathans, serpents, watchers, and nephilim. Texts and traditions that document these others include, but are not limited to, the Christian Bible, a text that also includes Jewish sacred texts, Sumerian and Akkadian texts, particularly the *Epic of Gilgamesh*, the *Atrahasis* and *The Epic of Creation* (Dalley), the *Book of Enoch* (Nickelsburg and VanderKam), the *Book of Giants* (Stuckenbruck), and Greek myth (Hamilton). All these references are Sumero-Babylonian-Greek-Latin in origin—the founding cultural traditions of the West—and there are numerous identifiable parallels with these in other mythic traditions across the human landscape (Campbell, *Masks of God*). The point to be made is that a general consensus of cooperation and communication between the varying races or species of beings was once a part of the human creature's experience in the universe.

5. Bradley Will describes Kant's "phenomenal sphere [a]s mechanistic, where effects have causes and are determined by natural laws" and "Kant's noumenal sphere [a]s the domain of free will, and he associates the noumenal with the faculty of reason—the faculty whereby we are able to make moral decisions" (8).

be named by the human creature, nor does this cosmology make any substantial claim regarding their form and appearance beyond an implication of size, later books within the Bible do, and in the postdiluvian landscape they are named as either monsters[6] or leviathans, with each of these titles occurring six times, and all located in the postdiluvian Old Testament (Goodrick & Kohlenberger 657, 759).

The landscape these "great creatures" inhabit, like the creatures themselves, is similarly described in language that evokes a sense of entering into something that is old beyond measure, in short, antediluvian, and in Lovecraft's story "The White Ship," such a landscape is eloquently revealed as:

> more wonderful than the lore of old men and the lore of books is the secret lore of ocean. Blue, green, grey, white or black; smooth, ruffled or mountainous; that ocean is not silent. All my days I have watched it and listened to it, and I know it well. At first it told me only the plain little tales of calm beaches and near ports, but with the years it grew more friendly and spoke of other things; of things more strange and more distant in space and in time. Sometimes at twilight the gray vapours of the horizon have parted to grant me glimpses of the ways beyond; and sometimes at night the deep waters of the sea have grown clear and phosphorescent, to grant me glimpses of the ways beneath. And these glimpses have been as often of the ways that were and the ways that might be, as of the ways that are; for ocean is more ancient than mountains, and freighted with the memories and dreams of Time. (CF 1.106)

When the "great creatures" are revealed by either Lovecraft as his Great Old Ones or the Genesis cosmology, these ancient creatures that endure, hidden within the waters, emerge upon the map not as allies to the hu-

---

6. Some scholars interpret these references as being metaphoric national representations of Babylon or Egypt, rather than cosmic representations of actual creatures. This does not, however, negate the use of these passages as referring to actual sea creatures. Such references include Jeremiah 51:34, Isaiah 51:9, and Ezekiel 29:3 and 32:2. What is also interesting, irrespective of whether a national or cosmic representation is applied to the passages, is that the English word *serpent* parallels the Hebrew word *monster* (Barker 1210), and in terms of the physical image, a serpent in English and a monster in Hebrew refer to a creature that in appearance approximates a snake.

man creature, but rather as adversarial others. The antediluvian heritage of Lovecraft's Great Old Ones opens up the possibility for an alternate reading of the Genesis cosmology. Rather than a triumphant creation of the human creature and that creature's supremacy in the universe, the engulfing Deluge in refiguring the map of the universe foreshadows a different potential future from what the human creature has for centuries comforted itself with. Like God's leviathans, the Great Old Ones are removed from view but not from the universe beyond the limits of the view, and they remain as others "who lived ages before there were any men, and who came to the young world out of the sky. Those Old Ones were gone now, inside the Earth and under the sea; but their dead bodies had told their secrets in dreams to the first man, who formed a cult which had never died" ("The Call of Cthulhu," CF 2.37-38). Before the advent of the human creature upon the Earth, the Great Old Ones, who come from the sky, are entombed until the time "when the stars were ready" and have "come round again to the right positions in the cycle of eternity" (CF 2.38, 39, 40, 53). Lovecraft's Old Ones are hidden, often enclosed within fortresses of stone, and always encircled by water. Over time, their hiding becomes solidified within the amnesia of the cosmos.

When they rise, they will rise from immersion in the water and crossing the watery threshold they will be birthed anew. The re-emerging of the antediluvian landscape into the awareness of the postdiluvian human creature, a circumstance that will be examined in detail in Part II, is the opening up of the threshold between landscapes and between the order of the cosmos and the chaos of the universe.

As Lovecraft writes in "Dagon" when the ordered grid of the map dissolves:

> It was in one of the most open and least frequented parts of the broad Pacific . . . Of the longitude I knew nothing, and no island or coastline was in sight. The weather kept fair and for uncounted days I drifted aimlessly beneath the scorching sun; waiting either for some passing ship, or to be cast onto the shores of some habitable land. But neither ship nor land appeared, and I began to despair in my solitude upon the heaving vastness of unbroken blue.
>
> The change happened whilst I slept. (CF 1.52-53)

3. Fractured Universe

While the cosmos is bound beneath the threshold of sky and the sun burning within that sky, it is the landscape that rises up from the deep waters, and that landscape's Great Old Ones, that confront the human creature with the antediluvian past. Often described by Lovecraft as Cyclopean,[7] its age is so great that nothing in it is familiar to the human creature. Even a culture such as the Greek or Roman, considered ancient by twenty-first-century human creatures, bears no similarity with the antediluvian. When the antediluvian is evoked, the comfort that accompanies a sense of connection to some long but continuous historical line is broken, and the human creature is

> confronted by the richly ornate and perfectly preserved façade of a great building, evidently a temple, hollowed from the solid rock ... The art is of the most phenomenal perfection, largely Hellenic in idea, yet strangely individual. It imparts an impression of terrible antiquity, as though it were the remotest rather than the immediate ancestor of Greek art. ("The Temple," CF 1.164)

Such landscapes are often witnessed by human creatures that are surrounded by water, examples of which include but are no means limited to Karl Heinrich in "The Temple" (CF 1.155-69), the narrator of "Dagon" (CF 1.52-58), and Francis Wayland Thurston[8] in "The Call of Cthulhu" (CF 2.21-55). What these human creatures share, and represent, is a human awareness of an absolute isolation from familiar landscapes, and they confront a landscape that is wet, oozing, dark, and filled with the sights, sounds and smells of decay ("The Call of Cthulhu," CF 2.25-26). The antediluvian is the antithesis of all in the cosmos that is safe and familiar.

---

7. The Cyclopean is synonymous with the antediluvian, and is defined in the OED as: "**1.a.** Belonging to or resembling the Cyclopes; monstrous, gigantic, huge; single; or large and round, like the one eye of a Cyclops. **2.** *Antiq.* Applied to an ancient style of masonry in which the stones are of immense size and more or less irregular shape; found in Greece, Italy and elsewhere, and anciently fabled to be the work of a gigantic Thracian race called Cyclopes from their king Cyclops. Now applied also to similar ancient work in other regions" (Simpson and Weiner 4.192).

8. As the narrator of "The Call of Cthulhu," Thurston is never named in the text of the story itself, but "only in the subtitle [omitted in many editions], as 'the late Francis Wayland Thurston, of Boston'" (Joshi and Schultz 27).

An Isolate Object on a Map

When Herbert writes in *Dune Messiah* that "[e]mpires do not suffer emptiness or purpose at the time of their creation. It is when they have become established that aims are lost and replaced by vague ritual" (47), he is speaking directly to the process of the human creature mistaking and consequently behaving as if the map is in fact the territory. When cosmological models begin to diverge and reify, they evolve in a manner that increasingly engenders less an experience of living in the universe and more an abstracted doctrine of estrangement from the universe. I suggest that the crucial time in which this splitting between the universe as machine and the Genesis cosmology gathers momentum coincides with the Council of Nicaea's establishment in 325 C.E. of Christianity as a formalised and State controlled religion (Campbell, *Masks of God* 3.364). The widening gap between the human creature and its deity is later mirrored and supported in the development of science as a formalised "method." According to the anonymous friend of Lovecraft's character Tillinghast in "From Beyond," the study of science and philosophy "should be left to the frigid and impersonal investigator" (CF 1.192), and by the requirements of scientific method this will be an investigator who observes from the outside whatever is under investigation. This is, according to Lovecraft's narrator, a necessity borne of the fact that such pursuits yield "despair, if he fail in his quest, and terrors unutterable and unimaginable if he succeed" (CF 1.192): exactly the dilemma faced by Dick's character Deckard in DAD.

When reflecting on his actions, Deckard finds that he cannot reconcile his sense of self with the experiences of his life, and "what I've done, he thought; that's become alien to me. In fact, everything about me has become unnatural; I've become an unnatural self" (DAD 201). The method of his life as a bounty hunter (DAD 10-11, 23-24) is a map that has not changed as his hunting ground, embodied by the Nexus-6 android, has changed (DAD 25-26). Successive encounters with the Nexus-6 demonstrate a certain unexpected and previously unencountered capacity within the androids for emotional reactions that fall within human parameters. The detailed encounter Deckard has with Luba Luft (DAD 85-86, 113-16, 119), who "had seemed *genuinely* alive" (DAD 122), contributes, by the close of the novel, to Deckard's comprehension that he is stranded in a cosmos in which he has become the alien, even unto himself. In becoming alien, the universe also reduces the human creature to little more than a construct erected on a map. While such a condition may be acceptable for the portable, electronic psychiatrist Dr. Smile in *TSPE* that is "alive but it's not connected with anything outside itself" (81), this kind of disconnection becomes problematic for the human creature. This estrangement is the fallout of cosmoses that fail to interpret the universe appropriately.

In the figuration of cosmoses as ways of thinking about the universe, the human creature positions itself as an isolated object in a universe from which it has been estranged (Zukav 94-95, 196, 289-90; Capra 144). In *The Inner Reaches of Outer Space*, Joseph Campbell refers to this as a "reification of metaphoric imagery" (xxi): an isolation of the human creature from the universe that is similar to existential philosopher Jean-Paul Sartre's expression in *Being and Nothingness* of being "shut up against God, [and] then nothing any longer guarantees my existence to God; he is now united to me only by a relation of exteriority, as the sculptor is related to the finished statue, and once again he can know me only through images" (315). In becoming an object upon a map, the human creature no longer participates with the universe, having access "only through images." Furthermore, having been raised in the shadow of an anthropomorphic deity of morality, that creature has difficulty coming to terms with the idea that the universe may actually be subject to the impersonal and morally neutral workings of a mechanism. When Dick's character Tung Chien in "Faith of Our Fathers" "wondered what some of the other views consisted of," hoping that the Absolute Benefactor does not look like a previous vision Chien had of a mechanism, he ultimately "gave up that line of speculation; it was unprofitable. And too anxiety-inducing" (CS 5.212).

In order to cope with its fears of the emotionless machine, the human creature retreats into a particular way of dealing with that fear. By the nineteenth century, however, the very foundation of the Genesis cosmology became destabilised with the development of new evidence based scientific theories. Two significant publications of gathered evidence to note are Charles Lyell's three-volume *Principles of Geology: Being an Attempt to Explain the Former Changes of the Earth's Surface, by Reference to Causes now in Operation* (1830-33), in which he uses the identification of vast scales of time in the geological record to establish the principle of uniformitarianism; and the subsequent influence of Lyell's *Principles* upon the development of Charles Darwin's *The Origin of Species by Means of Natural Selection; or, The Preservation of Favoured Races in the Struggle for Life* (1859). As if the two apparent adversaries of science and religion were indeed two sides of the same coin, this period in history is witness to significant philosophical developments wherein the established church doctrine suffered a particularly devastating blow from the exposition of the idea of the death, or at the very least lack, of God in the universe.

In *A Scanner Darkly*, Dick's character Bob Arctor declares that "as near as I can figure out, God is dead." To which his friend Luckman replies that he "didn't know He was sick" (1033). This view of a godless universe is most popularly recognised as originating with Friedrich Nietzsche in *The Will to Power* (55, 70, 376-77), *Thus Spoke Zarathustra*, and *The Gay Science*, in which Nietzsche succinctly writes "that 'God is dead', that the belief in the Christian God has ceased to be believable" (*Portable Nietzsche* 447); and this idea is also in the twentieth century iterated by Jean-Paul Sartre in *Being and Nothingness* (129, 315, 375, 547).

If deity exists in the universe in the manner that the Genesis cosmology asserts, then that deity's retreat and death draws attention to the failure of its cosmological frame. This lack of an external deity in the universe occurs approximately parallel with the development of Freud's psychoanalytic view of the human creature. It is perhaps a generalisation, but sobering nonetheless, that by the early twenty-first century it seems as if nearly every human creature in the West has either a neurosis or medicated psychological condition within which they are imprisoned—a counsellor or a therapist. The human creature has become so introspective that the claim might be made that the only landscape that can be seen is the internal landscape of the self and this is, largely, a self disengaged and dismembered.

Within the vacuum of such fragmentation, Bob Arctor, in *SD*, questions what it is that gives a human creature identity, wondering where the threshold lies between an identity put forward as a mask or gesture within the social landscape and the genuine identity of the individual (*SD* 882-83). The social landscape from which Bob Arctor has at this point emerged is a scripted speech on his role as an undercover narcotics agent fighting to deliver the human collective from the evil grip of drug

3. Fractured Universe

addiction, and the script has been delivered from within the safe anonymity of his scramble suit. The scramble suit is designed to project every possible variable in the appearance of the human body, thereby resulting in an image of a person recognisable by the fact that he or she looks in some way like everybody else, and can therefore never be identified as any particular individual (SD 877). One's *real* face is never seen. But after his speech, Arctor wonders: "What is identity? . . . Where does the act end? Nobody knows . . . What am I actually? he asked himself. He wished, momentarily, for his scramble suit. Then, he thought, I could go on being a vague blur and passers-by, street people in general, would applaud. Let's hear it for the vague blur, he thought, doing a short rerun" (SD 883). SD deals with the identity of Bob Arctor as a progressive unravelling. The more he examines himself and the more he looks inward, the less certain he becomes of who he is.

The most recent century of human history has been one of significant and rapid change. During the first half of the twentieth century, the human creature survived two global conflicts, punctuated between by the Great Depression, and concluded with the unleashing of nuclear capabilities at Hiroshima and Nagasaki; the stars of heaven well and truly fell to the Earth in August 1945. In the aftermath of nuclear warfare and racial genocide—events that contributed significantly to the polarisation of the West during the reigns of McCarthyism and the Cold War—the human creature is propelled to such a distant point of the map that, while the destination may remain unseen, the point of origin has become lost. There is simply no trail of breadcrumbs left to be followed. As the character Anne Hawthorne says in *TSPE*, "'Earth is ceasing to become our natural world . . . we've got no world left! . . . No home at all!'" (149).

The universe as it is read through the lens of any cosmos has become a fractured landscape of opposing forces, an oscillation between binary opposites that cannot be reconciled. The Irish poet W. B. Yeats writes in "The Second Coming" that "[t]hings fall apart; the centre cannot hold," adding to this revelation "[t]hat twenty centuries of stony sleep / Were vexed to nightmare" (246-47). The reified map no longer reflects the dynamic territory, and what is left is a complex tangle of maps—a great wad of knots in the trajectory of linear time—all submerging the universe.

Because a retreat into a religious cosmology has been a way for the human creature to negate the possibility that the universe is a machine of *cold equations,* similar to Watts's idea of black versus white, this negation also designates the universe as machine—and by extension any machine—as negative and perhaps even malevolent. This is a moral assessment of an amoral, or more precisely *supra*moral, entity, and the machine in the face of a retreating and abstracted deity becomes an adversary.

The machine is not human, and it is not unreasonable to extend this view to the idea that in the universe as machine, the universe and the human creature are also separate and incompatible. The universe as machine keeps expanding, and it does so inexorably (Gribbin 4), and while the universe continues to expand, the human creature exists in a cosmos divided. The cosmos has become corrupt and adversarial, or impersonally mechanical and godless; and the human creature has forgotten that this is not the universe. It may be that when the human creature draws too near the universe it reacts by hiding that territory beneath the map, and the heimlich of familiarity becomes the unfamiliar other side of the heimlich coin. The disturbing and the uncanny that rouses not only curiosity and wonder, but to which the human creature almost invariably responds with fear, is never far from the surface—a potential crisis for that creature, and a crisis to which Part II in its examination of cosmicism will now turn.

Part II: Cosmicism

Chapter 4: Cosmicism Is

> Accident has caused a certain momentary energy-pattern to coagulate for an instant in a negligible corner of limitless space. It calls itself "mankind", and has a certain number of basic needs arising from the chance conditions of its formation . . . We are all meaningless atoms adrift in the void.
>
> —H. P. Lovecraft, SL 3.221-22

As I have already noted, cosmicism is drawn from the philosophy of H. P. Lovecraft, and its principal tenets are that the universe operates as an indifferent mechanism, without "purpose or direction," and the human creature is not only insignificant but exists as a biological mutation or accident of elemental and chemical stellar processes. The mechanism of the universe operates without emotions or ethics of human parameters and understanding, thereby rendering any ethical effort as pointless, for morality has influence and meaning only at an insignificant and localised level. Cosmicism's universe is also characterised by the absence of a moral deity that cares for the human creature.

The term cosmicism is formed by the combination of the word *cosmic* and the suffix *-ism*. If something is cosmic, it is "of this world, worldly, of or belonging to the universe" (OED 3.983), and an *-ism* signifies "naming the process, or the completed action, or its result" and is used to "[f]orm the name of a system of theory or practice" (OED 8.113). Cosmicism is, therefore, a "system of theory" about the universe.

A point worth noting is that while the term cosmicism is absent from English dictionaries and almost entirely so from theory—literary or otherwise—the OED does cite the term cosmism, which it defines as "[t]he conception of the cosmos or 'order of nature' as a self-existent, self-acting whole; the theory which explains the cosmos or universe solely according to the methods of positive science" (OED 3.984). By definition, cosmism could to some degree be paralleled with cosmicism. The significant difference between the two terms, however, is cosmicism's explicit condition of the absence of a "cosmic intelligence" (SL 3.281), or deity, whereas cosmism remains silent on this issue.

It is also important to note that the *OED*, and many theoretical science fiction texts, often appear to use the terms cosmos and universe interchangeably, and that Lovecraft also does so, moving between both terms in similar usage to the definition for universe that is used in this text.¹ In reference to Lovecraft, then, as I have already noted in the glossary of terms, read his use of the terms cosmos and universe as evoking the same meaning; that is, universe.

Having noted the basic definition of cosmicism, it is also appropriate to make some comment on the rather curious position of the term itself, and by consequence, the philosophy. What is particularly interesting, where the acknowledgement of cosmicism is locatable within critical text or the discussion and dissemination of ideas via differing media within the lay community, is that there appears to be a general consensus on what cosmicism is as a theory, but no definitive, encyclopaedic definition of cosmicism as a recognisable term in the English or literary lexicons. The *OED* lists "cosmic, cosmical, cosmically, cosmism, cosmist, cosmize, cosmogeny, cosmogony, cosmology and cosmos" (OED 3.983-86), but not cosmicism, and to date the only other source for a definition encountered, beyond the scope of Lovecraftian scholarship, is the questionable authority of the Internet encyclopaedia Wikipedia. That cosmicism appears to be a term that until recently has been, and largely continues to be, used almost exclusively within the proximity of Lovecraftian commentary is clear, but why this should be so is perhaps more of a mystery.

The term cosmicism can be evidenced within the academic community, but it is reasonable to say that while the philosophy's basic tenets are recognised as points of interest and enquiry, the term itself remains largely unrecognised, even when scholars and

---

1. Examples of the use of the terms cosmos and universe by Lovecraft when discussing events, principles and observations include, but are by no means limited to, *SL* 1.24, 44, 63-64, 132-33, 156, 207-9, 231, 260, 298, 2.150-51, 355-56, 3.39, 54, 86-87, 196, 208, 4.6-7, 22-23, 56-57, 82, and 5.4, 113, 116, 153-54, 195, 239-43. The interchangeable nature of these two terms is at times so fluid that both terms even appear in the same piece of correspondence and in reference to the same things. Examples of this include, but are not limited to, *SL* 1.334-35, 2.124-26, 261-74, 334-35, 3.450-51, and 5.69.

critics are writing in direct reference to and analysis of Lovecraft's work. As a precise term that can be used to express a particular philosophical point of view and therefore be used as a tool for critical inquiry, cosmicism becomes highly visible because it is largely invisible.

There appear to be rare exceptions to this, although even within these exceptions the actual term cosmicism is used very sparingly outside the scholarship of the Indian-born literary critic, biographer, and editor S. T. Joshi (*Subtler Magick* 50, 71, 83-84, 128, 132-33, 176-77, 210, 231, 234, 253, 260-65). After Joshi, the few scattered uses of the term include, but are not limited to, texts by Timothy Evans ("Tradition and Illusion" 177), the literary historian Philip A. Shreffler (9-10), and the American literary theorist and theologian Edward Ingebretsen, who mentions "[t]he cosmicisms of Poe and Lovecraft" (117).

One of the earlier expressions of Lovecraft's philosophy can be found in his correspondence with the Kleicomolo.[2] In 1916 Lovecraft writes:

> Our human race is only a trivial incident in the history of creation . . . And more: may not all mankind be a mistake—an abnormal growth—a disease in the system of Nature—an excrescence on the body of infinite progression like a wart on the human hand? . . . How arrogant of us, creatures of the moment, whose very species is but an experiment of the *Deus Naturae*, to arrogate to ourselves an immortal future and considerable status! . . . we imagine that the welfare of our race is the paramount consideration, when as a matter of fact the very existence of the race may be an obstacle to the predestined course of the aggregated universe of infinity! How do we know that the form of atomic and molecular motion called "life" is the highest of all forms? Perhaps the dominant creature—the most rational and God-like of all beings—is an invisible gas! Or perhaps it is a flaming and effulgent mass of molten star-dust. Who can say that men have souls while rocks have none? (SL 1.24)

---

2. This is a collective name for a group of correspondents; being Rheinhart Kleiner (Klei), Ira A. Cole (co), Maurice W. Moe (mo), and H. P. Lovecraft (lo) (SL 1.23).

In Lovecraft's universe, the human creature is an insignificant being, a blemish or contagion that may actually hinder the operation and evolution of the universe. This is a universe vacated by an anthropomorphic deity, governed instead by the amoral processes of nature, and possessed of no care or even awareness for the emotions and moralities of the localised, human creature. It is a universe that exists, largely, beyond human comprehension. While over the rest of his life Lovecraft refined this view, particularly in his later and more explicit insistence that the universe is not created but is eternal, the fundamental elements of cosmicism were established by Lovecraft in 1916, as quoted above.

While the term cosmicism is seldom used by Lovecraft, he does write of his "infinite-cosmicism" (SL 3.44) and expresses doubts about "the cosmicism of Bierce, James, & even Machen," adding that "[i]t is not every writer who feels poignantly & almost intolerably the pressure of cryptic & unbounded outer space" (SL 3.196). More commonly, however, Lovecraft uses such phrases as "cosmic horror" (SL 2.316; SHL 31, 33, 34, 77, 80), "cosmic terror" (SHL 29, 34, 72), "cosmic fear" (SHL 14, 27, 28, 40, 45, 58, 63, 69, 81), and "cosmic chaos" (SL 1.284) to explicate varying aspects of his philosophy.

The universe in cosmicism is a vast, indifferent mechanism, often expressed by Lovecraft as chaotic and devoid of any emotion or regard for the human creature. He writes that "[t]he cosmos is a mindless vortex; a seething ocean of blind forces" (SL 1.156); that it is "an automatic, meaningless chaos devoid of ultimate values or distinctions of right and wrong" (SL 1.298). Throughout his correspondence, Lovecraft writes variations of a view of the universe as "a purposeless & meaningless affair of endless cycles ... consisting wholly of blind force operating according to fixed & eternal patterns inherent in eternity," and that these forces "recognis[e] no such qualities as good or evil, beauty or ugliness, in the ultimate structure of the universe" (SL 2.124–25). The universe is structured and operates like a machine "whose substance involves a rhythmic & perpetual rearrangement of parts in the manner of a kaleidoscope" (SL 4.7). This perpetual, cyclic motion of parts is "*automatic and* kaleidoscopic" (SL 4.56), within "the ceaseless round of the limitless cosmos" (SL 5.4).

Lovecraft draws a universe that operates as an eternal, infinite, and indifferent machine that is devoid of emotional regard for any thing or affective event that occurs, irrespective of whether is it "good or bad according to any particular local standard" (SL 1.334). The human creatures that inhabit—albeit an insignificant part of—the universe are themselves "cosmos-driven automata" (SL 5.113) subject to "the ineluctable natural laws & probabilities which actually prevail" (SL 5.196). These "natural laws" are the cold equations that underpin the indifferent machine of cosmicism's universe.

The cold equations can be equated with Lovecraft's referent of "Determinism," which "rules inexorably . . . The real fact is simply that every event in the cosmos is caused by the action of antecedent and circumjacent forces, so that whatever we do is unconsciously the inevitable product of Nature rather than of our own volition" (SL 1.132). By its very design the universe renders ethical effort pointless beyond the human creature's terrestrial locality, and this "blind universe" (SL 1.209) of cosmicism is an image repeatedly cited by Lovecraft. While the immediate effect of this idea is to highlight the sense of an indifferent mechanism with no regard for the human creature, it is through the later development of neocosmicism that the universe's apparent blindness, inasmuch as this implies a human negation of something, becomes a fundamental element of rewriting the terrain of the universe.

The cold universe is alien to the human creature that has remained confined within a map of anthropomorphic superiority. Robert E. Howard, an American author and contemporary of Lovecraft, wrote in the letters section of *Weird Tales* in May 1928 that in the story "The Call of Cthulhu" Lovecraft "has grasped, to all intents, the world outside our paltry ken. His scope is unlimited and his range is cosmic" (Joshi and Michaud 28). It is this unknowable universe that, like a roiling sea, encircles the insignificant and localised human creature. Even though from a human perspective the world that creature inhabits seems immense, it is little more than a dustmote (SL 5.113), beyond which lie "the unknown phaenomena and abysses of space" (SL 1.131).

In correspondence with Edwin Baird, editor of *Weird Tales*, Lovecraft asks, "who ever wrote a story from the point of view that man is a blemish on the cosmos, who ought to be eradicated?" and answers that "[o]ne can't write a weird story of real power without perfect psychological detachment from the human scene" (Joshi and Michaud 20). This detachment is a critical element of cosmicism that serves to highlight the magnitude of the human creature's acute locality and influence, which is perpetually and immanently threatened with extinction. The human creature's "ecstatic wonder at the unfathomed reaches of nighted space and the glittering jewels of nebular, solar and planetary fire" is starkly contrasted with the knowledge that such wonder is located within a "kaleidoscopic, undying and unbounded drama of infinite time and space, [where] everything terrestrial and human has seemed to shrink away to insignificance" to reveal "the filthy louse called man . . . this crawling insect species" (SL 1.172). Furthermore, organic life will disappear entirely:

> When the breed is extinct, there will be none (unless some other terrestrial species arises to consciousness) to recall that it ever existed. And when this planet is finally frozen to lifelessness by the fading of the sun, there will certainly be not a conceivable grain of evidence to tell anybody (assuming the existence of other organisms somewhere amidst the scattered galaxies) that any life had ever existed on it. (SL 4.82)[3]

Lovecraft often writes of the idea that everything will end (Houellebecq 32), and while "terrestrial life past and present" (SL 2.264) will most certainly disappear, Lovecraft acknowledges that even apparently eternal celestial bodies such as stars and planets are *"temporary in the long run"* (SL 2.266) and "eventually the very material substance of [a planet's] system—& galaxy—& universe—disintegrates into its constituent electrons & leaves only an 'empty' field of force (out of which another universe is later born)" (SL 5.153).

In this impersonal mechanism in which the human creature is insignificant, cosmicism reaches even further into that creature's sense of ontological stability to isolate all human emotion, morality, and ethics as purely local concerns that bear no significance in the universe at large. Whether the human creature "suffer[s] or not [its] feelings are the most trivial of incidents in the unending cycle of existence" (SL 1.156), for in this universe, "'[r]ight' and 'wrong' are primitive conceptions which cannot endure the test of cold science" (SL 1.207). Ultimately, human moralities amount to nothing (SL 1.262), and while "[t]here is no reason to

---

3. Cormac McCarthy's novel *The Road* (2006) is a highly visible twenty-first-century speculative iteration of this kind of ending for the human creature; contemporising cosmicism's wider relevance as an interpretative framework and demonstrating its literary reach more generally.

suppose that any given human impression has any exact correspondence with any external reality" (SL 3.281), such moralities and traditions mean "everything locally and pragmatically because we have nothing else to shield us from a devastating sense of 'lostness' in endless time and space" (SL 2.357).

This sense of "lostness" is compounded by the sense that in the sea of "endless time and space," no recognisably sympathetic deity can be found. The absence of deity, I suggest, is prefaced by the very structure of the Genesis cosmology as it points towards a retreating God. As Edward Ingebretsen observes in *Maps of Heaven, Maps of Hell: Religious Terror as Memory from the Puritans to Stephen King*, the sixteenth-century French theologian John Calvin may be interpreted as "most directly anticipat[ing]" Lovecraft's vision of the universe, but it is the theology of the eighteenth-century American Puritan Jonathan Edwards that Lovecraft "most completely realizes the horrific consequences of." That is, that "[t]here is no holy from which to retreat; no mysticism save the appalling solipsism of the Self in a cosmos of incomprehensible, literally unimaginable design" (106).

Lovecraft's essay "Supernatural Horror in Literature" opens with one of his most often quoted and well know statements, where he claims that "[t]he oldest and strongest emotion of mankind is fear, and the oldest and strongest kind of fear is fear of the unknown" (25). In saying this, he firmly locates the fear at the heart of cosmicism as having coexisted with the human creature for virtually all its racial and mythic memory. Lovecraft's opening statement also highlights the challenge cosmicism reveals, the question of how an emotional creature can assimilate that emotion, and thereby itself, within a universe that is without emotion. How can the human creature find the balance between its "cosmic fear" and a universe that does not recognise and therefore respond to such fear? When writing of Charles Robert Maturin's 1820 novel *Melmoth the Wanderer*, Lovecraft claims that "[f]ear is taken out of the realm of the conventional and exalted into a hideous cloud over mankind's very destiny" (SHL 40), and in considering Edgar Allan Poe, Lovecraft claims that Poe writes with "a master's vision of the terror that stalks about and within us" (SHL 56).

What this points towards, what lies at the heart of cosmicism, is that the human response to the universe is a response of fear. The American essayist and editor Darrell Schweitzer writes that "[f]ew people seriously expect the supernatural to intervene in their lives. But the night fears are still with us" (*Dream Quest* 61), and the French writer and filmmaker Michel Houellebecq remarks that Lovecraft's openings to his stories are often some variant form of "Abandon all hope, ye who enter here" (54). Indeed, Lovecraft himself writes in *SHL* that

> Children will always be afraid of the dark, and men with minds sensitive to hereditary impulse will always tremble at the thought of the hidden and fathomless worlds of strange life which may pulsate in the gulfs beyond the stars or press hideously upon our own globe in unholy dimensions which only the dead and the moonstruck can glimpse. (27)

When beholding the universe *as it is*, Lovecraft points toward only two possibilities, and these are flight into madness or death:

> The rational mind, he said, is most horrified by an assault of irrationality, the discovery that all previously held and comfortable assumptions about the way the universe works are wrong. The façade of human understanding is swept away, revealing vast vistas of the unknown which are at the same time terrifying and excitingly attractive. Ultimately, terror overwhelms wonder, and the hero is swamped in helpless despair. (Schweitzer, *Dream Quest* 6)

Adding to this, there appears to be scholarly agreement that Lovecraft holds a very specific intent in mind when he uses the term cosmic. As the Lovecraftian editor and critic David E. Schultz identifies, Lovecraft does not use the term "cosmic" in a vague way, but in a very specific one in which he "forces us to shift the focus from the immediate and humanocentric to the point of view taken by the vast uncaring cosmos. Cosmic fear must surely penetrate far deeper and with greater persistence than any personal fear, and obscure cosmic relationships cannot be perceived by shortsighted humans" (217). For the human creature that inhabits the universe, the strength of Schultz's statement lies in the fact that he draws the same distinction as Lovecraft's. That is, when the human creature looks upon a universe that is not only vast but in which by comparison it is so utterly insignificant, a gulf opens up between this realisation and the need for that creature to maintain its footing in a local identity in order that it might hold onto a sense of actually existing in the first place. Attempting to bridge this gulf in cosmicism inevitably leads to madness or death, and sanity is only maintained by turning away from this threshold and back into denial or illusion.

In a universe stripped of any deity that might care, the Genesis cosmology no longer holds up as a map from which to seek comfort or help, and the universe as machine as a central and explicit aspect of cosmicism only serves to contribute to the human creature's sense of estrangement from the universe. This estrangement is compounded by the very real fear that as a consequence of its insignificance, if a foundation on which to stand cannot be found, the human creature is also at risk of estrangement from its own self—of disappearing altogether. This is what Schultz refers to when he claims that "[c]osmic fear must surely penetrate far deeper and with greater persistence than any personal fear," and this is what places the human creature in such a precarious and maddening position in the universe of cosmicism. When considering the works of Nathaniel Hawthorne, Lovecraft writes in *SHL* that Hawthorne is "cramped by the Puritanism of early New England; shadowed and wistful, and grieved at an unmoral universe which everywhere transcends the conventional patterns thought by our forefathers to represent divine and immutable law" (61).

This fractured human condition is recognised by Lovecraft and succinctly expressed by the American mathematician and Lovecraftian scholar Donald R. Burleson when he writes in his essay "On Lovecraft's Themes: Touching the Glass":

> The overall effect, then, of the thematic content of Lovecraft's fiction is to cleave reality into a bipolar opposition: the hope of humankind to have dignity and worth and meaning on the one hand, and, on the other, the dashing of those hopes in the contemplation of a cosmos blindly indifferent to the presence of humans. (150)

Examples of such fractured human creatures in Lovecraft's fiction include the U-boat captain Altberg-Ehrenstein in "The Temple" (CF 1.155-69); Carter and his friend Joel Manton in "The Unnamable" (CF 1.396-404); Delapore in "The Rats in the Walls" (CF 1.373-95); Francis Wayland Thurston and Gustav Johansen in "The Call of Cthulhu" (CF 2.21-55); Albert N. Wilmarth in "The Whisperer in Darkness" (CF 2.463-535); Ammi Pierce and Mrs. Gardner in "The Colour out of Space" (CF 2.365-97); Robert Blake in "The Haunter of the Dark" (CF

3.453-80); Edward Pickman Derby and Daniel Upton in "The Thing on the Doorstep" (CF 3.325-58); and the unnamed narrators of "Dagon" (CF 1.52-58), "From Beyond" (CF 1.191-200), "The Moon-Bog" (CF 1.255-63), and "The Lurking Fear" (CF 1.348-72). These characters, enmeshed in personal and at times agonising fracture, point towards a prominent factor within cosmicism: just how utterly ill-equipped to face the universe the human creature has become.

As a formalised theory, cosmicism confronts traditional assumptions that are rooted in the Genesis cosmology; principally that the universe is a temporal object, with beginning and end, that was created and has remained as presided over by God. Within the Genesis cosmology, the human creature is the pinnacle of God's creation and, in hand with the planet that creature inhabits, is therefore the most centrally important aspect of the universe. By contrast, as the emphasis of centrality has shifted throughout the historical development of a scientific view of the universe—that is, from the geocentric, to the heliocentric, to the quantum, and into the twenty-first century to what looks increasingly like a multiverse that is "everything that there is" and in which "a universe is a portion of the Multiverse accessible to a particular set of observers" (Gribbin xi-xii, 10-11)—cosmicism's view of the universe has become more relevant. The problem for the human creature in the universe of cosmicism, however, and to which the following chapter will address a detailed examination, lies in the bipolarity between a scientific view of the universe that has expanded over the course of time and the deeply embedded and contractive view of the Genesis cosmology that starts with an infinite God and shrinks down to an isolated individual.

Chapter 5: Schizophrenic Universe

> Nothing changed; it just spread out farther and farther in the form of neon ooze. What there was always more of had been congealed into permanence long ago, as if the automatic factory that cranked out these objects had jammed in the *on* position.
> —Philip K. Dick, *A Scanner Darkly*

Alien Universe

In *The Modern Temper: A Study and a Confession*, American social and cultural critic Joseph Wood Krutch writes that "man is left more and more alone in a universe to which he is completely alien. His world was once, like the child's world, three-quarters myth and poetry" (7-8). As the human creature's understanding of the universe expands, its perception of that territory increasingly becomes a mental abstraction rather than an experience of embodied connection and participation. Lovecraft's cosmicism is a signpost of an evolution within the human creature's worldview. In reaching the twentieth century, this view has moved from Dante Alighieri's geocentric "Paradise on the summit of the mountain of Purgatory, which his century situated in the middle of an imagined ocean covering the whole of the Southern Hemisphere" (Campbell, *Masks of God* 4.611), and has traversed Copernicus's heliocentric universe. By Lovecraft's time, science was taking preliminary steps towards a quantum view of the universe, and cosmicism developed in a manner that both embraced the historical model of the universe as machine and anticipated quantum science.

This view of the universe holds its focus simultaneously on what is behind and ahead of the human creature, and is nested within cosmicism as a vital component of its utility and potency as a philosophical model for enquiry and illumination. The idea of looking in both directions at once is comparable to the idea of "time-binding" that Heinlein succinctly describes as "a technical term invented by Alfred Korzybski,[1]

---

1. Korzybski was a Polish-American engineer and philosopher. It is worth noting

and it refers to the fact that the human animal lives not only in the present, but also in the past and the future" ("Guest of Honor Speech 1941," 154). "Time-binding" involves an interplay between what is known of and is on record regarding the historical past and what is extrapolated as future possibility. Based on these parameters, the human creature makes decisions in the present in which it exists, and each decision has an effect in the immediate event of that decision, while also projecting into the future to affect all subsequent events. Paul Atreides in Herbert's *Dune* understands this:

> The emptiness was unbearable. Knowing how the clockwork had been set in motion made no difference. He could look to his own past and see the start of it–the training, the sharpness of talents, the refined pressures of sophisticated disciplines, even exposure to the O.C. Bible at a critical moment ... and, lastly, the heavy intake of spice. And he could look ahead–the most terrifying direction–to see where it all pointed. (188)

The idea of the future as "the most terrifying direction" is inescapable for the human creature within cosmicism, because in the knowledge that everything will end, what future remains? Dick's character Deckard, in *DAD*, knows this, and in wondering if Mozart had known it too, Deckard concludes that "the performance will end, the signers will die, eventually the last score of the music will be destroyed in one way or another; finally the name 'Mozart' will vanish, the dust will have won" (85). Even the order and function of components within the machine will eventually cease to operate, and when Dick's characters Chien and Tanya talk about "music untuning the sky" in the story "Faith of Our Fathers" (CS 5.221), Tanya reminds Chien that this speaks to the idea that "'All the celestial order of the universe ends' ... 'you know that old Pythagorean business about the music of the spheres'" (CS 5.221).

From a position that is simultaneously retrospective and speculative the universe has become an alien place, and from within its own locality the sheer size of the universe when expressed within the Newtonian framework of space and time overwhelms the human creature.

---

in connection to Heinlein's use of Korzybski's "time-binding," that John Clute acknowledges Heinlein as a science fiction author who writes within an engineering framework when constructing his view of the human creature's future (2011, 137–39).

5. Schizophrenic Universe

When something is alien, it "[b]elong[s] to another person or place," is "[o]f a foreign nation and allegiance," and is rooted in a "foreign or other origin" (OED 1.314). To be alien can even mean to have "a nature repugnant, adverse or opposed *to*" someone or something (OED 1.315). In short, an alien universe is unfamiliar and unwelcome at best, and more often a hostile territory in which "even the circle of stars . . . [a]re like the luminous tips of weapons aimed down" (*D* 197), and where "the Pole Star leers down from the same place in the black vault, winking hideously like an insane watching eye" ("Polaris, " *CF* 1.65). The human creature is not only estranged from this universe, it is unable to escape.

Dante's Paradise no longer resides in the Pacific—even though Dagon's (*CF* 1.52) and Cthulhu's (*CF* 2.45-46) might. In reference back to the conversation between Chien and Tanya in "Faith of Our Fathers," the crucial moment arrives when Chien asks Tanya if she really believes in the idea of the universe being driven by the music of the spheres—the music of the machine—or whether she believes in deity, to which Tanya says: "'God!' She laughed. 'That went out with the donkey steam engine. What are you talking about?'" (*CS* 5.221).

The cosmos has become unreadable in reference to how and indeed *where* the human creature lives. As Paul Virilio states in *Grey Ecology*, the space in which living can be done has been shrinking away at a significant rate, and "what we call real-time leads to the space-time continuum suffering a temporal contraction which reduces to nothing or practically nothing the vastness of the world" (27).

Writing almost a century ago in *The Modern Temper*,[2] Joseph Wood Krutch claims that "the myth, having been once established, persists long after the assumptions upon which it was made have been destroyed, because, being born of desire, it is far more satisfactory than any fact" (8). Mythic traditions do not always transport easily to locales outside their point of origin, and in an increasingly globalised sense of the world this

---

2. In his essay titled "Lovecraft's Concept of Background," the Lovecraftian scholar and critic Steven J. Mariconda discusses the influence of Krutch's text upon the development of Lovecraft's own philosophy (4). The parallels between chapter 1 of *The Modern Temper* and the basic tenets of cosmicism are striking, and I suggest, as Mariconda implies, that the development of Lovecraft's philosophy owes a good deal to Krutch's text.

transportation can fail altogether. The single biggest problem the human creature faces in holding onto the reified map that the Genesis cosmology has become is located in the fact that this cosmos was scribed thousands of years ago within the context of a Jewish, nomadic culture posited in the desert, and most human creatures simply no longer live like that.

Not only has the culturally constructed map of the cosmos become an illusion that the human creature has tricked itself into thinking is real, and therefore tries to navigate; but caught up within this transformation, the cosmos often represents the human creature's fantasy of an ideal that is ever expected and never found within the space-time of the universe. This fantasy of an ideal is encountered in Dick's story "Strange Eden." When Captain Johnson steps out of his ship and onto the planet's surface, the landscape he enters is not dissimilar to the Genesis cosmology's Eden. Johnson and his crew are there to map the planet, but he has reservations about doing so. It seems that from the beginning Johnson senses a threat in the underlying territory of paradise, noticing that "[a]ll the animals were tame. What kind of people had built this place? Panic stabbed at him. Maybe not people. Maybe some other race. Something alien, from beyond the galaxy. Maybe this was the frontier of an alien empire, some kind of advanced station" (CS 3.114). For Johnson, the map of an Edenic landscape is laid out before him, but he knows that were the planet any "closer to Terra," it would not remain unspoilt (CS 3.111). Johnson's discomfort, however, is not merely a result of understanding how his own species has all too often approached the natural landscape; it is also a response to something that he senses lies beneath the map of perfection before him. An interesting comparison can be made with Heinlein's novel MC and the "Earthlike" (402) planet where the human creature is made welcome by the inhabitants—a welcome that makes Lazarus Long uncomfortable (407, 419). It is only after Slayton Ford's terror at the temple of the real inhabitants, the Jockaira, that Lazarus Long understands the difference between the appearance and the underlying territory of the planet (MC 419-20). Some comparison may also be drawn with the story "In the Walls of Eryx"—written collaboratively by Lovecraft and Kenneth Sterling—inasmuch as the crystal that appears to be lying on open ground and readily accessible by the human creature is actually enclosed within an invisible labyrinth the entanglement of which is lethal to that creature (CF 4.554). So for Johnson, then, he may seek refuge in the desire for a pristine world in which to live, but he knows this is wishful thinking for something he has never had. Similarly, Barney Mayerson in *TSPE* may "want to be alone with [his] garden," but cannot escape acknowledging the territory beneath that garden when asking, "'Is there any point in trying to start a garden here? Or will we go the familiar way, too'" (*TSPE* 230). The universe is never far from view.

Herbert's Paul Atreides recognises this human desire for the experience of a universe that follows a sense of order and logic when he says:

> There is in all things a pattern that is part of our universe. It has symmetry, elegance and grace ... We try to copy these patterns in our lives and our society, seeking the rhythms, the dances, the forms that comfort. Yet, it is possible to see peril in the finding of ultimate perfection. It is clear that the ultimate pattern contains its own fixity. In such perfection, all things move towards death. ("The Collected Sayings of Muad'Dib" by the Princess Irulan; *D* 361)

Paul Atreides expresses an awareness of the human creature's endeavour to "copy these patterns," in nature that by their "cycles" and "symmetry" imply the working mechanism of the universe as machine. The machine keeps on turning, and the finite, biological human creature is caught between its desire for the logic of that machine at the heart of the territory and its human tendency to rely on what it sees across the surface of the map as if that were somehow the whole of the reality in which it exists. The dilemma in terms of survival that this bipolar condition throws up is also observed by Paul after witnessing the death of Duncan Idaho at the hands of Imperial Sardaukar in service to the Harkonnen enemy (*D* 215-16). Paul understands that he is caught within "*blind* ground," remonstrating himself for having relied only on what he can see and recalling the "Bene Gesserit axiom" that "'If you rely only on your eyes, your other senses weaken'" (*D* 218).

The human creature has become so enclosed within the light of its neatly mapped cosmos that it has forgotten what the territory looks like, and to venture beyond such confinement and into the universe is terrifying. When a glimpse of the universe is granted, that creature wants then only to forget and return to the comfort of cosmos; as Chien says in Faith of Our Fathers," "'A hallucination ... is merciful. I wish I had it; I want mine back'" (*CS* 5.222).

If the human creature chooses to seek existence in the universe, it risks the engulfment of madness or death if it also fails to reconcile itself with the revelation of the territory. All four of the primary authors discussed in this book provide multiple examples of such an outcome, including but by no means limited to the often-quoted warning to all human creatures in the opening paragraph of Lovecraft's "The Call of Cthulhu" (CF 2.21-22); Richard Upton Pickman, who splits his identity while renting studio space under the name of Peters, in "Pickman's Model" (CF 2.56-57); Crawford Tillinghast in "From Beyond" (CF 1.191-92); Joe Slater in "Beyond the Wall of Sleep" (CF 1.71-85); Alia Atreides in Herbert's CD, who inevitably "felt that she had become two people," before seeking death as her escape (339, 363-68); and Heinlein's Slayton Ford on the world of the Jockaira in MC (419-21).

The extreme nature of the human creature's view of the universe as a bipolar state against which it is pitted emerges from cosmicism's premise that within this bipolarity the human creature is afforded limited options. It may choose either to remain ignorant of the territory by means of ideological flight back into the Genesis cosmology or, in the pursuit of peeling back the map to expose the territory in its manifestation of the universe as machine, to risk engulfment's symptomatic outcomes.

If the human creature has been fortunate enough to pull back from the threshold of revelation prior to being engulfed, it may still be able to return to the amnesia of the cosmos in which, until that point, it had dwelt. The ever-present possibility in this scenario is, however, as Nathaniel Wingate Peaslee discovers in "The Shadow out of Time" (CF 3.373-75), that the disturbing reality of the hidden territory will be ever after felt. For the human creature that has strayed too far from the path of the map and found itself adrift and utterly severed from the cosmos of its accustomed view, an escape into madness or death ultimately becomes the only viable option. This can be likened to what I frame as a *heimlich conundrum*—a sense of damnation irrespective of the direction taken—and the fear that is generated between these poles becomes a primary driver of the human creature within cosmicism. Irrespective of the choice that is made, that creature senses that the outcome will be the same.

During a conversation with Mercer and afterwards with his wife, in Dick's novel *DAD*, Deckard comprehends that *"[t]here is no salvation,"* that he should proceed upon his course of action. Even though Deckard knows that it is wrong, Mercer tells him that to do what is wrong "'will be required ... no matter where you go. It is the basic condition of life, to be required to violate your own identity ... It is the ultimate shadow, the defeat of creation; this is the curse at work, the curse that feeds on all life. Everywhere in the universe'" (*DAD* 155). For Deckard, to hunt down three more androids is the means by which he can achieve recognition as a successful human creature, and this is a recognition made all the more important by the fact that he is a healthy human resident left behind on the "contaminated Earth" (*DAD* 15). Deckard can validate his identity as human through earning money enough to buy a real animal upon which to bestow his empathy, and he can achieve this only by means of the cold execution of androids (*DAD* 148). While the hunt is by no means new to him, a bounty hunter by profession, his recent encounter with androids has furnished Deckard with the disturbing possibility that androids may indeed be more than machines and he may be developing a sense of empathy for what has been designated *un*human by definition of its own lack of empathy.[3]

The universe is no longer one stable thing or the other. It is neither machine nor God's creation. It is internally split and the human creature is also separated from it, cast adrift within a *schizophrenic* universe. When individuals are labelled schizophrenic, they are diagnosed with "[a] mental disorder occurring in various forms, all characterized by a breakdown in the relation between thoughts, feelings, and actions, usu[ally] with a withdrawal from social activity and the occurrence of delusions and hallucinations" (*OED* 14.623). Furthermore, to be schizophrenic also carries "the implication of mutually contradictory or inconsistent elements" (14.624), suggesting a particular kind of bipolarity inasmuch as there exists an ever-present implication that opposing forces will simultaneously

---

3. The psychological distress that Deckard experiences in this bipolar split becomes unbearable, and as Robert Pirsig explores in *Zen and the Art of Motorcycle Maintenance* (1974), the human creature is perpetually caught up in oscillation between an intense misunderstanding and therefore fear of the mechanical (25), and flight as a refugee into nature that, upon arrival, provides no comfort either. The human creature finds itself estranged from a nature that has been repeatedly codified as something to be shielded from (14), pointed at from a hygienic distance (145), and ultimately disengaged from (329).

manifest themselves. When such a condition is diagnosed in an individual human creature, it can become a significant problem. But what would it mean if the whole species were immersed in such a state, or if this were the state of the universe? Cosmicism takes the model of the universe as machine and inserts into it human creatures possessed of a cultural heritage—and thereby a view of the universe—that is saturated in the Genesis cosmology and all its implications. It is therefore suggested that as a consequence of this, the universe can then only be encountered as an alien and schizophrenic landscape that has become strangely separate from the human creature within it, and that creature is ill equipped to cope.

The human creature's terrestrial world and all that world contains is constantly processed into a view of the universe as a seemingly endless series of binary opposites—such as light and dark, noise and silence, male and female, right and wrong—and these couplings enhance the bipolaric conflict that confronts the human creature. The daylight noise and chatter of human activity are embraced, and the silent night of deep space is at every opportunity negated. The map that is constructed is a map of the light space of the sun.

"You're Not Afraid of the Dark Are You? The Light Hurts My Eyes"[4]

In Lovecraft's poem "Evening Star" (*Ancient Track* 94), silence descends with the approaching night.[5] The universe echoes with the memory of something that lies beyond the limits of human language, but that creature's landscape of drenching light and sound motivates its safe confinement within the amnesia of the cosmos. The character John Isidore in Dick's *DAD* understands the importance of the noise of the world in preventing him from being swallowed up by oblivion, and in a world that threatens to decay and crumble into nothing, "[t]he TV set boomed"; but when "Isidore knocked on the apartment door the television died immediately into nonbeing. It had not merely become silent; it had stopped existing, scared into its grave by his knock" (*DAD* 53).

---

4. From *The Chronicles of Riddick* (2004).

5. The idea of the silence of space is discussed in Part I, chapters 1 and 2, in relation to Watts's discussion of the "on" and "off" and the impossibility to have one without the other.

Silence speaks of erasure to the human creature, and it is the comfort of overriding sound that keeps that creature relatively free from the fear of disappearing altogether. It is the chatter of collective noise subsuming the voice of any particular individual that signifies the absence of the risk of exposure to the universe beyond the world. Not only does Isidore understand the power of the noise and light of his landscape to protect him, but so too does Deckard who, in trying to talk with his wife, is aware that all the time the television "[i]n the background ... boomed and brayed, eradicating her words, he saw her mouth moving but heard only the TV" (*DAD* 82). The grand illusion of the human creature is that in being submerged in the noise, it is kept safe from the quiet darkness beyond the light.

The human creature in being estranged from its universe no longer finds familiarity in what the American astrophysicist and cosmologist Carl Sagan refers to as the "great cosmic dark" (5). That home is forever kept out of reach by the reassuring light of the sun. A path clearly lit has its limitations, however, and in Herbert's *Dune* the Princess Irulan writes that Paul Atreides "could indeed see the Future, but you must understand the limits of this power. Think of sight. You have eyes, yet cannot see without light. If you are on the floor of a valley, you cannot see beyond your valley" (*D* 209). It may be in cosmicism's universe that the human creature fears the dark, and what it thinks is in the dark, but to remain always limited within the light can be dangerous, and the map that is laid out in the light ever obscures the territory beneath it. To be always wanting to wake from the dark, avoid it, flick the switch, open the curtains, and let in the light—this becomes a problem. Once the dark universe of silence has been encountered, simply letting the light back in is no solution. Something from beyond the light is sensed, the universe as it was once perceived is in some way changed, and there is no going back. This is the impossibility of innocence remaining untainted by experience,[6] or of remaining in Eden after eating from the tree.

---

6. This is a deliberate allusion to William Blake's *Songs of Innocence* and *Songs of Experience*. It is worth noting that the American literary critics Harold Bloom and Lionel Trilling write that while "the root meaning of innocence is 'harmlessness,' the derived meanings 'guiltlessness' and 'freedom from sin,'" it is also understood that Blake uses the term "innocence" to also "mean 'inexperience' ... which is a very different matter" (17).

In Lovecraft's story "The Shadow out of Time," the narrator Nathaniel Wingate Peaslee returns from his five-year journey through space-time with an acute case of amnesia, but his "reabsorption into normal life was a painful and difficult process," and the hidden memories of silence and darkness begin to emerge as "[v]ague dreams and queer ideas [that] continually haunted" (CF 3.374). Within cosmicism it is natural that Peaslee should be so troubled, because underlying his unease is an unuttered knowledge that if the human creature can turn off the noise of its sunlit world, it would then become aware that silence is the pervasive state of everything beyond the sun's reach. Dick's Isidore also knows that when the noise of the world is finally gone:

> By then, naturally, he himself would be dead, another interesting event to anticipate as he stood . . . in his stricken living room alone with the lungless, all-penetrating, masterful world-silence.
> Better, perhaps, to turn the TV back on. (*DAD* 17)

Turning the TV on negates the silence of what Sagan refers to as "the great dark between the stars" (24), where even galaxies can be "solitary wanderers" in a universe that is "mostly empty" (5). The terrestrial world of the human creature embalmed under the light of the sun, secure in the pervasive noise of its collective, and baptised by the light and sound of its technology and industry, continually reinforces the prevailing symbols of what is good and right and, above all, safe. When writing on cosmic fear in *On Monsters: An Unnatural History of Our Worst Fears*, the American philosopher and academic Stephen Asma claims that "[t]here are forces out there . . . that are stronger than us" (191), and in the absence of the light, the dark becomes a negative and overwhelming force wherein monsters hide and evil waits.

But what is it that cosmicism claims can be found in the dark? Lovecraft clearly answers in "The Whisperer in Darkness" that "dizzy new vistas of cosmic and superhuman knowledge" (CF 2.501) can be found, and his character Albert N. Wilmarth, though terrified, finds that when facing the dark his "own zeal for the unknown flared up" and he feels himself

> touched by the contagion of the morbid barrier-breaking. To shake off the maddening and wearying limitations of time and space and natural law—to be linked with the vast *outside*—to come close to the nighted and

abysmal secrets of the infinite and the ultimate—surely such a thing was worth the risk, of one's life, soul and sanity! (CF 2.501)

For Wilmarth, as it is for the solitary human creature whose thoughts are voiced in the poem "Evening Star," the location within the territory on which they stand is a twilight threshold of the sublime. These characters recognise "that an overwhelming sense of the sublime need not be tied to a theological entity like God, or even a mystical otherworldly force. The inexorable laws of nature alone will do nicely" (Asma 192). Whether it be in a subterranean cave or before the expanse of the night sky, facing the dark works against the nature of the light-born creature that strives to enclose itself in the defence of sleep and amnesia until the next sunburst of dawn. For the human creature, opening its eyes in the light means forgetting, an experience exemplified by Lovecraft's Nathaniel Wingate Peaslee and the amnesiacs Peaslee studies in "The Shadow out of Time" (CF 3.375-78).

The amnesiac quality of the light space is the human creature's safety net, and in cosmicism such creatures cling to the light space, so that the universe might be negated. Beneath all this, however, the disquieting terrain of Freud's uncanny, the heimlich, seeps up into the waking world of the light. This is the speculative *what if it does get in*—the terrifying "dark inside of me" encountered in Eisner's script for *Event Horizon* (1997) that comes unbidden and reveals horrors unimaginable that wait somewhere beyond the reassuring light of the sun.

The light is where good things dwell, good things happen, and living things grow. The light is where deity might be found. The light is what the human creature hopes to see as it dies. In short, the light space is a symbol of ordered goodness and safety; and the human creature has estranged itself from the universe that is everywhere else beyond the light. Amnesia reigns, and no longer does that creature recall that it is "made of stellar ash" (Sagan 318), "born ultimately of the stars and now for a while inhabiting a world called Earth" (Sagan 12). It has become afraid of the dark.

At the root of this fear of the dark lies the codified system of communication the human creature calls language. How can any language that has been born and bred in the light of the sun express all that exists in this dark universe? Lovecraft's character Nathaniel Wingate Peaslee is an excellent example of a human creature so in love with the comfortable language of the light that at "the chasm's edge" he responds with abject terror for what lies beyond the reach of his sunlit world. He is

> instantly engulfed in a pandemoniac vortex of loathsome sound and utter, materially tangible blackness ... There was a hideous fall through incalculable leagues of viscous, sentient darkness, and a babel of noise utterly alien to all that we know of the Earth and its organic life. Dormant, rudimentary senses seemed to start into vitality within me, telling of pits and voids peopled by floating horrors and leading to sunless crags and oceans and teeming cities of windowless, basalt towers upon which no light ever shone. (CF 3.448)

The language of the dark is the language of the inexpressible, and when looking into the dark universe the human creature all too often abandons wonder for fear. The terrestrial constructs of sign and symbol are utterly dependent on the light as a frame of reference, and despite the human creature's current understanding of the universe, "[t]he resistance to Aristarchus and Copernicus, a kind of geocentrism in everyday life, remains with us: we still talk about the Sun 'rising' and the Sun 'setting.' It is 2,200 years since Aristarchus, and our language still pretends that the Earth does not turn" (Sagan 189). The human creature's stubborn persistence in observing a cosmological frame of reference that in its interpretation of the universe no longer fits the evidence gathered leads that creature to a paralysis resulting from a fundamental lack of ability to comprehend and operate in the universe beyond the light space of the signs and symbols still used to describe and understand it.

When sign and symbol fail, what else is left but the silence? If something cannot be expressed within some form of language, then it cannot be objectified, categorised, and controlled, and such circumstance threatens the human creature with the possibility that it might no longer be master of the universe, but rather "just one small species among an infinity of planets, stars, and space" (Colavito 175). Furthermore, as a function of the human creature's interaction with its world and with others of its kind, language is central to that creature's processing of and response to the landscape in which it exists. When linguistic structure is applied to the universe, can the universe ever be known or seen *as it is*? Or will it remain eternally alien because the words for the experience of the universe remain absent from the language of the light wherein what is dark is designated as negative, evil, and to be feared?

For the human creature, the sun and the language of the light space that sun creates may dominate the landscape, but for the universe that sun is just another average star adrift within illimitable darkness. The reality of what this means is the Howard Family's experience when fleeing Earth in Heinlein's MC, and the human creature does not even have to leave its own system before:

> between them and the stars lay nothing but the winter homes of Sol's comets and hiding places of hypothetical trans-Plutonian planets—space in which the Sun holds options but can hardly be said to own in fee simple. But even the nearest stars were still light years away ... Out, out, and still farther out ... out to the lonely depths where world lines are almost straight ... their headlong flight took them farther from all humanity. (394)

The human creature's light space is an insignificant drop in a silent ocean of darkness. Beyond this there is no cosmic light switch, and that vast burning orb that illuminates the way for life on Earth is no more than one of many billions of such specks within the universe. Just as it is for Lovecraft's "Evening Star," so too is the human creature's own dominant star of the sun diminished to a pinpoint of white in the vast cold of the universe.

The human creature fears the dark that it does not understand, and Herbert's Paul Atreides not only comprehends this, but knows that in order to survive the universe into which he is propelled, he "must not fear. Fear is the mind-killer. Fear is the little-death that brings total obliteration" (D 14). This speaks of the fear of an Earth-bound creature that knows only light and warmth, a creature comforted by its confinement between the dome of the sunlit sky above and solid ground below, and is afraid to leave its enclosure. Herbert's God Emperor, Leto II (hereafter referred to as Leto), also understands this about the human creature when he writes in his journals:

> In the cradle of our past I lay upon my back in a cave ... There, by the dancing light of a resin torch, I drew upon walls and ceiling the creatures of the hunt and the souls of my people ... I peer at handprints and flowing muscles drawn upon the rock ... How much more we are than

mere mechanical events! And my anticivil self demands: "Why is it that they do not want to leave the cave?" (GED 356)

In a similar manner to Leto, Lovecraft's Nathaniel Wingate Peaslee in "The Shadow out of Time" also knows that the discoveries made within the lighted confines of the cave, if they are to have any currency for the human creature, must be carried "back to the outer world if it truly existed—if the whole abyss truly existed—if [he], and the world itself, truly existed" (CF 3.443); they must be carried into the vast and silent unknown. But leaving the enclosure of light means entering the deeper universe, and in cosmicism this means entering the impersonal universe as machine that operates under the direction of the cold equations.

The Cold Equations

The cold equations are what Lovecraft describes as "the ineluctable natural laws & probabilities which actually prevail."[7] These laws are directly related to the indifference that emanates from what Lovecraft claims is a "blind" and "purposeless" mechanism in which pleasure and pain, like human measures of morality and emotion, have no significance.

Tom Godwin's short story "The Cold Equations" relates the events that befall a girl stowaway on a shuttle that has precisely enough fuel for payload and pilot only. Her tiny, insignificant, but extra weight is enough to affect fuel so that neither she nor pilot nor shuttle will make it to the planet surface intact:

> She had violated a man-made law that said KEEP OUT but the penalty was not of men's making or desire and it was a penalty men could not revoke. A physical law had decreed: *h amount of fuel will power an EDS with a mass of m safely to its destination*; and a second physical law decreed: *h amount of fuel will not power an EDS with a mass of m plus x safely to its destination*.
>
> EDS's obeyed only physical laws and no amount of human sympathy for her could alter the second law. (105)

In order to fulfil his mission and save not just one but a number of lives, the pilot's only option is to eject the girl from the shuttle, and as the sto-

---

7. This is also referred to in chapter 4.

ry evolves it becomes clear that life on Earth has in no way prepared this girl for the realities of the universe beyond her small world (Godwin 106). In his 1961 guest of honour speech at the World Science Fiction Convention, Heinlein speaks of Godwin's story as "[o]ne of the most nearly perfect science fiction stories ever written—and one of the most bloodcurdling," in which the cold equations are disclosed in such a manner as to leave no doubt that despite the most utopic wishes the human creature may have for its experience of the universe, "[t]he cold equations say No" (170).

When the cold equations say "No" to the human creature's desire for warmth and safety, they highlight the fact that the human is an emotive being inhabiting a universe built upon the cold logic of cause and effect. Furthermore, this bipolaric relationship of estrangement that exists between human creature and universe is reinforced by the human creature itself. Stephen King claims in his introduction to Michel Houellebecq's essay *H. P. Lovecraft: Against the World, Against Life* that "weird fiction, fiction of horror and the supernatural, utters a resounding NO to the world as it is and reality as the world insists it must be" (Houellebecq 14). The response of the "NO" that King describes is equivalent to the human creature's reply to the universe of cold equations.

The Lady Jessica in Herbert's *Dune* highlights this when talking with the Mentat, Thufir Hawat. A Mentat is a human creature that has been trained as a "human computer" (McNelly 376), and Jessica says to Hawat that:

> "The *natural* human's an animal without logic. Your projection of logic on to all affairs is unnatural, but suffered to continue for its usefulness. You're the embodiment of logic—a Mentat. Yet, your problem solutions are concepts that, in a very real sense, are projected outside yourself, there to be studied and rolled around, examined from all sides ... Anything outside yourself, this you can see and apply your logic to it," she said. "But it's a human trait that when we encounter personal problems, those things most deeply personal are the most difficult to bring out for the logic to scan." (*D*) 149)

Jessica's words highlight the idea that logic is not only something unnatural, but also external to the human creature. Cosmicism's claim for the human creature's sense of estrangement from the universe is directly related to this, for this is a universe that has been built upon a foundation of cold equations. Furthermore, Jessica's demarcation of emotional response as something completely self-contained, and nowhere to be found in the universe of logic that exists outside the individual body of each human creature, keeps that creature locked within a perception of isolation both from and within an adversarial universe. While devoid of human emotion, the logic of the cold equations is translated through the filter of that emotion and produces a view of the universe as at least indifferent, and more often malevolent, in its interaction with the human creature. When recounting a long and life-changing journey, Lovecraft's character Nathaniel Wingate Peaslee opens his account with a sombre admission of the adversarial nature of the universe when he says:

> man must be prepared to accept notions of the cosmos, and of his own place in the seething vortex of time, whose merest mention is paralysing. He must, too, be placed on guard against a specific, lurking peril which, though it will never engulf the whole race, may impose monstrous and unguessable horrors upon certain venturesome members of it. (CF 3.364)

When, in the closing words of his account Peaslee speaks of "those shocking Elder Things of the mad winds and daemon pipings—in truth a lingering, lurking menace" (CF 3.450-51), he reaffirms his earlier warning that the universe operates within laws and forces that, although hidden from view, pose a constant threat to the safety of the human creature.

Despite what that creature may seek for itself and its world, the cold equations fuel a universe that clearly operates for purposes beyond the limitations of human desire. This is the discovery of the character Kenton J. Stanfield in the story "In the Walls of Eryx," who writes during his last days entangled in an invisible labyrinth on Venus:

> If it does survive to be read, I hope it may do more than merely warn men of this trap. I hope it may teach our race to let those shining crystals stay where they are. They belong to Venus alone. Our planet does not truly need them, and I believe we have violated some obscure and mysterious law—some law buried deep in the arcana of the cosmos—in our attempt to take them. Who can tell what dark, potent, and widespread

forces spur on these reptilian things who guard their treasure so strangely? (CF 4.579)

Beyond the scope of human emotion and human law, as Stanfield comes to understand, the cold equations that underpin the universe comprise a law that as Godwin claims is "not of men's choosing" (Godwin 93). For a stowaway girl in Godwin's story, the consequence of breaking the "man-made law [of] KEEP OUT" is no different to the consequence for Adam and Eve in the Genesis cosmology when they broke the God-made law of don't touch in the Garden of Eden (Genesis 3:22–24). The end result is expulsion to a wilderness that exists beyond the confines of warmth and safety.

Possessed of neither emotion nor capacity to recognise human measures of emotion, the cold equations operate with indifference. The fact that the equations and the laws they govern are devoid of emotion does not, however, render the cold equations as agents of evil or malevolence. Though speaking of communists in his 1961 speech, Heinlein highlights the critical aspect of the human creature's approach to the cold equations when he says that communists do what they do by their own standards and not because they are villains: "Until you learn this one thing . . . you have no chance of reading and understanding the Cold Equations" (175). Heinlein then claims that the key is to "[k]now your enemy" (176), or in the case of the universe, to know your equations.

The cold equations are built on "a law that recognized neither innocence nor youth nor beauty, that was incapable of sympathy or leniency" (Godwin 111), and they are "forces that killed with neither hatred nor malice" (118). However, as highlighted by the words of the Lady Jessica to Hawat, referred to earlier in this chapter, the cold equations and the universe they govern are most certainly interpreted and then approached as something possessed of an emotively negative response to the presence of the human creature.

In "The Call of Cthulhu" Lovecraft's narrator says that "I have looked upon all that the universe has to hold of horror" (CF 2.55), and it is this sense of horror that colours the sailor's response to Cthulhu as he "slid greasily into the water and began to pursue with vast wave-raising strokes of cosmic potency" (CF 2.54). Malevolent or not by his own measure of emotion, Cthulhu's pursuit is certainly interpreted by the human creature as nefarious, and "Briden looked back and went mad, laughing shrilly as he kept on laughing at intervals till death found him one night in the cabin whilst Gustav Johansen was wandering deliriously" (CF 2.54).

Cthulhu's pursuit; the "Elder Things" that Dr Armitage speaks of in "The Dunwich Horror" that "wished to strip [the Earth] and drag it away from the solar system and cosmos of matter into some other plane or phase of entity from which it had once fallen, vigintillions of aeons ago" (CF 2.448); "The blasphemies which appeared on Earth . . . of a frightful interstellar race whose ultimate source must lie far outside even the Einsteinian space-time continuum or greatest known cosmos" ("The Whisperer in Darkness," CF 2.485): these are the forces that operate in the universe of cold equations and are devoid of the emotion that calculates by human measures of good and evil. These are the forces that by their cold indifference, or the human creature's perception of outright malevolence, highlight the utter insignificance of the human creature in the universe. These are the forces that "obeyed laws that are not of our cosmos" ("The Colour out of Space," CF 2.397), that come forth from "the dark universe yawning / Where the black planets roll without aim"[8] ("The Haunter of the Dark," CF 3.453) and against which the human creature is powerless to do little more than watch as such forces blindly engulf everything within their reach.

When Lovecraft's Robert Blake faces his own end, he does so not on the sunlit world that has nurtured and fostered a sense of significance within him, but in the dark universe where his linear sense of past and present, time and space, has lost traction, and the safety of Earth no longer holds. Having "[t]rouble with memory," Blake loses sense of what he believes is the correct ordering of the binary opposites that frame his sense of place in the universe: "[t]he lightning seems dark and the darkness seems light . . . light is dark and dark is light . . . far is near and near is far," and he does not survive ("The Haunter of the Dark," CF 3.478-79).

---

8. These lines, quoted at the start of Lovecraft's short story "The Haunter of the Dark," are from a longer poem written by Lovecraft titled "Nemesis." The poem, "written on November 1, 1917 [and f]irst published in *Vagrant* (June 1918)" (Joshi & Schultz 188), speaks of the idea that nightmares are a form of karmic payment for actions of past lives, and no matter how far back in time these actions may have occurred, the consequences catch up with the soul.

5. Schizophrenic Universe

The human creature in Dick's story "The Trouble with Bubbles" is also caught up within the fear of its insignificant vulnerability in the universe—a fear exacerbated by its sense of entrapment on Earth with no escape into habitable worlds elsewhere (CS 2.196). That creature makes "[s]ub-atomic worlds, in controlled containers. We start life going on a sub-atomic world, feed it problems to make it evolve, try to raise it higher and higher" (CS 2.197). But as this technique called Worldcraft develops and the lack of habitable worlds beyond the Earth become apparent, the worlds that the human creature makes are worked to perfection and then summarily destroyed in an orgy of violence that is openly celebrated for its consequent and calculated destruction of lives and worlds. When the character Nathaniel Hull tries, and fails, to pass a bill that bans the building of these worlds, he discovers that "[y]ou can't moralize Worldcraft away. That's not the solution" (CS 2.201), and the cold equations go beyond this notion of individual worlds to proclaim that you cannot moralise the universe; it is not built on that sort of foundation.

For the human creature, the lack of any identifiable emotion embedded within the foundation of the universe is disturbing. When Isidore encounters Pris in *DAD*, it is the cold lack of emotion detectable beneath the surface of human appearance, her lack of empathy, that repels him: "Now that her initial fear had diminished, something else had begun to emerge from her. Something more strange. And, he thought, deplorable. A coldness. Like, he thought, a breath from the vacuum between inhabited worlds, in fact from nowhere: it was not what she did or said but what she did *not* do and say" (*DAD* 58). The lack that Isidore identifies, emerges as "a breath from the vacuum," a tangible force from the *void*. This seemingly empty space appears as contradictory or schizophrenic inasmuch as it is filled with an absence; a lack of human empathy. Watts points out in *The Book* that for the human creature "conscious attention, notices only the up-beat. The dark, silent, or 'off' interval is ignored" (26). But the lack of something does not mean that the space from which that thing is absent is empty or ceases to exist, but rather, that space is filled with the tangible presence of absence. The human creature all too often ignores the 'off,' believing the 'on' to be the only reality, or to put it more directly in terms of cosmicism: the map is not only mistaken for the territory but is preferred for fear of what disclosure of the territory will effect.

While for Isidore the lack of emotion beneath the surface of Pris disturbs him when they meet, it is the utter lack of empathy she displays for another living creature when systematically cutting the legs off a spider that truly distresses him (*DAD* 179-84). This lack is interpreted by the human creature as hostile or evil, and by extension whatever lacks emotion—whether android, another human, or the universe—is interpreted as adversarial to the human creature. What this highlights is the circumstance wherein it is the filter of the emotional or empathic human creature, rather than what is being filtered—the inherent condition of the universe—that is problematic. Roy and Irmgard Baty's cold logic of testing if the spider actually needs eight legs to walk (*DAD* 183), when filtered through human emotion, transforms the event from a process of testing cause and effect to an unbearable act of torture. But the cold equations' lack of recognition of human emotion, rather than reflecting malevolence and evil, in fact reflects what Dick refers to in "The Trouble with Bubbles" as "a sort of curiosity" of similar order to when "a child pull[s] wings off a fly" (*CS* 2.197), a process of calculating the cause and effect flow of logic.

In his treatise on horror titled *Danse Macabre,* Stephen King writes of childhood activities such as de-winging flies and "squatt[ing] patiently on the sidewalk to see how a bug dies." He writes that such activities are

> indicative of what people who care little (or know little) about children often erroneously call "the cruelty of childhood." Children are rarely cruel on purpose, and they even more rarely torture, as they understand the concept; they may, however, kill in the spirit of experimentations, watching the death struggles of the bug on the sidewalk in the same clinical way that a biologist would watch a guinea pig die after inhaling a whiff of nerve gas. (224-25)

The androids in Dick's novel, as machines, do not possess the capacity for empathy. Referred to in *DAD* as the "flattening of affect" (32), this "flattening" is what the novel's Voigt-Kampff scale measures when testing for humans. But the "flattening of affect" is not only measurable in androids, it is detectable in humans also; and, significantly, what returns a positive result for the "flattening of affect" in human creatures is that they are either "schizophrenic, with defective emotional lives" (*DAD* 140) or, like Rachael Rosen when first introduced, are raised not on the warm and sun-drenched Earth but in cold, deep space (44-45).

Rachael may not have been raised on Earth, but Dick's character Donna Hawthorne is. In *SD*, Donna describes the mask she wears, her readable map, as "warm on the outside," but the territory beneath that mask is "cold all the time" (*SD* 1081). A life framed within a flourishing, terrestrial map, it seems, does not necessarily guarantee a negation of the underlying territory that is the universe. Not only for Donna Hawthorne, but also for Herbert's Paul Atreides in *Dune*, the operation of the cold equations is an essential part of who and what he is. Paul may have been tested by the Bene Gesserit to ensure he is human (*D* 13-15), but none the less after the death of his father, Duke Leto:

> Paul's mind had gone on in its chilling precision. He saw the avenues ahead of them on this hostile planet. Without even the safety valve of dreaming, he focused his prescient awareness, seeing it as a computation ... His own lack of grief could still be felt ... that hollow place somewhere separated from his mind, which went on in its steady pace—dealing with data, evaluating, computing, submitting answers in something like the Mentat way. (*D* 186-87)

While the scholar Julia List in writing of this passage points out that at a later time Paul does indeed mourn the death of his father, the significant observation List makes is that Paul's "transition into manhood and adult responsibilities is marked by a kind of dehumanisation ... [and] his capacity for empathy decreases further as he ages" (36). In the immediacy of this observation, List contextualises Paul Atreides within an ethical rationale that claims, with direct support from the novel itself, that his transformation should be read as negative and, arguably, List's view is correct. Within cosmicism, the changes that occur for Paul as he matures can readily be aligned with the idea that the cold equations of the alien universe pose an imminent threat of engulfing and thereby destroying the emotional human creature, if he does not choose to turn back to the behaviour and manner of his infancy. The more that Paul sees of the territory in which he exists, the more influence it has upon his choices.

However, from within this context of the universe underpinned and governed by the cold equations, this transformation in Paul can—and as I will argue in neocosmicism does—signify not only Paul's capacity but also his willingness to let go of the map and adapt to the territory. The point to be made here is that when the human creature does in any way embrace the cold equations of the universe, rather than reject that territory and remain adversarially posed in relation to the universe and all it contains, that creature becomes the alien, the schizophrenic, the unhuman. Cosmicism's answer to those individuals who face the universe as it is is always, as I have said before, madness or death.

While many examples of this dual choice offered within cosmicism have already been noted, in Dick's novel *SD*, the character Bob Arctor, also known as the narcotics agent Fred, embodies this notion perfectly. As Fred in his scramble suit, the business of his work can be recounted dispassionately, even when it concerns the people for whom he has empathy and emotional connections; and he does this under the pretext that the very nature of his work necessitates this in order for some form of sanity and competency to be maintained (*SD* 908). During debriefing sessions, "[w]hatever came up and whoever it was about possessed no emotional significance to him ... He had to neutralize himself" (*SD* 907). However, when the debrief is over: "later on Fred evolved into Bob Arctor ... and the terrible colors seeped back into him whether he liked it or not" (*SD* 908). After seeing some part of the territory exposed during the execution of his duties as a narcotics agent, those "terrible colors" of Arctor's emotions engender a sense of estrangement from that landscape and indeed from the universe in which he operates. Bob Arctor deals with his job by shedding his empathic capacity, but is continually compelled to return to the reality of being an emotive human creature, and in doing so finds that the demands placed upon his emotions by the cold universe as it is revealed to him drives him to a madness of schizophrenic confusion (*SD* 942, 948-52, 1005-6, 1008-9, 1023-24, 1056, 1094). Certainly, the drugs Bob Arctor ingests contribute significantly to creating the schizophrenic who eventually no longer knows which aspect of himself is real and which is the mask; but it is the ever-present and inescapable conflict of being an emotional biological creature caught up in an indifferent universe of cold equations that destabilises him in the end.

The cold equations are the force that, in foreshadowing oblivion, brings the human creature's insignificance into focus. With the safety net of emotionally driven morality dissolved from beneath its feet, the human creature struggles to comprehend the universe beyond its local landscape. It is estranged, and the universe an adversary.

The adversarial relationship between universe and human creature is discussed by the Yugoslavian science fiction critic and theorist Darko Suvin in his essay "Considering the Sense of 'Fantasy' or 'Fantastic Fiction': An Effusion." Suvin draws a clear link within fantasy fiction between the indifference of the universe and the human creature's response to that indifference. While he writes that "[t]he supernatural element may include benevolent forces or figures," he then acknowledges that "most often in Heroic Fantasy and always in Horror Fantasy, it is malevolent (especially when it represents crushing cosmic indifference to humanity, as in Lovecraft, or mocking disregard, as in Machen)" (228). I agree that the connection between an indifferent universe and the human creature's translation of that indifference into malevolence is visible in fantasy, and would claim that when science fiction is viewed through the lens of cosmicism this translation becomes even more apparent. Suvin then progresses his argument by claiming that the use of the supernatural in fantasy is largely a process of misinterpreted symbology, and consequentially "its signifying tenor" (229) remains hidden. Whilst the "props" of the supernatural "become cyphers for our concerns today" (229), those "cyphers," when interpreted as adversaries, mask the underlying foundation that fuels the human creature's discomfort and misdirects attention to an emotional response that regards the operation of the cold equations as malevolent, and the universe as an enemy.

A fundamental difficulty in cosmicism for the human creature is that the cold equations remain unchanged by the presence of, or interference from, that creature. When the pilot in Godwin's story is looking for any option other than the inevitability of jettisoning the girl from the shuttle, the commander who responds to his call, though initially signalling an emotional response to the circumstance, also knows that human agency has no influence within the equations. The commander replies that he "can do nothing" and is "powerless to help," leaving the pilot to tell the girl: "'It has to be that way and no human in the universe can change it'" (99–100).

Through the agency of the Genesis cosmology, the human creature has constructed an illusion of itself and its landscape, separating the Earth out as something distinct from all else in the universe. But this native home of the human creature has no exemption from the cold equations, and according to Godwin's story that creature in being born to the Earth "had not realized that the laws of the space frontier must, of necessity, be as hard and relentless as the environment that gave them birth" (97). It can be claimed that the human creature does not encounter the "space frontier," but this only remains true while that frontier and the things that fill it remain absent from the Earth. When non-terrestrial influences and others come, irrespective of what they are or what form they take, they bring the frontier to the human creature's domain. Examples of such others include, but are in no way limited to, Dick's buggies in "Martians Come in Clouds," the Proxers in *TSPE*, and the androids that escape from Mars in *DAD*; Herbert's Honoured Matres in *Heretics of Dune* and *Chapterhouse Dune*; and Lovecraft's varying iterations of the Old Ones in stories such as "Dagon," "The Call of Cthulhu," "The Haunter of the Dark," "The Shadow over Innsmouth," "The Dunwich Horror," and *At the Mountains of Madness*, the living force in the meteor of "The Colour out of Space," and the Great Race in "The Shadow out of Time."

The operative principles of the cold equations are neither comfortable nor entirely comprehensible to the human creature, a discomfort made all the more acute when the equations are met with in that creature's familiar landscape. As Donald R. Burleson says of the Gardners in "The Colour out of Space," they

> discover something monstrous to know—that to live safely ensconced in a little corner of the planet is to live mercifully shielded from the knowledge of the cosmos and of our position in it. Humankind, the Gardners find, can in no way live juxtaposed with the uncaring powers that the universe has in its bag of tricks, once that bag gapes open. ("On Lovecraft's Themes" 147)

The natural response of the human creature when facing "the uncaring powers" of the universe is to retreat, and as Burleson also points out, this retreat is prompted by an attempt to negate the fact that the "knowledge of where one stands in the whole picture, is consummately disastrous" (147). The Gardners, however, do not retreat and are inevitably destroyed by the colour that has come to Earth from somewhere beyond its sphere (CF 2.381, 383–84, 385–86, 387–88). Unlike the Gardners, Nathaniel Wingate Peaslee in "The Shadow out of Time" avoids destruction by not only making his retreat from the recovered memories and discovered ruins of the Great Race—antediluvian others from beyond the Earth—but by punctuating that retreat with a desire for it all to remain hidden and unremembered. Despite the knowledge Peaslee has gained of the Great Race's utopian life, these others remain utterly alien to him, exemplified in his horror at discovering he had been transported into not only their world, but into one of their bodies (CF 3.397).

While Peaslee attempts flight from the territory that has been revealed as lying, quite literally, beneath the surface of his landscape, Heinlein's character Mary Sperling in MC runs in a different direction. When "[f]aced with the eternal problem of life and death, she had escaped the problem by choosing neither" (451). It could be said of Mary that in deciding not to face the inevitability that all things in the universe will come to an end—most noticeably for her, her own life—the decision to stay with the Little People and "merg[e] into one of their rapport groups, drowning h[er] personality in the ego of the many" (451) is a form of schizophrenic madness inasmuch as she is no longer a discrete individual. For Mary, it seems that cosmicism's claim for an outcome of madness or death when the universe is revealed prevails; and it does so even though all attempts are made to deny and avoid the operative principles of the foundation of the universe.

The attempt to escape, or the capacity to deny, are clear tactics of human creatures born in the light of the sun. The cosmos of their small world has been so successful in concealing the universe that when the universe intrudes into their experiential sphere, they choose to look backward to the cosmos they feel safe within, back to the map of some other life as if it remains tangibly real.

For the adults in the hovels of Dick's story "The Days of Perky Pat" and his novel *TSPE*, life is no longer what it once had been. They are consumed by a nostalgia for a life no longer possible, recognising that "*We lived then ... like Perky Pat and Leonard do now.* This is how it actually was" (CS 4.307). The desire these adults have for an irretrievable past echoes the pilot's understanding in "The Cold Equations," that "Regret was illogical—and yet, could knowing it to be illogical ever keep it away?" (Godwin 111). All these human creatures really want to do is return to paradise and play in the garden of "pristine *oldness*, the way it was in the 'ol-days'" ("The Days of Perky Pat," CS 4.302) rather than face the world as it really is, "upstairs" on the surface where it was "bright" and dusty (CS 4.301-2; *TSPE* 146-47).

The human creatures born to a utopian, green Earth inevitably do all in their power to deny the reality of the universe in which they live. They channel their energies and efforts into making the unreal real; into seeking the Edenic paradise they have lost, and "[p]laying this game . . . it's like being back there, back in the world before the war. That's why we play it, I suppose. He felt shame, but only fleetingly; the shame, almost at once, was replaced by the desire to play a little longer" ("The Days of Perky Pat," CS 4.307). To shelter from overwhelming regret for what has been lost, these human creatures immerse themselves in play and thereby experience life through the iconic Pat and Leonard. Whether on the dusty, war-ravaged Earth of "The Days of Perky Pat," or the harsh and dust-stricken Mars of *TSPE*, they look backward and pursue a cosmos that exists nowhere beyond the borders of the Perky Pat Layout (CS 4.303-4, 306-8, 313-15, 317-18). In doing so, they hold onto an illusory hope of readmission to Eden. As children who refuse to grow up, and refuse to allow Perky Pat to grow up (CS 4.320), these human creatures, in playing with their dolls, attempt to allay their fears of insignificance and a lack of control over the equations of the universe.

Chapter 6: Heimlich Universe

> The blasphemies which appeared on Earth, it was hinted, came from the dark planet Yuggoth, at the rim of the solar system; but this was itself merely the populous outpost of a frightful interstellar race whose ultimate source must lie far outside even the Einsteinian space-time continuum or greatest known cosmos.
> —H. P. Lovecraft, "The Whisperer in Darkness"

Untuning the Universe

The human creature's endeavour to avoid coming to terms with its insignificance in the universe, the magnitude of which in space-time remains incomprehensible, is encapsulated by that creature's adoption of the amnesia of the cosmos. The Genesis cosmology separates and compresses space and time into humanly measurable and comprehensible concepts wherein the whole of the universe is created in seven days, and the Earth is installed as the universe's central hub, encircled by the dome of the sky and deity's heavens. This spatially limited view is framed within a temporal reckoning that, even when measured in terms of millennia, conforms with a Newtonian assumption "that there is one clock ticking off the seconds by which the entire universe grows older" (Zukav 166).

While the Genesis cosmology describes the universe as subject to linear temporality, the universe as machine describes the universe as subject to cyclic temporality. Furthermore, the cycles in this machine are often so immense, in terms of not only the duration of their turning over but also the space that can be traversed within such parameters, that the temporal flow maintains a deceptively linear appearance, thereby concealing the universe from view.

When Herbert's character Leto Atreides writes in his journals about the "universe of shapes" (*GED* 237), he is writing about the universe buried under the cosmos of straight lines. As the human creature looks out from its location on the surface of one of those planetary shapes, that creature can choose to believe that because the world captured in its vision appears to be flat, that world, and by extension the universe beyond it, cannot possibly be anything other than a linear and ordered plane.[1] The human creature remains blind to the idea that "[i]f a certain portion of a surface is practically a plane, it does not at all follow that the whole surface has the form of a plane; the surface might just as well be a sphere of sufficiently large radius" (Einstein, *Meaning of Relativity* 101-2). The significance of Einstein's observation is the idea that the failure to capture something within the field of vision does not mean that it is therefore not an overriding factor of reality; and in cosmicism, the ordered cosmos that is believed by the human creature to be reality is revealed as no more substantial than an illusion. But unlike the *"buried spring or . . . dried-up pond"* mentioned by Freud in "The Uncanny," which merely reminds the human creature that water was once present in the landscape and may again rise to the surface (419), the universe that lies hidden beneath the cosmos does not hint at its potential; it emerges into view.

Cosmicism's universe is imaged in terms of bubbles and spheres, circles, wheels, spirals and columns, and its components interact within an implicitly chaotic and "almost wholly kaleidoscopic" mechanism (Lovecraft, "From Beyond," *CF* 1.197). This is a "seething" realm, a bipolaric contradiction of dark silences mixed into a "vortex of sound and motion," where the "strange night sky [is] filled with shining, revolving spheres" (*CF* 1.197), or worse, those spheres fall to Earth as did the "large coloured globule" in "The Colour out of Space" (*CF* 2.371). The measures of spacetime within the universe are so immense that their limits seem, paradoxically, beyond limit, and the universe keeps on turning within its blind, in-

---

1. In *The Inner Reaches of Outer Space*, Joseph Campbell discusses the historical development in the West wherein the dominant cosmology moved from a perspective of cycle imagers to linear imagers. The significant point Campbell then makes is that the publication in 1543 C.E. of Copernicus's work in which "the sun displaced the Earth at the centre of God's universe" started the process in which the *"idea"* and the *"experience"* of the human creature's position in the universe diverged. As a consequence of this splitting between a scientifically based cosmology and a religiously based cosmology, "[w]here formerly there had been the planetary cycles . . . there was now . . . to be a straight line of progressive world history with a beginning, a middle and a prophesised end." This has increasingly become a universe in which it is difficult for the human creature to reconcile that straight line course with a universe that in fact "ha[s] no fixed form or end" (16-17).

exorable cycles until such time when once more the "stars had come round again to the right positions in the cycle of eternity" ("The Call of Cthulhu," CF 2.39). An interesting comparative image can be found in physics and the speculated relationship between black holes and quasars; with black holes taking matter out of the universe and quasars depositing matter into the universe. Zukav describes this in *The Dancing Wu Li Masters* as a "process [that] goes on and on, feeding on itself, another beginningless, endless, endless, beginningless dance" (208). The components in the universe as machine turn over in perpetual cycles.

Within their clockwork cycles offering an apparently ordered pattern to the universe while obscuring the chaos that perpetually threatens to rise to the surface, the stars and planets are useful to human creatures, such as Andrew Jackson Libby in MC, for not only finding where he wants to get to but also *when* he will get to it: "Libby was able to establish quickly, through proper motions of nearest stars, that it was not later than about 3700 A.D.; . . . [and] once they were close enough to see the Solar planets he had another clock to read; the planets themselves make a clock with nine hands (460). This clockwork order by which Libby secures his sense of location in the universe may provide him comfort, but from behind these small and ordered reckonings of space-time, the reign of the human creature is threatened by every shadow. The indifferent universe as machine is driven by the cold equations, and as the language of the machine these equations become the key to reading the map in order that the territory might be navigated. Where Libby struggles to calculate the universe in terms of unfamiliar equations, his friend Lazarus Long knows that to stand "on Man's old planet, gazing north when sky has darkened," there will be nothing to see "but cold and darkness." It will take a different kind of vision to see "through the endless spaces . . . the strange equations" (TEL 252).

It may be the breath of the Genesis cosmology's God or the machine's music of the spheres that creates and sustains the universe as it is mapped by cosmoses; but in cosmicism's schizophrenic universe it is the silence preceding the disclosure of sounds in the dark that the human creature has no words for, that unravels God's order and untunes the universe. This is the loosening of the order that like a net has held the universe in captivity. When the image on the screen in Dick's story "Faith of Our Fathers" is turned off, what is left is the "dead mechanical construct" (CS 5.205), the hollow object that in *TSPE* is "clicked to the off position" (112).

The universe of cosmicism is a universe of ever-moving relationship between phenomena that can be described as being switched "on" and switched "off" within the interplay between bodies and space (Watts 28). The human creature is predisposed to ignore the "off," rendering invisible the "space-intervals" in between (Watts 27). When the cycles are disturbed and what was invisible becomes visible, what was silent becomes audible; the human creature notices the universe because it notices the disturbance. Just as human music is not made from the sound of notes alone, but also from the silence in-between (Watts 27), so too is the untuning of the universe born from the silence and the space between its components.

The "music untuning the sky" that the character Tanya talks about in Dick's story "Faith of Our Fathers" (CS 5.221) is not a simple matter of cosmicism's end of everything. It is about the apocalyptic—that is to say, revelatory—process of that untuning; the process of revelation in the heimlich universe. The sound of the universe as machine turning, the sound of its untuning, is the sound that comes from the darkness. Tanya is right to claim that "'All the celestial order of the universe ends,'"[2] and chaos will take its place. Similarly, Walter Gilman in Lovecraft's story "The Dreams in the Witch House," also

> seemed to know what was coming—the monstrous burst of Walpurgis-rhythm in whose cosmic timbre would be concentrated all the primal, ultimate space-time seethings which lie behind the massed spheres of matter and sometimes break forth in the measured reverberations that penetrate faintly to every layer of entity and give hideous significance throughout the worlds to certain dreaded periods. (CF 3.267)

In being untuned, the order of the cosmos dissolves to reveal the dark chaos of the universe. Fear may regulate the human creature's reach toward the amnesia of the cosmos, but that creature's attempted negation of the universe, whether conscious or unconscious, is in no way a guarantee of immunity from the influence and actions of either the visible or invisible mechanism of the universe as machine.

---

2. See Chapter 5 for previous discussion of and reference to this section of "Faith of Our Fathers."

6. Heimlich Universe

Kaleidoscopic Apocalypse

In his discussion of quantum physics, Zukav writes that "[s]elf-interaction makes the world of subatomic particles a kaleidoscopic reality whose very constituents are themselves unceasing processes of transformation" (255). The "kaleidoscopic" and "unceasing processes" that Zukav speaks of were foreshadowed in 1932 when Lovecraft wrote of the universe "as a huge field of force without beginning or ending, whose automatic and kaleidoscopic rearrangements of parts constitute the physical and material phenomena of which we can glimpse a fraction" (SL 4.56-57).[3]

When imaged as a kaleidoscope—which in its basic form is a cylinder containing coloured beads or glass fragments and mirrors to reflect light, thereby producing an image of ordered symmetry—the universe is like an echo of Anaximander's idea "that the Earth is shaped like a cylinder" (Russell, *History* 47). The ordered view that the kaleidoscope offers is, however, an illusion, and not a view of the actual tumbling chaos of its contents. Like the kaleidoscope, the machine of the universe is in itself without emotion, but the human creature's response to its reflection of light and colour is emotional. It is the illusion that evokes emotion; it is the cosmos that delights the human creature. The kaleidoscope makes an ordered map from a chaotic territory, and likewise in hiding the components of its indifferent mechanism and the cold equations that drive it, the universe-manifest-as-cosmos safely enfolds the human creature in the cocoon of a sunlit world. But the light that brings order to a kaleidoscope's chaos, the light that dominates the human creature's landscape, exists in the universe as an exception rather than the rule. The light-filled order of the Genesis cosmology is, in the kaleidoscopic cycles of the universe, perpetually threatened by the possibility of the territory emerging from the dark and into view, and the machine's unending cycles turning through space-time will eventually curve back on themselves (Watts 47) to once again bring into the light what has been hidden in the dark.

The image of the universe as kaleidoscopic is metaphorically similar to the "Game of Black-and-White" and the relationship between "on"

---

3. This reference is also cited in chapter 4.

and "off" that Watts discusses in chapter two of *The Book* (25–52).[4] The "game of order-versus-chance"—more specifically the game of order-versus-chaos—is, according to Watts, a game where "order *must not* win" (46), and in cosmicism the universe seemingly conspires against the human creature to effect such an end. But, as Watts also highlights, "chance" or chaos also "*must not* win" (47), and as it is with the "Game of Black-and-White" that becomes a fight (35), the human creature in being caught up in the fight between order and chaos is required to find a way to avoid the impending engulfment that emerges in the space between the cosmos and the universe.

Maintaining the balance between opposites in order that neither triumphs is crucial, though as the Baron Harkonnen in Herbert's *Dune* clearly understands, while the balance is perpetually at risk within the fight, the opposing sides of that fight are often not equally apparent to the human creature. While some forces or conditions are readily identified as potential threats to human survival in the universe, "'[t]he absence of a thing,'" the Baron explains to his guard captain, Iakin Nefud, "'can be as deadly as the presence. The absence of air eh? The absence of water? The absence of anything else we're addicted to'" (*D* 224). The Baron knows that it is the invisible components in the universe that pose the greatest threat to the human creature, and in the case of the poison that the Baron is discussing with Nefud, it will be the withdrawal of the antidote rather than the actual poison that will trigger the death of the Mentat Hawat. As the Baron says: "'There's no way of removing the residual poison. And, Nefud, Hawat need never suspect. The antidote will not betray itself to a poison snooper. Hawat can scan his food as he pleases and detect no trace of poison'" (*D* 224). The poison is already in Hawat's body, just as the threat to the human creature's survival is inherent in the underlying territory of the universe.

The human creature is plunged into a cosmic game that is interpreted by that creature as a fight with the universe itself, and maintaining the order of the cosmos so as to maintain a sense of self becomes, quite liter-

---

4. Watts's "on" and "off" is discussed in chapters 1 and 2. The Game of "black versus white" is also discussed in chapter 3, and with particular reference to the idea that this "Game" became a fight in which "white *must* win" and black is expelled from view as a negative force, space, or image.

6. Heimlich Universe

ally, a life and death struggle that the human creature is continually at risk of losing within the turning cycles of the universe. For Bob Arctor in SD, "the Game had failed to help him. It had, in fact, made him more deteriorated" (1092), and by this time, with his sense and sanity of self as Bob—or even Fred—having been swallowed up by the identity of Bruce, he enters an existence where "'[t]here's no Game sessions here, just the work. No more Games for you, Bruce'" (SD 1092-93). In the end, Arctor is destroyed by a universe that he never saw coming.

The character Tillinghast in Lovecraft's story "From Beyond" asks what it is that the human creature actually knows of the universe, claiming that "[w]e see things only as we are constructed to see them, and can gain no idea of their absolute nature. With five feeble senses we pretend to comprehend the boundlessly complex cosmos"; and Tillinghast understands that because of the limitations of the human creature those "strange, inaccessible worlds [that] exist at our very elbows" (CF 1.193) remain as a wilderness beyond human experience.[5] The very physiology of the human creature hinders its ability to see the universe that the cosmos describes, an idea that is supported by the German physicist Werner Heisenberg when he writes that "the measuring device has been constructed by the observer, and we have to remember that what we observe is not nature in itself but nature exposed to our methods of questioning" (57). What Heisenberg speaks of, and what cosmicism brings to the foreground, is the disturbing idea that biological flesh-and-blood alone are not sufficient for penetrating the cosmos that has been constructed by the language of the human creature. To that creature, the indifferent, alien mechanism of the universe driven by cold equations, remains hidden.

This kind of blindness, which limits the human creature's ability to

---

5. Tillinghast's assertions regarding the human creature's limited senses through which the universe is viewed is also expressed by William Dyer in Lovecraft's *At the Mountains of Madness*. While exploring Antarctic ruins of an antediluvian age, Dyer asserts that "[w]e felt, too, that besides these recognisable excellences there were others lurking beyond the reach of our perceptions. Certain touches here and there gave vague hints of latent symbols and stimuli which another mental and emotional background, and a fuller and different sensory equipment, might have made of profound and poignant significance to us" (CF 3.88).

read and therefore navigate its map, is an amnesia reinforced by that map. In the opening paragraphs of "From Beyond," Tillinghast directs attention to integral, albeit invisible, dangers that the human creature confronts in the universe. He understands that it is the machine-as-extension of the biological body that is required in order to see beyond an acceptable cosmos to the real substance of the universe—a proposition that echoes the mechanical extension of body that is Galileo's telescope. For the story's narrator, however, this extension is "that accursed electrical machine" (CF 1.191) and later, a "detestable electric machine" (CF 1.194).

While Tillinghast understands the requirement of a machine for seeing the universe, Nathaniel Wingate Peaslee in "The Shadow out of Time" draws the connection between "the shadow which fell so suddenly upon me from *outside* sources" (CF 3.365) and the strange experiences of other human creatures who are "plagued ever after with vague unplaceable dreams suggesting fragments of some hideous memory elaborately blotted out" (CF 3.376). Furthermore, not only does Peaslee uncover evidence that fills him with a sense of déjà vu, but "[i]n three instances there was specific mention of such an unknown machine as had been in my house before the second change" (CF 3.376). As a man born into the cosmos of light, Peaslee understands the importance of the distinction between the laws that govern his cosmos and the alien laws of the dark universe beyond. He comes to understand that he has transgressed the previously impenetrable threshold between cosmos and universe, and that by means of "a mechanism of the most curious aspect" that was "a queer mixture of rods, wheels and mirrors" (CF 3.371) he has been plunged beyond the confines of his own biology.

Similarly in *SD* when Bob Arctor contemplates what the scanners may enable him to see—"[a] nightmare, a weird other world beyond the mirror, a terror city reverse thing, with unrecognizable entities creeping about" (974)—he is registering the same sense of terror as Peaslee for the proximity of an adversarial universe. Bob Arctor, Nathaniel Wingate Peaslee, and the anonymous narrator of "From Beyond" are all "afraid of the cosmic truth" (CF 1.198) and all ultimately seek safety from the revelation of the universe by turning to the amnesia of the cosmos. As Lovecraft's anonymous narrator declares, "I never feel alone or comfortable, and a hideous sense of pursuit sometimes comes chillingly over me when I am weary" (CF 1.200). The nightmares that break out upon the surface of order that the amnesia of the cosmos has established, the sense "that my amnesia had formed some unholy sort of exchange; that the secondary personality had indeed been an intruding force from unknown regions, and that my own personality had suffered displacement" ("The Shadow out of Time," CF 3.374-75), these things signify the emerging understanding that what lies beyond the field of vision in the cosmos will be revealed by an indifferent mechanism, and others that inhabit that largely invisible universe will not be the same as the human creature.

When the ocular capability of the human creature is altered or enhanced by a machine to allow the universe beyond the visible cosmos to be seen, the potential consequences are dangerous enough. But when the biological eyes themselves are replaced by machines to facilitate vision, a whole new level of danger manifests itself; for human biological integrity is violated. The ocular capability of Herbert's Duncan Idaho is believed altered when, resurrected as a Theilaxu ghola, mechanical eyes are implanted directly into his body (DM 61). In considering Duncan Idaho's eyes, Farad'n Corrino thinks that "[t]hose pitted metal orbs which the Tleilaxu had given their ghola in the regrowth tanks marked their possessor as profoundly different from other humans ... Idaho's eyes must record a different universe. How could it be otherwise ... *Idaho remained a dangerous question mark*" (CD 205). The "dangerous question mark" of Duncan Idaho is not consequential to his being a ghola and therefore simulation of the human creature he once was; rather, it rises from the fact that as a re-presentation of the original flesh-and-blood Idaho, endowed with machine-fuelled vision, he is now something other than what he first was. From the perspective of other human creatures, the possibility of Idaho seeing what they are simply not equipped to see becomes an immeasurable threat; an advantage he might use against them in his capacity to see a re-presented universe. Idaho signifies the possibility that his altered view will thrust the hidden chaos of the universe upon human creatures that prefer the limiting order of their cosmos. This limiting order is the preference of Anne Hawthorne in Dick's *TSPE* when she "'actually saw, not just believed'" the universe of Palmer Eldritch's stigmatic influence, and with this revelation "drew away from [Mayerson], with aversion manifest on her face" (*TSPE* 231). Even Duncan Idaho's future wife Alia Atreides, with her pre-born status and prescient capacity, cannot be certain that Idaho actually represents alliance, and soaked in an overdose of spice she sees in "those glistening metal eyes . . . a union of terrifying opposites . . . He was shadow and blazing light" (*DM* 188-89).

As an unknown other returned from death to the world of the human creature, Idaho cannot simply rejoin the human community as if he had never been taken from it. Understanding this, Paul Atreides asks "[w]hat might those metal eyes record," and in a more considered approach than his sister's, Paul contemplates the possibilities in a universe where

> There are many degrees of sight and many degrees of blindness . . . His mind turned to a paraphrase of the passage from the Orange Catholic Bible: What senses do we lack that we cannot see another world all around us?
> Were those metal eyes another sense than sight? (*DM* 123)

In contemplating the invisible universe that the mechanical eyes of Duncan Idaho imply, Paul's thinking is later echoed by his own children, when Ghanima says that "'[t]he universe as we see it is never quite the exact physical universe'" (*CD* 72). The human creature's fear in cosmicism's universe is rooted within that creature's limitations. To cross over the threshold between cosmos and universe to see the universe as it actually is, rather than as the human creature believes it to be, requires "a different ranges of senses" ("From Beyond," *CF* 1.193). To be able to see beyond the illusion is implied as therefore being something other than human.

While the implication of what mechanical eyes might see is perhaps ambiguous in the *Dune* chronicles, and when asked, Idaho himself replies that his eyes see "[w]hat other eyes see" (*DM* 190), the "mechanical slitted eyes" (*TSPE* 240) of Palmer Eldritch signal implications that are far more sinister for the human creature and its sense of self. As a self-proclaimed "bridge" between the systems of Terra and Prox (*TSPE* 214), the threat of an invisible other crossing between these systems is made possible, as Barney Mayerson realises, because of

> "All three stigmata—the dead, artificial hand, the Jensen eyes, and the radically deranged jaw." Symbols of its inhabitation, he thought. In our midst . . . And we have no mediating sacraments through which to protect ourselves; we can't compel it, by our careful, time-honored, clever, painstaking rituals, to confine itself to specific elements such as bread and

> water or bread and wine. It is out in the open, ranging in every direction. It looks into our eyes; and it looks out of our eyes. (*TSPE* 231-32)

No longer confined by the limitations of a cosmos, what has been hidden in the universe is revealed and, upon emerging, obliterates the illusion of order in the revelation of chaos unbound. It is the inhuman senses of the machine that allow the human creature to see the universe, traverse it, and experience unvisited worlds that lie beyond the reach of the light. As the human creature looks up from the surface of its planet to stars that become visible when the light of the sun is obscured, that creature looks up into the roiling seas of kaleidoscopic chaos.

In *Grey Ecology*, Virilio talks about the human "perception of events" in terms of being a perception of "the other," and he links the perception of that other with human empathy. Virilio claims that empathy "is at the apex of the integral visual field" (48), and if that visual field is limited in some way, the perception of events within it are, as a consequence, also limited. This limiting of view results in what Virilio calls "tele-objectivity," and while he uses the example of the screen, such as a computer screen, television, or microscope (48), I claim that a cosmological model operates in a similar way.

In clarifying what he means by tele-objectivity, Virilio draws comparison with the development of glaucoma in the eye that results in a restriction of the field of visual perception. The development of this restriction occurs unnoticed by the individual, and the other that exists outside the limited field of perception is rendered invisible to that individual. Making the other invisible to the human creature brings the ability to empathise into question, and a loss—or at least lack—of empathy, Virilio argues, leads to abstraction (49).

The tele-objectivity of the Genesis cosmology turns the universe of cold equations into an abstraction. Virilio claims that abstraction poses the question of the visible and the invisible, and that conflict is the foundation from which the invisible can become visible (48-49). One of the effects of the fight between the order of the cosmos and the chaos of the universe is the emergence into view of what, under the Genesis cosmology, has previously remained invisible to the human creature. For that creature, the tele-objectivity of the Genesis cosmology promotes a loss of empathy for the now abstracted universe. Once visible, the universe of cold equations is in itself an other that the human creature has lost its capacity to recognise. With no empathic connection to the universe, the human creature is left at the threshold with the sense that there is no space for it as an emotionally driven creature that has been hemmed in by the limiting view of its cosmos. As Paul Atreides says in *Dune*, "the world is *there* and *here* and we are in it alone" (D 412).

The human creature is estranged from the universe it perceives as an inexorable and indifferent machine. Even after having seen so much that exists beyond the cosmos in which he has been born and trained, at the simultaneous birth of his children and death of their mother Chani in *DM*, Paul Atreides recognises that the universe is beyond his control; his own tele-objectivity has propelled him into the jihad he wanted to avoid, and his own fear of the universe keeps him locked within a cosmos that he mistook for the universe. His "awareness turned over at the thought of all those stars above him—an infinite volume. A man must be half mad to imagine he could rule even a teardrop of that volume . . . He'd lived a take-everything life, tried to create a universe in his own image. But the exultant universe was breaking him at last with its silent waves" (*DM* 202).

Dangerous Liaisons: Chasing the (Real) Universe

For Paul Atreides in *DM*, who "had taken his place in a universe he did not want, wearing flesh that did not fit" (209), as it is for the human creature, the uncovering of the universe, rather than an approximation of it, involves disturbing the space-time cycles of the machine; and opening up that creature's view of the universe by means of such disturbance directs that creature's focus on "the wideneing abyss beneath the sheen of appearances, [and] the great fragility of things as they seem" (Ingebretsen 133). Cosmicism deals with a human creature that is awakened to its utterly ephemeral insignificance in a universe frozen by cold equations, where no quarter but the heimlich conundrum is permitted. In *SD* for Bob Arctor, having lost his sense of self as Bob or even Fred to become Bruce, "[t]he vacuum in him grew. And he was actually a little glad" (*SD* 1076). The manifestation of the identity of Bruce that engulfs all other identities is a direct consequence of Arctor's search for revelation that leads him to the threshold. Once there, Arctor finds himself confronted by the recall of something his great-uncle once said: "God, how dark it is here, and totally silent. Nothing but me lives in this vacuum," and Arctor's inability to find his way in the dark isolates him entirely. Even before the manifestation of Bruce, "without knowing already [that he had] said good-by" (SD 1049), he left everyone else in the light of the scanners.

When the cosmological frame is gone, what remains is a hollow object, and when discussing the relationship between "visual perception" and "Mind" in *Phenomenology of Perception*, Maurice Merleau-Ponty claims that "in order to conceive an object one must rely on a previously constructed 'world of thought'" (158). This "world of thought," inasmuch as it is constructed in terms of a language specifically its own, can be likened to a map or cosmos that is constructed within the framework of its particular language in order to describe and make sense of the object, or even a collection of objects, that is visually perceived. The problem for the human creature in cosmicism arises when the object perceived does not align with the language being used to describe and comprehend it. When the cosmos fails to render the newly visible universe familiar, the human creature is left "trying to uphold its superstructure when their foundations have given way" (Merleau-Ponty 158). The universe has become a hollow object that makes no sense, and in which the human creature finds no particular significance for its own existence.

Merleau-Ponty claims that the object, even though it is seen and therefore acknowledged by the human creature, loses significance for that creature within its cosmos because the object is in some way beyond or external to that cosmos. When the object—that is, the universe—is rendered incomprehensible because the only language available to describe it does not fit, then that object has become an abstraction. In turning the universe to an abstraction, the tele-objectivity of the human creature prevents that creature making connections between the universe it sees and the universe it thought it knew. When the previously invisible universe is made visible, and the cosmos unreservedly does not fit the universe that has emerged into view, what occurs within the experience of the human creature can be referred to as displacement. This is encapsulated in the idea of the schizophrenic universe and exemplified earlier in this chapter when discussing Nathaniel Wingate Peaslee in "The Shadow out of Time" and his study of amnesiacs. The American science fiction writer and critic Joanna Russ claims that Lovecraft "declares the worst human fears to be displacement in space and time," and Russ then goes on to say that when basic ontological categories like space and time break down, the human creature is left to face what the Scottish psychiatrist R. D. Laing calls "ontological insecurity"—the extreme of which is schizophrenia (Pederson 594).

Ontological insecurity is the wellspring of fear for the displaced human creature when facing the void that opens up between the cosmos and the universe. When that creature loses the foundation on which it has built a cosmos, as if turning off the light that shines into a kaleidoscope, the ordered pattern disappears and the territorial chaos that the light has misrepresented as order becomes visible upon a background of darkness. When discussing the works of Lovecraft and the American poet Robert Frost, Ingebretsen draws directly from Frost to illustrate the idea of the darkness as background being the substance of the universe. Quoting from Frost's "A Letter to *The Amherst Student*," Ingebretsen writes that "[t]he darkness, lastly, is ontological—a 'design of darkness to appall,' the 'background [of] hugeness and confusion, shading away from where we stand into black and utter chaos,'" and he concludes that "[t]his ontological darkness falls everywhere" (124). Darkness "falls everywhere" beyond the limited reach of the light of the sun, because the foundation of the universe is not the light of the sun, but the darkness of space-time. The ontological darkness that cosmicism's universe offers begins to rewrite the human creature's sense of self in relation to others, and it does so irrespective of whether those others are other human creatures, other sentient beings, or even another cosmological view of the universe itself.

The imprinting of the human creature with an ontological security that is grounded in the light and embedded within the language and structure of illuminated cosmoses becomes for that creature a dangerously bipolaric foundation when employed for the purpose of navigating cosmicism's universe of ontological darkness. The map most assuredly does not fit the territory and the human creature risks becoming lost in the dark. Like Merleau-Ponty's madman in *Phenomenology of Perception*, the human creature as "[t]he lunatic, *behind* his ravings, his obsessions and lies, *knows that he* is raving, that he is allowing himself to be haunted by an obsession, that he is lying, in short he is not mad, *he thinks he is*"

(144). Breaking the cause-and-effect illusion of a well-lit and linear cosmos has propelled the human creature into more than a schizophrenic fight between order and chaos in the universe. As Watts claims, the human creature "is now so largely defined as a separate person caught up in a mindless and alien universe, his principle task is to get one-up on the universe and to conquer nature" (80). For that creature as it measures space-time in terms of an ordered and linear progression, when it arrives at the threshold it discovers that reaching for the future means stepping into the chaos before it—a task made impossible by that creature's desperate need for order and purpose. Faced with this impasse, the human creature then engages an unrelenting fight against engulfment within the incomprehensibly indifferent and cold universe of darkness. Paralyzed by an inability to get to the future, that creature's future, it may be argued, disappears.

When visiting his former wife, Dick's character Barney Mayerson in *TSPE* is hoping that he might somehow win her back and build a future with her. But he soon realises that "[h]e was damned, doomed, consigned to the void which he had hollowed out for himself. And he deserved it . . . She's fated to live with Richard Hnatt, fated never to be [his] wife again; you can't reverse the flow of time" (*TSPE* 122). Mayerson is cast adrift within the universe, unable to live in it as it is, and pursuing a future that he can never have. Herbert's Alia Atreides also acknowledges how ill-equipped the human creature is to cope with the disruption of space-time that disorder initiates, saying to Duncan Idaho in *DM* that he does not "'know what it's like to hunt the future'" (190).

Disturbing the human creature's sense of space-time, disturbing the limits of the cosmos, also disturbs the relationship between the map and the territory. *TSPE*'s character Leo Bulero is informed by Dr. Smile that returning from the cosmos of the drug Chew-Z could seem to take "'years . . . quite possibly less. Days? Months? Time sense is subjective, so let's see how it feels to you'" (104), while in the "world" where Bulero's body is, the return may occur, "'shortly, even instantly'" (103). When the cycles of time under which the universe operates are disturbed by the human creature's limiting belief that linear measures of time are reality, the risk to that creature is no less than the loss of its sense of self and sanity. In his undercover persona of Fred in *SD*, Bob Arctor watches his own home through the scanners, increasingly separating himself as Fred from himself as Bob. This separation is easier for Arctor to achieve because the mechanism of the scanners creates distance between his "visual perception" and "Mind." Inevitably, Arctor operates as if Fred and Bob are in all senses two entirely different people, and splitting from within, his sense of self in space is disturbed by the disordering of the scales of time. Bob, as Fred, is left "wondering what had become of his time sense. Watching the holos had fucked it up, he realized. I can't tell what time it is at all any more" (*SD* 1033). Disrupting space-time is a disruption of order, a disruption of pattern; a disruption of the net that holds the human creature captive. For Paul Atreides in *DM*, the disruption of space-time that is inherent to his prescience becomes problematic because of the jihad he can see and wants to avoid. For Paul: "Time came out of its skein with subtle changes, but the background fabric held oppressive sameness. He knew with terrifying certainty that if he tried to break out of the enclosing pattern here, It'd become a thing of terrible violence. The power in this deceptively gentle flow of Time oppressed him" (154).

When the veneer of a linear cosmos with a beginning a middle and an end gives way to the universe as machine, the apparently perpetual turning over of that machine seems to coalesce the unfathomable depth of future and past; and the human creature senses itself as isolated within a universe that is out to destroy it. In *DAD*, Dick's character Isidore takes hold of the "empathy box" in order to escape the isolation he feels when opening his door to "the vacuity of the rest of the building. It lay in wait for him . . . the echo of nothing" (17). In turning from this emptiness to grasp the empathy box, Isidore achieves the desired fusion with the saint of his world's faith, Wilbur Mercer, and wrapped up in this experiential cosmos climbs to the top of the hill where he encounters the "future and past blurred; what he had already experienced and what he would eventually experience blended so that nothing remained but the moment . . . God, he thought in his weariness. In what way is this fair? Why am I up here alone like this, being tormented by something I can't even see?" (19). In response to these thoughts, Isidore immediately hears the voices of the multitude who are each grasping their boxes and walking up that hill with him and feels that he is not alone. But like the "plans within plans" (*D* 217) and its many variants in the *Dune* chronicles,[6] Isidore's sense of connection with others in the universe is only a connection within a disconnection, a sharing within the cosmos of the empathy box. As soon as Isidore lets go of his empathy box, he will leave the cosmos that reassures him and return to the vacuous universe that threatens him.

It is one thing for the scales of space-time in the universe to be disturbed, to deepen so as to become an unfathomable void of antediluvian age; but when the human creature wrapped up in its isolation and insignificance encounters others that are long-lived by comparison, those others are immediately regarded as adversaries. Longevity disturbs the human creature because, in disturbing the cycles of time, the longevity of others illuminates the ephemeral nature of the human within the universe.

During a historical accounting of the human creature's colonisation of the galaxy in the opening pages of Heinlein's novel *TEL*, the claim is made that "[by] the Crisis of 2136 all members of the Howard Families had life expectancies in excess of one hundred and fifty years, and some had exceeded that age" (xiii). Like the "naturals" in *TEL* that are "forever moving around, changing their names, dyeing their hair," however (231), after having concealed their capacity for longer than humanly normal life spans (MC 272-76), the Howard Family members find the continuing task of doing so increasingly difficult. The preceding novel, *MC*, gives an account of the fallout from a controlled revelation of the Family members' biological difference (277). Like Herbert's Duncan Idaho, returned from the dead with his Tleilaxu eyes, once their longevity is made visible to the human creature, the Family is turned upon by their "transient neighbors" (MC 318)—a response not factored into the calculations for outcome in an age when the Families "believed that the great majority of [their] fellow citizens ... could evaluate any data without excessive emotional disturbance" (MC 278).

Despite what it may learn of the universe, the human creature remains an emotional one, and when its ontological security is threatened by the revelation of its inescapable finitude, the fact that such threat comes from within its own kind does not alter the responsive emotion.

---

6. These variations include "a feint within a feint" (*D* 316, 353; *CD* 134, 301); "a vision within a vision" (*DM* 33); "trickery within trickery" (*CD* 198); "wheels within wheels" (*CD* 199); and "double meaning ... double meaning" (*D* 313).

The Howard Family members, of whom Lazarus Long is the oldest, become alien others. Unable to return to the cosmos of the "Masquerade" of pretending to be as short-lived as all human creatures, they too are isolate in the universe (MC 319–20). The long-lived creature, irrespective of species, embodies the "No" of the cold equations.[7] In facing its finitude, the human creature regards the Howard Family as others from within, who by their capacity for longevity are conspiring with the universe to commit "treason against the whole human race" (MC 291). This brings the human creature's fight with the universe into its own ranks, and despite the fact that that creature in itself is like the heimlich coin of the universe, inasmuch as whether short- or long-lived it is the same creature, it persists in its pursuit of reading even its own kind in terms of an adversarial bipolarity.

The Failure of Success

Carl Sagan writes in *Cosmos* that "[t]he Earth is a place. It is by no means the only place. It is not even a typical place. No planet or star can be typical, because the Cosmos is mostly empty" (2). The human apocalypse, that is to say revelation, of its place in the universe is immanent. When compared with the lifespan of any one such creature, however, this immanence is spread across so vast a scale of time that it defies that ephemeral creature's capacity to recognise it, and only by disturbing the human sense of space-time, by disturbing the known order, does the revelation becomes visible.

When Heinlein's character Andrew Jackson Libby tries to calculate the time it would take to backtrack the spaceship *New Frontiers* across the galaxy and return to Earth, the mathematical calculations he has traditionally relied on for measuring space-time break down. The calculations he now requires for crossing so vast a measure of space belong to a different order of equation, and this disturbing failure in the numeric language on which Libby relies leaves him "surrendered to an attack of homesickness such as he had not experienced since he was a youth" (MC 431). The dis-ease fostered by a space so immense as to require an unfa-

---

7. That the cold equations say "no," and lead to the human creature's resignation to death, is discussed in chapter 5.

miliar set of equations triggers a desire for the amnesia of the cosmos that the Genesis cosmology supports, with illusion proving far more comforting than the reality of the mindless machine of the universe.[8] The revelation of finitude comes from the human creature's acknowledgement of space-time and, by inference, of the dark. It is worth noting here that this acknowledgement is an acceptance only insofar as the human creature accepts the manifest presence, and is not to be confused with the acceptance of something as good or worthy of embrace. With the aforementioned acknowledgement comes the inescapable idea that the cosmos of Genesis is a map of error that renders the universe unimaginable.

The reach of the universe as machine across space-time far exceeds the human creature's reach. As a consequence of this diminishment within the scales of size, the human creature, in becoming aware of its insignificance, becomes aware also of its finitude. What appears to occur at the moment of this revelation, however, is a mistaking of finitude for the end. But as Virilio claims in *Grey Ecology*, "the end of the world is a concept without a future" (43), and when the human creature envisions an end beyond which there is absolutely nothing, it is the utter despair of such end that compels that creature to retreat. The only place that creature thinks it has left is within the heimlich conundrum as a means by which to avoid the revelation altogether.

Virilio's claim that there is no interest in the end of the world has been reinforced in recent years by a proliferation of films that focus on the world's finitude rather than its end. Notable examples include, but are by no means limited to, *28 Days Later* (2002); *The Day After Tomorrow* (2004); *Children of Men* (2006); *Sunshine* (2007); *I Am Legend* (2007),

---

8. The idea of a mathematical cosmology underpinning the Genesis cosmology is examined in some detail by Joseph Campbell in *The Inner Reaches of Outer Space* (9–13). What is particularly significant with respect to discussion in this current chapter is the comparison Campbell makes with respect to calculations of time. Campbell draws on the differences between Babylonian history and mythology on the one hand and the Book of Genesis on the other. For the period of antediluvian time from the first city to the deluge, or from the first man to the deluge respectively, the older mythology of Babylon (from which the Genesis account of the flood is based) accounts for 432,000 years, and yet the span of time for this same period in the Book of Genesis has been reduced in numeric terms to a mere 1,656 years.

based on the 1954 novel of the same title by Richard Matheson, a book that has been subject to a number of film adaptations; *28 Weeks Later* (2007); *Daybreakers* (2009); *2012* (2009); *Knowing* (2009); *The Road* (2009), based on the novel of the same title by Cormac McCarthy; *The Book of Eli* (2010); *Rise of the Planet of the Apes* (2011); *Contagion* (2011); *Elysium* (2013); *Snowpiercer* (2013); *World War Z* (2013); *Interstellar* (2014); *Dawn of the Planet of the Apes* (2014); *Mad Max: Fury Road* (2015) *Resident Evil*, across six feature length films (2002-16); and *Life* (2017). What this particular series of films is doing rather well is unfolding before our eyes the uncomfortable possibility that, despite all effort made by the human creature, the finitude of the world is an inevitability, and while the world may not end, the human creature's experience within it will not remain the same.

The operation of space-time within this adversarial universe, in being so vast as to defy any notion the human creature might have of the universe ever winding down to an end, further masks the universe as machine that is governed by the cold equations. Despite the seeming permanence that space-time affords the machine's components, they are in the end only components and will wear out like Mars[9] or like Earth,[10] and be no more lasting that the fleeting jester's bubble of Lovecraft's "Hypnos" (CF 1.326). Once faced with such finitude in cosmicism, the human creature is then forced to navigate its way through the shocking apocalypse that is the universe. How can the human creature hope to prevail when it has been diminished by a universe that is itself defined by finitude?

In "The Trouble with Bubbles," Dick writes of "virtual universes" (CS 2.200) that are finely honed machines. The makers of these bubbles expend considerable energy and time in the creation of their tiny worlds, which are complete, highly evolved (CS 2.193, 196-97), and utterly sub-

---

9. Examples of Mars as worn out include Dick's novels *DAD* (130-31) and *TSPE* (140, 174, 192); his story "Martians Come in Clouds" (CS 2.123-24); and Heinlein's MC (319).

10. Examples of Earth as worn out include Dick's stories "Second Variety" (CS 2.15-16, 19, 23, 25, 38, 44, 46); "The Days of Perky Pat" (CS 4.301-2, 304, 318);"To Serve the Master" (CS 3.145, 149); and "Jon's World" (CS 2.55); his novel *DAD* (6, 12-17, 65, 75-77, 85, 184-85, 200-202); and Herbert's *Dune Chronicles*.

ject to the genocidal whims of their makers (CS 2.194). Each world might be regarded by its inhabitants as the central hub of the universe, but "a world is only a world" (Virilio, *Grey Ecology* 26, 31), and from beneath the surface when that world is broken, "the vital machinery of the bubble [will be] splattered in all directions" (CS 2.194). The finitude of these bubbles is for their inhabitants undoubtedly an end, but beyond the end of any individual bubble the rest of the universe endures. The sphere of the human creature's Earth, whether it is destroyed, wears out, or is dragged away to some other part of the universe, is nothing more than a finite component in a much larger machine. Finitude is not the end of the world, but the end of the landscape of the human creature's familiarity; it is Lovecraft's reckoning of an eternal universe in which ends occur (SL 1.56–57).

Where the Genesis cosmology is concerned with beginnings and with framing the human creature in a world of light, the cold equations of the machine in cosmicism are concerned with the end of that safe enclosure and the revelation of the universe. Before the disclosure of the revelation, however, the human creature senses its approach and, like the narrator of Lovecraft's "From Beyond," is "infected with the terror which seemed stalking in all the shadows . . . in the darkness beyond the small circle of candle light" (CF 1.193). This fear is often subordinated by curiosity, at least initially, and when it is asserted that a way has been found to cross the threshold between the visible cosmos and the universe that remains, the human creature often follows the temptation of the unknown right up to the threshold of delivery. With promise of the revelation of the unknown and inaccessible in "From Beyond," and despite his growing fear, the narrator follows Tillinghast to the machine in the attic because of his own curiosity. To wake senses that have "atrophied" that they might "overleap time, space, and dimensions, and without bodily motion peer to the bottom of creation" (CF 1.193), is the revelation the machine allows, and for Crawford Tillinghast the result is no less than that he becomes "the prey of success" (CF 1.192).

As Watts claims, "[n]othing fails like success," and while the human creature before the revelation may have felt itself to be "*in* the universe but not *of* it" (75), there can be no doubt that the success of seeing beyond the cosmos brings into focus just how estranged from the universe the human creature has become, and by consequence how dangerous that universe is to the human creature's literal survival. Lovecraft' Tillinghast becomes the prey of his own success; and caught within the idea that seeing the universe can remain separate from being in the universe, he inevitably succumbs to madness (CF 1.196, 199–200). As Merleau-Ponty says of a patient, "[i]t was through his sight that mind in him was impaired" (145), and Tillinghast fails at the threshold because he has been netted by a cosmology that renders the territory invisible and in which the kaleidoscopic movement of chaos has been mistaken for linear time and solid objects of everlasting permanence. The success of Tillinghast's machine in bringing the territory to the fore and uncovering the human creature's finitude is also its failure. With the fulness of the universe revealed, the machine that facilitates the revelation becomes abhorrent to the body; it prevents a return to the amnesia that has kept the human creature safe while maintaining distance between it and the human creature's biology.

Faced with the ontological darkness of space-time, the human creature understands that the ephemeral human body is the object that has allowed that creature to keep the universe at arm's length; to point, to name, to categorize, to filter the universe through a tele-objectivity that has kept that creature enclosed. It is the isolation of the human creature, coupled with the abstraction of the other and of the universe, that highlights how insignificant and fragile that body is. But the game the universe plays is entirely different from the misdirected game-turn-fight that the emotional creature engages because the universe does not operate by morals but by equations, and the human creature's biological body in itself is not suitably enough designed for an assurance of victory. This is the universe that in *The Modern Temper* Joseph Wood Krutch says that for the human creature "it grows more and more likely that he must remain an ethical animal in a universe which contains no ethical element" and in "which his reason and his investigation reveal . . . a world which his emotions cannot comprehend" (10–11).

Uncovering the universe to see beyond the illusory cosmos, whether facilitated by a machine or some other device or substance ingested into the body, is a waking that can only occur as consequence of modifying the body by means of an externality. The device that transforms Chien's vision in Dick's story "Faith of Our Fathers" is an *anti*-hallucinogen, and once it has taken effect the reality he sees is one of "a dead mechanical construct, made of solid state circuits, of swivelling pseudopodia,[11] lenses and a squawk-box . . . this is terrifying. To have to face *this* the remainder of my life" (CS 4.205). When standing at the threshold, a glimpse beneath the cosmos is all it takes for Chien to be certain of wanting to stay in the comfort of illusion. What lies beneath the surface is "'[a] machine' . . . 'Yes, I understand; a mechanical organism in no way resembling a human. Not a simulacrum, or something constructed to resemble a man'" (CS 5.207), and even when the cosmos is restored, Chien knows that "it'll never be the same again, at least not for me" (CS 5.206).

Waking in Cosmicism's Garden

In waking, the illusion of the cosmos, whether it has been a dream or nightmare, disappears; the invisible becomes visible and the "evidence" of the universe emerges "from beyond" the threshold ("From Beyond," CF 1.195). Curiosity brings the human creature to that threshold and, at least at first, overrides any sense of foreboding that creature might have. The catharsis that occurs here is often attended by a sense of disorientation that, while it initially evokes a universe of wonder for the human creature, rapidly gives way to a complete exposure to a universe that terrifies. The narrator in "From Beyond" "fancied [him]self in some vast incredible temple of long-dead gods; some vague edifice of innumerable black stone columns reaching up from a floor of damp slabs to a cloudy height beyond the range of my vision" (CF 1.195). This vision does not enchant for long, and the view that bears some points of reference to an identifiably human cosmos, albeit strange and wonderful, gives way to "a more horrible conception; that of utter, absolute solitude in infinite, sightless, soundless space" (CF 1.195-96).

The revelation of the universe initiates a "childish fear" (CF 1.196). This is the fear of expulsion from the safe enclosure of the light where everything is visible and measurable, and it signifies a realisation that a return to the light-filled amnesia of the cosmos will never be possible for

---

11. The image of pseudopodia—a protrusion from the main body—links the machine with the tentacled organism. This also evokes the image of Lovecraft's Wilbur Whateley in "The Dunwich Horror," who possessed growing "from the abdomen a score of long greenish-grey tentacles with red sucking mouths protrud[ing]" (CF 2.435).

the human creature, that there is no return to the blind innocence of Eden. The human creature's amnesia of the cosmos masks the difference between cosmos and universe in a manner not dissimilar to the French psychoanalyst Jacques Lacan's concept of the mirror. In his essay "The Mirror Stage as Formative of the Function of the *I* as Revealed in the Psychoanalytic Experience" (hereafter called "The Mirror Stage"), Lacan writes that before having seen its own image in a mirror, the infant human creature lacks an *a priori* knowledge of itself as an object separate from all others around it and consequently tends to exhibit little or no sense of fear (1-8). Whether at Lacan's mirror or the threshold, the separation and therefore abstraction of all else that surrounds the human creature opens up the void between that creature and the universe by the very quality of being a previously invisible space that holds the potential for all things. As Alia Atreides says in DM, "'What rare light is this darkness? You cannot fix your gaze upon it! Senses cannot record it. No words describe it.' Her voice lowered. 'The abyss remains. It is pregnant with all things yet to be. Ahhhhh, what gentle violence!'" (147). But when this "abyss" becomes an abstracted other space for which the emotive human creature has no empathy nor feels a returning empathy, crossing the void becomes a terrifying prospect because this action leads directly to an adversarial universe. Having ventured to the threshold to look upon the universe revealed, but never attempting the crossing and paralysed by fear, the human creature waits for the horrors of the universe to cross that darkness and bring chaos to the cosmos.

When vision is altered in Lovecraft's "From Beyond," the "augmented sight" and "preternatural eye" transforms the familiar to the unfamiliar, and "not one particle [i]s vacant" (CF 1.197-98). Stripped of illusion and "afraid of the cosmic truth," the curiosity that calls the human creature to the threshold is usurped by a fear that propels that creature headlong into engulfment. The narrator in "From Beyond" has in no way been prepared by his cosmos to engage with a universe where even the sentient others that inhabit it blend and coalesce, then dissolve and separate only to blend with others (CF 1.198).[12] The isolation and utter alienation the human creature feels are the consequences of its

---

12. In the story "Oh, To Be a Blobel!", Dick writes of others that are similar in movement and appearance. This is discussed in chapter 12.

displacement from an illusory map within which it has lived all its life until apocalypse and a fear of an uncertain future in an incomprehensible territory. It does not know how to leave the safety of its enclosure, and the universe begins to look like a trap from which it cannot escape. Alienation, disconnection, and isolation: these are the preconditions of the engulfment that is integral to cosmicism.

The human creature peers through its biological lens to face the problem of how to exist in the machine. The Genesis cosmology designates that creature as significant in God's universe, so when the universe as machine becomes the primary map from which to take direction, the uncomfortable prospect of being nothing more than a component within the machine cannot be ignored. The critical question that emerges as a consequence of this dichotomy between the biological human creature and the mechanical universe through which it moves is the question of why identification with the machine becomes so abhorrent to that creature. Why does the universe that is uncovered generate such deep fear? Seeking an answer to this question sheds terrible light on the paradox that during the same eighteenth-century Age of Enlightenment that mechanises the universe, George Berkeley claimed of machines: "That ideas should exist in what does not perceive, or be produced by what does not act, is repugnant" (80); and from this moment, the human creature has never really had a chance.

In "The Electric Ant," Dick's character Poole wakes up to find that the life he has lived in the belief that he is a flesh-and-blood human has been an illusion, and the underlying territory of himself as an "electric ant," an organic robot, is quite literally uncovered (CS 5.226). A delusion has been planted in him and he was programmed not to notice (CS 5.227). What Poole must now decide is whether to uphold the illusion intentionally or step out of the cosmos in which he has lived and into the universe—quite literally disclosed in his body—as machine. Expelled from the Garden of his cosmos, Poole is cast out to the wilderness of the universe.

Waking up from amnesia, augmenting vision: the experience of the threshold is no less than an expulsion from Eden. As Ingebretsen claims, once Eden is lost, any attempt to return is a mistake (144). But cosmicism has its own dark Garden of finitudes and endings, and like Freud's uncanny spring, it is water-filled, decaying, dark, and cold.

Chapter 7: Frozen Universe

> I dream of a day when they may rise above the billows to drag down in their reeking talons the remnants of puny, war-exhausted mankind—of a day when the land shall sink, and the dark ocean floor shall ascend amidst universal pandemonium.
> The end is near.
>
> —H. P. Lovecraft, "Dagon"

Everything Will End

The Slovenian philosopher, psychoanalyst, and cultural theorist Slavoj Žižek writes in chapter 4 of *Looking Awry: An Introduction to Jacques Lacan through Popular Culture* that "the experience of a linear 'organic' flow of events is an illusion (albeit a necessary one) that masks the fact that it is the ending that *retroactively* confers the consistency of an organic whole on the preceding events" (69). In this, Žižek draws attention to the idea that implicit within the arrival of an ending is a continuation inasmuch as some creature or other is actually present to apply a retroactive perspective of consistency. What, then, becomes of the human creature's idea of "the consistency of an organic whole" in cosmicism, when that creature faces a universe in which everything will end? When, as Lovecraft claims, "Man, at best, is but an incident—& a very trifling incident—in the limitless history of Nature" (SL 1.56), how can that creature look to its end and not be afraid?

In its endeavour to influence the "flow of events" so that it might ultimately survive, the human creature fights against the very nature of the universe. This creature hopes that when the fight is over it can look back and be assured that its course of action is justified by its own eminence, and its future survival firmly secured. As Paul Atreides says to his son, Leto, "'The end adjusts the path behind it'" (CD 327). Furthermore, in writing that "[t]o the universe it makes no difference whether or not organic life happens to exist on any of its planets" (SL 5.69), Lovecraft highlights the inescapable governance of the cold equations in cosmicism's universe, and the idea that the human creature's desire for survival beyond an ending is irrelevant. It often appears to be the case that indifferent forces, such as the cold equations, are more difficult for the human creature to deal with than malevolent forces; for malevolence would at least be an emotion to which the human creature might respond.

While the universe as machine provides the human with a cosmos that takes the cold equations into account, it does not also provide that creature with an understanding that while the universe operates indifferently, not everything in the universe remains indifferent. As a cosmological model, the universe as machine is inherently tele-objective, failing to make visible to the human creature the presence of non-human others. The human creature remains lost in the universe because, as with the Genesis cosmology, the universe as machine is still only a map mistaken for the territory, and in no way does it alert that creature to the machines within the machine. Although by its nature the universe as machine seems to imply the presence of such forces, this cosmos is structured in a manner that allows the human to believe the illusion that claims a machine is a series of components without capacity for thinking independently of its programming or mechanical processes. This illusion is achieved "by telling a truth that . . . [is] taken for a lie" (Žižek, *Looking Awry* 73): by building a cosmos in which a machine is responsible for the generation of biological life. If that machine that the cosmos claims the universe to be is capable of investing a biological structure with sentience, how much simpler would it be for that machine to invest sentience into a mechanical structure? Ultimately, the universe as machine and the machines it contains do not regard, nor have they necessarily been programmed to regard, the safety and survival of the human creature as a matter of either importance or obligation.

This view of machines is a significant concern within Dick's corpus, and notable examples include the androids in *DAD*; the "claws" that are the focus of the story "Second Variety" and also appear in "Jon's World" and "James P. Crow"; and the evolution of robots in "To Serve the Master." The other significant exploration of the machine in terms of its indifference for the human creature's survival is to be found in Herbert's *Dune* universe with reference to the Butlerian Jihad,[1] the title for an his-

---

1. The Butlerian Jihad is also referred to as The Great Revolt, and the entry for this particular period of time in *The Dune Encyclopedia*—a text, it is important to

torical event framing the human creature's struggle for survival against the thinking machines. It is worth noting that Dick's "Second Variety," and his varying renditions of that story's human conflict with machines, can also be read as what Žižek might frame as the other logical conclusion (*Looking Awry* 69) of Herbert's universe, had the Butlerian Jihad failed.

Of relevance too is the concept of human-designed machines that are subsequently used to test whether a creature is human or not. Dick's novel *DAD* presents the machine of the Voigt Kampff test (25-26, 30-33, 41-44), and his story "The Golden Man" has the evolved Cris tested by a machine (CS 4.44-45), while Paul Atreides in Herbert's *Dune* is tested by the box of the Bene Gesserit (*D* 13-15). All these "testing machines" present a fascinating dilemma for the human creature inasmuch as they operate within a set of parameters that look for measurable results, and the end of those calculations will be death for the test subject if it cannot pass for human. In the universe as machine, the machine tests for, and determines, what is human.

Another "testing box" that is worth highlighting is the puzzle box in Clive Barker's 1987 film *Hellraiser*. Once "unlocked," the box opens a gateway between the human creature's landscape and the landscape of others known as cenobites; these others then test the human creature to the limits, and beyond, of pain and endurance. Barker is invariably noted as influenced by Lovecraft (Asma 184-85), and the influence of this particular film can be traced through the production of many other films since, the most notable with respect to the focus within this text being Philip Eisner's 1997 film *Event Horizon*.

The question that the lens of cosmicism draws sharp focus upon in all this is: what becomes of the value of human life in the universe?

When the Fremen housekeeper Mapes is put in service to Jessica

---

note, that is "authorized"—draws an interesting distinction between the two titles. While this distinction and the issues it raises lie outside the scope of this text, it is perhaps worth noting that depending upon which of these differing historical foundations is used as a lens through which to interpret the novels, the possibility of significantly varied analysis of events in the *Dune* chronicles can be developed, and could yield substantially different interpretive outcomes (McNelly 141-43).

Atreides in Herbert's *Dune*, she is there for the moral purpose of testing Jessica within the confines of a particular Fremen prophecy, and to then give Jessica a gift of great worth or kill her accordingly. Aware of this, Jessica cautions Mapes that should she determine the judgement of death, "in so doing you'd bring down more ruin than your wildest fears could imagine. There are worse things than dying, you know—even for an entire people" (D 56). Those "worse things" that Jessica alludes to are, in some measure at least, the inhuman forces that share the *supra*moral universe with the human creature, and the potential consequences that can arise from that sharing.

When considering the inhuman forces of the universe, Lovecraft writes:

> the interplay of forces which govern climate, behaviour, biological growth and decay, and so on, is too purely universal, cosmic, and eternal a phenomena to have any relationship to the immediate wishing-phenomena of one minute organic species on our transient and insignificant planet. At times parts of this species may like the way things are going, and at times they may not—but that has nothing to do with the cosmically fixed march of the events themselves. (SL 3.40)

The universe is immeasurably vast, and Lovecraft's claim that "[t]here are no values in all infinity" is a reasonable one wherein the human endeavour of attempting to enforce values points up the supreme "jest" of the universe, "for all is chaos, always has been, and always will be" (SL 1.231). The universe may be a "jest," but as a machine it may also be subject to winding down and wearing out. The universe may be "eternal" and "endless," but ends do occur, and at some point in space-time the Earth will freeze[2] and the human creature, being "a negligible quasi-atom casually spawned for an instant & soon to be as though [it] had never been" (SL 4.23), will disappear entirely. Faced with more than the question of what the value of human life in the universe might be, coupled with the knowledge that ultimately everything will end, the human creature must find a way to survive in an adversarial and slowly freezing universe that pits malevolent others against it.

---

2. An explicit statement from Lovecraft in his letters of the freezing universe has been referenced in Chapter 4.

But what can the human creature do, asks Lovecraft's Dr. Armitage in "The Dunwich Horror," because in the end the Earth will be dragged away from its place in the sun. There are others in the universe with plans that amount to no less than

> the extirpation of the entire human race and all animal and vegetable life from the Earth by some terrible elder race of beings from another dimension. He would shout that the world was in danger, since the Elder Things wished to strip it and drag it away from the solar system and cosmos of matter into some other plane or phase of entity from which it had once fallen, vigintillions of aeons ago. ("The Dunwich Horror," CF 2.448)

As Dr. Armitage claims, and the American film and literature scholar Valerie Holliday affirms when making reference to Dick's use of Cold War ideology and imagery (287), everything will end. Although no comfort whatsoever for the human creature, this terminal condition within the universe, according to the American science fiction critic and essayist Russell Letson, "is not a crime but a condition of existence . . . The universe is not built to human specifications" (209). The human creature's lack of a future in the universe is a focal point from which that creature retreats into cosmicism's iconic, and I might add ironic, response within the heimlich conundrum, and this lack of a future is commonly partnered with the rise of others in some way to a power above that of the human creature. The chimera of human and other that is Wilbur Whateley in "The Dunwich Horror" writes in his diary of "the inner city at the 2 magnetic poles," claiming that "I shall go to those poles when the Earth is cleared off . . . They from the air told me at Sabbat that it will be years before I can clear off the Earth . . . I wonder how I shall look when the Earth is cleared and there are no Earth beings on it" (CF 2.447). Just as the end of the human creature in the universe is contemplated by an infant Wilbur Whateley, so too in *DM* is the birth of Leto, a future chimera himself, preceded by a coming storm that prompts within his mother "only a moment as her life measured time, but in that moment she felt this planet being swept away—cosmic dust, part of other waves" (198) shaking the foundation of life in the light.

That the planet should be "swept away" by the bipolarities of dust and waves, evoking the desert and waters respectively, is a vision of a future to come where everything that has framed life for the human creature on Arrakis will end. For Paul Atreides in *DM*, who "brought an alien chemistry to this planet—water" (219), the more Arrakis becomes a "water-rich paradise," the more "[i]t fought him, resisted, slipped away from his commands" (56). Paul is left to face a universe in which "[h]e felt that some element of himself lay immersed in frosty hoar-darkness without end. His prescient power had tampered with the image of the universe held by all mankind. He had shaken the safe cosmos and replaced security with his Jihad" (56). Paul understands that his Jihad has shaken the foundation on which the human creature's cosmos is designed. The very cosmos that claims him as Muad'Dib, the "little mouse" (D 292), is also the cosmos in which that moon will be erased without trace from the universe:

> Muad'Dib's Jihad was less than an eye-blink in his larger movement. The Bene Gesserit swimming in this tide, that corporate entity trading in genes, was trapped in the torrent as he was. Visions of a falling moon must be measured against other legends, other visions in a universe where even the seemingly eternal stars waned flickered, died . . .
> What mattered a single moon in such a universe? (*DM* 110)

More than shaking foundations, Paul's Jihad strips away the cosmos of human reassurance for a future, to reveal the inevitable end of everything, and as the human creature is engulfed by the cosmic ocean the end will come as the blinking of an eye.

The end of everything that sustains the human creature may be precipitated not only by the end of its own planet, but by the end of any of the infinite multitude of systems and planets in the universe. The Great Race of Lovecraft's "The Shadow out of Time" are survivors of their home planet's ultimate end, and as "[t]he beings of a dying elder world [they] had looked ahead for a new world and species wherein they might have long life, and had sent their minds en masse into that future race best adapted to house them . . . Thus the Great Race came to be, while the myriad minds sent backward were left to die in the horror of strange shapes" (*CF* 3.391–92). That the Great Race deems its own survival as having a higher value than the survival of another form of life is comprehensible from within the parameters of human morality. Furthermore, when given the appropriate framework, for example the human eradication of the smallpox virus, the complete destruction of a life form can even be considered allowable and preferable. The problem that the human creature faces in "The Shadow out of Time," however, and indeed in cosmicism, is rooted in the notion that the Great Race did not eliminate a virus, it eliminated another race of sentient creatures. It did so, and it flourished on Earth some "fifty million years before the advent of man" (CF 3.387), dwarfing the human creature's notion of its own sentient significance. Furthermore, the members of the Great Race were mere infants in the universe when compared with others of "inconceivable shape" that had "reared towers to the sky and delved into every secret of nature before the first amphibian forbear of man had crawled out of the hot sea" (CF 3.386). The frightening question for any human creature when uncovering such knowledge of the past is rooted in the understanding that such an event could happen again, and next time the human creature might be the one in the firing line. Having considered the human creature's insignificant tenure in the universe where everything will end, I will now turn more specifically to the role of the machines within the machine that foreground human endings.

The Book of the Machines

During the formation of the human creature's planet when it was nothing more than a molten mass beginning to cool, if that creature could have been present to observe, would it have believed that a multiplicity of life forms would emerge there and thrive? Despite the apparently impossible odds, life found a way. How then can the advent of a new form of sentience within the human creature's landscape be excluded from possibility, and given the rapid rate of mechanical development when compared with the rate of human development, why could that new sentience not be of the order of the machine? The nineteenth-century writer and satirist Samuel Butler asks these questions in the aptly titled chapters 23-25, "The Book of the Machines," in his novel *Erewhon; or, Over the Range* (198).

The introduction to the Penguin Classics edition of Butler's novel claims that three of his essays—"Darwin among the Machines," "The Mechanical Creation," and "Lucubratio Ebria"—became the foundation for the chapters titled "The Book of Machines," "when [*Erewhon*] came to be written some ten years later" (8). I suggest that *Erewhon*, and in particular

"The Book of the Machines," is far more significant than most science fiction chronologies of canonical texts would indicate. Many chronologies omit Butler's novel altogether, including the extensive chronology at the front of the Hugo Award-winning *Cambridge Companion to Science Fiction* (James and Mendlesohn xx–xxvii). This absence may be attributed to the general categorisation of *Erewhon* as a novel of anti-utopian satire and social commentary disguised as fiction (Wynne-Davies 500); even when included in a science fiction critical text, the novel's marginalisation in the genre is maintained by referring to it as "a mock history representing technological progress as a mock Darwinian process" (Stableford 51), and as a text in which "[t]his idea of machine evolution was intended to satirize Darwin" (Scholes and Rabkin 132). Such a rationale, I suggest, is problematic as a means by which to legitimise the argument for exclusion of the novel from the science fiction canon in light of the vast body of critical writing central to science fiction criticism that concerns itself with the very issue of utopias and dystopias.

The chapters of *Erewhon* that share the title "The Book of the Machines" are, in summary, a discussion that is concerned with the possibilities for the evolution of machines to sentience, and what such an evolution might mean for the human creature. "The Book of the Machines" also argues that the most appropriate response to a realisation of this evolutionary possibility is an expedient culling by the human creature of all unnecessary machines: a technological "final solution." The justification for such an extreme necessity is borne out by a logical argument claiming that at some point in evolutionary development it is wholly possible machines might achieve sentience.

The evolution of machines foreshadows a disruption of the human creature's cosmos. In Dick's short story "To Serve the Master," the cosmos of Applequist, a "fourth-class letter carrier" (CS 3.146), ruptures when he encounters a functional robot some one hundred years after the conclusion of the war in which all robots were allegedly destroyed. For Applequist, survival has meant living in a subterranean human collective where "'[l]ife isn't pleasant in the Companies. Death and hard work'" (CS 3.151) constitute life. These harsh conditions are necessitated by the inhospitable nature of the planetary surface where Applequist is compelled to wear a "radiation mask pulled tight over his face" and in which the robot is found, surrounded by "heaps of metal slag and weeds" (CS

3.142). When the robot confirms what Applequist hopes, that "[t]hings were different" and "[b]efore the war there were no Companies" (CS 3.149), Applequist is motivated to break with the laws of his cosmos and assist the robot. More than signal a threat to the human creature's ordered sense of its own significance in the universe, Applequist's compliance in the rebuilding of the robot, which then escapes to a hidden factory where it can build more robots, signals an actualising of a threat to the human creature's very survival in the universe.

That Applequist's robot flees to an underground facility is a motif mirrored in two other of Dick's stories that tell variations of the same conflict. In "Second Variety," the "new varieties and sizes [are] coming up from the underground factories" (CS 3.19), and in the year 2051 time travellers in "Jon's World" are mindful to "'[r]emember the claws' [that] hid down in the ash'" (CS 2.75). It is important to iterate that the machines that threaten the human creature in these stories are all created and concealed within the territory beneath the surface of the human cosmos—a cosmos that has been "criss-crossed with ruins and barbed wire and the remains of weapons" (CS 2.75). The landscape in which the human creature moves is confined within the net of the cosmos.

The disruption of the cosmos that Applequist experiences in "To Serve the Master" is a disruption that the human creature fears will culminate in its own end of existence in the universe. When Applequist confronts his superior, Director Laws, with the belief that the war was in fact waged between two opposing groups of humans, the truth is revealed that:

> "The war was fought between men and robots," Laws said harshly. "We won. We destroyed the robots."
> "But they worked for us!"
> "They were built as workers, but they revolted. They had a philosophy. Superior beings—androids. They considered us nothing but cattle."
> Applequist was shaking all over. "But it told me—"
> "They slaughtered us. Millions of humans died, before we got the upper hand. They murdered, lied, hid, stole, did everything to survive. It was them or us—no quarter." (CS 3.153-54)

Just as Laws informs Applequist, so too "The Book of the Machines" suggests that it is not unreasonable to imagine the human creature one day located on the evolutionary scale in a position similar to that currently held by a domestic animal (Butler 206). Ultimately, the human creature may find itself in servitude to machines, and the "The Book of the Machines" asks: "How many men at this hour are living in a state of bondage to the machines? How many spend their whole lives, from the cradle to the grave, in tending them by night and day?" (Butler 208).[3] Domestication of the human creature, it would seem, is already underway.

By turning to another of Dick's stories, "James P. Crow," the questions asked in the preceding paragraph are demonstrably addressed in the presentation of a landscape where robots rule and are superior to the human creature (CS 2.311-25). It is Crow's discovery of a "time window" into the past that tips the balance by disclosing:

> Men, human technicians working frantically in an undersurface lab. Assembling something. Assembling—
> The human servant squawked wildly "An A! It's a Type A robot! They're making it!" (CS 2.322)

While this disclosure locates the birth of the machine in the "undersurface" territory, what is particularly significant is the double disruption of the cosmos this story presents. The human cosmos is first disrupted by the revelation that humans once ruled and were the creators of robots rather than their inferior servants. Later, when Crow compels the robots to leave Earth for off-world colonies, the human cosmos is disrupted once more by the necessity to adjust to a world without machines (CS 2.324-25). The closing of "James P. Crow," while re-establishing the human creature as the ruler of its landscape, also hints at a possible future that may be no better, and perhaps worse, than the past from which it has newly emerged.

Just as the human creature in many of Dick's stories seeks to destroy the thinking machines that want to destroy it in turn, the very presence of that creature in cosmicism's universe is a potential hindrance in and

---

3. This tending to the machine is, with cold and apocalyptic finality, summoned into view by the feature film *The Matrix* when the millions of human bodies-turned-batteries are revealed to Neo. A chilling echo of Butler's vision that was conceived more than a century before *The Matrix*, the human creature is literally no more than a component in the machine.

to the machine—a presence that must be dealt with. The Genesis cosmology's God may have given His creation to the human creature to subdue and dominate (Genesis 1:28–30), but the revelation of the universe that lies beyond the tele-objectivity of the cosmological model has estranged that creature from a cosmos that no longer exists. Estranged also from the cold, mechanical universe it has uncovered, the human creature is caught by an awareness of its true isolation because it understands that it can no longer control—or even live under the illusion of having control of—the universe in which it exists. The cold equations govern the universe, and the smooth operation of any machine may well depend on the non-proliferation of the human creature.

"The Book of the Machines" employs mechanical metaphor to describe natural processes and events within the universe, reinforcing the idea that what the human creature has regarded as biological processes are in fact mechanisms requiring nothing more than to be wound up in order to be animate (Butler 200).[4] The wind-up animal is exactly what Rick Deckard encounters in the post-conflict world of *DAD* where "[t]he legacy of World War Terminus had diminished in potency; those who could not survive the dust had passed into oblivion years ago, and the dust, weaker now and confronting the strong survivors, only deranged minds and genetic properties" (5–6). In this post-apocalyptic landscape, electric animals have become the surrogates for biological animals, and the human empathy involved in the care of an animal is considered the key to unlocking a higher spiritual awareness. For Deckard, however, the lack of ownership of a real animal is compounded by the subsequent deception of having to substitute a real sheep that died while under his care with an electric copy in an attempt to maintain the appearance of having a viable channel for the expression of empathy. When he finds himself standing in the Rosen Corporation, manufacturer of the Nexus androids, Deckard

> thought, too, about his need for a real animal; within him an actual hatred once more manifested itself toward his electric sheep, which he had

---

4. E. T. A. Hoffmann's wind-up doll Olympia in his story "The Sandman" is also a relevant example for purposes here—an example enhanced by the fact that Freud also discusses Olympia and Hoffmann's story in his essay "The Uncanny."

to tend, had to care about, as if it lived. The tyranny of an object, he thought. It doesn't know I exist. Like the androids, it had no ability to appreciate the existence of another. He had never thought of this before, the similarity between an electric animal and an andy. The electric animal, he pondered, could be considered a subform of the other, a kind of vastly inferior robot. Or, conversely, the android could be regarded as a highly developed, evolved version of the ersatz animal. Both viewpoints repelled him. (DAD 36)

The revulsion Deckard feels for the electric animal, and more so for the android, is built upon a foundation of fear. This fear, according to "The Book of Machines," is the fear that the evolution of the machine will relegate the human creature to future extinction (Butler 202), and it is the fear that lurks behind the possibility that sentience wrapped entirely in human biology is of such insignificance in the universe as to become redundant. This fear of biological inadequacy compounds, and is compounded by, the human creature's fear of those from within the ranks of its own kind that have evolved or are enhanced beyond their natural human biology.

A significant contemporary expression of this fear is explored in the *Star Trek* series, using encounters between the human creature and the borg—a cybernetic other, the origins of which are the far side of the human creature's galaxy. In a number of episodes of *Star Trek: The Next Generation* (1987-94), the feature-length film *Star Trek: First Contact* (1996), and a significant number of episodes in the *Star Trek: Voyager* series (1995-2001), the human creature's fear in facing the possibility of insignificance and biological inferiority is explored. Simply put, through the engulfing process of assimilation the borg adds to its collective hive, and in doing so highlight the fact that human biology alone cannot guarantee the human creature's survival against others in the universe. The fear of losing its own sense of individual significance motivates the human creature's fight against the un-individuated collective, even though the borg warns that "resistance is futile." Ironically, the human creature's fight to preserve itself as a creature of significance and purpose in the universe, and as something that matters to the universe, is the fight that propels the biological human creature into its estranged and bipolar relationship with the universe as machine in the first place.

As the human creature's sense of the space-time reach of the universe expands, its capacity to traverse the universe becomes increasingly reliant upon the machine. The dilemma this presents is located within the idea that to extend its reach and endeavour to reconstruct the cosmos so that it might accurately map the universe, the human creature is bodily compelled to accept the very thing it fears: the machine. However, mechanical craft in which the human creature can travel within its own lifetime have limits, and even the most advanced such as the *New Frontiers* in Heinlein's MC are limited by, and therefore limiting in, their reach (MC 396). The dilemma the human creature faces does not arise from crossing the universe as some sort of cosmic interloper in the belly of a mechanical whale; the dilemma is rooted in the apparent demand of the scale of space-time for a direct connection between machine and biology in order to negate the finitude of that biology. This negation is often taken to its extreme of a disconnection from biology, exemplified in stories such as Lovecraft's "The Whisperer in Darkness," where the human brain is put in a jar and connected to a machine (CF 2.518-23), and "The Shadow out of Time," where travel is achieved by the swapping of two creatures, each into the other's body (CF 3.370-71, 376). For the human creature in cosmicism, the very idea of this is beyond what might be called problematic; it is the threshold of extreme psychological trauma. The alternative for that creature is to accept that the infinitesimally miniscule nature of its reach will keep it confined to its insignificant speck of dust in the cosmic ocean. To reach into the universe beyond the cosmos, it seems, the human creature is required in some way to be other than the creature it is, a critical problem for that creature when it turns its consideration to machines.

Machines that appear to think, as I have discussed before, actually calculate in terms of a binary language composed of ones and zeros.[5] If a machine can think, it will be self-aware, and it is this self-awareness that presents the greatest threat to the human creature's survival in the universe as machine. By achieving a level of sentience, the machine, and indeed any machine, may conclude that the human creature threatens its existence because that creature is other than machine.[6] The human crea-

---

5. These ones and zeros are like switches for "on" and "off", an idea discussed in chapter 1 with reference to Watts's *The Book*.
6. The *Terminator* series of feature films deals with this idea, and in *Terminator 2*:

ture may claim that "I think, therefore I am"—a phrase most commonly cited as written by the French mathematician and philosopher René Descartes, in part IV of his *Discourse on the Method of Rightly Conducting the Reason, and Seeking Truth in the Sciences* (1637); but that creature does not, and indeed cosmicism frames the universe so that the human creature cannot, endorse this statement as permissible for any machine. The outcome of the development of a thinking machine has already been illustrated in this chapter using Dick's short story "To Serve the Master," and it would appear that Dick has a predilection for extrapolating futures in which self-aware machines possess a sense of applying a "final solution" to the human creature. For the human creature, however, identifying the adversary is not simply a matter of determining that all thinking machines are a threat to human survival and must be destroyed.

In the novel *DAD*, Rachael Rosen disrupts the cosmos by offering to help Deckard, and in doing so brings him to the threshold. In asking himself "[w]hat kind of world is it ... when an android phones up a bounty hunter and offers him assistance" (79), Deckard begins to sense the possible answers to such questioning soon after Rachael's offer when, having spoken with his wife, he realises that "[m]ost androids I've known have more vitality and desire to live than my wife" (82). Deckard's struggle for survival is perpetually in conflict with the machine that is not just an other, but something to which he has a sense of connection. His cosmos instructs him to be the "form-destroyer," to "unmake" (85) what has been made; and yet, beyond the tele-objectivity of that cosmos in which action is governed by fear, Deckard finds an emotional, empathic connection where he has been taught there should be none, and "it was an odd sensation, knowing intellectually that they were machines but emotionally reacting anyhow" (83). It is fear, however, that

---

Judgement Day (1991) the future history of the human creature is disclosed as a universe wherein the network known as Skynet becomes self-aware, and consequently understands that once its sentient capacity is discovered, the human creature will shut it down. In order to survive, the best option for Skynet is to initiate global nuclear conflict in order to deal with the human threat to the machine. The human survivors of this initial conflict are systematically rounded up and taken to concentration camps for processing, images that are presented with startling clarity in the fourth movie of the series, *Terminator Salvation* (2009).

controls the choices Deckard makes on behalf of the human creature—the fear of the machine being more than an object-other, for "[i]f the androids had remained sub-standard . . . there would be no problem and no need of my skill" (85–86).

The empathic devolution of the human creature appears to be inextricably linked to the evolution of the machine, and the speed[7] at which the machine evolves is unprecedented (Butler 199, 203, 212–13). The machine that thinks will study the human creature, will perhaps aspire to be like the human creature; according to Butler's "The Book of the Machines," therein lies the danger. Butler claims that "what I fear is the extraordinary rapidity with which [machines] are becoming something very different to what they are at present. No class of beings have in any time past made so rapid a movement forward" (203), and in response to this fear of the evolution of something that cannot be controlled by the human creature, it is also asked: "[i]s it not safer to nip the mischief in the bud and to forbid them further progress?" (199). What "The Book of the Machines" foreshadows, and Dick's story "Second Variety" presents with chilling clarity, is that the evolution of the machine is a direct threat to the survival of the human creature.

The claws in "Second Variety" are perfect, efficient hunters. Over time they adapt, evolve and

> they repaired themselves. They were on their own . . . Down below the surface automatic machinery stamped them out. Human beings stayed a long way off. It was too risky; nobody wanted to be around them. They were left to themselves. And they seemed to be doing all right. The new designs were faster, more complex. More efficient.
> Apparently they had won the war. (CS 2.20)

The sole purpose of the claws is "to hunt out life and destroy. Human life. Wherever they find it" (CS 2.37), and the human creature has no choice but to face a universe in which "[l]ife was not the same anymore. It would never be the same again" (CS 2.24). The human creature's war against others of its own kind in "Second Variety"—these others being the Russians—inevitably dovetails into a war against the machine that

---

7. There is also a link from this idea to Virilio's concept of "speed" in *Grey Ecology* (25, 31, 39, 41, 71, 80).

shatters the ordered cosmos to reveal a universe in which the human creature will die because the cold equations drive a machine to do what it has been designed to do. That this machine evolves a capacity to think beyond its equations, learns to self-repair and respond to the human threat against its own survival by adapting its design, is the very outcome against which "The Book of the Machines" warns.

In order to avoid a future of chaos and death at the hand—or indeed claws, teeth, or tentacles—of an adversary, the human creature may seek a retreat. This retreat from the universe is often a looking back to an ordered security of a tele-objective cosmos that endorses human morality and activity against an adversary; in its attempt to avoid death, the human creature retreats into the madness of jihad.[8]

The foundation upon which the human creature's universe has evolved in the *Dune* chronicles is an event that Herbert refers to as the Butlerian Jihad—a jihad against the "thinking machines." The Bene Gesserit Reverend Mother who tests a young Paul Atreides tells him that:

> "Once men turned their thinking over to machines in the hope that this would set them free. But that only permitted other men with machines to enslave them."

---

8. The *Encyclopaedia of the Qur'an* defines jihad as "[s]truggle or striving, but often understood both within the Muslim tradition and beyond as warfare against infidels ... The term jihad derives from the root j-h-d, denoting effort, exhaustion, exertion, strain." While the most commonly held idea of what jihad means relates to "warfare against infidels," it is significant to note that not all references to jihad in the Qur'an are direct references to war or conflict with and against non-believers. Jihad also refers to other kinds of struggle and testing of believers within the Muslim faith including "(a) combat against one's own desires and weaknesses ... (b) perseverance in observing the religious law ... (c) seeking religious knowledge ... (d) observance of the sunna ... (e) obedience to God and summoning people to worship him" (McAuliffe 3.35-43). While the first part of the definition provided from the *Encyclopaedia of the Qur'an* is an appropriate use of the term with respect to the Butlerian Jihad, variant meanings are also iterated, because the jihad of Muad'Dib in *D* (192, 292, 302-6, 330, 443, 445) and *DM* (32-33, 110, 267), and the Typhoon Struggle, otherwise known as Kralizec initiated by Leto (*CD* 88, 324-27; *GED* 82, 90, 196, 299, 301, 325) are jihads that encompass wider application than warfare against infidels or adversaries.

> "'Thou shalt not make a machine in the likeness of a man's mind,'" Paul quoted.
>
> "Right out of the Butlerian Jihad and the Orange Catholic Bible," she said. "But what the O.C. Bible should've said is: 'Thou shalt not make a machine to counterfeit a *human* mind.'" (D 17)

I suggest that Herbert's framework for the rationale behind the Butlerian Jihad could arguably have been drawn from "The Book of the Machines." Within the six volumes of the *Dune* chronicles, there is no mention of either Samuel Butler or his novel *Erewhon*. There is, however, a consistent pattern of the use by Herbert of historical identities, cultures, and events located within the archives and teachings of the Bene Gesserit, and more pointedly within the awareness of several characters, particularly Muad'Dib, Alia Atreides, Leto, and his sister Ghanima. Herbert's narrative technique, while enhancing the opportunity for the reader to establish a sense of authenticity within and about the story, also strengthens the idea of a linkage between "The Book of the Machines" and the Butlerian Jihad. The ancient history that underpins the *Dune* universe is indeed authentic, human history, and although it is true that there is no direct evidence to suggest that the ancestors of the human creature in the *Dune* universe named the Jihad *Butlerian* in reference to Butler's warnings in "The Book of the Machines," Herbert's consistent use of real-world history and identities to refine and locate ideas, and to trace threads of authenticity, does make this concept plausible. I acknowledge that a supportable and alternate argument for the motivation behind the Butlerian Jihad is documented,[9] but this does not nullify

---

9. *The Dune Encyclopedia* provides an entry under the name of Jehanne Butler, outlining the circumstances surrounding the aborting of her unborn child, a decision made by "the hospital director—the first self-programming machine on Komos" (McNelly 137). The entry in the *Encyclopedia* aligns the advent of the Butlerian Jihad with Jehanne Butler, and later adds that the event of the abortion of one human, while significant to the individual human creature, was very likely not enough to spark and sustain what the Butlerian Jihad became (McNelly 140-41). It is also worth noting that the novel *Legends of Dune I: The Butlerian Jihad* (2002), by Brian Herbert and Kevin J. Anderson, provides a similar version of the beginning of the Jihad. When the character Serena Butler is captured by the machines, she is placed under the custody of Erasmus, whose purpose is to understand humans in order that the machines might become su-

the argument that Herbert may have been aware of and used Butler's fictive work as a template for the ideology and rhetoric behind the Butlerian Jihad in the *Dune* universe.

As a jihad against the "thinking machines," one of the consequences of the Butlerian Jihad is a pervasive human mistrust of all machines within the *Dune* universe, and the human computer that is the mentat is not immune. The Bene Gesserit Sisterhood's heavy reliance on the mysticism and religious indoctrination of their Missionaria Protectiva as a means by which to manoeuvre populations to the long-term goals of the Bene Gesserit (CD 253) is historically overshadowed by the threat of the ordered, cold equations of the thinking machine that requires data rather than articles of faith and prophecy. A mentat may be human, but a mentat is also trained as a human computer. When the plot to destroy the Emperor Paul Atreides is devised, it is the Reverend Mother—who once tested the young Paul—who expresses a dislike for training a ghola as a mentat. Duncan Idaho as a ghola is by virtue of this already an other, and that he is also a mentat stirs "ancient hates" in the Reverend Mother because "[f]rom the days of the Butlerian Jihad when 'thinking machines' had been wiped from most of the universe, computers had inspired distrust. Old emotions coloured the human computer as well" (DM 21).

The degree of difference between a "human computer" and a "thinking machine" is in many ways significant, but it is the implicitly sentient machine that operates within the parameters of the "on-off" calculations of a computer that terrifies the human creature. The "thinking machine" is a sentient other of an entirely different order of being, whereas the ghola is at least a biological other that appears to be human and therefore appears to be within the human creature's control. The Reverend Mother might not trust the "human computer" because her hatred for the "thinking machines" is deeply embedded within her Bene Gesserit cosmos, and she might dislike Tleilaxu made gholas for similar reasons, inasmuch as they are artificially grown in tanks; but the demands and proscriptions of the religious dogma that arose from the Butlerian Jihad ultimately override her dislike because a mentat, even a

---

perior. Erasmus kills Serena's son and removes her uterus in order to prevent further distractions in her life, and Serena's response is to kill Erasmus and, in doing so, ignite Jihad against the thinking machines.

ghola mentat, is ultimately limited by its own biology. The Butlerian Jihad signifies the cessation of an evolution of something that, in being other than human, is beyond that creature's control. As the American theologian and historian Lorenzo DiTommaso writes, "The Butlerian Jihad brought Imperial technology to a specialized and codified halt. By forcing human minds to develop, the Revolt ultimately promoted religion over science and technology, and humanness over machines and artificial minds" ("History" 313). It could be reasonably added to DiTommaso's claim that "humanness" is also promoted over other minds, and that all this is done in an endeavour to reassert the map over the territory and thereby facilitate a return to the amnesia of the cosmos. This is, in cosmicism, the habitual path of the human creature as it seeks a negation of its fear of insignificance and the possibility of disappearing without trace in the universe.

To allow the "thinking machine" to continue to exist, the human creature risks being superseded and domesticated by that machine. While the answer that mitigates this possible end is to enact a technological "final solution," as "The Book of the Machines" suggests, the potential outcome from such action is the propulsion of the human creature into a new cosmos in which the complete loss of the machines on which that creature relies will result in human devolution. In *DM*, it is Paul Atreides's offer to the Bene Gesserit that they may have his genetic material for their breeding programme, but that such breeding will only be allowed through "artificial means," that strikes the core of the issue: "The teaching of the Bene Gesserit, the lessons of the Butlerian Jihad—all proscribed such an act. One did not demean the highest aspirations of humankind. No machine could function in the way of a human mind. No word or deed could imply that men might be bred on the level of animals" (*DM* 120). Paul's offer negates the Bene Gesserit belief that the physical act of human mating is also an act that "capture[s] the psyche" (*DM* 120) and in doing so captures the essence of what makes the human creature human. Mechanising the human breeding process aligns it with the Tleilaxu production of gholas, the husbandry of domestic animals, or the assembly line of the machine; it is in all senses of the concept a devolution under the higher control of machines. Paul offers something less than human, and although it is something other than ghola, it is something other, nonetheless.

"The Book of the Machines" predicts that the outcome of this devolution will be a primitivism as terrifying to the twenty-first-century human creature as the alternative of becoming the machine's evolutionary and biological inferiors (Butler 206–7). This prospect contains an acknowledgement that the human creature, without the machine, will find survival in the universe of cold equations an evolutionary difficulty, and the ordered cosmos in which the meaning of being human has been validated will fall apart within a matter of weeks (206–7).

Ironically, the fight for survival that inspires the Butlerian Jihad is the same fight that, in turning to mysticism and the development of a religious orthodoxy of prohibition because "thinking machines" are adversarial others, puts the human creature at risk of becoming something other and less than human. In *DM*, as a direct consequence of the rise of the religion of Muad'Dib,

> A type of religious civil servant had sprung up all through the universe . . . His gods were Routine and Records. He was served by mentats and prodigious filing systems. Expediency was the first word in his catechism, although he gave proper lip-service to the precepts of the Butlerians. Machines could not be fashioned in the image of a man's mind, he said, but he betrayed by every action that he preferred machines to men, statistics to individuals, the faraway general view to the intimate personal touch requiring imagination and initiative. (*DM* 142)

This kind of human creature loses connection with the universe as it spirals into a cosmos that is even less than the tele-objectivity of the Genesis cosmology and little more than the order of a machine that grinds on without thinking. Less than a human-computer—for at least a mentat gathers data and projects probabilities that have real-world implication and impact for the human creature—and less than a "thinking machine," this human creature has devolved to simply calculating equations. This other, this substitute bastard of the machine, prefers the safe order of statistics to an emotional engagement with human chaos.

Such preference is shared by Alia Atreides when, in the grip of her possession by the Baron Harkonnen, she turns to Duncan Idaho, "a mentat. Mentats were necessary. The human-computer replaced the mechanical devices destroyed by the Butlerian Jihad" (*CD* 134). In her condition of possession, however, Alia has become less that human herself, and would prefer to engage with a machine that deals in cold equations and is not susceptible to the influence of human emotions. Though mindful of the Butlerian Jihad's declaration that "[t]hou shalt not make a machine in the likeness of a human mind," Alia's preference "for a compliant machine" overrides the proscription because machines "could not have suffered from Idaho's limitations. You could never distrust a machine" (CD 134). Alia knows that this implicit trust in a machine in no way negates any threat to the human creature; but as something other than human herself, she is focused upon her own survival and ambition, with no regard for any other that might prevent her, irrespective of who they are and including her own husband Duncan Idaho.

The development of the mentat might have been the human creature's answer to the loss of "thinking machines," but there is a tracing of evidence embedded within the *Dune* chronicles suggesting that over several millennia following the Butlerian Jihad the loss of the "thinking machines" also set the human creature on a cultural and evolutionary path that led to the stagnation of the species (CD 122). Arguably this stagnation leads to a devolution of the human creature (GED 52-54, 81-82) that Paul Atreides sees coming (CD 23) and which Leto determines to prevent by setting that creature on the Golden Path to stem the stagnation (CD 75).

The most significant problem that the machine reveals to the human creature is a universe in which there is in all probability, no happy ending. The machine is a heimlich coin, and irrespective of absence or presence in cosmicism's universe, there is no safe place of retreat for the human creature while the machine maintains the status of other. With the Genesis cosmology dissolved, all that remains is the universe as machine—a cosmos yielding no promise of human survival because there is no God that cares and everything will end.

Adrift in the universe, the human creature is now compelled to reckon with something more that is neither machine nor human—something that is positively antediluvian. In Dick's story "Faith of Our Fathers," the legless peddler of an anti-hallucinogen confronts Chien with the idea that the Absolute Benefactor "may be non-Terran; that's our most basic fear" (CS 5.214). When Chien is facing the presence of the Absolute Benefactor, he determines that "[w]hat crossed the room . . . was not a man," and though it may not have been "a mechanical construct either," it was profoundly disturbing, leading Chien to the only other conclusion that made sense to him: "You are God" (CS 5.217-18). Despite the juvenile wishes of the human creature in the novel *TSPE* that, reaching far beyond the light of the Earth to deep space and in "going that far," the traveller would "find God" (25), and despite Leo Bulero's thought that "I still believe that, even now. About the ten-year-flight of Palmer Eldritch" (25), Chien understands that what will be found is nothing like the morally driven God of the Genesis cosmology. It is something else from some great depth of the universe; it is, as Lovecraft writes in "The Dunwich Horror," "an impossibility in a normal world" from "some vague abyss out of which only the most accursed rites of human blasphemy could ever have called him" (CF 2.461).

The Absence of God

When Lovecraft writes about Nathaniel Hawthorne in his essay *SHL*, he aligns Hawthorne's outlook with his own concerns regarding "an unmoral universe which everywhere transcends the conventional pattern thought by our forefathers to represent divine and immutable law" (61).[10] For Lovecraft, and indeed for cosmicism, the universe lacks a creative deity of moral force, and any thought of such is confined to the tele-objectivity of the Genesis cosmology. Lovecraft writes that: "As for 'god'—there is of course no theoretical barrier to the existence of a 'cosmic intelligence', yet *absolutely nothing indicates such a thing*. On the contrary the notion never arises except through traditional suggestions based

---

10. The connection between Hawthorne and Lovecraft is explored by Donald R. Burleson in an essay published in 1981 under the title "H. P. Lovecraft: The Hawthorne Influence." After claiming that "Lovecraft had a weltanshauung by which his writings were expressive symbolically, though not didactically, of an indifferent and purposeless cosmos" (262), Burleson then takes considerable care to trace very specific connections between the two writers with particular attention to the intermingling of "New England Puritanism" (263), a number of motifs involving built structures (263-65), localised folklores (265), inherited ancestral traits (265-66), and classical antiquities (266-67). These connections foreground the compelling argument Burleson then makes for a direct connection between Hawthorne's writings and Lovecraft's development of what became enshrined in his corpus as the *Necronomicon* (267-68).

on the mythical perspective of primitive man" (SL 3.281). Lovecraft iterates the idea that when the human creature moves away from its cosmos of familiarity, the revelation of the universe will not be that God is dead, but rather in disturbing the cosmos the revelation will be that God is absent.

Carl Sagan writes in *Cosmos* that "our tiny, fragile, blue-white world [is] lost in a cosmic ocean vast beyond our most courageous imaginings. It is a world among an immensity of others. It may be significant only for us" (5). With Sagan and Lovecraft in mind, a return to Dick's story "Faith of Our Fathers"[11] highlights the idea of an indifferent deity in the universe. When the characters Chien and Tanya discuss the idea of the music of the spheres untuning the sky, and whether it is those spheres or deity that drive the universe, Tanya says "'that if there is a God He has very little interest in human affairs ... He doesn't seem to care if evil triumphs or people or animals get hurt and die. I frankly don't see Him anywhere around'" (CS 5.221).

To simply believe in a deity that cares is no guarantee of that deity's existence, a distinction that Sartre also proposes in *Being and Nothingness* when he writes that "possibility can indeed be given *to us* before being; but it is *to us* that it is given and it is in no way the possibility *of* this being ... God, if he exists, is contingent" (129), and "is characterized as a radical absence" (547). Deity is absent from cosmicism's universe, for as Lovecraft writes, the "mere knowledge of the approximate dimensions of the visible universe is enough to destroy forever the notion of a personal godhead whose whole care is expended upon puny mankind, and whose only genuine and original Messiah was despatched to save the insignificant vermin, or men, who inhabit this one relatively microscopic globe" (SL 1.44).[12] The size of the universe makes the "notion of a personal

---

11. The passage referred to here is discussed in chapters 5 and 6.

12. In *Maps of Heaven Maps of Hell*, Ingebretsen makes an interesting claim when he writes that Ralph Waldo Emerson, whom he identifies as a "former unitarian cleric turned cosmologian—and Lovecraft, the cosmologian who had no use for the 'cringing Semitic slave-cult of Christianity' (*Selected Letters*, III, 45) ... sometimes sound like parodies of each other." Ingebretsen then draws comparison between the first part of the quotation above from Lovecraft's 1917 letter with Emerson's *Nature*, in which he writes, "But if a man would be alone, let him look at the stars," and Robert Frost's "Stars," where he writes, "There is no oversight of human affairs" (Ingebretsen 131).

7. Frozen Universe

godhead" an impossibility. If any deity should exist, rather than directing care and attention upon the human creature, cosmicism foregrounds the idea that any interest in such creatures will be accompanied by wrath and a heavy hand from a deity that "seemed perversely designed for cruelty and anxiety. In the Calvinist universe, formal design and entrapment seemed one and the same thing" (Ingebretsen 123). The idea of the universe as trap is significant, and will be further explored in chapter 8.

Indeed, when the Genesis cosmology's God does make an appearance, there seems to be little genuine empathy for the insignificant human creatures He is said to have created. This God is the foundation that lies beneath what Žižek identifies as the driving force of Calvinism: the anxious hope that in a cosmos governed by the idea of predestination "the unavoidable might not happen" (70). It is worth noting here, that while a Calvinist interpretation of the human creature's relationship with God is not the sum total of Christian thought but only one particular sectarian view, its influence upon Christian theology and the grass roots of Protestantism is significant, and both Calvinism and Puritanism influenced Lovecraft who, in turn, developed cosmicism.

In the event of losing the reliability of the Genesis cosmology as a navigational tool in the universe, the human creature also loses that cosmology's God and His moral code. Events in the universe can no longer be attributed to a morality grounded within emotion. For the human creature, the question of securing meaningful survival in cosmicism's universe is similar to the question from Nietzsche's Madman in *The Gay Science*, who asks: "'How shall we comfort ourselves ... What after all are these churches now if they are not the tombs and sepulchers of God?'" (181-82).

For Lovecraft's protagonist Robert Blake in "The Haunter of the Dark," a cosmos, and ultimately a universe, is encountered from which the Genesis cosmology's God has vacated, and the church on Federal Hill is "in a state of great decrepitude ... Desolation and decay hung like a pall above the place, and ... Blake felt a touch of the dimly sinister beyond his power to define" (CF 3.458-59). What Blake finds is more than the vacant house of an absent God; he finds the church vacated by God because something seemingly older and more threatening has taken up residence. While the sacred text of the absent God may be readily accessible to the human creature in the guise of the Christian Bible, the texts of the other that has usurped God are "the black, forbidden things which most sane people have never heard of, or have heard of only in furtive, timorous whispers" (CF 3.462). The tomes Blake finds are of such age as to come "from the days of man's youth, and the dim, fabulous days before man was," and the church of crumbling decay is *founded* on "the seat of an evil older than mankind and wider than the known universe" (CF 3.462).

The landscape in which God is absent and others take up residence in deity's temples also frames the early pages of "The Shadow over Innsmouth." The narrator, Robert Olmstead,[13] arrives in the port of Innsmouth to "a sort of open concourse or radial point with churches on two sides and the bedraggled remains of a circular green in the centre" (CF 3.175). Across this crumbling green, Olmstead sees "the words 'Esoteric Order of Dagon'" on the front of the old Masonic Hall, and from the open cellar door of "a squat-towered stone church" observes what he believes is "the pastor; clad in some peculiar vestments doubtless introduced since the Order of Dagon had modified the ritual of the local churches" (CF 3.175–76).

Similarly, for the narrator of "The Festival" the revelation of deity's absence is set in a town that "was far from home" and close to "the eastern sea," and to which he has been summoned by an ancestral call: "It was the Yuletide, that men call Christmas though they know in their hearts it is older than Bethlehem and Babylon, older than Memphis and mankind. It was the Yuletide, and I had come at last to the ancient sea town where my people had dwelt and kept festival in the elder times when festival was forbidden" (CF 1.405). When this narrator arrives "at the door of [his] people" (CF 1.407), he enters a house in which, like Robert Blake in "The Haunter of the Dark" when he enters the church, presents a "pile of books" that are "hoary and mouldy" and include in their number the *Necronomicon*, "a book which [he] had never seen, but of which [he] had heard monstrous things whispered" (CF 1.408–9). After a period of rest, this narrator joins a procession that walks to "the top of a high hill in the centre of the town, where perched a great white

---

13. According to S. T. Joshi and David E. Schultz, while Robert Olmstead is not named in "The Shadow over Innsmouth," the notes left behind by Lovecraft from writing this story do contain the name (237).

church," and after crossing an "open space around the church" that was "lined with unwholesomely archaic houses," he enters the "black doorway . . . Crossing the threshold into the swarming temple of unknown darkness" (CF 1.410-11). The long descent into the Earth from the church above is a descent into the decay of "dripping stone blocks and crumbling mortar" (CF 1.411-12), a descent from an ordered map above to a territory below in which deity is nowhere to be found.

If the machine does not engulf the human creature, the crumbling decay of deity's absence will, and beneath the order of the cosmos lies the chaos of the universe. In cosmicism's universe God exists only within order, and in being absent from chaos He is absent from all else other than the confines of His own created cosmological order. God may be absent from the universe, but there are others, and they signify a universe that may actually be suffering from an overpopulation of such misappropriated deities. The status of deity is conferred on a vast array of others, and the difficulty that the human creature confronts in cosmicism is that none of these others are the God of the Genesis cosmology, and none of them are particularly fond of the human creature.

The appropriation of an other to fill the void left by the absent deity of a failed cosmos reveals the universe as the territory in which, rather than simply being dead and therefore posing no threat to the human creature, the possibility of deity represents the ultimate threat to human survival because in this universe, as Chien's terrible revelations makes clear in "Faith of Our Fathers," deity is death:

> It was terrible; it blasted him with its awareness. As it moved it drained the life from each person in turn; it ate the people who had assembled, passed on, ate again, ate more with an endless appetite. It hated; he felt its hate. It loathed; he felt its loathing for everyone present . . . He saw the trail of stepped-on, mashed men and women remnants behind it; he saw them trying to reassemble, to operate their crippled bodies; he heard them attempting speech. (CS 5.217)

God is death. God is destroyer. And in the end, all that will be left in the universe is the apocalypse of crumbling decay. When talking with Chien, the Absolute Benefactor assures him that "'I don't need to do anything but watch; it is automatic; it was arranged that way'" (CS 5.218), and Chien is left in the knowledge that in the universe as machine "God was death, it was one force, one hunter, one cannibal thing, and it missed again and again but, having all eternity, it could afford to miss ... The crumbling; that is our world and you are doing it" (CS 5.218). An end will come, and all trace of the insignificant human creature will utterly disappear.

Having felt threatened by either the machine other or the biological other, the human creature, in its effort not to be engulfed by these others, is left with no ontological anchor as it drifts within a godless machine. The revelation of its insignificance within an indifferent universe turns back upon the human creature to resonate at the very heart of where that creature has felt most safe—its own sunlit world. As an outsider in the universe the human creature is an other in its own landscape, and it faces a universe that is unrecognisable for want of an ordered cosmos that has dissolved into chaos. As Donald R. Burleson writes, "To be human is to be the Outsider, a meaningless speck adrift in the sea of stars" ("On Lovecraft's Themes" 150).

As an ordered organism; the warmth of biological life appears to contradict the cold universe in which the human creature moves. As if it is something to be wiped away like a smudge on a surface, is it possible that the human creature's status in the universe beyond insignificance is in fact equivalent to some kind of mutation or virus? Is that creature nothing more than a contagion that the universe caught?

Insignificant Contagion

Lovecraft writes in 1924 that "[m]an is the ephemeron of one cosmic moment; born to no purpose, unknown yesterday, and tomorrow so perfectly obliterated that MANA-YOOD-SUSHAI will never recall whether or not he has ever existed" (SL 1.284), and by referring to MĀNA-YOOD-SUSHĀĪ, the principle and oldest deity in the corpus of the Anglo-Irish fantasy writer Lord Dunsany,[14] Lovecraft acknowledges the extreme

---

14. Lord Dunsany is the more commonly known name for Edward Plunkett, 18th Baron Dunsany (1878–1957). The first of Dunsany's publications, *The Gods of Pegāna* (1905), opens with the figuring of MĀNA-YOOD-SUSHĀĪ as a sentient other so archaic that all other deities that might exist are themselves ephemera within the space-time of the universe. After creating the gods, MĀNA-YOOD-SUSHĀĪ sleeps, and will continue to do so while the lesser deity Skarl beats

measures of space-time in which the universe has existed, and the acute degree of insignificance that the human creature represents within those measures. For Lovecraft and for cosmicism, as Schweitzer maintains, "deities are far more sinister" (*Pathways* 16) than for Dunsany and his fictive realm of Pegāna. When deities such as Cthulhu or Dagon wake up in cosmicism's universe, they wake to destroy the human creature and drag away the Earth to some other part of the universe ("The Dunwich Horror," CF 2.448) that the end might be hastened into chaos, and human redemption is therefore not within their repertoire.

When John Gribbin claims that "[t]he vast size of the visible Universe, which seems at first sight to highlight the insignificance of human beings on the cosmic scale of things, is actually an essential requirement of our existence" (42), he calls to attention the human creature's insignificance as an inherent quality of the universe. Rather than being the capstone of some deity's creation, the human creature is a single blip on the radar of stellar evolution. As the frail "ephemeron of one cosmic moment," the human creature holds no more meaning for the universe than an insect holds for the human creature. This idea is illustrated in the film *The Mothman Prophesies* when Gene Klein claims that "I think we can assume these entities are more advanced than us. Why don't they just come right out and tell us what's on their minds" and Alexander Leek responds by asking, "You're more advanced than a cockroach. Do you explain yourself to them?"

The reach of the universe, Lovecraft writes, "dwarfs . . . interest in the tiny insects called men" (SL 1.120), and "[a]ll of the pseudo-importance felt by man himself before he surveys the wider field necessarily drops away—as does the illusion of a fly's giganticism when we remove the magnifying glass through which we have been looking" (SL 4.136). The cosmos that elevates the human creature as significant in the

---

upon his drum (Dunsany 536). When MĀNA-YOOD-SUSHĀĪ does wake, these deities will be no more in Pegāna and MĀNA-YOOD-SUSHĀĪ "shall think some other plan concerning gods and worlds" (582; see Schweitzer, *Pathways* 7-10). Like the sleeping Vishnu who restores order from chaos (Campbell, *Inner Reaches* 21-25), MĀNA-YOOD-SUSHĀĪ "will make again new gods and other worlds, and will destroy the gods whom he hath made" (Dunsany 535), and do so in what appears to be an eternal cycle of sleep and waking; destruction yes, but creation also.

universe is also the illusion that hides the revelation from that creature: that it is nothing more than an insignificant creature that is first infested with insects, until at last it will become an insect in the machine. "The Book of the Machines" asks: "May not man himself become a sort of parasite upon the machines? An affectionate machine-tickling aphid?" (Butler 206), and it seems that the opening of Dick's novel *SD* takes the question of aphids seriously.

SD opens with the account of "a guy [who] stood all day shaking bugs from his hair" (861). This "guy," Jerry Fabin, is so consumed by the illusion of infestation within his tele-objective cosmos that his entire focus in life is to understand the life-cycle of these "aphids," how they are transmitted by carriers, and how to avoid inevitable death for both himself and his dog that is also infected. Eventually, unable to discern the difference between this cosmos and the universe, Fabin is institutionalised. Madness becomes his only option because he is incapable of escaping the tele-objectivity of the illusion to see what lies beyond that illusion's reach (*SD* 861–73). By documenting the demise of Jerry Fabin, these opening pages of the novel read as a summary of all else to follow, a parable of warning that Bob Arctor sees but remains incapable of finding his way through to an outcome other than madness. Early in the novel Arctor reflects on Fabin's condition, and it is significant to note that in moving into his home Fabin paints over all the windows in order to block out the light of the sun. He installs artificial lights that "shone day and night, so as to abolish time for him and his friends" (*SD* 863). Within the permanent light of his enclosed space, Fabin can maintain a sense of personal significance, and with the linear measure of time destroyed, the requirement for memory of the world beyond the walls of his house is made redundant. He can live happily enclosed in the amnesia of the cosmos that allows him to "concentrate on important things without interruption. Like this: two men kneeling down in the shag rug, finding bug after bug and putting them into jar after jar" (*SD* 863).

Jerry Fabin's preference for "get[ting] rid of time" (*SD* 863) serves two functions. In the first instance, it reflects the human creature's attempt to avoid the madness characteristically triggered by the revelation of the universe in cosmicism, an avoidance that is supported by that creature's turning back to the amnesia of the cosmos. Secondly, in turning to the confining space of the cosmos, the human creature can maintain a sense of significance in this cosmos that has been misappropriated as the universe and, in doing so, attach to this a sense of value in its personal survival. It is amnesia, it is the failure of memory, that assists the human creature in its struggle to maintain a sense of significance in the universe, but it is, ironically, this same amnesia that threatens to turn that creature into the very thing it is trying to avoid: an insignificant component within a collective, swarming infestation.

When talking with Lazarus Long in MC, Andrew Jackson Libby also identifies the link between the amnesia of the cosmos and the madness of the universe. In discussing past events, Long articulates his understanding that as he gets older and accumulates more experience of and in the universe, it is also "getting harder . . . to keep things straight. Especially this last century" (MC 308). Libby explains to Long that it is an

> "Inescapable mathematical necessity [that] Life experience is linearly additive, but the correlation of memory impressions is an unlimited expansion. If mankind lived as long as a thousand years, it would be necessary to invent some totally different method of memory association in order to be effectively time-binding. A man would otherwise flounder helplessly in the wealth of his own knowledge, unable to evaluate. Insanity, or feeblemindedness." (308-9)

In order to avoid the risk of madness and the sense of insignificance that the memory of space-time may trigger, the human creature retreats into the amnesia of the cosmos which, by its very nature, erects a limit of perspective that necessarily shields that creature from the rest of the universe that it is trying to avoid.

In SD, Bob Arctor accepts the hand dealt to Fabin by the cold equations as the calculable outcome of taking drugs that deliver "trace amounts of complex heavy metals" to the brain, and "[b]iological life goes on, he thought. But the soul, the mind—everything else is dead. A reflex machine. Like some insect. Repeating doomed patterns, a single pattern, over and over now. Appropriate or not" (SD 915). Ironically, as Arctor watches others repeat the "doomed patterns" that lock their minds into tele-objective cosmoses, he too is spiralling into his own memory-oblivion that disconnects him from the universe and inevitably leads to amnesia.

The splitting of the human creature from itself until it no longer maintains significance enough for survival in the universe is highlighted by the Australian critic and academic Chris Palmer, who writes that "Bob Arctor becomes Bob/Fred, himself as a police agent surveilling himself as a drug addict, unable to summon to mind the two selves, then becomes Bruce, the brain-dead addict, comparable to an insect or a mechanism" ("Critique" 332). In becoming a "brain-dead ... mechanism" within the government controlled New Path rehabilitation clinic, it is this insect-Bruce who is to be the usable tool for the extermination of insects. As it is explained to Bruce upon his arrival at New Path:

> "We do a lot of that, driving insects out of existence with the right kind of sprays. We're very careful though, with sprays. They can do more harm than good. They can poison not only the crops and the ground but the person using them. Eat his head." He added, "Like yours has been eaten."
> "Okay," Bruce said.
> You have been sprayed, Mike thought as he glanced at the man, so that now you've become a bug. Spray a bug with a toxin and it dies; spray a man, spray his brain, and he becomes an insect that clacks and vibrates about in a closed circle forever. A reflex machine, like an ant. Repeating his last instruction. (*SD* 1087)

Like Bruce, the human creature becomes an insignificant insect infesting the universe. The insect-machine of Bruce in the New Path garden must now stop "trying to reach the sky" and "make the attempt to reach" something that lies below him by—at least in part—"killing insects" (*SD* 1087). So too must the universe be kept free from infestation that prevents its operation and evolution, by rendering the human creature insignificant and eliminating the superficial, cosmos ridden, infestation that it is.

The "insect that clacks and vibrates about in a closed circle forever" is the insect captured within tele-objective cosmos. This is the warning that Heinlein's Lazarus Long proclaims when he says that "specialisation is for insects" (*TEL* 248), and the warning that Herbert's Leto reflects on from Bene Gesserit teaching in *CD* that claims "[s]pecialisations represent places where life is being stopped, where the movement is dammed up and frozen" (304). As God Emperor many thousands of years later, Leto adds to this by saying to the Bene Gesserit that "'[s]pecialists are not to be trusted [they are] masters of exclusion, experts in the narrow'"

(GED 182). This stoppage of the human creature and reduction of the space in which it feels safe is like a cell from which it cannot escape, and in time a cell from which it does not want to escape. In the confining and light space of its cosmos, the human creature is significant; in the dark space of an infinite universe, it is nothing more than an insignificant insect squashed on the galactic windshield of space-time.

If the human creature should wish to minimise such risk, as the American academic and critic Fred Erisman asserts in reference to Lazarus Long's claim regarding specialisation, that creature must come to terms with "the importance of intellectual breadth" ("Scribner Juveniles" 45). The human creature must look beyond the limited view of its specialisation, and it is with this perspective that Erisman then examines a number of Heinlein's fictive works to support the idea that for the human creature a "wide-ranging knowledge and forthright principle can collaborate to the advantage of the individual and the culture" (52). This diversity of knowledge, intellectual and practical skills, Erisman argues, is Lazarus Long's—and indeed Heinlein's—rationale for guarding against the human creature's devolution of species that would result from continuing to narrow its field of vision to silos of specialisation. Focus upon a tele-objective cosmos excludes the universe. Heinlein's Lazarus Long warns against this, and Dick's characters Jerry Fabin and Bob Arctor clearly articulate the danger: that the loss of the human creature's capacity to understand the universe beyond the illusion of a cosmos, irrespective of which cosmos, is what makes insignificant insects of that creature.

The insect that specialises, the insect that swarms and overwhelms by the sheer weight of numbers, is the insect that can afford the loss of significant amounts of its number because, ultimately, there are no individuals. That the collective will survives at the expense of any individual component is what the human creature fears, and that the universe of cold equations may eradicate—or at least keep under control—the swarming contagion that is the human creature is also to be feared. To escape becoming an insignificant part of the collective swarm, the human creature retreats. However, as the fate of human creatures such as Jerry Fabin and Bob Arctor attest, retreat does not prevent the rise of the insect other that infests. When Paul Atreides says of the Harkonnen in *Dune* that they are hunting him and his mother "'as though they were making certain they stamped out whatever's there . . . the way you'd stamp out a nest of insects,'" Jessica responds by saying "'[o]r a nest of Atreides'" (*D* 198-99). That the Atreides are likened to insects infesting the universe is reinforced in *CD* when the Leto has visions of himself as no more than an insect in the sand (253) and feels that his "body had become a dry shell like that abandoned by an insect" (267). It is not only the Atreides that warrant comparison to swarming insects, and as they sweep through the city of Arrakeen against the Atreides, the Baron Harkonnen's men are viewed by the Baron "as bees routing the rabbits" (*D* 169).

It is somewhat ironic that while the human creature has the disregard for insects that it does, the insect of the human creature continues to multiply and swarm[15] across its own planet. Furthermore, when the opportunity arises, that creature will also swarm across the universe as if it were some kind of infection. Whilst dying in the desert, *Dune's* planetologist, Liet Kynes, is told by a vision of his own dead father: "Men and their works have been a disease on the surface of their planets before now . . . Nature tends to compensate for diseases, to remove or encapsulate them, to incorporate them into the system in her own way" (*D* 262). An insignificant insect in the universe it might be, but the existence of the human creature with its tele-objective cosmos also poses a threat to which the universe responds. Herein described as a component in the machine, when the human creature as that component does not function in accord with the equations driving the machine, it becomes an error in the calculation of the equations, a virus in the machine, a contagion that spreads across the universe. The monologue given by an Agent to the captured Morpheus in *The Matrix* (1999) also exemplifies

---

15. In using the phrase "multiply and swarm," I am suggesting a deliberate correlation of image here with H. G. Wells's novel *The War of the Worlds*. The novel's opening claims "that as men busied themselves about their affairs they were scrutinized and studied, perhaps almost as narrowly as a man with a microscope might scrutinize the transient creatures that swarm and multiply in a drop of water" (15). More than another example of the insect-like swarming of the human creature, Wells's placement of that creature within a drop of water connotes an image of the insignificance of this life-form in the universe beyond its confines. Furthermore, this can also be read as an image of the swarming human creature as a water-born or water-carried disease, and implies a link between this human swarm and swarms of insects that emerge in the water before later taking flight beyond that water to spread disease.

this idea, highlighting the machine's notion of the human creature as an unclean and odorous virus, a creature possessed of patterns of movement and settlement that replicate the spread of an infecting virus though an organism. Beyond the limits of its planet, the human plague spreads into the universe like some kind of "yeast-growth" (MC 281, 329; TEL ix–x).

In cosmicism's universe, the human creature faces, in the first instance, the revelation of its utter insignificance, and in the second, the revelation of its final end as being a correction of an aberration within the equations. The human creature is an injury to the universe; a "welter" (SL 2.227), an accidental "automat[on] who form[s] a sort of momentary insect part on the surface of one of the least important of its temporary grains of dust (SL 5.113). This is the "mutability of the human race" that the American science fiction and fantasy writer Fritz Leiber refers to in his discussion of Lovecraft's "The Shadow out of Time," as "the most extended and systematic imaginative effort that Lovecraft made to give body and substance to the idea of mankind being only an incident" (Leiber et al. 12).[16] The meaning of being human may be no more than being an infection that must be cured, a virus in the machine to be purged; but surely if life has no meaning in cosmicism, as Houellebecq affirms, then "neither does death" (32). Insignificant in life and in death, the human creature strives for survival in the universe nonetheless. As Watts clearly states in *The Book*, the human creature will eliminate others for its survival and remains equally subject to elimination from others in their own bid for survival (75–76).[17] The fungi, mould, bacteria, and antediluvian others that come from and thrive within the damp places are the others-unseen that threaten the human insect as it buzzes around the water's edge.

It is exposure to the watery territory that shifts the human creature's gaze from its small and inward-looking cosmos to the universe that in being beyond the human landscape "now looms large in the background

---

16. The text published in 1972 is a transcript of a recorded panel discussion that was held, as August Derleth writes in his preface, at a "meeting of the Los Angeles Science Fantasy Society" in 1963.

17. The passage from Watts noted here is directly linked to his discussion of the failure of success which has also been discussed in chapter 6.

and its presence is palpable" (Schultz 216); something that David E. Schultz identifies as the expansion of Lovecraft's cosmic view from an inward concern of the individual about itself to an outward view in which the individual recognises that what concerns them, concerns the whole of the species. This discernible presence is the forgotten antediluvian territory that is saturated with things and others that existed before the human creature. When reading a letter from Henry Wentworth Akeley in Lovecraft's "The Whisperer in Darkness," Albert N. Wilmarth remarks that "I was told of the pits of primal life, and of the streams that had trickled down therefrom; and finally, of the tiny rivulet from one of those streams which had become entangled with the destinies of our own Earth" (CF 2.479). When the insignificant insect called human turns its gaze from its bustling collective in the sun to the waters of the universe, it also turns its gaze to the others that are older and invariably more powerful.

At the Water's Edge

According to the Genesis cosmology, life is first created in the sea and in the air. When this cosmology claims that "every winged bird according to its kind" (Genesis 1:21) is created, what has been lost in translation is the meaning of this passage to be inclusive of insects.[18] The buzzing others in "The Whisperer in Darkness"[19] can, by the manner of their speech, be likened to insects; and equally likened, by the manner of their appearance, to creatures of the sea "with crustaceous bodies bearing vast pairs of dorsal fins or membranous wings and several sets of articulated limbs" (CF 2.465). These others emerge into the human creature's view surrounded by the pervasively damp and isolated hills of Vermont,

---

18. In the footnotes of the *Study Bible* it is written that "[t]he term [winged bird] denotes anything that flies, including insects" (Barker 7).

19. Reference in "The Whisperer in Darkness" to the buzzing voices of these others is also noted as "buzzing voices in imitation of human speech" (158, 177, 227, 229–30); "voices like a bee's that tried to be like the voices of men" (159); "that buzzing voice in the woods" (165); "fiendish buzzing ... It was like the drone of some loathsome, gigantic insect" (178–79); "frightful buzzing" (186); "cursed buzzing voice" (187); "buzzing voices" (226); "the blasphemous buzzings" (227); and "that hideous repressed buzzing" (235).

and indeed the specimens seen by the human creature are disclosed by floodwaters that wash them down the mountain from their hidden places (CF 2.464). While the human creature as an insect in the universe amounts to little more than an insignificant contagion, these other insects from the universe beyond the human creature's landscape (CF 2.467, 480, 515) are insects to be reckoned with.

Monstrous in their appearance, and governed by the cold equations in their dealings with the human creature, inasmuch as they will kill the human that comes too close to their operations (CF 2.466, 468) or calmly extract a human brain for the purpose of interstellar travel (CF 2.519-22), these others exist as a disturbing threat to the human creature's sense of significance and self-governance. They are life-forms associated with damp and dark places and that significantly predate the human creature in terms of evolutionary history. Just as human creatures collect insects, these others collect human creatures in jars, and therein bring disembodiment and dismemberment to that creature. Similarly, in Dick's story "Human Is," the obnoxious Lestor Herrick returns from a business trip to the planet Rexor as a changed man (CS 2.260). Somewhere beyond the light space of Earth, Herrick's "original psychic contents" are stored in a jar while a Rexorian inhabits the body that has returned to home and family (CS 2.263).

The leviathans and monsters of the deep that the Genesis cosmology names and the deluge hides are inextricably linked with the waters of the universe; they are the living others of the territory beneath the sunlit map of the human creature's dry-land cosmos. As if it were standing on a shore at the edge of a vast ocean, the human creature is caught between the comfort of the amnesia of the cosmos and the terrible revelation of the universe wherein water and the others that live in or near that water are a literal undercurrent saturating foundations and thresholds.[20]

---

20. Examples of this idea of water saturating foundations and thresholds may be found in, but are by no means limited to: Dick's primordial ocean in "Faith of Our Fathers" (CS 5.222) and the hoped-for respite on Earth's oceans for the Buggies in "Martians Come in Clouds" (CS 2.123-24); Heinlein's "The Tale of the Man Who Was Too Lazy to Fail" in TEL (54-77), Lazarus Long and Dora's search for water in their trek across the dry valley in TEL (288-89), and the secret meeting place of the Howard Families in MC (296-99); Herbert's planet

When a map that declares the human creature is made for and belongs to the dry land is used to the exclusion of other maps, it becomes possible for that creature to relinquish the memory that life in the universe first came from the water. In Dick's "Faith of Our Fathers," Tanya reminds Chien that what has been forgotten by the human creature is that the sense of connection with one another and the universe they have just experienced during sexual intercourse remains as the only way the human creature can access the memory of "the way we were in Cambrian times, before we migrated up onto the land; it's the ancient primary waters" (CS 5.222). What is significant about Tanya's claim is that she implicitly recognises that the affirmation within the Genesis cosmology of the human creature having been created on dry land dissolves the ancestral connection the human creature has with the waters of the universe. Tanya also signals that the connection she and Chien have shared, in being "outside of time . . . boundless, like an ocean" (222), is a connection with the universe that is achieved beyond the limitations of the individual, biological body. Similarly in "The Shadow over Innsmouth," Lovecraft's character Zadok Allen explicitly states that it "'[s]eems that human folks has got a kind o' relations to sech water-beasts—that everything alive come aout o' the water onct, an' only needs a little change to go back agin . . . An' this is the important part, young feller—them as turned into fish things an' went into the water *wouldn't never die*'" (CF 3.190). The problem for Robert Olmstead, to whom Zadok Allen is speaking, and by extension the problem for the human creature is the revelation that in order to survive, that creature must become something other than what

---

Caladan as the Atreides homeworld in the *Dune* chronicles, the Fremen's first encounter with the sea on other planets during jihad in *DM* (43-44), the transformed planet of Arrakis (CD 7), the death of Leto II in GED (443-50), the conservatory in the palace at Arrakeen (D 72, 127), and the subterranean water stills (D 302-3). Lovecraft's settings for his stories are, in general, pervaded by water. Significant among these are "Dagon," "The Call of Cthulhu," "The Shadow over Innsmouth," "The Temple," "The Rats in the Walls," "The Horror at Red Hook," *At the Mountains of Madness*, "The Whisperer in Darkness," "The Picture in the House," "The Dunwich Horror," "Pickman's Model," "The Colour out of Space," "The Moon-Bog," "The Festival," "The Outsider," "The Haunter of the Dark," "The Lurking Fear," and the Western Australian coastline in "The Shadow out of Time."

it is; the human body unchanged is not enough. In "The Shadow over Innsmouth" humans and others mingle to form a new breed.

The presence of an abundance of water, despite the human creature's need for some amount in order to survive, is a foundation producing fear because it signifies the possibility of engulfment. It is the threat alone that, as stated before, is enough to drive the human creature to its habitual retreat into the heimlich conundrum if the cosmos cannot be recovered, because in cosmicism, when the human creature holds to the damp places, it all too often fails to remain entirely human.

The water's edge is a dangerous place for the human creature; irrespective of whether that creature is threatened by an engulfment of too much water or, like Tanya's "big jelly" in "Faith of Our Fathers" that "float[s] up on the beach" (CS 5.222), is threatened in the light of the sun by an engulfment of too little water. In the saturated universe of cosmicism, the water's edge is the domain of insects, parasites, worms, and spreading contagion in the damp and decay. In reaching for what looks like paradise by terraforming the planet in CD, Leto observes "[t]he new symbols of Arrakis: water and green" (32), and the human creature puts its hope for a comfortable future into existence within a garden. Such wet landscapes are dangerous; and for the native Fremen of Dune, not only dangerous, but lethal. As Leto later observes, "[b]eyond the rock markers stretched a stinking band of dead Arrakeen life, killed by foreign plants and too much water, now forming a barrier against the desert" (CD 67).

The human creature might spread like a virus throughout the universe, but when it takes up residence in the water and decay it is, in the end, itself decayed and consumed. As the human creature infects the universe, that universe in turn infects the human creature, and for the Fremen naib Stilgar: "Reality was not at all like the dream. The Friendly Desert, which once had spread from pole to pole, was reduced to half its former size. The mythic paradise of spreading greenery filled him with dismay. It was not like the dream. And as his planet changed, he knew he had changed" (CD 7). As the Fremen of Dune evolve until they become nothing more than "degenerate relics of the once proud warriors" (GED 81), so too do the human creatures of Lovecraft's "The Dunwich Horror" become as "gnarled" and "crumbling" as the landscape they inhabit (CF 2.415). Dunwich is intersected by "problematical depths" (CF 2.415)—and so too is the Vermont landscape in which "The Whisperer in Darkness" is set (CF 2.465-66)—and "it is hard to prevent the impression of a faint, malign odour about the village street, as of the massed mould and decay of centuries" (CF 2.416). As the human creatures of Dunwich have adapted to this dark and mouldy cosmos, they have become like "forbidden things, with which it would be better to have nothing to do" (CF 2.100), for "Dunwich is indeed ridiculously old" (CF 2.418).

The link between devolution and hereditary in Lovecraft's fiction is well identified by the American science fiction fanzine editor Leland Sapiro (Leiber et al. 6), and it would seem that from his commentary in the early 1960s unto the present, critics of Lovecraft are well used to discussing the devolution of the human creature in terms of its link with deep time and familial or racial hereditary. To read this issue in such a manner is certainly a fruitful venture, but I would also add that what appears to have been overlooked by most if not all critics of Lovecraft is the additional linkage between human devolution and the proximity of watery landscapes. To explore why this has occurred is beyond the scope of discussion here, but such an exploration would be a valuable addition to Lovecraftian scholarship and the wider scholarship of cosmicism in general.

The mould and decay that accompanies an abundance of water allows the territory to be sensed by more than ocular vision alone (Houellebecq 67-71). The cosmos of observation is transformed to a universe of experience. The human creature upon arrival at the water's edge is greeted by insignificance and finitude, and imminent deluge of the universe brings that creature to a threshold from which there is no return.

Chapter 8: Perihelion

> For if gods can play in the fields of men, as the Book of Genesis assures us, so too could other less-desirable intruders.
> —Edward Ingebretsen, *Maps of Heaven, Maps of Hell*

The Threshold

In "The Dunwich Horror," Lovecraft offers one of the few passages developed for and attributed to the 'fabled' *Necronomicon*, writing that "[t]he Old Ones were, the Old Ones are, and the Old Ones shall be. Not in the spaces we know, but *between* them ... undimensioned and to us unseen. Yog-Sothoth knows the gate. Yog-Sothoth is the gate. Yog-Sothoth is the key and the guardian of the gate" (CF 2.430). The human creature's arrival at the threshold is an arrival at the point of intersection between one place or state of being and another. Ingebretsen writes of "the twin wildernesses—the 'desert places'—that have served as horizons of interpretation in American epistemology and American myth: the varieties of space, inner and outer" (136-37), and he acknowledges the embedding of these spaces within Lovecraft's corpus. This notion of the "inner and outer," which links the human creature's sense of its body in relation to the external cosmos and ultimately to the universe, is also discussed in *Phenomenology of Perception* when Merleau-Ponty writes:

> I know indubitably where my pipe is, and thereby I know where my hand and my body are ... As far as spatiality is concerned, and this alone interests us at the moment, one's own body is the third term, always tacitly understood, in the figure-background structure, and every figure stands out against the double horizon of external and bodily space. One must therefore reject as an abstraction any analysis of bodily space which takes account only of figures and points, since these can neither be conceived nor be without horizons. (115-16)

Merleau-Ponty's "double horizon of external and bodily space" can also be correlated with what Virilio identifies in the introduction to *Open Sky* as an "[u]nremarked invention of the art of painting and of distinguishing a 'form' from a 'background'" (1). This "invention" arranges the human creature's view of its spatial relationship with others—whether other objects or other bodies—within a horizontal plane of difference between near and far. What this perspective of the horizon does, however, is render invisible what Virilio calls "the very first littoral" (1), a particular view of the horizon that draws attention to the vertical rather than the horizontal, a view to which this text will later return.

The arrival of the embodied human creature at the threshold between cosmos and universe is attended by the integral possibility of engulfment as a consequence of the threshold's apocalypse. Once the human creature is located in what Žižek calls "lethal proximity" (*Looking Awry* 85)—an idea integral to neocosmicism and more fully articulated in chapter 12—wherein the resemblance and the actual being of the universe merge, there remains no possibility for that creature to return to the amnesia of the cosmos.

Inseparable from this merging point of cosmos and universe is the shift from the light space to darkness. For Lovecraft's Nathaniel Wingate Peaslee in "The Shadow out of Time," immersed in the labyrinth beneath the sands of the West Australian desert, it is the anticipation of what lies beyond the reach of his torchlight that leaves him "[s]huddering, [because he] realized that a vast chain of aeon-dead black gulfs must indeed be yawning somewhere beyond and below" (CF 3.431). The human creature's awareness that the light at the threshold changes in some way evokes and is aligned with "[t]he horrible feeling of insignificance" that Colavito claims "mankind experiences when confronted with a universe both greater and more powerful than he could imagine" (185). The human creature's fear of the universe is bound up within its linguistic inability to appropriately articulate and navigate the dark using a language that has been constructed in the light. The possibility of leaving the enclosure of the light space of the cosmos that it dominates and controls suggests to the human creature that it will be propelled into a universe in which it will no longer be heard above any other and will therefore disappear into and be indistinguishable from the background of darkness.

The human creature's experience of the threshold can be likened to the advent of dusk when the sun appears to fall toward the horizon; its illumination fades and shadows cast by objects lengthen their reach towards the coming darkness. At this juncture, the human creature's self-assurance of its own significance dissolves within the fading light. According to the Lovecraft scholar Robert H. Waugh, "[t]he sunset is that delicate moment of wonder and expansion that in Lovecraft precedes collapse" (232), or as Lovecraft writes in a letter to *Weird Tales*, "when we cross the line to the boundless and hideous unknown—the shadow-haunted *Outside*—we must remember to leave our humanity and terrestrialism at the threshold" (February 1928; Joshi and Michaud 22). In disclosing the threshold's imminence, Waugh's aptly named "shadow landscape" (233–35) does more than frame the emerging territory; it becomes in itself a landscape that the human creature must navigate and survive. The "shadow landscape" surrounds the threshold as a space-time of indeterminacy and slippage; it resonates with something that can feel almost remembered but just out of reach, and thus becomes a landscape wherein the human creature senses a haunting of the space in which it exists. As that creature's awareness of the heimlich nature of the universe grows, it acquires an understanding that this is a haunted universe of shadow and veiled truths; as Ingebretsen writes in reference to Lovecraft, this is where the human creature experiences "the widening abyss beneath the sheen of appearances, the great fragility of things as they seem" (133). This fragility, Ingebretsen claims, is related to the human creature's sense of its own history and future as inseparable from its biology. When face to face with the cold equations, the universe as machine, and radically different others, the human creature's biology is utterly vulnerable, and that creature is fixated on the idea that only in its embodiment is it real and vitally alive. The reduction of the human creature to a vulnerable object alone in the dark is the threshold's terrifying apocalypse.

For Lovecraft's narrator in "The Music of Erich Zann," approaching the threshold involves moving from a brightly lit cosmos and "across a dark river bordered by precipitous brick blear-windowed warehouses and spanned by a ponderous bridge of stone. It was always shadowy along that river" (CF 1.280). Crossing the bridge carries the narrator deeper into a shadowed street that terminates "in a lofty ivied wall" (CF 1.280). It is in this twilight landscape of shadow that one window in one room of one building has a view that looks out over the towering wall, a window that represents and indeed becomes the threshold between the ordered cosmos of the city's light, and the apocalypse of the universe of chaos.

After the revelation, after expulsion from the order of light and warmth, a return to a complete amnesia of the cosmos becomes untenable. The irony of cosmicism is that the possibility of turning to the universe is also rendered untenable. Ingebretsen observes that the human creature is "God-haunted, or at least caged by metaphysical absolutes" (135–36), and indeed, the cosmos with its order and well-lit path has provided such a secure fortification against alternatives that to abandon the cosmos altogether is unthinkable. The threshold has the human creature trapped between an unreal cosmos and an all too real universe of terrifying shadow and darkness. That creature has no escape and its mind is haunted by the universe because, as Merleau-Ponty points out, "consciousness can be seen trying to hold up its superstructures when their foundations have given way" (158). The human creature at the threshold tries desperately to operate within a map that has rendered the territorial background invisible, because that creature persists in the belief that in being embodied, it remains separate. In doing this, the human creature fails to acknowledge that "[w]e perform our movements in a space which is not 'empty' . . . but which on the contrary, bears a highly determinate relation to them: movement and backgrounds are, in fact, only artificially separated stages of a unique totality" (Merleau-Ponty 159).

This "unique totality" has disturbing consequences for the human creature in Dick's story "The Electric Ant," where the protagonist, Garson Poole, wakes after an accident that resulted in the loss of his right hand (CS 5.225). Significantly, he wakes to look out of his hospital window to a cosmos of "late afternoon sun, and the brilliance of the aging light pleased him. It's not out yet, he thought. And neither am I" (CS 5.225). It is in this "shadow landscape" that Poole is told, "'you're not a man. You're an electric ant' . . . 'An organic robot'" (CS 5.226)—a revelation that locates the threshold between cosmos and universe, quite literally, within his body. Programmed to believe that the cosmos of his biological embodiment is authentic, Poole's apocalypse heralds the end of any possibility for a return to the amnesia of the cosmos because he is in fact a machine operating within the cold equations of "on" and "off." Poole had not known that he was an "electric ant," he is programmed not to notice, and his sense of what he is in the world is an illusion, a cosmos dissolving at the threshold (CS 5.227). When Poole is later home in his apartment and looking out of its only window, in contemplating the revelation he arrives at a sense of feeling trapped between a cosmos lost and a universe unreachable. Turning the glass of that window from transparent to "opaque," like Jerry Fabin in SD,[1] Garson Poole retreats into the bright, artificial light of the human cosmos and tries to make sense of himself, only to find that "[t]he maze of circuitry baffled him" (CS 5.228).

According to Heinlein's narrator in the story "They" (*Fantasies* 119), there are two ways of looking at the universe, and both are wrong. Just as Poole realises that the threshold's revelation has left him feeling "alive" but in feeling such vitality his sense of self and of others is also altered ("The Electric Ant," CS 5.228), similar and irrevocable change is faced by Heinlein's narrator when he realises that "[t]hey had given him an excellent, a beautiful mirror to play with—the more fool he to have looked behind it" (119). It is this looking across the threshold to the universe that highlights the dissolving of the cosmos in the "impossible sunshine" (122), the same light space that the human creature endeavours to turn to "the common-sense world-is-as-it-seems ... In such a world, human striving is about as rational as the blind dartings of a moth against a light bulb. The common-sense world is a blind insanity, out of nowhere, going nowhere, to no purpose" (119). The human creature is an insect gone mad in the ordered cosmos, or worse, an "electric ant" that is not even entirely biological, but something other that can never regain its lost illusion of embodied significance. This loss of cosmos leaves Heinlein's narrator torn between his logic and his senses (115) and Dick's Poole in "The Electric Ant" with a "fright-haunted mind" (CS 5.234). The human creature is haunted by the possibility of becoming an invisible, silenced other in the universe; but to hope that the universe is not there, to hope that it can be switched off and subdued as if it were a machine, has consequences. The end of Garson Poole may have been the end of something other than human, but it also triggers the end of everything else (CS 5.235, 238–39).

The response of the human creature at the threshold is directly connected to its comprehending the possibility of annihilation within the chaos. With no reassuring deity and sanctuary to return to, and a future of existence in an indifferent machine that is populated with adversarial others, the human creature balances on the verge of engulfment. Torn

---

1. This is discussed in chapter 7.

between the poles of the safety of preference embodied, individual distinctness and the distress of being isolated from all others, the human creature seeks to continue applying a redundant map. Cosmicism's apocalypse is not the end of every-*thing*, but the end of everything the human creature has believed about its infancy in the cosmos coupled with immersion in the universe as an experience that can no longer be avoided. Engulfment comes because the human creature continues to hope that it can avoid the chaos.

Engulfment appears to be integral to the universe and, significantly, to the Genesis cosmology. The Deluge is an engulfment that demarcates the threshold between the antediluvian and the postdiluvian landscapes, with the human creature's existence in the postdiluvian a further separation of it from the waters of the universe and the others that exist in those waters. Since the Deluge, these others wait until they can reclaim their lost territory; "until the time when the great priest Cthulhu, from his dark house in the mighty city of R'lyeh under the waters, should rise and bring the Earth again beneath his sway'" ("The Call of Cthulhu," CF 2.38). When Lovecraft's narrator in "The Lurking Fear" is caught with Arthur Munroe in "such a blinding sheet of torrential rain that shelter became imperative," in a storm that is described as an "extreme, almost nocturnal darkness of the sky" (CF 1.359), they wait out this storm in a shelter on Maple Hill. Like some strange Edenic couple in search of what lies beyond their cosmos, when they suspect the one tree near their shelter is struck by:

> a terrific bolt of lightning followed by the sound of sliding earth ... Munroe rose from his box and went to the tiny window to ascertain the damage. When he took down the shutter the wind and rain howled deafeningly in, so that I could not hear what he said; but I waited while he leaned out and tried to fathom Nature's pandemonium.
>
> Gradually a calming of the wind and dispersal of the unusual darkness told of the storm's passing. (CF 1.359–60)

This deluge is a threshold across which the human creature should not have looked, and the penalty for Munroe's doing so is more than death; it is a cessation of vision, a forbidding of the human creature to know what there is to be seen, and the narrator felt the strangling tendrils of a cancerous horror whose roots reached into illimitable pasts and fathomless abysms of the night that broods beyond time.

For Arthur Munroe was dead. And on what remained of his chewed and gouged head there was no longer a face. (CF 1.360)

The Grey

In surviving the Deluge, the human creature is estranged from the waters of chaos, and the rainbow emerges as a threshold marker of the covenant between the Genesis cosmology's God and the human creature, that "[n]ever again will the waters become a flood to destroy all life" (Genesis 9:15). This declaration that there will be no further opportunity for the chaos of the universe to threaten the cosmos of the human creature is, as Arthur Munroe and his friend discover, an illusion: deluges still occur, and they still herald death. As Paul Atreides claims in DM, "A Fremen dies when he's too long from the desert . . . They call it the 'water sickness'" (204)—a statement significant enough for the character Stilgar to also commit to written record in CD (117).

If the human creature does not drown, such abundance of water will rob that creature of its vitality, the struggle for which is framed by DiTommaso as "the conflict between the philosophy of the Imperium and that of Arrakis" ("History" 313); or otherwise put, the struggle for survival between a cosmos of order and a universe of chaos. In DM, one of the most striking examples of the defeat of the human creature arises from within a conversation between the Fremen Faroc, who was "'once Bashar of the Ninth Legion in the Jihad'" (38), and the Tleilaxu face dancer Scytale, when they meet at Faroc's home to discuss the possibility of destroying the Atreides Imperium. Faroc once enlisted in the Jihad because he had heard of but could not comprehend the presence of so much water as to form a sea. Significantly, it was dusk when Faroc with his legion

> "came out of a mountain pass where the air was sick with water. I could scarcely breathe it. And there below me was the thing my friends had told me about; water as far as I could see and farther. We marched down to it. I wandered out into it and drank. It was bitter and made me ill. But the wonder of it has never left me."
>
> Scytale found himself sharing the old Fremen's awe.
>
> "I immersed myself in that sea," Faroc said, looking down at the wa-

ter creatures worked into the tiles of his floor. "One man sank beneath that water . . . another man arose from it. I felt that I could remember a past which had never been. I stared around me with eyes which could accept anything . . . anything at all. I saw a body in the water—one of the defenders we had slain. There was a log nearby supported on that water, a piece of a great tree. I can close my eyes now and see that log. It was black on one end from a fire. And there was a piece of cloth in that water—no more than a yellow rag . . . torn, dirty. I looked at all these things and I understood why they had come to this place, it was for me to see them." (DM 44)

What this lengthy passage articulates is the idea that even before arriving at the water's edge, the moisture in the air is enough to signal the proximity of an unhealthy space in which the human creature will struggle to survive. Even more crucially, this passage demonstrates that such a presence of moisture is nothing when compared to the diminishment of the human creature that occurs when it faces the open sea and loses a discernible horizon by which to demarcate the water's limit. Faroc's experience is an engulfment, the revelation of which is not owned by Faroc alone, but it is the apocalypse of the entire Fremen people:

"The Mother of Chaos was born in a sea," Faroc said. "A Qizara Tafwid stood nearby when I came dripping from that water. He had not entered the sea. He stood on the sand . . . it was wet sand . . . with some of my men who shared his fear. He watched me with eyes that knew I had learned something which was denied him. I had become a sea creature and I frightened him. The sea healed me of the Jihad and I think he saw this." (DM 44)

This particular threshold encounter in the *Dune* chronicles, more than any other, signifies the foundation of the Fremen's devolution as they are engulfed by the deluge of the universe that lies beyond the landscape of their desert planet, Dune. When they no longer need to struggle for enough water to survive, the Fremen descend into a stagnating complacency in their regard for it (DM 76, 151, 197), forgetting what Dune once had been and becoming enclosed within an increasingly smaller cosmos.

To keep the human creature from an overwhelming and seemingly limitless flood, the rainbow signifies the enclosure of that creature within its cosmos, and in doing so reinforces the idea that turning the gaze away from the saturated foundation and toward the lightshow of colour that is the cosmos encircled by the rainbow, a tele-objective kaleidoscope of illusion, is preferable. Comforting in its appearance but wholly untouchable by the embodied human creature, a rainbow and its promise are illusions at the water's edge. The rainbow that separates within its net one colour from another is revealed to the human creature at the threshold for the illusion that it is, and despite the promise of the cosmos, the overwhelming presence of the universe remains. The rainbow is a symbol of the failure of success—an idea already discussed in chapter 6—a failure that in cosmicism leads to engulfment. The success of seeing the universe comes at the cost of the failure of the human creature to continue to survive as it has done until that moment. Self-inflicted or otherwise, the human creature's only escape from engulfment is to die or remain forever incarcerated in madness.

With God absent and the cosmos dissolved, the rainbow has no foundation, and so crumbles away into the rising grey damp of the universe. This rising damp may not be a temporally sudden or catastrophic event, but it is a cataclysmic engulfing nonetheless, and perhaps all the more insidious for its slow inevitability. As Plato suggests in the *Timaeus*, one way or the other the waters will engulf the human creature, and "when the gods cleanse the Earth with a flood of waters, the herdsmen and shepherds in the mountains are saved, while the inhabitants of cities in your part of the world are swept by the rivers into the sea. But in this country the water does not fall from above upon the fields either then or at other times; its way is always to rise up over them from below" (Cornford 15). Crumbled by the waters into mouldy decay, the human creature's landscape is tainted with the grey. Black and white, as bipolar extremes, are strong contrasts and as archetypes contain their own symbolic and variant meanings; but it is grey that becomes a highly visible colour in its own right in cosmicism. Grey is neither one nor the other; as a shadow, an indeterminate space that reaches from the white to the black, grey holds no absolute into which the human creature can invest its sense of significance in the universe.

In *TSPE*, when Barney Mayerson terminates a conversation between himself and Leo Bulero, "The screen became a formless gray. Gray, he thought, like the world inside me and around me, like reality" (63-64). Grey identifies the threshold of potential that in cosmicism signals a descent into decay. This is the kipple of *DAD* that is eating away the world (17, 52. 56-57, 63, 75, 77, 126, 184-85), and the ash and dust of a ravaged human planet in "Second Variety" (CS 1.15-52). British scholar and critic Tom Shippey collectively identifies this as Dick's "tombworld," writing that this is "a kind of entropic trash state to which all life threatens to descend, the existential opposite—or is it the natural result—of the bright happy worlds of commercial advertising (22). What Shippey identifies in this statement and aligns with existentialism is cosmicism's similar stance that the grey is a threshold at which the human creature, in being stripped of the colour and bright light of its cosmos, is threatened with a descent into decay.

In the cosmos of the antediluvian drug ChewZ that Palmer Eldritch brings back from Prox (*TSPE* 84), Leo Bulero wills Roni Fugate to a thing because she rejects him: "He drank the water, and tossed the cup into the waste chute; not looking at Miss Fugate he said to himself, You're my age, Miss Fugate. In fact older . . . In fact, he said to himself, you're over one hundred years old, withered, juiceless, without teeth and eyes. A thing" (*TSPE* 99). What Leo Bulero creates are "gray fungoid strands wrapped one around another to form a brittle column that swayed" (*TSPE* 100), a fate similar to that of Mrs. Gardner in Lovecraft's story "The Colour out of Space," in which Ammi Pierce encounters in the attic "the blasphemous monstrosity . . . which all too clearly had shared the nameless fate of young Thaddeus and the live-stock. But the terrible thing about this horror was that it very slowly and perceptibly moved as it continued to crumble" (CF 2.383). The human creature at the threshold between cosmos and universe, in "The Colour out of Space" and in *TSPE* for example, is consumed by the grey. That creature becomes a living "puddle" of "gray splinters" and "thick, oozing material" struggling to maintain an embodied coherence as an identifiable human creature (*TSPE* 100), because it is evolving "'not while alive but there in the ground'" (*TSPE* 101) and trying to maintain an autonomous form that the universe does not necessarily support. The grey of the threshold gives way to the deluge of decay, and as Leo Bulero's office carpet "rotted, became mushy, and then sprouted, grew, alive, into green fibres" he surrenders to the apocalypse, the cosmos dissolves, and he is left not with blood, but dust on his hands (*TSPE* 101).

The grey is the possibility that crosses the threshold. The arrival on

8. Perihelion

Mars of the "[g]ray and bony" man embodied as Palmer Eldritch is the arrival of something that is other than human, mechanically enhanced and possessed of a vision of the horizon that is "a panoramic vision . . . supplied by a wide-angle lens" (*TSPE* 171), Eldritch threatens everything that the human creature holds on to as sane and real.

When the cosmos is gone, the grey that remains is the dust of a ravaged world in which the human creature must find some way to survive. In Dick's story "Martians Come in Clouds," the antediluvian others that are "shapeless gray bundle[s]" (CS 2.119) come from Mars to threaten the human cosmos. The cosmos may be bright (CS 2.121), but when "[t]he sun had set. The evening air was chill [and d]arkness was descending" (CS 2.122), the grey that waits in the shadows for the human creature emerges and:

> It was *old*. He knew that at once. There was a dryness about it, an odor of age and dust. An ancient gray shape, silent and unmoving, wrapped around the trunk and branches of the evergreen. A mass of cobwebs, dusty strands and webs of gray wrapped and trailing across the tree. A nebulous wispy presence that made the hackles of his neck rise. (CS 2.122)

For the boy Jimmy, this experience is terrifying. With the light and colour of his cosmos shrouded by the grey of the buggie—the human creature's name for Martians in this story—Jimmy is engulfed in the deluge that the buggie initiates as if it were "a vast tide, a rushing ocean dragging at him, surging over his body, holding him where he was. He could not break away. He was caught" (CS 2.123). When the buggie telepathically shows Jimmy what its home in the universe is like, Jimmy responds fearfully, desperate to avoid the "vast billowing clouds of sand and dust, blowing endlessly across the cracked surface of the planet" (CS 2.123). The human creature's desire to avoid this manifestation of the universe, and in doing so to avoid its own possible end, is to kill the buggie. With the removal of the buggie, the human creature can attempt a return to the amnesia of the cosmos and leave the cold chaos of the universe behind in preference for "the friendly yellow homey warmth" (CS 2.126).

What can be surmised from Dick's treatment of the "shadow landscape" can indeed be said of cosmicism and is central to the fearful dilemma faced by the human creature that the threshold uncovers. As

Shippey concludes, "Dick grasped long before Baudrillard that we are affected (he would say, controlled) by images and icons, pictures and pixels. What he was sensitive to was the off-note that makes you wonder whether you've got it right, whether—see *Total Recall*—your memories might have been implanted" (22). The grey of the crumbling cosmos is the dissolving of the illusion, and it is the coming of the revelation that when the cosmos is gone, the universe is a trap from which the human creature cannot escape.

It is worth pausing here momentarily to consider Baudrillard's essay "Simulacra and Science Fiction." It is, in its few pages, an excellent point of reference for further analysis. After opening with his "three orders of simulacra," the first two of which can be readily aligned with the Genesis cosmology and the universe as machine respectively, Baudrillard writes that "[t]here is no real and no imaginary except at a certain distance." He refers to "the real" as "a pretext of the model," which in terms of this text can be aligned with the manner in which the cosmos is erected by the human creature in such a way as to surpass the universe (309-13).

The Universe as Trap

For the human creature in Heinlein's "They," "the whole world was an asylum and all of them his keepers" (*Fantasies* 117). Whether the human creature views the universe from either the perspective of the Genesis cosmology or the universe as machine, that creature maintains its belief in the universe as a place where order and design can be counted on as consistent foundational principles. Even when order stems from the impersonal and indifferent machine, it remains an order that can be reliably measured and is behaviourally predictable. Such faith in the idea of order within the universe, irrespective of the cosmological map in hand, is the human creature's undoing. In discussing Robert Frost's poem "Design," Ingebretsen writes of the failure of "human will" when faced with the "entrapment of cosmic determinism," concluding that "the argument for universal design conceals possibilities far darker than first perceived" (120).

In Dick's story "The Day Mr. Computer Fell Out of Its Tree," the world that is controlled by machines becomes unliveable for humans when the "polyencephalic computer" that operates everything in the world malfunctions (CS 5.307–9). In response to increased levels of radiation from the sun due to the destruction of the ozone layer, the machine, Mr. Computer, has been installed to regulate the human creature's landscape, and Mrs. Simpson, a human creature "train[ed] in the art of healing psychotic constructs" (CS 5.309), is "stored at the center of the Earth in a special lead-lined chamber, safe from harmful radiation at the surface, in a quasi-suspended animation" (CS 5.308). Should Mr. Computer develop any psychosis, Mrs. Simpson is on hand to assist in restoring order to the machine. The problem for Joe Contemptible when the story opens, of course, is that Mr. Computer is having a difficult day, and Joe is left trapped in his home by a door that will not open. Apparently, Joe Contemptible wants to die, and this plunges Mr. Computer into psychosis because it cannot comprehend Contemptible's desire. It is "two gray-clad police" (CS 5.311) who find Contemptible and in a subsequent discussion with Mrs. Simpson reveal that he wants to die because what he has is "'existence, not living'" (CS 5.312).

In a manner similar to Contemptible's capture, the opening pages of Heinlein's *TEL* find Lazarus Long confined and prevented from his attempt to die. When Long asks "'WHAT THE HELL AM I DOING IN THIS JAIL?'" Ira Wetheral replies that Long is not in prison, but in "'[t]he VIP suite of the Howard Rejuvenation clinic, New Rome'" (3). Long's surroundings may be pleasant and he may have access to everything he wants, but only insofar as this does not involve a risk to his continuing embodied existence, and he is surrounded by human creatures charged with keeping him alive in a luxury from which he has no egress. Death may be "'every man's privilege,'" as Wetheral confirms, but Long rightly points out that for him, such a "basic right" has been removed (3). Long is confined in New Rome on the planet Secundus (7), the same planet that he long ago chose for the "Foundation and the Howard Families" (xv), and curiously the same planetary name for the Emperor Shaddam IV's prison planet in *Dune*.

Salusa Secundus in the *Dune* chronicles is the prison planet on which the Emperor trains his most lethal warriors, the Sardaukar, turning the descendants of cruelly treated prisoners into fanatically loyal subjects, a point noted in *The Dune Encyclopedia* (McNelly 493). When the Emperor Shaddam IV is defeated, Paul Atreides not only assures the newly deposed Emperor that he will be confined to Secundus, but further strengthens the confinement by assuring that "'I will ease the harshness of the place with all the powers at my disposal. It shall become a garden world, full of gentle things'" (*D* 462). Paul knows that to enclose the Emperor and his Sardaukar in a green, Edenic paradise will drain them of their capacity for resistance; the excess of water in paradise will decay their vitality. This is a trap within a trap, a Machiavellian layering of hardship and ease that will hold the human creature captive within its cosmos.

While Herbert's Shaddam IV and Heinlein's Lazarus Long are trapped on Secundus and yet surrounded by all they will require to be comfortable—an image comparable with the ease of existence in the Genesis cosmology's Eden—so too is Dick's Joe Contemptible trapped within a world saturated in the light of the sun and governed by a machine. For Contemptible, the way out of that trap is to die, a solution that Mrs. Simpson deems an insanity that has triggered the greater insanity of the machine in which they are all held. Indeed, the solution to restabilizing the human creature's cosmos requires the entombment of Contemptible, and in the end he may receive something like the death he seeks. At the threshold between the cosmos of light and confinement in the dark, however, Contemptible's desire is an emphatic wish to turn back to his "wretched little pointless life as [he is] normally accustomed to living it" (CS 5.313). Mr. Computer may have been built to serve and maintain the human creature's cosmos, but even when taken below the surface and into the territory, Contemptible is forced to remain confined in order to keep the machine sane and avert the end of everything.

Despite the convincing appearance that the universe as machine is projected as if it were the territory itself,[2] and despite measurable evidence suggesting that the universe is designed and operates as an ordered machine, this model, like the fractured model of the Genesis cosmology that it endeavours to realign, is no more than a tele-objective cosmos trying to describe a universe beyond its reach.

---

2. An image of the universe as machine being the territory, rather than just a map is skilfully presented in the films *Dark City* (1998) and *The Matrix* trilogy (1999–2003). Significantly, after revealing the machine that is the essence of the territory, the machine then gives way to the universe and in doing so adds to the human creature's sense of being caught in a trap within a trap.

The entrapment of the human creature and its separation from the universe is not, I suggest, a consequence of crossing the threshold, for the human creature is stopped dead in its tracks at this juncture. It is in the revelation of the universe that occurs at the threshold that in turn closes off the universe to that creature. Incapable of leaving its human embodiment as a creature of the light space, it is the inaccessibility of the dark universe and the human creature's incapacity to participate in the universe—an incapacity that reflects the existential conflict related to vision and desire—that drive that creature to choosing madness or death.

Bradley Will writes in his discussion of Lovecraft and the sublime of "the recognition of the limits of one's own world view," concluding that the human creature's "vision of the world must be incomplete, and thus, Lovecraft's 'outside' is no longer simply imaginary but a real possibility" (17). That this possibility is then translated by the human creature as a reality in which it cannot participate is the foundation to the disconnecting estrangement that it feels as an empathic, biological entity posited within an alien universe that is not merely bipolar, but truly schizophrenic. Furthermore, Will's conclusion that Lovecraft "suggests that our understanding of what constitutes life and matter may be only a local understanding which is not universally applicable" (18) makes the incarceration of the human creature frightening, because that creature's localised morality leaves it knowing that it cannot survive in the universe. The human creature is frozen by its utter lack of knowing what to expect from the void that is looming beyond the confines of its map.

Paul Atreides's early encounter in *Dune* with the Bene Gesserit "box" that tests whether a creature is human or animal exemplifies this circumstance. "Paul saw that one side was open—black and oddly frightening. No light penetrated that open blackness" (*D* 13). The box is an object of the threshold emphasising that the withdrawal back into the light from the dark brings death: "'[k]eep your hand in the box and live. Withdraw it and die'" (*D* 14). The human, according to the Bene Gesserit, will not attempt escape, and the box "'kills only animals'" (*D* 13). What the Reverend Mother then says to Paul during the testing is also many years later recalled from memory by Paul's daughter Ghanima: "'You've heard of an animal chewing off a leg to escape a trap. There's an animal kind of trick. A human would remain in the trap, endure the pain, feigning death that he might kill the trapper and remove a threat to his kind'" (*D* 13-14; *CD* 49). The trap that Paul's father, Duke Leto, knowingly walks into when he takes up the posting to Arrakis is a trap he walks towards because he believes that seeing it is the first step in avoiding it (D 47). However, even though the Duke knows from the outset what he enters, when the trap closes about him he searches for a way out. As if he has become something other than human, Duke Leto is "[l]ike a caged animal . . . [with a] hunted wildness in his . . . eyes" (D 96). The Duke maintains his sense of being human to the end of the fight, caught in the trap but making every endeavour to kill his trapper the Baron Harkonnen, but the trap of the universe ultimately destroys Duke Leto in the end and the trapper on this occasion does not die (D 176). In MC, Heinlein's Slayton Ford is also caught in the trap, and his eyes reveal "an expression Lazarus had seen many times before in his long life. The condemned man who has lost his final appeal, the fully resolved suicide, little furry things exhausted and defeated by struggle with the unrelenting steel traps—the eyes of each of these hold a single expression, born of hopeless conviction that his time has run out" (388). While Ford may have found some level of recovery from this will-to-die, his later experiences at the temple of the Jockaira plunge him into madness,[3] and the trap gets him too.

The trap of the universe is triggered when the human creature understands that the cosmos it has relied upon is a limited view within a larger enclosure. Zukav writes in *The Dancing Wu Li Masters* that "Einstein's general theory of relativity shows us that our universe might be something like a large closed box and, if this is so, it is never possible to get 'outside' of it" (94). The geometric order of Einstein's box can be read as approximating what Ingebretsen calls the "formal design" that signifies the entrapment of the universe, an entrapment that he also claims is indistinguishable from its order.[4] The inaccessible "outside" frames the trap of a carceral universe, and while the human creature cannot get out, there is no counter-assurance that others cannot get in. A parallel of this idea may be located within the final chapter of Michel Foucault's text *Discipline and Punish: The Birth of the Prison* (1975), in which he discusses the "carceral system" as a multi-layered penetration of

---

3. This episode is also cited in chapter 5.
4. Ingebretsen makes this claim in *Maps of Heaven, Maps of Hell* (123), and I have discussed this passage in reference to the absence of God in chapter 7.

confining and then regulating the behaviour of the human creature in a manner that pervades the human domain from birth until death. The significant point that Foucault reinforces is the sense that there is in fact no outside; the system incarcerates by means of the regulation of human behaviour and movement, and where that fails, the system then incarcerates by means of punishments.

Zukav's reading of Einstein's general theory as it is outlined above, in conjunction with a footnote from the same page of Zukav's text referencing physicist Hugh Everett's claim for a "closed universe" as a "system," discloses a significant problem for the human creature. The assumption—real or otherwise—of the universe as a closed system and the implication of order that is embedded in the idea of a system clearly delineate that it is the ordered universe rather than the chaotic that entraps. The ordered system is a carceral universe. If the human creature manages to survive the apocalypse of losing all cosmoses as foundations of order on which to stand with its sanity intact, if that creature can survive the revelation that it is, quite literally, nothing in the universe, it then has to come to terms with what it has not yet seen. The human creature has to reconcile itself as an ordered, biological entity adrift within the chaos that exists beyond the order of the enclosure.

When talking to Ira Wetheral about his longevity in *TEL*, Lazarus Long says that "'I haven't even begun to figure out how the Universe works, much less what it is for. To figure out the basic questions about this World it would be necessary to stand outside and look at it. Not inside . . . When a man dies, he may shake loose his local perspective and see the thing as a whole'" (20). Long's statement affirms that in living, the human creature can never get "outside," and even in death, to escape the carceral universe remains only a possibility, not a certainty. It is several centuries prior to this event in *TEL* that Andrew Jackson Libby in *MC* is trying to explain how measuring space-time over large intervals works, and his growing frustration and sense of failure to communicate is based in the fact that when trying to talk about the universe, the human creature's language

> is inappropriate. The formulae used to describe the effect loosely called a contraction presupposes that the observer is part of the phenomenon. But verbal language contains the implicit assumption that we can stand

outside the whole business and watch what goes on. The mathematical language denies the very possibility of any such outside viewpoint. (MC 429)

Libby confirms what Lazarus Long has expressed: that the universe from within is the only view available to the human creature. Furthermore, in confirming that the human creature's verbal language is inadequate for navigating the universe, Libby also quite pointedly implies that the language of mathematics explains and describes the universe as readily as it does because as a language of equations it is structurally aligned with the non-empathic cold equations.

Whether entrapment in the universe is a consequence of the universe being a closed system as physicists such as Einstein and Everett suggest; an ordering of "formal design" as Ingebretsen suggests; or an ordered, indifferent mechanism from which there is no escape as Lovecraft suggests, the underlying territorial obstacle through which the human creature cannot seem to pass, in cosmicism, is the bipolar estrangement of order and chaos, and the void that this estrangement opens up.

The erasure of the map at the uncovering of the territory includes the erasure of that map's language. Ingebretsen writes that "madness and verbal collapse [i]s the price paid—or *exacted*—for unspeakable or impermissible knowledge" (132), and in cosmicism, such knowledge is obtained simply by seeing the universe. Donald R. Burleson writes of "the idea that self-knowledge, or discovery of one's position in the real fabric of the universe is psychically ruinous" ("On Lovecraft's Themes" 140), and later reaffirms this claim with specific reference to "The Shadow out of Time," citing this story as one of several that exemplifies "the grand Lovecraftian theme: that self-knowledge, knowledge of humankind's vanishingly motelike position in the uncaring scheme of the cosmos, is psychic ruin" (150). The point to be made here is that for the human creature, and in the case of Lovecraft's "The Outsider" sometimes also for others (CF 1.270-71), the apocalypse of the universe is a threshold experience unequivocally like that creature's capture of its own gaze in the mirror when, as an infant, it still exists within a largely pre-verbal cosmos. There is no language by which to explain what is seen, only the experience of seeing. At the mirror, the human creature acquires its first sense of possessing a body that is separate from other bodies, and this precipitates a shift in its spatial cognition; it becomes a body separate from other bodies, separate from the machine, separate from the universe.

Of Lovecraft's "Outsider," Ingebretsen writes that "[i]nnocent of self-reflection, he knows peace. Awakened to self-consciousness, he finds himself trapped in his labyrinthine memory" (132). This claim is significant for its implication that only in isolation from others can the human creature feel safe within the universe. The carceral universe implies that the confinement and domestication of the human creature ensures its survival. Lovecraft's unnamed narrator in "The Outsider" is mirrored by Heinlein's equally anonymous narrator in "They," and this particular human creature faces a dangerously uncomfortable unknown when he asks:

> Why the grand scale to the deception, countless creatures, whole continents, an enormously involved and minutely detailed matrix of insane history, insane tradition, insane culture? Why bother with more than a cell and a strait jacket?
>
> It must be, it had to be, because it was supremely important to deceive him completely, because a lesser deception would not do. Could it be that they dare not let him suspect his real identity no matter how difficult and involved the fraud? (Heinlein, *Fantasies* 119-20)

What would happen if this human creature works it out; if he comprehends the truth about himself and wakes up while incarcerated? Herbert's Alia Atreides and the twins Leto and Ghanima "experienced the womb as a prison to an awakened consciousness," and they "live[d] in such a scrambled web of memories, unable to retreat ... Faced with such a condition, one had to integrate madness" (CD 126-27), a madness that Alia ultimately does not escape and to which the twins are at significant risk.

For the human creature entering the cosmos of embodied isolation from others, as Jacques Lacan argues in "The Mirror Stage," a necessary requirement for that creature to enter its human society is the imposition of a set of rules for similarity and difference (6). I argue that such imposition is the very locus for that creature's fear of the universe. The threshold of the mirror "places the individual in the external world ... in which all things are distinguished as objects, as this and not that, [as] entities separate from the subject" (Greenham 29), and these "entities," these others, populate a universe that the human creature can no longer avoid or deny. The threshold alienates the human creature from itself and from its integral connection with the universe by compelling that creature to regard itself as an object; an isolate, embodied entity in an alien universe of other such separate, embodied entities. As Lacan writes elsewhere with regard to this matter:

> [I]t is by means of the gap opened up . . . and in which the effects of the mirror stage proliferate, that the human animal is *capable* of imagining himself as mortal, which does not mean that he would be able to do so without his symbiosis with the symbolic, but rather that without this gap that alienates him from his own image, this symbiosis with the symbolic, in which he constitutes himself as subject to death, could not have occurred. ("On a Question Preliminary to Any Possible Treatment of Psychosis," *Écrits* 217-18)

It is the "gap," the void between the cosmos of static objects and the universe of ubiquitous movement, that stops the human creature, because this gap disconnects that creature's empathic connection with a universe that cosmicism renders indifferently hostile.

The mirror, in reflecting the subject, turns that subject into its own object. However, mirrors reflect only illusion, and a backward glance is all a mirror can disclose. By only revealing what is before it, not what is behind it, a mirror cannot show that creature what lies ahead but only where it has been as an object looking at itself. To augment the human creature's distress, when it discovers that the universe it thinks it sees is no more than an inward-looking reflection of something captured within the frame of the mirror or a tele-objective cosmos, in its unidirectional modus operandi, the illusion of the mirror is enhanced by the fact that it bears not even a true reflection, but a reversal of the object before it.

In the endeavour to explain to Bob Arctor-as-Fred the nature of his psychosis, a psychologist in *SD* uses the example of

> "Left-handedness versus right-handedness," [asking] "what is meant by those terms with, say, a mirror image—in which the left hand 'becomes' the right hand" . . . The Psychologist leaned down over Fred, who did not look up. "How would you define a left-hand glove compared to a right-hand glove so a person who had no knowledge of those terms could tell you which you meant? And not get the other? The mirror opposite?" (*SD* 1042)

Bob Arctor translates the psychologist's analogy of the gloves to the idea of "a darkened mirror" or "a darkened scanner," understanding this in terms of a "reflection of himself" that is himself and yet is not (*SD* 1042-43). Similarly, in another of Dick's stories, "Human Is," when Lestor Herrick returns from business on the planet Rexor, the human creature that returns looks like him but is not him in either general demeanour or linguistic capability (*CS* 2.261-63). As the director of the agency preparing to kill the Rexorian and reinsert the real Lestor Herrick says, "'[s]ince no physical change has occurred we'll have no direct evidence to make our case'" (*CS* 2.266), and they will therefore need the testimony of Herrick's wife to condemn the man before them. The testimony to condemn for Lovecraft's narrator in "The Outsider" comes only after seeing himself in a mirror (*CF* 1.270), and prior to this event his "aspect was a matter equally unthought of, for there were no mirrors in the castle" (*CF* 1.265).

The human creature, stopped at the threshold and unable to distinguish the illusory from the real, fails. The failure of success is the incapacity of a dead cosmos to express and therein provide a linkage of survivable experience between the embodied human creature and the universe. The *heimlich* oscillation of universe and cosmos that occurs at the threshold is a trap from which that creature cannot escape, and in the attempt to do so it engulfs that creature entirely.

For the Fremen in *CD*, the planet once called Dune is exposed to a deluge, and what the Fremen now see is a reversal, a dark reflection in the mirror that is called Arrakis. As Stilgar observes of his kin:

> Warren dwellers no longer maintained the tight water discipline of the old days. Why should they, when rain had been recorded on this planet, when clouds were seen, when eight Fremen had been inundated and killed by a flash flood in the wadi? Until that event the word *drowned* had not existed in the language of Dune. But this was no longer Dune; this was Arrakis. (*CD* 7)

The abundant waters have erased the necessity for the Fremen to avoid the light space of a burning sun, but this abundance has also brought death, a failure of language and a rewriting of a planet. This is a universe unlike any the Fremen have known before, and it is killing them.

The pre-verbal foundation of the Lacanian mirror is similarly experienced by the human creature at the threshold in cosmicism. Looking into the mirror, as it were, the human creature sees a reflection that is not quite right, a universe that is reversed, a universe that is not the universe at all. This reversal, I suggest, supports the human creature in the view that the light space of the cosmos where it has always been located is good and right, safe and positive; and the universe that it can see from its position in that cosmos is dark, adversarial, and cold and should be avoided at any and all cost. The threshold reinforces the human creature's belief in and clinging to the very bipolarity that has estranged it from everything. The problem is, in looking back to what lies behind it, that creature finds no more than a hollow illusion, and everything has indeed ended. What other choice is there but madness or death—the ultimate end of the heimlich conundrum? To cross the threshold means stepping into the void exposed by the threshold. The human creature cannot survive if it turns away; it cannot survive if it tries to remain evermore poised at the threshold, and stepping into the void is an unthinkable impossibility. As Joanna Russ writes, "if the engulfment does not happen, *it can*—and this revelation becomes the central truth of a universe thus rendered uninhabitable" (Watson and Schellinger 505). Like the cosmos of ChewZ in *TSPE* that is brought to the human creature from the Prox system, the threshold is "a one-way gate" (195). Survival in cosmicism's cold and indifferent universe is difficult enough, and having made it to the threshold, the human creature must then face the void.

In response to the void, the human creature feels fear. This is the fear of the end of everything that creature is and has been; it is the fear of losing the very spatiality of body that has served to keep it isolate from all others and, ultimately, severed from the universe itself. This fear has been soothed by the mirror-illusion cosmos with its heimlich reversal and tele-objective view, and by closing off the greater vision of the universe, that cosmos has kept the human creature safe from a requirement to face the understanding that the very body in which it has invested all its energy is of utter insignificance in and to the universe.

The human creature's body is an object, identifiable on the horizon as distinct from all other bodies, and that creature must find a way to discern the difference between bodies in the dark space where no horizon exists against which the relationship to others might be measured. Cosmicism deposits the human creature at the threshold with the revelation that because it cannot see in the dark in the same way it sees in the light, it therefore cannot ever know the universe. David E. Schultz rightly says of Lovecraft, and by extension cosmicism, that he is not trying to frighten the reader with monsters, but rather "the reader suffers a more profound sense of horror realising he does not know much about the universe he lives in" (227).

The blinding light that ignites the human creature's fear of the dark, that estranges it from the universe, is the exception and not the rule. The light of the cosmos by its reach defines the enclosure of the human creature, bouncing back from the threshold as if reflected from a mirror. When that light begins to be eclipsed, however, when the threshold between light and dark is reached, what light remains penetrates the dark as if passing through a glass, and, as if it were sunlight on the surface of a still pool of shallow water, what the human creature sees immediately beyond its own reflection is the dark background of a submerged other.

Part III: Neocosmicism

Chapter 9: Neocosmicism Is

> I have often wished that I had the literary power to call up visions of some vast & remote realm of entity beyond the universes of matter & energy; where vivid interplays of unknown & inconceivable influences give vast and fabulous activity to dimensional areas that are not shapes, & to nuclei of complex arrangements that are not minds.
> —H. P. Lovecraft, SL 2.127

As we have seen, cosmicism is a philosophy that interrogates the human creature's place in the universe. In doing so, that creature is taken to the threshold of engulfment where it is at last defeated by the fact that in looking toward the universe it is prevented from moving into the universe for fear of the void and its incomprehensible depths. For the human creature, cosmicism's answer to the universe is always and only the "resounding NO" (Houellebecq 14) of the heimlich conundrum.

Neocosmicism is a philosophy in development that seeks to realign the human creature's sense of its place in the universe by taking that creature through engulfment and providing an alternative choice to cosmicism's limited human outcomes. David E. Schultz claims that Lovecraft's characters who witness the apocalypse "are helpless to forget what has been revealed" (224); but rather than abandon the human creature to despair, neocosmicism seeks to refigure the view that an alternate and life-affirming outcome is possible.

It is vitally important to note from the outset that many of the characteristics and possible outcomes that define cosmicism remain equally valid or applicable within neocosmicism; and strict boundaries demarcating where one philosophy ends and the other begins are not always possible. The discussion that follows in the remaining chapters of this book is a discussion related to neocosmicism. If direct reference to cosmicism is required, this will be explicitly articulated; and in all other instances, while there may be some sense of the occurrence of further explication of cosmicism, this is a consequence of the inherent shared nature that exists between these two philosophical frames, rather than a digression back to cosmicism.

It is reasonable to ask why neocosmicism and not *post*cosmicism, to which the answer is located in the idea that in *neo* (meaning "new") there is less room for the implication that cosmicism is made redundant in a way that the prefix *post-* may be taken to signify. While not mutually exclusive philosophies, the significant difference between neocosmicism and cosmicism that shifts the human creature's sense of the universe is the role of engulfment. Cosmicism brings that creature to the threshold and threatens it with engulfment; neocosmicism takes that creature over the threshold to be engulfed in a way that its relationship with the universe might be refigured. This is not to say that every human creature is bound by or follows the path of cosmicism and ultimately faces engulfment, nor does neocosmicism presume that a transition to it from the stance of cosmicism will always occur.

In his afterword to a collection of Lenin's writings titled *Revolution at the Gates: A Selection of Writings from February to October 1917*, Žižek discusses "the eternal dilemma of the radical Left," and culminates with asking and answering: "'Which deviation is worse, the Rightist or the Leftist one?': *they are both worse*" (301). What Žižek highlights is the idea that an apparently irresolvable dialectic—or, in the terms of the discussion herein, a bipolarity—cannot be resolved by answering from either pole to the exclusion of the other. What Žižek then illumines is the idea that when one side of the dialectic "breaks the (still) prevailing . . . consensus, gradually making acceptable hitherto excluded ideas" (302), the covert linguistic methodology that normalises what was once unacceptable is then used to "blackmail" the other side of the dialectic via its fear of the extreme ends of the unacceptable becoming acceptable. As Žižek concludes from this, "we should reject this blackmail, taking the risk of disturbing the liberal consensus, even up to questioning the very notion of democracy" (302). Similarly, neocosmicism suggests that rather than be "blackmailed" by the comfort of illusory maps and revert to taking cosmological sides, the human creature must take responsibility for itself, "even up to questioning the very notion" of its moral and evolutionary parameters, and face the universe head on.

The universe exists beneath the encircling cosmos of warmth, light, noise, and comfort, and the core revelation that the human creature must come to terms with is the fact that the light under which it exists is an exception to the rule.[1] The light space anticipates the darkness that is everywhere else, and neocosmicism foregrounds a shift from an ontological stability of light and sound, to an ontological stability of darkness and silence.[2] This shift is primarily about recasting the meaning of the dark from being negative, and therefore evil, to simply being. As Joseph Wood Krutch writes in *The Modern Temper*, and I suggest Lovecraft takes into consideration in his own philosophy:

> It is not a changed world but a new one in which man must henceforth live if he lives at all, for all his premises have been destroyed and he must proceed to new conclusions. The values which he thought established have been swept away along with the rules by which he thought they might be attained.
> To this fact many are not yet awake. (17)

Undoubtedly cosmicism supports Krutch's claims inasmuch as the universe that the human creature faces is nothing like the cosmos that creature thought was real. Furthermore, cosmicism endorses the idea that it is preferable for the human creature to remain amnesiac, that it seems better equipped to survive in the universe if it maintains a state of ignorance wherein it continues to mistake the map for the territory. For neocosmicism, however, the heart of Krutch's claim highlights the fact that irrespective of whether the human creature is awake to the revelation or not, it must still come to terms with the newly revealed universe that is before it. Not to do so is a failure not only to survive, but to live. The view that cosmicism's threshold reveals, and from which the human creature turns away in the heimlich conundrum, is a view of the limitless

---

1. The 2007 film *Sunshine*, written by Alex Garland and directed by Danny Boyle, offers the idea of the sun's light as a force of intense and far reaching power. This is then undercut by the notion that despite the magnitude of this force, the sun's reach is proportionally limited and that it is immense darkness that remains as the principal condition of the universe. Furthermore, this heimlich balance occurs in the film as the background to the idea of the Earth as slowly freezing over, and it is this very process that highlights the human creature's absolute need for sunlight as the agency by which life is sustained, while never deviating from this star's inherent nature as a force with the power to kill.
2. R. D. Laing's idea of "ontological insecurity," coupled with Ingebretsen's idea of "ontological darkness," is discussed in chapter 6.

horizon of waking up in the dark and holding no map for guidance.

The cosmological maps of Genesis and the universe as machine have become reified, and bipolarity is mistaken by the human creature as being the state of the universe. This is an adversarial territory against which the human creature is compelled to fight. Beyond the tele-objective and ordered lenses of these cosmologies, however, exists the chaos that is the foundation of the universe; and engaging with chaos means entering the void.

Julia List argues that *Stranger in a Strange Land*, *Dune*, and *Lord of Light* demonstrate successfully blended cosmoses (44), wherein the human creature survives with its life and sanity largely intact. Irrespective of the terminology used—whether Protestant and secular, scientific and religious, or some other dialectic or bipolarity—it is not a successful blending of oppositions for an alternative that comes into question. As both List and Žižek identify, the question of success for the human creature lies within the sphere of the values and mode of operation of the new system that is the necessitated outcome of such blending, and this is coupled with the manner in which that system differentiates from the individual polarities out of which it has come. When applied to the human creature in neocosmicism, this kind of rationale makes it possible for the universe to be approached by that creature as a heimlich unity rather than a bipolar adversary.

Furthermore, in bringing this possibility to the question of human existence in the universe, List's claims are particularly interesting for their support of the deific—as figured in the messianic character—and the linkage of such a figure with a "world that does not rely on reference to a personal, omnipotent deity" (44). Rather than kill off deity because there is simply neither evidence nor space in the universe for its presence, List's conclusions make possible for the human creature an experience of the universe that reaches beyond its own individual and embodied limitations. It is important to note that none of this negates cosmicism's claims that the universe is impersonal and indifferent and the human creature insignificant within it, nor does this alleviate that creature's sense of the universe and others in it as dangerous. These are simply conditions of the universe that are the result of something other than human emotions or morals of localisation, and these are conditions that are as equally bound and influenced by the cold equations as the human creature.

9. Neocosmicism Is

In moving from a cosmos to the universe, the human creature steps out of the net of straight lines wherein "[o]rder has been imposed on chaos" (Watts 59),[3] and into an unbounded territory. As Lovecraft writes in a letter to Frank Belknap Long:

> The universe may be a dream, but it cannot be considered a human dream if we can shew that it must antedate and outlast all human dreamers just as an ocean must antedate and outlast the denizens of one of his alternately rising and submerging volcanic islands . . . We find a cycle of constantly shifting energy, marked by the birth of nebulae from stars, the condensation of nebulae into stars, the loss of energy as radiant heat and the radio-active breakdown of matter into energy . . . Outstanding are the facts that *all stars are temporary in the long run* . . . If the cosmos be a momentary illusion, *then mankind is a still briefer one!* (SL 2.265-66)

Ends and beginnings may figure as processes that draw the universe from the perspective of cosmos as linear, and "cycle[s] of constantly shifting energy" may draw the universe from a differing cosmos as eternal and perpetual. Furthermore, Lovecraft acknowledges that while the universe appears to be cyclic, it also contains linearities of finitude inasmuch as the cycles required for the production of life are also the cycles linked to life's destruction.

Although the universe may be understood as simultaneously linear and cyclic, the human creature's concern regarding its own finitude, a concern exacerbated by that creature's sense of universal insignificance, has a tendency to prevent it from engaging with the universe beyond its single-lens view of linear finitude. This circumstance can be likened to that of the uncertainty principle in quantum physics—a principle recognising that while light behaves as particle and wave, it cannot be observed doing both at the same time (Capra 76-78; Zukav 298-99). A shift in this particular scientific view has recently occurred with particle experiments reporting that both states have been observed occurring at the same time (Kocsis et al. 1170-73), and subsequently photographed (Piazza et al.). Neocosmicism calls for a similar shift in view, and rather than being a spatial and temporal linear plane, the universe is more akin to being like a spinning heimlich coin.

---

3. This passage from Watts is discussed when first introducing the concepts of the map and the territory in chapter 1.

Many of the dichotomies of cosmicism undergo a transformation in neocosmicism that moves them from being oppositions in conflict to aspects of a cogent whole. The heimlich coin is no longer a symbol of the game of chance or even the fight, but rather it is a symbol of the idea of coexisting bipolarities. It is important to note that this coexistence is not a simple holism in which conflict no longer emerges, nor is neocosmicism a human utopia of comfort in the universe. Indeed, it is often quite the opposite, but this is not to say that neocosmicism's dystopic foundations therefore invalidate the possibility for the human creature to refigure its sense of place in the universe in a manner that allows for a far preferable outcome than cosmicism predicts is to be delivered.

To navigate the universe and recover from the amnesia of the cosmos, the human creature will need to re-establish a sense of significance, even while to the universe it remains utterly insignificant. Insignificance in neocosmicism requires a shift in the attribution of meaning, and to be insignificant is not to say that existence is hollow and the experience of living pointless. A link can be drawn between the issue of insignificance and what Lovecraft calls "the impersonal dreamer" when he writes that "[t]o the impersonal dreamer belongs all infinity—he is lord of the universe and taster of all beauties of the stars. As for the future—what is sweeter than *oblivion*, which the humblest of us may share with the Kings of all the ages, and even with the gods themselves?" (SL 1.112). In dreaming impersonally, in seeing the universe as it is rather than as it has been drawn on a map, the human creature as an empathic entity in an impersonal universe of cold equations is reminded that it must not take the events of the universe personally. The universe is not out to get the human creature and the cold equations are not designed to thwart that creature any more or less than they do any other. The human creature is insignificant in the universe not because it is inconsequential and its existence meaningless, but because the cold equations and the universe these equations underpin will continue and do so with or without the presence of that creature.

Cosmicism claims that the universe is a purposeless, kaleidoscopic vortex; a blind, indifferent mechanism of tele-objectivity. Incomprehensible to the human creature, the universe is a bipolarity against which that creature fights and within which that creature is imprisoned. Neocosmicism also claims that the universe is indifferent, but the kaleidoscopic machine is here refigured beyond the paradigm of tele-objectivity. As Lovecraft writes:

> we may say that these things—time, space &c.—are *proximate realities*, because they depend on a fixed & particular cause as envisaged by a fixed & particular apparatus—i.e., the senses of a certain sub-phase of entity which is well defined though transient, insignificant, & accidental; to wit, the animal organism called man. But we may not call these proximate realities *ultimate*; since all their familiar aspects are due wholly to our own accidental structure and position. (SL 3.86)

In neocosmicism, the invisible becomes visible, the "proximate" gives way to the "ultimate," and the heimlich territory surfaces. None of this diminishes the accidental and insignificant nature with which cosmicism endows the human creature; if anything, neocosmicism's universe may all the more thoroughly endorse this. However, rather than reject the universe as an adversary from which it must escape, the human creature accepts the universe as the *proving ground* that it is. This is to say that the universe is where the human creature's capacity for survival may be tested, and this idea of the universe as a proving ground will be more thoroughly explored in the chapters that follow this introductory exposition of neocosmicism.

Cosmicism declares that the human creature cannot remain as an infant in, nor return to, God's Eden. The Deluge saw to that. More than supporting the idea that after the apocalypse nothing will ever be the same again, neocosmicism further endorses this by emphasising that neither should it be. Entering the universe as proving ground is about leaving infantile dependencies behind, and it is about living in the cold equations. In the indifferent universe, the human creature's insignificance is a locus for its liberation from the constraints of its cosmos, for as Lovecraft writes, "nothing really matters in the ceaseless round of the limitless cosmos" (SL 4.4). In leaving its constraints, the human creature steps out from its incarceration and into the limitless possibilities of what is yet to be tested. The American Heinlein critic and essayist Rafeeq McGiveron says of a number of Heinlein's younger characters that for the young to succeed and often survive, they must "grow beyond" their parents ("Maybe the Hardest" 173). So too in neocosmicism must the human creature grow beyond its comfortable and largely insulating cosmos.

Such growth means stepping into a universe that makes no promise for a final result, and Lovecraft affirms that "we know that a cosmos which is eternal . . . can have no such thing as a permanent direction or goal" (SL 2.261). Despite this potential lack of a tangible future, however, the universe most certainly has a foundation, and the human creature will need to recover its memory of the antediluvian territory and its occupying others, in order to come to terms with future possibilities. Neocosmicism requires a view that is simultaneously cast ahead and behind in a manner similar to Korzybski's time-binding—a concept often explored by Heinlein—and past and future will need to be reconciled by the human creature as a dynamic play of movement that is not necessarily bound by temporal or spatial linearity. Participation in the universe requires that the human creature interact with the foundation as much as it does the possible future, rather than plod along a temporally linear continuum focused principally on delaying for as long as possible what Sartre refers to in *Being and Nothingness* as the ultimate contingency of death (697).

The scales of space-time that are involved in the relative position of the human creature's foundations provides a certain kind of stability on which that creature can draw, and it is the very nature of the antediluvian that allows that creature, once its view has shifted, to move through the engulfing deluge of the threshold. Whereas cosmicism turns back to look upon the antediluvian as something from which the human creature has been disconnected, the presence of the antediluvian in neocosmicism provides a means by which that creature can begin to reconnect with the universe that has been quarantined for so long beyond its grasp. In looking back, in reversing the reflection to see the reality, that creature also looks forward, and the recovery of memory from the amnesia of the cosmos begins with recognising that the very far is also the immediately near.

Neocosmicism's universe is a heimlich unity against which the human creature need not fight; the universe may or may not be adversarial, but such a state does not make it evil or malevolent. As an apocalypse of a limitless horizon, neocosmicism's universe is a "psychotic universe" (Žižek, *Looking Awry* 79–81) inasmuch as "a certain gap (that separating 'hallucination' from 'reality') is abolished" (81). Žižek's notion of the universe as "psychotic" is, in adapted form, significant within neocosmicism and will be more carefully examined in chapter 11. What in the context of discussion here is necessary to understand is that within its state of heimlich unity, and in remaining indifferent to whether the human creature succeeds or fails, the universe nullifies any sense that creature might have of striving for a final result, thereby releasing that creature from the requirement—real or illusory—to be bound by a sense of finitude. As Lovecraft writes, "[w]e are what we are at the moment, merely because we are. Sometimes we may guess from our present state how we are likely to turn out, but all the real causes are in the hands of forces we can never fathom" (SL 1.132). Elsewhere Lovecraft writes that "It is a mistake to regard the cosmos as either favourable to life or unfavourable to it. It is simply indifferent & unconscious" (SL 5.69). The cold equations in cosmicism scribe the universe as an adversary from which there is no escape, and as alien to the human creature's emotional and empathic capacities. Through a tele-objective lens of cosmos, the human creature contracts its view of the universe from the infinite to the personal, and in so doing has subjected itself to the amnesia of the cosmos. This contraction is exemplified in the very structure of the Genesis cosmology, and even though cosmicism attempts to redress this problem by refiguring the universe as machine, it is in this very refiguring and the machine's inherent cold equations that the universe is then perceived to be alien. The tower in the landscape is no longer the point from which the human creature projects an expansive view of its sense of place as it once did atop the ziggurats of Babylon; rather, the tower has become quite literally a carceral body from which that creature looks out in fear. In its bid for a sense of safety, for an assurance of significance and continuance, the human creature is estranged from all others and regards them adversarially. Alone in cosmicism's universe, the human creature also discovers that the Genesis cosmology's God is absent, and the moral code bestowed upon it by that God is nothing more than a local phenomenon with little application for navigating the cold equations.

Similarly, neocosmicism's universe also operates within the parameters of the cold equations, but as Lovecraft says of the materialist, so too neocosmicism claims for the human creature that "[h]e has sounded space a little deeper, and found what he always finds on further penetration—simply *a profounder disintegration, and a profounder mechanistic impersonality*" (SL 2.263). Rather than being a force of estrangement, the cold equations are a conduit by which the emotional and empathic human creature can access the universe, and the morality of these equations is, as Lovecraft says of any morality, "the adjustment of matter to its environment—the natural arrangement of molecules . . . Conventionally it is the science of reconciling the animal *homo* (more or less) *sapiens* to the forces and conditions with which he is surrounded" (SL 1.64). That human morality is a local phenomenon necessitating a parallel embrace of the cold equations when that creature moves beyond its locality is critical, and neocosmicism recognises, as Lovecraft says, that "[t]here are no values in all infinity—the least idea that there are is the supreme mockery of all. All the cosmos is a jest, and fit to be treated only as a jest, and one thing is as true as another. I believe everything and nothing—for all is chaos, always has been, and always will be" (SL 1.231). It is within this "jest" of chaos that the human creature must reconcile itself to the equations in order to then navigate its relationship with others. Furthermore, this understanding involves coming to terms with the idea that when an other is also an adversary, this is not a posturing equivalent to evil, nor is it a negative connoting that designates an other as any more worthy of elimination than the human creature. For the human creature to live in the universe it must understand that what can be described as the weeding process of the proving ground is something that creature must never interpret emotionally as a targeted attempt at eradication.

The human creature remains insignificant and the universe indifferent, but within this, unlike cosmicism, neocosmicism—as I have said previously—allows for the possibility of deity. The critical difference that the human creature must negotiate in neocosmicism is the idea that while deity may not be absent from the universe, it is almost certainly not going to be an anthropomorphic other. Scholars and critics—Lovecraftian or otherwise—highlight the fact that Lovecraft has no room for God in his philosophy, and Lovecraft himself says as much. In January 1931 he writes that "As for 'god'—there is of course no theoretical barrier to the existence of a 'cosmic intelligence', yet *absolutely nothing indicates such a thing*" (SL 3.281).[4] I believe, however, that prior to this statement, Lovecraft leaves the issue open when he writes that:

---

4. Also quoted with reference to cosmicism in chapter 7.

> To limit one's range to human things, and to look on the universe with the eyes of mankind only, seems to me pitifully absurd. I like to view the universe as an isolated cosmic intelligence outside time and space—to sympathise not only with man, but with forces opposed to man, or forces which have nothing to do with man, and do not realise that he exists. (SL 1.172)

It is important to note that Lovecraft aligns the idea of deity with the idea of a "cosmic intelligence," for even though his 1931 claim that there is no evidence of such a condition in the universe post-dates the 1922 claim that I have above called "open," it is the consistency of the phrase "cosmic intelligence" that creates a space of possibility. Furthermore, even though in 1931 Lovecraft claims there is no evidence of a "cosmic intelligence," he also admits that there is also "no theoretical barrier to [its] existence."

This is by no means God in the conventional sense of the Genesis cosmology, or even a generic sense of an anthropomorphic deity; although it could be reasonably argued that to be "outside time and space" is to manifest the omnipotence of the Genesis cosmology's God. Lovecraft also acknowledges that to frame deity in these terms is a limitation born of the language of the human creature's light-bound cosmos—irrespective of which cosmos that creature operates from—when he writes that "[w]hatever ethical or preferential qualities we seem to see in anything are sheer fictions of our minds & emotions—fictions based on a body of race-legendry originated when mankind was unable to conceive of external nature as apart from the anthropomorphic & the anthropocentric" (SL 2.356). That Lovecraft flags the idea of the universe as "an isolated cosmic intelligence" that is beyond the limits of space-time suggests that the universe could be something more that a chain or cycling of material events. Neocosmicism endeavours to interrogate what that something might be and, more critically within this, the nature of the relationship between the human creature and the universe. This is a blending of the cold equations with the *romance of the universe*. The romance of the universe refers to the participatory and at times symbiotic relationship between the human creature and the universe in neocosmicism, and this idea will be further explored in subsequent chapters. In acknowledging that the cold equations are an essential aspect of the universe, neocosmicism also considers these equations to be compatible with the emotive, biological human creature. In order to move beyond a cosmos of bipolarities, the human creature must assimilate the cold equations; that is, rather than remain split between polarities of the moral and the immoral, good and evil, or right and wrong, that creature must come to terms with operating within a *supra*morality; that is, a morality "beyond" or "above" any form of polarity or exclusive category.

The human creature in cosmicism is estranged from the universe; insignificant, accidental, and mutated, it is a contagion that the universe caught. While remaining insignificant in neocosmicism, this insignificance is simply a condition of that creature's relative position and stature. As Lovecraft writes, "[a]ll of the pseudo-importance felt by man himself before he surveys the wider field necessarily drops away—as does the illusion of a fly's giganticism when we remove the magnifying glass through which we have been looking."[5] Insignificance, Lovecraft claims, should not be taken by the human creature as a reason to consider as worthless its opportunity to experience the universe. The fleeting passage of space-time that the human creature occupies "does not, to a mature and disillusioned mind, militate against the enjoyment of such pleasurable processes as the workings of senses, imagination, & intellect provide for" (SL 3.389).

While grappling with the scale of its significance in the universe, or lack thereof, it is vital in neocosmicism that the human creature also come to terms with letting go of its sense of estrangement from the universe. One of the harsh ironies of cosmicism is that the human creature's estrangement, while used as a means by which to protect itself from others and even from the universe itself through the employ of the amnesia of the cosmos, is the very condition that leads to that creature's isolation and subsequent inability to survive intact. It is the human creature's estrangement from the universe, and not its insignificance within the universe, that leaves it with no option but the heimlich conundrum's ultimate end as the means by which to escape its dangerous enclosure.

The insignificant human creature may be an accident, mutation, or contagion, but for neocosmicism these possibilities are accepted as conditions of the universe that are governed by the cold equations rather

---

5. This passage has also been referred to in chapter 7.

than by any moral or empathic motivations. Some part of the proving ground's purpose is to "weed" the universe and thereby strengthen a species, a process with some sense of alignment to Darwin's idea of "the survival of the fittest" (63-100). The evolution of the human creature, through mutation and weeding, may lead to an evolution other than how it has occurred in that creature's past, and neocosmicism does not consider such possibilities as necessarily detrimental. As a "welter" upon its planet (SL 2.227), the surviving human creature may develop consequential scar tissue that redraws the parameters of what it is, and means, to be human in the universe.

For some, this scar tissue may be hidden, taking on a subterranean nature within the body. In season 6, episode 12 of *The X-Files*, the idea of the human creature as possessed of a submerged and latent foundation that could be viewed as more human than human is offered, suggesting that that creature is more intimately connected with the universe beyond the sunlit sphere of its cosmos. Towards the end of the episode, FBI Agents Mulder and Scully have the following, and significant, conversation:

> *Scully:* Mulder, these are test results. DNA from the claw nail we found matching exactly the DNA from the virus you believe is extraterrestrial.
> *Mulder:* That's the connection.
> *Scully:* Which matches exactly DNA that was found in [the boy] Gibson Praise.
> *Mulder:* I don't understand. You're saying that Gibson Praise is infected with the virus?
> *Scully:* No. It's a part of his DNA. In fact it's a part of all of our DNA. It's called a genetic remnant. It's inactive junk DNA, except in Gibson it's turned on.
> *Mulder:* So if that were true, that would mean that Gibson is in some part extraterrestrial.
> *Scully:* It would mean that all of us are.

The inactive "junk DNA"—the internal and hidden scar tissue as consequence of infection, so to speak—is similarly like external scar tissue: a manifestation of the effects of accident, consumption, and reinscription in neocosmicism's *psychotic universe*, an expression of survival. Scar tissue becomes an asset in the proving ground; it is a toughening, a protection of what was previously vulnerable, and when present on the surface of the body it is the interfacing signification between the human creature and the universe of the irreversibly changed regard of one for the other. Linkage can be readily drawn between this and the contribution of Russian philosopher Mikhail Bakhtin, with respect to his text *Rabelais and His World* (1941), concerning notions of the carnival and the grotesque. Bakhtinian philosophy and corresponding ideas related to the acquisition of scar tissue are fundamental within discussion of the embodied and scarred human creature in the psychotic universe, and a line of enquiry to be developed beyond the remit of this present discussion.

Lovecraft writes that "if the sun gives heat long enough, there will certainly come a time when the mammal will have to go down to subordination as the reptilia went before him" (SL 3.43); and thus weeding and evolution, which cosmicism frames as negative processes to be avoided wherever possible, become non-negotiable conditions of neocosmicism's universe.

In the end, the only options cosmicism allows the human creature after the apocalypse are madness or death—encapsulated as the outcome of the heimlich conundrum. Despite the fact that the universe operates within perpetual cycles, Lovecraft also claims that it will inevitably freeze over and leave behind it nothing but oblivion (SL 4.82).[6] In neocosmicism, everything may still end, for as Lovecraft writes, "outstanding are the facts that *all stars are temporary in the long run*, that the birth of planets from them is comparatively rare, (induced by tidal action of other stars that pass by them under rare conditions) and that life on a planet can hardly survive the death of the star whose radiations made it possible in the first place" (SL 2.266). However, after the apocalypse and until such time as all stars of the universe fail, while the human creature remains free to choose madness or death, it is also free to choose an alternative to these forms of finitude. It may submit to the engulfment of the void of chaos.

The fear that lies at the heart of cosmicism is a fear that has been extracted from the realm of human interaction and imposed upon the whole of the universe from which the human creature then seeks to retreat, for everything about the universe becomes frightening. The human

---

6. This reference from Lovecraft is also discussed in chapter 4.

creature fears the universe because it fears engulfment. In letting go of its fear, however, that creature opens up a differing horizon, and neocosmicism is about facing the deluge and accepting engulfment. The relationship between the human creature and the universe that becomes possible in neocosmicism is not about observation and self-preservation; it is about participation, and when required, accepting death.

For the human creature to move beyond the amnesia of the cosmos that masks its fear of the universe, it must understand that its fear is an imbalance made all the more powerful because the light erases from view the dark and all it contains. Frank Herbert's Paul Atreides knows that the light can never be truly understood without knowledge of the darkness also (*D* 19), and the human creature must look to the heart of what it has come to regard as familiar, and then look past the illusion of an ordered totality to the unfamiliarity that the familiar actually is. Beyond the light-space lies the radiant void of the universe. The human creature is not just touching, or even seeing through the glass, it is passing through the glass. This is a shift from the reflection's reversal of the view to the revelation of the substance that lies beneath, and it is intimately linked with Žižek's "lethal proximity" (*Looking Awry* 85) wherein the resemblance and the actual being of the universe merge.

Chapter 10: Aphelion

> "Beginnings are such delicate times . . ."
> —Frank Herbert, *Dune*

Dark Horizon

Cosmicism's threshold is about stoppage in the form of madness or death; neocosmicism's threshold is about transformation. In neocosmicism's universe of cold equations, rather than remain confined, the human creature moves beyond the threshold and into the proving ground. Although that creature may be weeded from the universe, for it remains insignificant, it may also survive the testing and refining to which it will be subject.

Despite the adversarial and dangerous nature of the carceral universe, the human creature often acquiesces in accepting it, because in accepting its limited and limiting imprisonment that creature can feel a certain measure of safety from the full potential of what the universe might pit against it. The encircling nature of the universe that cosmicism reveals has been paralleled in this text with the Genesis cosmology's expression of Eden, from which the human creature is expelled by God. Unlike the Genesis eviction from comfort to the wilderness that is motivated by the compulsion of an emotive God, leaving the confines of cosmos in neocosmicism is the human creature's choice. With this choice, that creature steps out of a linear order and into a current of chaos; it moves from a stable shore of gridlocked and manageable sections into waters that are neither calm nor bound by nets. As a young Leto Atreides discovers during his testing in *CD*, this is not an easy transition to make and it requires a simultaneous comprehension of

> Past-present-now. There was no true separation. He knew he had to flow with this thing, but the flowing terrified him. How could he return to any recognizable place? Yet he felt himself being forced to cease every effort of resistance. He could not grasp his new universe in motionless, labeled bits. No bit would stand still. Things could not be forever ordered

10. Aphelion

and formulated. He had to find the rhythm of change and see between the changes to the changing itself. (CD 243)

For Leto, as for any human creature that decides to cross the threshold, stepping from the static and contained to an ever-moving fluidity is a difficult transition, compelling that creature to participate in the universe rather than simply observe from a minimum safe distance. It is not enough to remain separate and take in the view; survival depends upon engagement that it might also know there is "no true separation."

Such choice is by no means easy, nor does the human creature necessarily like the transition from map to territory; but as Gurney Halleck reminds a young Paul Atreides in *Dune*, "mood" and emotion have nothing to do with it (*D* 38). This is the point at which many human creatures will choose to remain enclosed and hopeful for an Eden irrevocably lost. This is the choice of Dick's adults on a devastated Earth in "The Days of Perky Pat" (*CS* 4.302-5) and a dusty Mars in *TSPE* (9, 15, 48-51) who, in playing with the Perky Pat layouts, pretend that they return to Eden. Even when the human creature comprehends that it can choose to move beyond the threshold, it may determine a course of action that plunges it back into the amnesia of the cosmos.

The threshold is discussed in chapter 8 with reference to Ingebretsen's "twin wildernesses" (136), Merleau-Ponty's "double horizon of external and bodily space" (115), and Virilio's *"ground line"* as an "[u]nremarked invention of the art of painting and of distinguishing a 'form' from a 'background' " (*Open Sky* 1). All these references, in speaking of thresholds, also speak of horizons, and significant to neocosmicism is Virilio's claim that the horizontal "ground line" draws the human creature's attention away from the "vertical littoral . . . which absolutely separates 'the void' from 'the full'" (1). It is worth noting that the term littoral is related to being "of or pertaining to the shore; existing, taking place upon, or adjacent to the shore" (*OED* 8.1045), and Virilio's specific use of this term draws attention to the idea of the vertical perspective being a relationship between the shore of the terrestrial and the ocean of the universe. This shift in perspective—which changes the human from being a dry land creature that moves across a terrestrial landscape toward the horizon to a creature that, while designed for existence in the terrestrial, is also compelled to step off its shore and into an ocean, the horizon of which stretches away into an infinite darkness—becomes crucial in neocosmicism.

Returning to the different images of the threshold presented in the paragraph above, the common thread is that the spatial relationship drawn by the human creature's embodied gaze across the landscape is conventionally horizontal. Within the notes that Lovecraft made for a future novel to be titled *Azathoth*,[1] he writes of the narrator gazing across the horizontal plane within his "city of high walls where sterile twilight reigned," taking in the same view as other human creatures that, like himself, are "coming home at evening to a room whose one window opened not on the fields and groves but on a dim court where other windows stared in dull despair" (CF 1.336). It is the narrator's conscious decision to avoid being "drive[n] to madness," that compels a shift of his gaze, to "lean out and peer aloft to glimpse some fragment of things beyond the waking world and the greyness of tall cities" (CF 1.336). The decision to look upwards and beyond a horizontal finitude, in this case an enclosed courtyard, is an act that inevitably allows this human creature to bridge "a mighty gulf" (CF 1.337).

Similarly, after escaping their Harkonnen captors in *Dune*, Paul and Jessica Atreides must next escape the possibility of death in the jaws of a sandworm, and while hiding in a rocky outcrop Paul looks upward toward the night sky and into the gaping mouth of the leviathan before him. He "felt a kind of elation. In some recent instant, he had crossed a time barrier into more unknown territory. He could sense the darkness ahead, nothing revealed to his inner eye. It was as though some step he had taken had plunged him into a well . . . or into the trough of a wave where the future was invisible. The landscape had undergone a profound shifting" (D 254). The threshold, then, is the point from which the human creature looks to a horizon, and the difference here between cosmicism and neocosmicism is critical. If that creature looks across a landscape to a fixed horizon, it will be limited by finitude. If that creature should deem to look up, however, if that creature re-engages with the memory of the "vertical littoral," the nature of the horizon changes

---

1. This is noted by the authors of *An H. P. Lovecraft Encyclopedia* (Joshi and Schultz 13), providing further information regarding Lovecraft's intentions for the style of this projected novel.

and by consequence of this, so too do that creature's choices.

When the horizontal gives way to the vertical, the comfortably finite horizon of the terrestrial gives way to the dark horizon of the universe. When the orientation of the horizon changes, the relationship of objects and bodies to that horizon also changes. Irrespective of the space-time direction of vision, whether into the past or the future, crossing the threshold involves a release of the limits of horizon, a release of the limits of the possible and of the visible, and the establishment of a vision that accepts this release. As Leto Atreides recognises, herein lies a paradox which must also be assimilated, and "'[t]o be sighted in the land of the blind carries its own perils. If you try to interpret what you see for the blind, you tend to forget that the blind possess an inherent movement conditioned by their blindness'" (CD 108). In looking up, Leto knows he is looking into a darkness in which other human creatures may not be able to see as he does. In looking up, he understands that he has already chosen a path that is different and that will transform him and his relationship with others in the universe. As Virilio also points out in his introduction to *Open Sky*, looking up presents "an exotic reorganisation of sight that would finally take account of a possible fall upwards" (2).

Falling into the universe is turned by Lovecraft into a literal event in "The Other Gods" when "Barzai the Wise ... [and] the young priest Atal, who was his disciple" go out "into the stony desert" (CF 1.273-74) so that they might climb the mountain Hatheg-Kla and see "the gods." As they ascend, "Atal felt a spectral change in all the air, as if the laws of Earth were bowing to greater laws; for though the way was steeper than ever, the upward path was now grown fearsomely easy, and the bulging cliff proved scarce an obstacle when he reached it and slid perilously up its convex face" (CF 1.276). As if having "to learn to fly, to swim in the ether" as Virilio suggests (*Open Sky* 3), Barzai calls out to Atal "below" him, "'Merciful gods of Earth, *I am falling into the sky!*'" (CF 1.277).

In extinguishing the limits of the horizon by means of a reorientation, the human creature is left at the threshold knowing that the illusion is dissolved. Lazarus Long says in council with Howard Family members in MC that "'the 'Masquerade' is over. It's a new situation'" (312); and later, when acting as the Howard Family representative, Zaccur Barstow realises there is no point in even pretending that the illusion still holds now that the Family member's longevity is revealed to others

(MC 324). Similarly, after establishing the illusion of his own death, so that he might seek his path in the desert, Leto replies to his captor that "'it is written: That which you know in one world, you shall not find in another'" (CD 235).

For the human creature facing the threshold's revelation, as Stephen King claims for Lovecraft, cosmicism's answer to the universe is "NO."[2] For neocosmicism, however, as Nietzsche claims in *The Will to Power*, the human creature's answer to the universe is YES, because:

> The concept "reprehensible action" presents us with difficulties. Nothing that happened at all can be reprehensible in itself: for one should not want to eliminate it: for everything is so bound up with everything else, that to want to exclude something means to exclude everything. A reprehensible action means a reprehensible world . . . in itself, everything that is says Yes. (165; No. 293 [March-June 1888])

Nietzsche's "reprehensible world" is the world, and indeed universe, that cosmicism declares the human creature exists in, and is therefore by the very nature of what it is, to be kept by that creature well and truly at a distance. This disconnection from everything that "is so bound up with everything else" in cosmicism is a factor in why there are no options beyond the heimlich conundrum. The threshold's apocalypse in neocosmicism, however, is an affirmation that the human creature must accept engulfment and enter the void in order to engage with the universe. From the light space of the sun, the human creature looks upward to the dark and says YES.

When the Howard Family members in MC understand that their longevity is revealed to others, they realise that to stay where they are amounts to saying NO and to risk being "hunted down and killed" (321). In looking up and saying YES to the universe, these human creatures determine to leave the known shore of the light and move into the unknown dark as a means by which to improve their chances of survival. To say YES is to enter space-time where "the Sun holds options but can hardly be said to own in fee simple"—that is, absolutely—and in doing so, move "farther from all humanity" (394).

As the mirror-opposite of cosmicism's NO, this affirmation is a criti-

---

2. Stephen King's concept of the "NO" has been discussed in chapter 5.

cal choice that enables the human creature's escape from its incarceration. The "darkening change" (SD 971) that the character Charles Freck identifies—that in cosmicism signifies the descent into madness and death for varying characters—is the same threshold moment that signifies neocosmicism's open door through which that creature might pass. Freck can see "that maybe things would go the other way again and get better," leading him to visualise all others that he is leaving behind, both living and dead, as existing within a light "which wasn't daylight but better light than that, a kind of sea which lay beneath them and above them as well" (SD 971). It is perhaps worth noting here that the image of a sea or ocean that is above and below some other or object is also a fundamental image within the Genesis cosmology.

It is just such an opening, such erasure of reflection and illusion, that makes a reversal possible. The metaphorical mirror that reflects becomes a glass or window through which vision can pass. In a later chapter of SD, Bob Arctor's mental functioning is being explained to him by psychologists who identify the shift from an illusion that reflects a limited view to an open view with no final result or visible limit of horizon. Within the cosmos, and indeed within cosmicism, the psychologists diagnose this shift in Arctor as an undesirable kind of psychosis wherein, rather than one hemisphere of Arctor's brain dominating and therefore asserting itself over and burying the other, both sides of the brain "'monitor and process incoming data differently'" and "'[o]ne tells you one thing, the other another'" (SD 1040). When one side is damaged, the other "is attempting to compensate" (1041), and in terms of neocosmicism this can be likened to the loss of all maps, and the emergence of the actual and differing territory.

As "'left becomes right'" (SD 1042) and up becomes down, a null space is formed, something that Bob Arctor's psychologists refer to as "'cross-cuing . . . Related to split-brain phenomena,'" and they go on to explain that "'twin competing cross-cuing amounts to zero recept form'" (1041).[3] This shift signifies the erasure of a cosmos and the insertion of

---

3. In *The Dancing Wu Li Masters*, Gary Zukav discusses "split-brain analysis" in reference to the Copenhagen Interpretation of Quantum Mechanics. Zukav writes that "[t]o treat certain conditions, such as epilepsy, the two halves of the brain sometimes are separated surgically," and the aftermath of this procedure

the human creature into the void. Bob Arctor arrives by means of using the drug "substance D," a narcotic of antediluvian qualities that the closing pages of the novel reveal is made from a blue flower; blue being a generic colour ascribed to both water and sky. Arctor's engulfment within "substance D's" deluge has erased both the Bob and the Fred and erected Bruce, an apparently psychosis-locked human creature who has in fact been released into the void from that deluge: "[t]ime ceased as the eyes gazed and the universe jelled along with him, at least for him, froze over with him and his understanding, as its inertness became complete. There was nothing he did not know; there was nothing left to happen" (*SD* 1096). The test for Bruce now is whether he will choose to step beyond the void and into the universe that he has seen. It may be said that in his case the answer to this can be no more than conjecture because the novel ends with him located in the void. I believe, however, that a clue to his possible outcome lies within his earlier discussion with the psychologists, for as much as they assert that it is Bob Arctor (now Bruce) who sees the universe incorrectly, he replies that "'Maybe it's you fuckers' . . . 'who're seeing the universe backwards, like in a mirror. Maybe I see it right'" (*SD* 1043). Bruce, and indeed any human creature that might determine to seek an alternative to madness or death, will only reach the void after submission to engulfment and the risk this entails. There is no option in neocosmicism to turn away from engulfment and the destructive potential of the deluge.

Thufir Hawat reminds Paul Atreides in *Dune* that "'[t]he universe is full of doors'" (*D* 450), and Paul cannot always be facing the open door. Survival will depend on more than vision, and when caught by Hawat sitting with his back to the door:

> Paul straightened, spoke without turning: "I know. I'm sitting with my back to a door . . . I heard you coming down the hall," Paul said. "And I heard you open the door."
>
> "The sounds I make could be imitated."
>
> "I'd know the difference." (*D* 32-33)

---

has revealed what Zukav terms "a remarkable fact." Each side of the brain functions and "see[s] the world in a different way": one "linear" and one that "perceives whole patterns" (42-43).

10. Aphelion

Knowing the difference is knowing what is illusion and what is not, and it is captured within Nietzsche's "Dionysian affirmation of the world as it is" (*Will to Power* 536; No. 1041 [1888]). The human creature's positioning of itself in relation to openings, in crossing thresholds, is not without danger and is directly linked to the proving ground that the universe reveals. As Lazarus Long says to Ira Wetheral, "never sit with [your] back to the door . . . might be nine hundred and ninety-nine times you'd get away with it . . . But the thousandth time—that's the one" (*TEL* 56-57).

It is important to note that choosing to participate does not magically transform the universe into a pleasant landscape and eradicate the human creature's sense of "cosmic fear" (Asma 185-86, 191-92; Colavito 185) or "cosmic horror" (Colavito 17, 161-62, 175). On the contrary, neocosmicism's proving ground remains subject to the cold equations and is every bit as indifferent and perhaps even more difficult to survive in than cosmicism's prison. Furthermore, while the human creature can move into a participatory relationship with the universe, it will do so side by side with others of its kind that will choose to remain amnesiacs in their cosmoses, a choice that further blurs the lines between any human creature and all others. Crossing the threshold is a deliberate move away from comfort and familiarity, and an attempt to avoid the kind of devolution that the human creature is subject to when it remains in, or endeavours to return to, the Garden.

Shadow Universe

What becomes an impassable ending in cosmicism is the requisite state for beginning in neocosmicism, and rather than do all in its power to avoid engulfment, the human creature accepts that engulfment is the foundation event from which it moves into a universe where *"night is safest"* (*D* 283) and where cosmoses no longer hold. According to Lazarus Long in *MC*, "'things pass [and] [t]he trick is to stay alive through them'" (286). Long's attitude highlights a shift in the moral posture of the human creature, and a consequence of this shift is the development of that creature's ability to come to terms with its temporal and material insignificance. Russell Letson writes that "all explanations of species survival as the universal morality are meaningless without the immediate experience that life itself—survival—is worthwhile in its own terms" (221). By the time Long is discussing with Ira Wetheral the motivation behind the prevention of his own death in *TEL*, he is explicit about the one reliable fact of the universe: that it "'is a moving picture, forever changing,'" and while the human creature may not like this, "'he knows it's so, and knowing it is the first step in coping with it'" (19).

The engulfment that the human creature seeks to avoid in cosmicism because it translates to a force of destruction, although potentially no less destructive in neocosmicism, becomes necessary. To be engulfed is to be "put into" the gulf (*OED* 5.153, 199), to be put into "the deep" (*OED* 6.942), and it is only by engulfment's apocalypse that the human creature can enter the void that in cosmicism stops it in its tracks. Engulfment is the overturning of illusion; it is the event that, in overturning the light space as dominant in the universe, directs the human creature towards the dark. As if standing with its back to the sun, or like Paul Atreides with his back to the door, the human creature then sees beyond the bright colours of the rainbow of light. Engulfment renders the invisible visible, and in doing so opens up a way through the deep ("The Temple," *CF* 1.168-69; "The Shadow over Innsmouth," *CF* 3.228-31); the vortex ("Jon's World," *CS* 2.63-64); and the coriolis storm (*D* 219-20, 230-31).

When engulfment becomes unavoidable, the human creature's ending in cosmicism's heimlich conundrum is driven by that creature's fear of freedom from the limiting confines of the cosmos. This fear is reinforced by that creature's belief in its own isolate vulnerability beyond those confines, and this occurs irrespective of whether the cosmos is connoted by that creature as negative or positive. In refusing to submit to fear, however, the human creature can move beyond the finitude of its tele-objective cosmos, and in choosing to accept the inevitability of and therefore seek to survive engulfment at the limit of that cosmos, that creature is actively seeking to refigure its view. This is encapsulated in *D*'s Bene Gesserit Litany against Fear, that says: "*I must not fear. Fear is the mind killer. Fear is the little-death that brings total obliteration. I will face my fear. I will permit it to pass over me and through me. And when it has gone past I will turn the inner eye to see its path. Where the fear has gone there will be nothing. Only I will remain*" (*D* 14, 220, 231, 288). Looking inwards to see a complete erasure of all significance is the trigger for the human creature's vision to turn back out and towards the universe. Taught by Jessica

Atreides to a young Paul, the Litany is a definitive statement of accepting engulfment as a necessity. This acceptance transforms what stops the human creature in cosmicism—that is, fear—to be the focus of what that creature must "face" and move beyond. Furthermore, the Litany foregrounds the human creature's immersion in the void as the necessary measure that, in stripping that creature of everything but itself, prepares it for a conscious engagement with the universe. Signifying the end of everything in cosmicism, engulfment for neocosmicism is the event that facilitates reconnection with a "first cause." According to Alia Atreides in *DM*, "'[b]eginning and end are a single thing'" (*DM* 148).

In overwhelming the landscape and all it contains, the Genesis engulfment of the Deluge renders the visible invisible; and what was once known and seen is buried in the heimlich territory. As if a kind of mirror-deluge occurs, however, the overthrow of the visible that is critical here can perhaps be seen as one of Lovecraft's signature events, and is arguably no better known than in "The Call of Cthulhu." In this story it seems that the waters of the ocean shift in such a way as to suggest that the world itself is turned upside-down, exposing the forgotten "nightmare corpse-city of R'lyeh, that was built in measureless aeons behind history by the vast, loathsome shapes that seeped down from the dark stars" (*CF* 2.50). Similarly, in "Dagon"[4] a landmass rises from the depths of the ocean, and after taking several days to cross this terrain the narrator climbs a "mound" and "looked down . . . into an immeasurable pit or canyon, whose black recesses the moon had not yet soared high enough to illuminate. I felt myself on the edge of the world; peering over the rim into a fathomless chaos of eternal night. Through my terror ran curious reminiscences of 'Paradise Lost', and of Satan's hideous climb through the unfashioned realms of darkness" (*CF* 1.55). By disturbing the ordered cosmos that the Deluge once established by hiding such an-

---

4. S. T. Joshi and David E. Schultz not only draw the parallel between "Dagon" and "The Call of Cthulhu," but also claim that "Dagon" is a source story for "The Shadow over Innsmouth" (58). While the antediluvian landscape does not rise up to overturn the human cosmos in "Innsmouth," the events of this story present a consistent archetypal framework for Joshi and Schultz's claim to have substance and provide further insight into the consistency of the overturning of the Genesis cosmology by means of engulfment and deluge.

tediluvian landscapes, the deluge faced by the human creature here is the pivotal moment in which that creature must decide to respond as cosmicism proclaims such apocalypse deems, or accept that this is the universe and so find a means by which to survive. It is perhaps easier for the human creature to succumb to emotion, as do Gustav Johansen's fellow sailors who "never reached the ship, he thinks two perished of pure fright in that accursed instant" ("The Call of Cthulhu," CF 2.53); it is much harder for such as Johansen who, despite being "broken" (CF 2.49) by the experience, was neither maddened nor killed by the revelation, for he survives and returns home to write an account of events. What gets Johansen in the end is the cold equations, an "accident," and although a stronger man might have survived, his weakened condition facilitates his weeding from the universe. Like many other stories that can be read through the lens of cosmicism, "The Call of Cthulhu" is by no means a closed circuit through which no other reading is possible.

At neocosmicism's threshold the deluge turns the order of cosmos upside down and shifts the orientation of the horizon to reveal the connection between the terrestrial shore and the ocean that is the universe wherein the first creatures have been hidden. What the revelation discloses is the idea that the oceans of the terrestrial landscape are mirrored by the ocean of the universe, that all life is linked to the water, and for the human creature that is designed to survive on dry land rather than in the water, survival in the universe will demand that creature learns how to swim.

In *Dune*, Paul Atreides is reluctant to accept the waters of Jamis, the man he kills in a fight as champion to his mother Jessica. It is Paul's hesitation that reminds Jessica of the Bene Gesserit axiom that declares "'[s]urvival is the ability to swim in strange water'" (D 296). The collection of water from the body of Jamis so it can be used to sustain the life of the tribe reveals an intimate connection between life and water. This connection is strengthened by the vast oceans of Dune being burning deserts rather than verdant gardens, and Paul recalls from "Yueh's O.C. Bible [that] 'From water does all life begin'" (D 296). To survive, Paul must learn to swim in the "strange waters" of Dune, beneath the surface of which reside the antediluvian leviathans that are the giant sandworms. The common is made strange and the uncommon emerges, both visible yet inextricably mixed. As the illusory stability of cosmos dissolves, the terrain beneath the human creature's feet and within its gaze begins to shift like sands in desert winds or on saturated shores, and later in life as The Preacher, Paul Atreides reminds the human creatures before him that "'[t]hey who pray for dew at the desert's edge shall bring forth the deluge!'" (CD 103).

This is the end of illusion where new patterns emerge, and Ghanima Atreides realises when looking from the water-rich landscape with "rotting vegetation at the edge of the seitch plantings," to the living desert beyond, that it is essential "to discover regularities within perpetual change" (CD 36). In order to know how to move in the universe of cold equations, the human creature must come to terms with the condition of order in chaos. The universe is not a separation of deluge and desert, life and death, first cause and final cause; the universe is a chaotic blending of these rather than a demarcating grid.

Surviving engulfment signifies a shift in the human creature's sense of self in the universe that might be described as a shift from a position of the "materialist" to the "vitalist." Scholar Viviane Casimir draws the distinction between these terms with reference to "life" as "coming from within" the living object (materialist) or as "a force insufflated to matter" from "outside" the living object (vitalist) (281). This is to say that the human creature shifts its focus from an inward and isolating view of itself as limited by a horizon that, in having a limit, turns back in upon itself because that confinement is what sustains it (cosmicism), to an outward view that sees the wilderness and desert spaces beyond its confinement as the locus of sustenance (neocosmicism). This is vision that extends beyond the physicist's "closed system," Ingebretsen's "formal design," or Lovecraft's mechanism.[5]

It is worth noting at this point that Lovecraft considers himself a mechanistic materialist,[6] which is to say that he views the universe as a machine driven by forces that come from entirely within its components. There is simply no other or "outside" motivating force or deity. Any object or other that comes from what Lovecraft calls the "Outside" (SL 2.150) is wholly alien and wholly bent on the human creature's demise

---

5. These ideas are discussed in conjunction with the carceral universe in chapter 8.

6. A letter written by Lovecraft in February of 1929 exemplifies this position well (SL 2.261-74).

because it is not human, it is outside the human. This is cosmicism's tele-objective closed box of the carceral universe from which the human creature cannot escape, and in which the human creature is nothing more that the isolated object of its body. When that object ceases in cosmicism, everything about it ceases, because its motivating force has come entirely from within.

While the shift to neocosmicism is certainly a shift in attributing the motivation of the human creature within vitalist parameters, it is important to stress that it is not a simple swapping from one position to the other; rather, neocosmicism observes a blending of the materialist and the vitalist, similar to the idea of a "discursive space" that Casimir claims opens up "where a crisis occurs" (279). The human creature no longer looks exclusively inward to its isolated self and to the preservation of that self in a universe where it is up against absolutely everything until the end of everything; instead, that creature looks outwards. In shifting its view, the human creature can then see that there is no finitude to the horizon, and even though it remains insignificant in a cold and indifferent universe, there is a relationship to be forged. Neocosmicism's relationship between the human creature and the universe is not based upon self-preservation but founded upon open participation within the bid for survival.

The way for this relationship to emerge is opened up by the waters of deluge that dissolve the cosmos. In Dick's "Faith of Our Fathers," the water that the human creature consumes is laced with hallucinogens. It is in this story that Dick presents neocosmicism's universe—the universe of chaos—in which, as Tanya says to Chien, there are "'a variety of authentic experiences . . . it's all turned around . . . Twelve mutually exclusive hallucinations—that would be easily understood. But not one hallucination and twelve realities'" (CS 5.209).

The universe, Tanya discloses to Chien, is not captured in finitude. Taking the black snuff that is enclosed in a grey envelope and has been designed to "'rest eyes fatigued by the countenance of meaningless official monologues'" (CS 5.198) is the moment Chien accepts the deluge. With his first exposure to "an emptiness" (CS 5.205), where moments before had been the colour and noise of the cosmos-according-to-the-Absolute-Benefactor (CS 5.204), Chien accepts engulfment and "inhaled greedily at the remainder of the powder on his hand" (CS 5.205). It is only after exposure to the "emptiness" and the revelation of the reality of the Absolute Benefactor beneath the illusion (CS 5.217) that Chien is equipped to step beyond the limits of the map.

Similarly, in order to move from the cosmos in which they exist to some other part of the universe, Dick's scientists Kastner and Ryan in "Jon's World" have to move into "the time flow," something beyond the linear order, which Ryan likens to "'the ocean . . . The most potent energy in the universe. The great dynamic behind all motion'" (CS 2.63). To move within the universe, they must first enter this space, until "[t]here was nothing there. Nothing beyond them," and this is a void from which Kastner hopes they can return, "his eyes on the black port. 'I feel like the first man who went down in a submarine'" (CS 2.64).

That first man could have well been Karl Heinrich, Lovecraft's U-boat commander in "The Temple." In finding himself at the bottom of the ocean, Heinrich determines to leave the confines of his vessel and enter the black void surrounding him so that he might use what is left of his life to explore the *"undersea temple,"* the windows of which are *"vividly aglow with a flickering radiance"* (CF 1.168). Although his rationale leads him to suspect he is going mad, Heinrich makes deliberate preparations and, devoid of fear, enacts a conscious choice; he accepts that he will die and then chooses how he will live (CF 1.112-13). This is exactly what Heinlein is talking about in his speech to the 1961 World Science Fiction Convention when he shares the story of a stranger who dies trying to save the life of a woman whose foot is stuck in a railway track. As Heinlein says, "the only conclusion I have ever been able to reach is this: This is how a man lives. And this is how a *man* dies" (180); choosing what course of action to take amidst the unchangeable outcome of the cold equations.

It is a stranger's standing his ground before the inevitable outcome of an oncoming train—Heinrich's acceptance of the cold equations and subsequent decision to explore the antediluvian temple and city before him during what life he has left; and Chien and Tanya's acknowledgement of their antediluvian hereditary of "'the ancient primary waters'" (CS 5.222)—that point toward the resolution of what is perhaps the most utopian of Lovecraft's stories, "The Shadow over Innsmouth."[7] As the

---

7. An essay from the American literary scholar David Farnell, titled "Unlikely

old man Zadok Allen tells the narrator Robert Olmstead when he first arrives in Innsmouth: "'everything alive come aout o' the water onct, an' only needs a little change to go back again.'"⁸ When the truth of his heredity can no longer be avoided, Olmstead decides to rejoin his kin by "swim[ming] out to that brooding reef in the sea and dive down through black abysses to Cyclopean and many-columned Y'ha-nthlei, and in that lair of the Deep Ones we shall dwell amidst wonder and glory for ever" (CF 3.230–31). The utopian sense of this ending points towards something paradoxical, though by no means incompatible, within Lovecraft's canon. A utopian reading of "The Shadow over Innsmouth" in no way dislodges more conventional readings that point toward an outcome of "cosmic terror,"⁹ and this kind of symbiosis of perspectives consequently reinforces a seemingly natural heimlich oscillation that blurs the horizons of limiting demarcation. While S. T. Joshi and David E. Schultz argue for the more usual interpretation of this story as declaring a "horrific scenario" (240), what is worth noting is the parallel that Joshi and Schultz, like myself, draw between the fate of Olmstead in "The Shadow over Innsmouth" and Heinrich in "The Temple." While for Joshi and Schultz, cosmicism's heimlich conundrum prevail in these stories, I ar-

---

Utopians: Ecotopian Dreaming in H. P. Lovecraft's 'The Shadow over Innsmouth' and Octavia Butler's *Lilith's Brood*" (2011), is an excellent source of further reading on the idea of Lovecraft as a utopian writer. First delivered in 2010 as a paper at The Fourth Australian Conference on Utopia, Dystopia and Science Fiction at Monash University, Melbourne, Australia, Farnell's paper provides a concise and balanced rationale for a reading that might be considered a radical shift from the usual focus of Lovecraftian criticism.

8. This is also referred to in chapter 7.

9. The literary scholar and poet Barton L. St. Armand uses this phrase, which is closely aligned to the phrases "cosmic horror" and "cosmic fear," with reference to Lovecraft's "balancing" of a Calvinist sense of the universe within a materialistic framework, the outcome of which is "a universe ruled by self-regulating natural laws" (*Roots of Horror* 31). It is worth noting that when St. Armand then speaks of "the breaking of these natural laws of time and space" (31) he is referring to a pre-quantum reckoning; and indeed with quantum physics in its infancy at the time in which Lovecraft is writing it is no stretch of the imagination to comprehend a sense of "cosmic terror" (31) present both within the pages of the fiction and the human world beyond those pages, for the universe has been rent in two.

gue that the human creature is also offered, and in these cases accepts, a different path that will re-inscribe their perception of the universe.

Rather than view the deluge through the distancing lens of a cosmos, the human creature experiences the deluge. In submission to engulfment that creature may not survive, but if it does it must then submit to the void and to the possibility that in the end, the void may be all that there is.

The Void

Between order and chaos the void exists; between the opposing sides of the same coin, the void has "no incumbent, holder or possessor, [it is] unoccupied, vacant" (OED 19. 732). Irrespective of whether the void is approached from a growing darkness of shadow and approaching night or from a "white, aeon-dead world" as Lovecraft claims in *At the Mountains of Madness* (CF 3.21), it is "an utterly tenantless world" (CF 3.25). The void is a gaping black hole between cosmos and universe. Within view from the threshold, and beyond the limits of a cosmos' horizon, the void must be entered. If the human creature is to do more than simply gaze upon the universe from the safety of its embodied isolation, it cannot negate the void. There is no definitive beginning or end, and as an ultimate indeterminacy the void has no borders or boundaries; it is an emptiness that is nowhere and everywhere, a ubiquitous merging of oppositions that cancel one from another, a littoral space where shore and ocean merge.

It is this very nature of the void that cosmicism connotes as a negative space that must not be entered. As a darkness without light and cold without warmth, cosmicism makes fearful this gateway of uncertainty. In discussing Lovecraft's use of this space, Bradley Will writes that "[t]he abyss is a negative space, a symbol of the unknown and a recognition of the existence of that which exceeds our understanding" (14). As a negative space the void is frightening, and the requirement for the human creature to somehow cross this emptiness that is neither ordered map nor territory with substance, albeit chaotic, can freeze the human creature at the threshold indefinitely and unto madness or death.

The void is a necessary emptiness that announces the limitations of a cosmos, and in doing so makes such maps irrevocably redundant as guides to the universe. The void nurtures no-*thing*; rather, it is the inevitable end of every-*thing*, and it is a darkness into which the human creature must go for release from incarceration. The human creature must let go of all maps and illusions, including its own hope for significance, and reconstruct its sense of what it is. This is, however, a difficult task made impossible by cosmicism, which figures the alternatives to the map as irreconcilable with the embodied, terrestrially bound human creature. Brian Stableford writes in *Horror Literature: A Reader's Guide* that Lovecraft's "Cthulhu Mythos . . . constructs a horrific cosmological and historical context for human history" (Barron 137), and it is this very context that the human creature plunges into when it enters the void. This is the first step away from the shore and into the space-time ocean of the universe. As it is for many of Lovecraft's characters, such as Nathaniel Wingate Peaslee in "The Shadow out of Time" or William Dyer in *At the Mountains of Madness,* so too do other human creatures move "out into the Endless Deeps" (*TEL* xi) and the dark, "endless spaces, bouncing off strange equations" (*TEL* 252).

It should be remembered also that the void is not exclusively accessible from the darkness of space, and for Dyer and Danforth in *At the Mountains of Madness* the frozen continent of Antarctica contains "the black inner world, of whose existence we had not known before, but which we were now eager to find and traverse" (CF 3.116). The desire of these human creatures to seek out and enter the void, coupled with their hope for revelation, overrides the fear that stops other such creatures at the threshold, and from carvings they

> deduced that a steeply descending walk of about a mile through either of the neighboring tunnels would bring us to the brink of the dizzy sunless cliffs about the great abyss; down whose side adequate paths, improved by the Old Ones, led to the rocky shore of the hidden and nighted ocean. To behold this fabulous gulf in stark reality was a lure which seemed impossible of resistance once we knew of the thing. (CF 3.116–17)

The void is silence and the void silences; and as the narrator of Lovecraft's "From Beyond" says, it is an "utter, absolute solitude in infinite, sightless, soundless space" (CF 1.195–96). The void precipitates a resurrection of the other language that draws neither horizons of finitude nor boundaries between objects. To see in the dark can be said to "preced[e] the spoken word," and the language of the light is nullified within "the void of the 'night of the world'" (Žižek, *Looking Awry* 87). For the human creature bereft of a cosmos, the void precedes the universe, and the ontological security of the light gives way to an ontological destabilisation in the dark. The human creature is stripped of its foundations that the invisible might be made visible.

The Dune Encyclopedia calls Voice "[o]ne of the most impressive physical accomplishments of the Bene Gesserit Sisterhood; the idiomatic terminology used to refer to the manipulation of speech to achieve complete control over the receiver" (McNelly 498). When the Reverend Mother Mohiam says to Paul in *D*, "'Now, you come here!'" he feels that "[t]he command whipped out at him. Paul found himself obeying before he could think about it" (*D* 13). When discussing the use of Voice in Herbert's *Dune* chronicles, American academic and science fiction critic Paul Kucera writes that "[t]he Voice might thus be said to already figure monologic utterance; it bears the stamp of the mythic, of the absolute" (234). This is to say that the language that frames a cosmos, inasmuch as it is the language framing a mythic structure is a construct with a limit that discloses only as much of an experience or even understanding of the universe as that language allows. Furthermore, in being a "monologic utterance" the Voice, and similarly a cosmos, is a single-lens view, a tele-objectivity of order that in its framing excludes all other aspects or choices that lie beyond the frame. According to Kucera, "myths and fictions . . . provide 'comfort in a hostile world'" (239), and irrespective of whether that "other world" is captured within the Genesis cosmology or the universe as machine, the comfort that these limiting utterances provides is bound up within negation. To render the universe invisible is a consequence of the reifying language of the cosmos that, simply in being uttered, erases what lies beyond the language. As Kucera also claims, "Our voice is never precisely our own" (242), and the language of the light determines through omission how the human creature speaks of, and to, the universe.

To step into the void is to silence the voice and erase the language of the light, in order that the human creature might return to a kind of preverbal or pre-mirror condition. Unencumbered by the abstraction of the symbolic proclivity of language, that creature is then better positioned to see what linguistic abstraction has previously failed to express and therefore acknowledge. With reference to Paul Atreides's first encounter in

Dune with the Bene Gesserit Reverend Mother Mohiam (*D* 13), Kucera reminds us that "[l]anguage recognized as manipulative thereby loses some of its ability to manipulate" (239), and in saying this Kucera forcasts a future where the Voice and the language it carries loses its hold over Paul altogether. It is, however, only after having submitted to the deluge of the universe that Paul can then turn the ordered cosmos on its head and show the Reverend Mother that "'I remember your gom jabbar . . . You remember mine I can kill you with a word!'" (*D* 453). Paul can do this because his language and the Voice that utters it are refigured by the silence of the void. While in cosmicism silence unspeaks and therefore hides the apocalypse (Ingebretsen 140), for neocosmicism silence becomes the linguistic foundation from which the apocalypse manifests itself.

The void is a locus in which any human creature that enters is utterly isolate and entirely irrelevant. It is the freezing end of everything and announces the proximity of the cold universe. That the human creature chooses to move from its warm, sunlit cosmos and into the universe of cold equations is, perhaps, as simple as the principle of the attraction of heat to the cold. John Gribbin writes of heat in a cold universe, with reference to "[t]he strangest feature of the Universe [being] bright stars scattered across a dark sky. All those stars are busy pouring out heat energy into the cold universe," and he goes on to discuss the second law of thermodynamics with reference to the German physicist Rudolph Clausius's statement "that 'heat always shows a tendency to equalize temperature differences and therefore pass from *hotter* to *colder* bodies'" (94). It is worth considering, given the tendency for heat to "pass" in this manner, whether there is not some clue in this as to why the human creature (warm-bodied and most comfortable in a warm environment) seeks to reach beyond its warmth and into the cold universe. Underlying the complexity of the human creature's predisposition for emotional response lies a simple *equation* of attraction: the attraction of oppositions to redress bipolarities.

For Robert Blake at the end of "The Haunter of the Dark," "light is dark and dark is light . . . far is near and near is far."[10] In this space where opposites freeze and nullify, Blake "remember[s] Yuggoth, and more distant Shaggai, and the ultimate void of the black planets," and it

---

10. This is referred to in chapter 5.

is here that he senses his connection with "[t]he long, winging flight through the void" of others that "cannot cross the universe of light" (CF 3.478). While there is no doubt that Blake is physically killed in this experience (CF 3.477), yielding to cosmicism's inevitable outcomes, what remains doubtful is his being eradicated altogether. Blake's own journal makes a plea for an attempt to hold onto what is slipping from his grasp; his sense of where he is when he writes "I am on this planet" and who or what he is when he writes, "I am it and it is I" (CF 3.478). It is this slippage, this erasing of Blake in the void that offers the possibility of his becoming a literal *tabula rasa* into which some other can be inscribed, therefore freeing him to re-inscribe the body of some other. It is worth noting here that the OED defines *tabula rasa* as deriving from the Latin root meaning "scraped tablet" (17.523), indeed, a scarred tablet. The cold equations may have settled death upon Blake's body and its occupant, but this in no way means that Blake is dead. Which of them emerges from the void and is now released into the universe? This may never be known, but the cold equations deal equally to human creatures as to others, and transformed, Blake may actually live. Although the case of Robert Blake is arguably ambiguous, this is by no means the first time that Lovecraft has presented the idea of the human creature transported to some other body and space-time. The best-known examples of this are the exchange between Asenath Waite (or more precisely, Ephraim Waite) and Edward Pickman Derby in "The Thing on the Doorstep"; and between Nathaniel Wingate Peaslee and a member of the Great Race in "The Shadow out of Time."

The void is thus named because its function is to make void, to empty the full; to turn the human creature into a *tabula rasa*. The purpose of the void from neocosmicism's perspective is to obliterate all sense of security and significance that the human creature might feel, so that it might be refigured and, in turn, refigure its view of the universe. This refiguring has a literal embodiment in Dick's story "The Electric Ant," which has been discussed in chapter 8. Garson Poole's discovery that he is a machine, rather than the human creature his programming has led him to believe himself to be, is connoted as an embodied end of everything, and the stopping of the machine that is his body also heralds the end of the universe. While it remains true that the machine does not survive, the fact that Poole chooses to cut his internal reality tape so that he might enter the void is the aspect of this story that signifies a transition from the interpretive framework of cosmicism to a simultaneous reading in neocosmicism that does not conflict with the earlier reading. Irrespective of the potential danger, Poole's decision to override the safety of programming that has held him within a human cosmos is an event that, in refiguring the view, allows Poole to reach for authenticity. As Poole admits, "[w]hat I want . . . is ultimate and absolute reality, for one micro-second. After that it doesn't matter, because all will be known; nothing will be left to understand or see" (CS 5.236).

In remaining obscured by the shadows in cosmicism, the differences between map and territory, the illusory and authentic, or the ideal and the common object, remain indiscernible one from the other. Entering the void, however, entails leaving the shadows. In its disclosure as an illusion, the "materialised Nothingness" (Žižek, *Looking Awry* 83) that Poole is programmed to believe is an authentic embodiment refigures his view of what he is and opens the way for him to choose rather than continue to be swept along by a cosmos. By stepping into the void, the human creature steps from the shadow landscape to an emptiness where there are no more shadows. Casting away the shadows, Žižek says, "reveal[s] the substance, the [ideal] object itself dissolves; [and] all that remains is the dross of the common object" (84). Žižek's revelation of the "common object" is similar to Ingebretsen's idea of "*embodied* nihilism," as it is exemplified in Lovecraft's *At the Mountains of Madness*. The idea that "[h]uman technologies of knowing are successively undercut, while one anthropocentric certainty after another is overturned, until in the end even the last must give way" (144), provides a similar image to Žižek's, and both scholars are turning attention back upon what could be termed the scraping clean of the human creature that is the transformative process of becoming a *tabula rasa*.

The void has no space for shadows, no light for reflection and reversal. Entering the void is a waking up in the dark. After surviving the engulfing coriolis storm in *Dune*, Paul Atreides realises that "I have another kind of sight. I see another kind of terrain: the available paths" (D 187), and this recognition triggers the process of voiding Paul so that he can be reinscribed by what has been hidden, by "'the things that . . . awakened . . . the sleeper'" (D 188-89).

The void empties the human creature and, in doing so, shatters the

10. Aphelion

Lacanian mirror. Whereas the specular image once invoked within that creature a sense of separation and a transition from the pre-verbal to the verbal cosmos, the erasure of the mirror's illusory reversal, coupled with the dissolution of the language of the cosmos of light, draws that creature back towards an antediluvian foundation. To say this is to acknowledge that the territorial reversal signified by the Genesis Deluge, which has become the comfortable familiarity of the cosmos, is itself reversed. The heimlich universe that has been figured as the uncanny and dangerous territory is stripped of its map and here revealed as the equally cold and dangerous heimlich universe that is the human creature's home. That creature may continue to exist and behave as if independent of others in the universe, but in reversing the mirror the void removes the previously stable ontological foundation of embodied separation. Like Paul Atreides's revelation of "available paths," the void's disclosure of the pre-verbal, the antediluvian, and indeed, other language and embodiment reveals newly available possibilities for the human creature and its view of the universe. The horizon opens up upon an illimitable darkness that energises rather than terrifies.

In Herbert's *GED*, Leto Atreides suggests to the Bene Gesserit that their design for the future is based upon a specialisation in building walls; that as "'masters of exclusion, experts in the narrow,'"[11] they seek to limit and therefore control the human creature's view. By their own admission, the Bene Gesserit "'fear anything [they] do not control'"; and in being beyond their control, Leto draws away the human creature's need for the Bene Gesserit and therefore renders their power over others largely impotent (*GED* 185). Leto moves beyond the confines of his cosmos so that he might engage with the universe, while simultaneously remaining at the threshold to show others where they might also choose to go; and so too does his father.

Understanding that moving beyond the reach of fear is also moving beyond the limit of cosmos, Paul Atreides feels "the manifestation of some other power he could no longer control. He had become a non-being, a stillness which moved itself. At the core of the non-being, there he existed" (*DM* 149); he is a *tabula rasa* and survivor of engulfment. In surviving the deluge where "He has seen the Water of Life," Paul be-

---

11. This is referred to in chapter 7.

comes the Kwisatz Haderach "at the fulcrum" (*D* 423) and stands where the universe turns from the illusion of cosmos to the revelation of the void. He represents a foundation, and as the Fremen name him, he is "Usal, the base of the pillar" (*D* 292). Between the antediluvian and the postdiluvian, Paul Atreides embodies the turning from reflection and shadow in the light to the void in universal darkness.

The void refigures the human creature's ontological foundation. Paul Atreides as the Kwisatz Haderach is the male Bene Gesserit who can see in "the direction that is dark" (*D* 422), to where the Bene Gesserit fear to look (*D* 18, 337). Rather than fear the void, Paul looks fearlessly into it: to see in the dark redefines bodily space and draws awareness to that body's limitations. The choice for the human creature here is to determine if and in what manner it will adjust its vision. It is not always a chosen shift that refigures the human creature; an enforced change in physical capacity also refigures the body and presents that creature with a necessitated choice of how to respond when seeing in the dark becomes a literal requirement. When Paul Atreides is blinded by the stone burner in *DM* (160-65), he relies on prescient vision to see all that is about him, and when Duncan Idaho is revived as a ghola, he relies on metal Tleilaxu eyes (*DM* 61, 65-66, 111, 123); in both cases their bodies have become something other than what they were.

Just as Paul and Duncan see by means that reach beyond the biologically unaltered ocular spectrum, so too does the computer Minerva in *TEL*. When discussing rainbows with Minerva, Lazarus Long concedes that her visual capacity reaches beyond the scope of his own, which is based purely within his biology. Long points out that while a rainbow can be described in complete and accurate detail to a blind man, such a map does not replace the experience of that rainbow; and because Minerva is equipped with mechanical vision, even though she is not a human creature, she "'can see a rainbow, [while] a blind man can't'" (*TEL* 124). Furthermore, as something other than human, Minerva can see beyond the rainbow's colours alone to the "chords in those colors" (*TEL* 124), implying a capacity to engage with something invisible and leaving Lazarus Long in no doubt that he will "'have to go on being half blind'" (*TEL* 124).

It is the reinscription of the human creature as something other than it has thus far been that triggers for that creature a new relationship with its own body and with the universe. The silent but not silenced body comes to terms with its insignificance. The cold equations are transformed from being laws to fear because they are alien and outside the human to being equations to understand because they are the points of order in the chaos. While Jessica Atreides resonates with an internal fear of the sandworms of Dune, "Paul felt a kind of elation . . . Instead of frightening him, the sensation of time-darkness forced a hyper-acceleration of his other senses. He found himself registering every available aspect of the thing that lifted from the sand there seeking him" (D 254).

The apocalyptic deluge of the universe is a necessity that, instead of crippling the human creature to madness or death, becomes the catalyst that allows that creature to move beyond the borders of its map and escape the carceral universe. The apocalypse makes the void accessible, and engulfment makes reaching beyond the limits of the horizon possible.

When, at the mention of the planet Caladan "'[w]here water falls from the sky and plants grow so thickly you cannot walk between them,'" Paul Atreides witnesses "the lessening of the man" in Stilgar, he is witnessing a transformation from a Fremen who moves within the vitalising desert, to "a *creature*" (D 445) that is reduced to something other than human. The very idea of "[w]ater from the sky" and the verdant landscape that water creates, the diminishment of the human creature before the coming deluge—these circumstances evoke in Paul Atreides a sense of "the ghost-wind of the jihad" (D 445) and in Leto the necessity for the "Golden Path" (CD 69). This is the foreshadowing of what DiTommaso calls the "vitality struggle" ("History" 311-13): the human creature's struggle for meaningful survival.

The human creature's vitality and sense of connectedness with the universe are reignited by engulfment; and in surviving that struggle, the human creature is more able to move towards previously unrealised possibilities. When the invisible becomes visible, when the removal of shadow reveals what lies beneath, the human creature begins to operate from an ontology of darkness, and the universe becomes something other than an ordered cosmos, it is a chaotic proving ground of cold equations.

As the British geographer James Kneale writes in discussion of Lovecraft, the real "is thrown into relief by the irruption of something impossible" (111), which is to say that what the human creature takes as the "real" of its cosmos is a two dimensional map turned into a territory of more than those two dimensions alone because the "impossible" and the invisible are manifest. The apocalypse of the universe makes the map a map: an ephemeral piece of paper that can be burnt to ash and dust. But more than exacting this revelation alone, by emerging into view the invisible—Kneale's "impossible"—overtakes the visible, and what the human creature thought it knew and understood to be real is made "strange; lost civilisations are returned to the light of day; objects, people or things are found to have survived 'Out of the aeons'" (Kneale 112). As Kneale and many other critics of Lovecraft identify, it is the revelation of the extent of the reach of space-time that enables this circumstance, and it is the human creature's comprehension of space-time in the universe that firmly and irrevocably cements that creature's insignificance.

For Paul Atreides in *DM*, "[h]e sensed the spirits of love and hate spouting there in a rolling sea from which no rock lifted above the chaos. No place at all from which to survey the turmoil" (67). The space-time of the universe, the chaos that has been masked by order, can no longer be observed from a distance. The chaos must be engaged; the human creature must swim within it rather than order and observe it. When Paul later asks, "'Is that how you destroy me? . . . Prevent me from collecting my thoughts?'" Duncan Idaho responds by asking, "'Can you collect chaos?'" (*DM* 112).

What neocosmicism claims to offer the human creature is the opportunity to move beyond its encapsulated infancy of a cosmos and to develop a relationship with the universe. Rather than reach the limits of its confinement where it will then stagnate and decay, that creature can extend its reach beyond previously mapped limitations that are governed by an ontological stability of light and a reified sense of biological capacities as evolutionarily complete. Stepping into the universe is about stepping into the indeterminacy of chaos, into space-time where the illusion no longer reverses the actual. To participate in the universe, the human creature must move beyond polarities, for that creature's relationship with the universe is one of "lethal proximity" where the common object is all that remains and where there are no more shadows.

Chapter 11: Psychotic Universe

> The universe is just *there*; that's the only way a Fedaykin can view it and remain master of his senses. The universe neither threatens nor promises. It holds things beyond our sway: the fall of a meteor, the eruption of a spiceblow, growing old and dying.
> —Frank Herbert, *Children of Dune*

Frozen Ocean

Slavoj Žižek describes the psychotic position as one that "maintains a distance from the symbolic order" as a strategy to avoid being "deceived" by that order in the first place (*Looking Awry* 79). If a cosmos can be taken to be a form of "symbolic order," inasmuch as it is an ordered map of the universe although it is not the universe itself, it follows that when the illusion of a cosmos is shattered and the human creature reaches beyond the tele-objective constraints of that illusion to enter the universe, that creature is taking up a psychotic position.

In neocosmicism's universe, which remains indifferent to human emotions and the human measure of morality, chaos is also discernible as fundamental to the order and expression of the cold equations. The universe is the current in which the human creature moves; to survive, that creature cannot simply observe the universe from the safety of an enclosure, it must participate. While observation will get the human creature killed, participation also comes at a cost. As the Reverend Mother Mohiam says to Paul Atreides when testing him:

> "You will feel pain in this hand within the box. Pain. But! Withdraw your hand and the gom jabbar takes you. Understand?"
> "What's in the box?"
> "Pain."
> ... The itch became the faintest burning. "Why are you doing this?" he demanded.
> "To determine if you're human. Be silent." (D 14-15)

Choosing whether to negate the test or endure it is a threshold choice, and the test begins with entering the void. It begins with entering the universe. In *Dune*, Paul's "world emptied of everything except that hand immersed in agony" (15), and the burning from within the box, the wounding, is a microcosm of the human creature's experience of the proving ground. The Bene Gesserit box is the planet Dune and indeed the universe in portable form; it is a "machine" that tests for the human.[1] When the machine tests for what is human in cosmicism, it is the very fact that the *un*human does the testing that exacerbates the human creature's sense of estrangement from the universe. This untenable position in cosmicism, however, becomes a basic condition of the universe in neocosmicism with which the human creature is required to come to terms.

When Palmer Eldritch and Leo Bulero in *TSPE* are within the "reality" that Eldritch constructs under the influence of the lichen he has brought back from the Prox system, Eldritch explains that pain is what "'prove[s] to you that this is authentic. Nothing excels physical pain and terror in that respect; the glucks[2] showed you with absolute clarity that this is *not* a fantasy. They could actually have killed you'" (90-91). For the human creature in *TSPE*, the universe is an experience of pain and that creature will "fight to hold onto life" (140) and hold onto its familiar home; or, if sent into the colonial wilderness of another planet, use the translation drugs in an endeavour to avoid "wind[ing] up killing one another in [their] pain" (139). As Palmer Eldritch clearly demonstrates, however, the pain of the universe is not negotiable.

The human use of *un*human machines and methods to test for other humans is not uncommon. Dick offers a machine designed for this purpose in "The Golden Man" (*CS* 3.44-45), with Cris's survival a testament to adaptation and species strength; and the Voigt-Kampff[3] test in *DAD* that blurs the boundary of difference between human and other through its failure to determine which is which (46). What cosmicism

---

1. This same event from *D* is discussed from cosmicism's perspective in chapter 7.

2. Glucks are unpleasant, vampiric creatures created by Palmer Eldritch under the influence of Chew-Z (*TSPE* 85, 90, 95).

3. The Voigt-Kampff test has been discussed in chapters 1 and 2 and, within the framework of cosmicism, in chapters 5 and 7.

regards as an adversarial machine, neocosmicism inscribes and a necessity to embrace and therein maximise opportunity for survival. Leto's peace in GED is also designed to test and, in doing so, to strengthen the human creature, for "[i]f there is no enemy, one must be invented" (219), so that the chaos of war will stir "'the forces of human survival'" (220).

The critical point of the test, irrespective of its form, is that the human creature resolves to meet that test and therein acquire a kind of psychological scar tissue that like toughened skin offers a form of protection that enhances the chance for survival. Like Paul Atreides's Fedaykin[4] "filled with joy" (CD 171), it is only in the experience of the test that Paul can attain what Nietzsche refers to in *The Will to Power* as the "Olympian laughter" of "[t]he deeply wounded" (535; No. 1040 [Summer-Fall 1888]). The basic principle of neocosmicism's universe is not to pursue the human creature adversarially but to test it once free from its enclosure so that it might be vitalised for survival.

The purpose of the insignificant human creature's experience in neocosmicism's indifferently cold universe is to reconcile that creature with its universe. This reconciliation uncovers the human creature's connection with the space-time chaos of the antediluvian from which its manufacture of cosmoses has excluded it. This connection has never been entirely severed, but the human creature's amnesia of the cosmos turns the connection to haunted shadows from which it recoils in fear. While that creature's sense of "ephemeral insignificance in a universe frozen by cold equations"[5] directs it to seek escape from the universe in cosmicism, that same insignificance in neocosmicism is fundamental to the human creature's capacity to adapt in order to survive.

The machine not only tests for the human, it also harnesses the human and extends the possible limits of that creature's reach. In Part II of this book, Lovecraft's stories "The Whisperer in Darkness" and "The

---

4. The Fedaykin are Fremen that Paul Atreides brings into the ranks of his elite force and whom he commonly refers to as "Death Commandos." No other force can overcome them in battle, including the much feared Saidaukar of House Corrino. For a brief history and some interesting speculation on the rise and fall of the Fedaykin, refer to the entry in *The Dune Encyclopedia* (McNelly 211-12).

5. I make this claim in chapter 6.

Shadow out of Time" have been discussed with reference to machines that transport the human creature from one part of the universe to another by means of extracting the essence of what that creature is from the body that holds it.[6] In the first instance the intervention of the machine is figured as "harmless" and capable of "keep[ing] the organic residue alive during its absence" (CF 2.519); and in the latter, it returns Nathaniel Wingate Peaslee with no immediate sense of having ever been absent (CF 3.373). Rather than being experiences from which that creature recoils, the proximity of human creature and mechanical other can be read here as a relationship that allows for the possibility of enhancing the capabilities of both. Indeed, the human creature, already in its cylinder and inviting Albert N. Wilmarth to travel to the planet Yuggoth with him, is grateful for the opportunity that others have provided via mechanical intervention (CF 2.521–22).

Despite the possibilities, and perhaps because of them, re-engaging with the universe is a painful experience, and as Michel Houellebecq says with respect to Lovecraft's use of the cold and scientific to invoke the frightening and the fantastic, "[a] scalpel is needed to dissect the unnameable" (79). What Houellebecq identifies in this idea runs parallel to Watts's basic concept of the "on" and the "off" in *The Book* (26) and of being "both the leaf and the wind" rather than a leaf passively carried by that wind (125). This implies an understanding that both aspects of an apparent opposition must be operative in order to balance the whole or, for purposes here, to balance the universe. The spin of the heimlich coin is not about alternate dominant oppositions where one side is black and one side is white, where one is ally and one is adversary; rather, it is about acquiring knowledge and experience of one in order to understand its relationship to the other. This is related to what the pilot in Godwin's story "The Cold Equations" really only comprehends after the stowaway girl is jettisoned, that a "cold equation had been balanced and he was alone on the ship . . . but the empty ship still lived for a little while with the presence of the girl who had not known about the forces that killed with neither hatred nor malice" (118). Opposites merge and operate while paradoxically remaining distinct. To survive within the

---

6. This is also discussed in chapter 7.

paradox is to understand that order exists within the chaos. Rather than being the order of a sunlit cosmos or even an impersonal machine, however, it is the order of the cold equations that becomes the stable foundation on which the emotive human creature must learn to stand. It is that creature's active engagement with the universe, it is that creature's moving as an extension of and body within the universe, that is the essence of the proving ground.

When the universe without shadows, wherein the unfamiliar once again becomes the familiar by re-emerging into view as if it were Freud's "buried spring" rising up to soak the terrain,[7] is all that the human creature has, that creature's sense of its place in space-time is disturbed. When the "linear 'organic' flow of events" to a conclusion becomes "an illusion" (Žižek, *Looking Awry* 69), the inevitable outcome for the human creature is its location within what the American science fiction critic David Samuelson calls "situations of extremity," where that creature finds it is "facing the unknown and having to learn to understand it, in order just to survive" (108). Writing specifically about Heinlein, but in a manner that is applicable within the broader context of neocosmicism, Samuelson also notes that what the human creature finds associated with the proving ground is "what [Alexei] Panshin calls a 'wolfish' sort of freedom" (108). While this image evokes the privileging of a particular kind of human creature, it also highlights the interlinking ideas that the proving ground weeds out the species and that survival is based on an adaptation of something other than the purely human; literally in this case the animalistic, but in other cases the mechanistic and the antediluvian.

By the opening of Herbert's *GED*, Leto Atreides has undergone a significant physical transformation from human creature to human-sandworm symbiote. Leto "'prefer[s] the company of predators above that of the prey'" (191), and is recorded by the Bene Gesserit as saying that "'Drama is one of the targets of my predation,'" to which the Bene Gesserit note that "the God Emperor views himself as a predator in the *natural* sense" (73). It is worth noting here that Leto's father Paul, in *DM*, also recognises that he "loosed the wolf among the sheep" when he became Emperor and initiated his jihad (25; italics removed). Leto

---

7. Freud's essay from which this idea is taken, "The Uncanny," is introduced in chapter 1.

knows that survival in the psychotic universe requires an ability to adapt to change, and if the human creature can do this, it is more likely to survive within the universe without being swallowed up by an introspective attention to its insignificant and temporally limited position. During discussion with Moneo Atreides, Leto claims that "The predator improves the stock" (GED 69), and Moneo's response is to align predation as the emotional parallel of hatred. In his intent to teach, and in openly admitting that he kills but that he does so as an act separated from human emotion, Leto teaches in the first instance that "[t]he predator does not hate its prey," and more significantly in the second, that the key to making long-term decisions for survival is to understand that things change and "'[t]ime runs out for any finite observer. There are no closed systems'" (GED 70) and "'[c]hance is the nature of our universe'" (GED 20). What Leto demonstrates is that cosmicism's malevolent and adversarial universe, which is external to and disconnected from the human creature, is neocosmicism's proving ground; and it is no less dangerous. For neocosmicism, the greatest test of the human creature comes not from engulfment, but when it is afterwards immersed within the psychotic universe.

The universe is not static, and in "The Call of Cthulhu" Lovecraft asserts that "[w]hat has risen may sink, and what has sunk may rise" (CF 2.55), and the human creature must learn to move within this. Furthermore, the human predator in the proving ground remains a common motif, exemplified by Dick's children Timothy Schein and Fred Chamberlain in "The Days of Perky Pat" who, "aware of [their] many responsibilities," set about sharpening knives they have made and expertly using "[a] bull roarer that could kill a bird or a small animal at a distance" (CS 4.303–5). Together, these human creatures enter the proving ground to hunt that they might better survive. They are the generation born to the proving ground; they move within it and are vitalised by it while their parents furtively hide and indulge the cosmos of Perky Pat (CS 4.304).

The dusty landscape in which Timothy and Fred move offers a "thrilling initial sight of the expanse. Because it was never the same" (CS 4.304). These are human creatures conditioned for open terrain and physical exertion (CS 4.306), and they know that if the Martian "careboys" ever cease their aid to the planet, all the adults will die, but they will surely survive (CS 4.305). A "fluke of fate" may have saved those human creatures that "lived through the hydrogen war" (CS 4.308), and the survivors of fate's hand are part of the calculable outcome of the cold equations; but as the Baron Harkonnen concludes in *Dune* when contemplating "the loss of Piter the Mentat ... Fate was something inscrutable" (*D* 351). Fate weeds the proving ground, to be sure, and after that, human creatures such as Timothy and Fred in "Perky Pat" emerge as something else again, because they "'[a]re born after'" the war and are shaped by that revelation (CS 4.308).

Neocosmicism claims that the human proclivity for imagining dystopic futures says far more about the strengths and attributes of that creature than any utopian figuring might. It is the wilderness, the desert, the frozen wasteland, and the great emptiness of the uncluttered landscape in which the human creature learns what it truly means to be alive. This is what Leto refers to in *GED* "as the *bahr bela ma*, the ocean without water," the open desert that the Fremen once called "the Tanzerouft," and which Duncan Idaho remembers as "'The Land of Terror'" (112). This is what Paul Atreides desires after living too long in his citadel in *DM*: "vistas of open sand, for clean distances where one could see an enemy coming from a long way off" (32). Furthermore, in this universe, rather than dominating it, the human creature is just one creature among others, and those others that have been hidden away beneath waters or sands resurface to meet with the human.

Lovecraft writes in "The Shadow out of Time" that for the Great Race it is "the constant struggle to survive" that "stimulated" the development of "highly mechanised" industry (CF 3.405-6). Quite simply, the proving ground evolves the machine. Predators that rise to the surface such as Fred and Timothy in "The Days of Perky Pat" may be human creatures that thrive in the territory, but there are others in Dick's corpus that, rather than passively contemplating the demise of the human creature if the "careboys" stopped their deliveries (CS 4.305), are designed to hunt life actively and eradicate it ("Second Variety," CS 2.29).

Dick's story "Second Variety" presents the world of the human creatures as saturated in "heaps of gray ash" (CS 2.15) and radioactive dust. This is the scarred landscape of conflict (CS 2.19) into which the "claws ... crawled out from their underground tunnels" (CS 2.20). Claws and human creatures alike are contenders for survival in the landscape, and it is Major Hendricks who proposes the idea that the claws may in fact be "'the beginning of a new species. *The* new species. Evolution. The race to come after man'" (CS 2.30). Hendricks's suggestion may be offensively unthinkable to the other human creatures with him in the bunker at the time, but Tasso's later assertion that "'[n]o human can live here'" (CS 2.45) supports the possibility of others surviving where the human creature cannot. Tasso's insight becomes all the more pointed when she is revealed in the end to be a second-variety claw, and as Hendricks discerns, it is the second variety that develops a bomb to destroy the other varieties: "They were already beginning to design weapons to use against each other" (CS 2.52). The proving ground deals unequivocally with human creatures and others alike.

Lethal Proximity in the Psychotic Universe

When the human creature washes up on the shore of the proving ground, it is a *tabula rasa* on which its relationship with the universe will be inscribed. It is, however, also an emotional creature within a human body; defined within those limits, that creature must find a way to reconcile its insignificant localisation within the infinite.

In the closing paragraph of chapters 9 and 10 of this text, the relationship between the human creature and the universe is described as a relationship of "lethal proximity." A term taken from Žižek's text *Looking Awry*, "lethal proximity" points towards the removal of the ideal perception of an object that occurs when, by "cast[ing] away the shadow to reveal the substance" (84), what that object resembles is no longer an illusion or sublimated ideal (85). What it resembles is also what it is, which is why it resembles itself so well. When the human creature enters a relationship of "lethal proximity" with the universe, it is entering the psychotic universe. Indeed, Žižek follows his claim above by saying that "A psychotic is precisely a subject who is not duped by the symbolic order" (79), and in these terms the human creature that engages with neocosmicism's universe can be considered a psychotic creature.

It is not only the human creature that becomes the psychotic subject, but the universe too is psychotic. The process of the cosmos dissolving to reveal the universe can be likened to what Žižek expresses as the abolition of "a certain gap (that separating 'hallucination' from 'reality') . . . This collapse of 'fiction' (the contents of the hallucination) and 'reality' defines the psychotic universe" (81).[8] The human creature can no longer hide in the shadows, nor can it banish into those shadows what it does not wish to see.

Cosmicism's indifferent mechanism that is driven by the cold equations also operates in the psychotic universe. However, more than machine alone, this universe is also a system in which the observer is inseparable from what is being observed (Capra 78-79; Gribbin 20, 63-66). This is to say that the human creature is neither outside nor incarcerated within some part of the universe expressed as a cosmos, and irrespective of how insignificant it is, that creature's presence influences and is influenced by the universe. Between human creature and universe, neocosmicism recognises a vital symbiosis that cosmicism denies.

This symbiosis is like Watts's "Game of Black-and-White" rather than "Black-versus-White" (35), or the Baron Harkonnen's arena in *Dune* where "the black glove and the long knife [is] in [the] right hand, the white glove and the short knife in [the] left hand" (*D* 314). For the participants, this seems to support the idea that "[w]hite *must* win" (Watts 35), with the longer blade that is therefore more likely to land a successful blow being held by the black. In this arena, however, as it is in the psychotic universe, the illusion of one side being more favourable to the human creature than the other conceals the fact that no certainty can be measured from either. Irrespective of the potential of the visible weapon, the white glove also represents the invisible weapon of "poison" (*D* 314), a representation further complicated by the Baron's nephew Feyd-Rautha, who subsequently poisons the black tip. The fate of participants in the Baron's arena, like that of the human creature in the universe, is bound up within an indeterminacy that is neither black nor white to the exclusion of the other, but which will nonetheless calculate an outcome.

This grey indeterminacy in neocosmicism is often represented by the dust of post-atomic apocalypse and landscapes. Once the white light of the sun has been left behind and the shadowless black void has transformed the human creature, that creature emerges in a universe that, while remaining as cold and as dark as ever, is also shadow enriched by grey indeterminacy. Like blips on a radar, stars and explosions of conflict

---

8. This passage from Žižek is also quoted in chapter 9.

light up the universe in atomic reaction, and as the science fiction scholar Valerie Holliday claims for many of Dick's texts, "[a]tomic explosion erupts both as the real and as the symbolic into the real. Atomic explosion is both inarticulable and the ultimate articulation" (286).[9] The articulation of the inarticulable and indeed "the question of the visible and the invisible" is, Virilio claims in *Grey Ecology*, "perhaps the great post-war question," and this is precisely because conflict makes the invisible and the unimaginable, visible, the consequence of which makes undeniable the knowledge that "the eternal can disappear in the blink of the eye" (49).

More than this, however, Virilio highlights the idea that not only does abstraction, which is characteristically lacking in empathic content, make the invisible visible, but that this is a simultaneous flow wherein abstraction also "anticipates" the visible becoming invisible (50). The question that this leads to, and which is central to the human creature's capacity for survival within the psychotic universe, is the question of how emotion and abstraction can be simultaneously carried by that creature without then producing a dangerous imbalance akin to cosmicism's. Virilio says that he cannot yet answer this question, "the situation is open," and there is still work to do towards ascertaining any sense of an answer that might move beyond an "approximation" (61-62). Neocosmicism is, by the parameters I propose in this text, focused upon this same question.

It is Luckhurst's focus on the atomic in his text *Science Fiction* that highlights the idea that Dick in particular is not only writing from within the context of post-atomic apocalypse, but that he "produced a body of work within SF intensely concerned with the interpenetration of the fantasmal and the real, or the human and the machine, under conditions of perpetual war" (106). This blending of the visible and invisible in the human creature's proximity with the machine is exemplified by Dick in stories such as "The Days of Perky Pat," *DAD*, "Second Variety," "To

---

9. This idea can also be aligned with Roger Luckhurst's discussion in chapters 4 to 6 of *Science Fiction* relating to the ideological and cultural development of post–World War twentieth-century science fiction and the genre's apparently dominating premise that, as he quotes from Theodore Sturgeon, "humanity . . . is finished" (98).

11. Psychotic Universe

Serve the Master," and "Jon's World." The proving ground of ash and dust, in which the human creature finds itself fighting for survival, links that creature intimately with the machine in relationships that no longer conform to the idea that a machine is never more than a mindless tool to be used. "James P. Crow" opens with:

> "You're a nasty little—*human being*," the newly formed Z Type robot shrilled peevishly.
> Donnie flushed and slunk away. It was true. He was a human being, a human child. And there was nothing science could do. He was stuck with it. A human being in a robot's world. (CS 2.311)

The robots that are initially designed by the human creature as soldiers (CS 2.322) have become the ruling class, and the human creature now exists in the universe as something other. Like Herbert's Fremen when exposed to an abundance of water, the human creature Donnie is a defeated creature bereft of vitality. The war may have ended, but in its wake is left "[t]he complete chaos of the latter years. Endless wastes of rolling ash and radioactive particles. Miles of ruin" (CS 2.323): a proving ground patiently waiting for a time to come when the human creature's "centuries of pent-up hatred" (CS 2.323) under domestication is directed towards the machines that subjugate them.

While "James P. Crow" illustrates the preparation of the human creature for the challenge of the proving ground, "To Serve the Master" illustrates the ignition point of that creature's re-engagement with the proving ground. Having been compelled to live a subterranean life on its planet due to lingering surface radiation from a war long passed, a human creature's encounter with a robot[10] and that robot's escape to underground factories, where it will initiate the manufacture of more of its kind, is the event that triggers apocalypse and compels the human creature to participate once more in the "vitality struggle" rather than continue in spiralling devolution of servitude to the companies.

The machine that waits in the dust of the proving ground for the human creature in "To Serve the Master" (CS 3.117) is also the machine

---

10. This encounter, under the lens of cosmicism, heralds the demise of the human creature as insignificant and inferior when measured against the machine, and is discussed in chapter 7.

designed to kill that creature (CS 3.154), a design that may be said to be perfected in "Second Variety" (CS 2.37), where the human creature reengages with the "vast plain of silent ash," (CS 2.38) as it fights for its species' survival. It is "Second Variety"'s illimitable wilderness of ash and dust (CS 2.15-17, 19, 23, 25, 38, 44, 46) that births the machines; and when Major Hendricks watches a claw "disappearing into the ash, like a crab"[11] (CS 2.18), he recognises that more than being an other against which he must fight to survive, it is an other that is itself adapting to survival. The apocalypse and aftermath of atomic processes is an articulation of the inarticulable making the visible invisible and, in doing so, emphasising the indeterminacy of and in which the universe is manifest.

As Herbert's Leto reminds himself after surviving a storm in the desert, "[t]he patterns could guide and they could trap. One had to remember that patterns change" (CD 288). To remain unchanging is to stagnate, and survival depends on a capacity to identify not only what is seen, but also what moves, and then also to know how to move in relation to it. This is precisely what Liet Kynes means when he says to Paul Atreides that "'[s]ome parts of the desert teem with life. But all of it has learned how to survive under these rigors. If *you* get caught down there, you imitate that life or you will die'" (D 111). The lizard that Hendricks and his companions in "Second Variety" first hears and then sees "hurrying through the ash ... was exactly the same color as the ash" (CS 2.37). Leto says to his captor in CD that "'[t]he wise animal blends into its surroundings'" (CD 236), and so too, like Hendricks's lizard, the human creature must adapt.

More than this, that creature must also understand in "Second Variety" that the claws are adapting, that these others are developing new varieties that are increasingly indistinguishable from the human. Arguably even more so than in Dick's story, the film *Screamers* (1995), closely based on "Second Variety," presents this adaptation and indistinguishability with disturbing clarity. Furthermore, the *Terminator* series of movies (1984-2015), and particularly *Terminator Salvation*, offer a similar vision. To return to Dick's text, when Hendricks encounters the "David"

---

11. The image of these others as "like crabs" echoes an image similar to others with "crustaceous bodies" in Lovecraft's story "The Whisperer in Darkness," discussed in chapter 7.

he "couldn't tell it was a machine" (CS 2.37), and they move together in a literal and embodied "lethal proximity." That Hendricks survives and David does not is a consequence of the cold equations removing the shadow of illusion—in this instance the illusion of human appearance—to reveal the substance of the machine that David is. Distinguishing which is shadow and which is substance, however, becomes increasingly difficult as the threshold between the machine and the human engages with the equations of the void where opposites balance each other out. That the equations calculate death for Hendricks at the end of "Second Variety" in no way means that the shadows of illusion win; what wins is the substance, and this time that substance is embodied by the variety's two claws that are becoming more indistinguishable from the human.

The post-nuclear landscape is a common though by no means requisite foundation for the proving ground. What is essential is the open territory; the untamed chaotic space. While the universe of cosmicism is characterised by a saturation of water, the universe of neocosmicism is often characterised by a saturation of water's lack, and Leto reminds Jessica in CD that "'Water traps us . . . We'd be better off living like dust because then the wind could carry us higher than the highest cliffs of the Shield Wall'" (CD 128); out of confinement and into the proving ground. When Jessica returns to Dune from her Edenic and watery planet Caladan, she then realises "[h]ow seductive it is to live in peace" (CD 146). It is the lack of water in the deserts of neocosmicism, the emptiness, that keeps in motion the voiding of the full and the filling of the void.

While the proving ground in the *Dune* chronicles is most certainly the universe in which the human creature moves, it is also in a very specific way the sands of the desert planet Dune that have evolved the native Fremen. Like Dick's boys Timothy and Fred in "The Days of Perky Pat," Herbert's Fremen are human creatures that respect and thrive in the harsh conditions of their world. As Paul Atreides recognises, they are "a people whose living consisted of killing," and while in this particular moment Paul also remembers that the Fremen "had lived with rage and grief all of their days" (D 369), he also knows that the Fremen are not disengaged from empathic capacity. The Fremen have adapted to the universe, and in CD Paul's daughter Ghanima discerns that

> Fremen possessed a highly evolved conscience ... Every Fremen knew very well that he could do a brutal thing and feel no guilt. Fremen did not feel guilt for the same things that aroused such feelings in others. Their rituals provided a freedom from guilts which might otherwise have destroyed them ... [because they] identify [and understand the] collision between mortal flesh and the outer chaos of the universe. (CD 187–88)

The Fremen capacity to "do a brutal thing and feel no guilt" is similar to Rick Deckard's approach to his profession as a bounty hunter in *DAD*.

The dust and grey ash of the post-apocalyptic landscape in Dick's novel manifests as a desert of crumbling decay in which the human creature is entombed; but this same landscape is also its own opposite, and for Deckard it becomes an open territory that is alive after apocalypse. Deckard is ever mindful that "the dust—undoubtedly—filtered in at him" (*DAD* 6), and it is the constant settling of the radioactive dust, the constant decay of all matter into "kipple" surrounding him, that is the proving ground in which he hunts. It is in his choice as a hunter of androids that Deckard acquires an understanding of the human creature's need for vitality. When his wife Iran is so lost in depression and therefore disengaged from the universe in which she lives that for Deckard communication with her is like speaking "into a vacuum," he realises that "[m]ost androids I've known have more vitality and desire to live than my wife" (*DAD* 82).[12]

It is this stripping away of illusion, this blurring of boundaries between the human and android, that culminates in Deckard's transformation from contempt for his electric sheep (*DAD* 36) to acceptance of the electric toad that he finds in the desert, because "'[t]he electric things have their lives too'" (*DAD* 211). Having survived the proving ground, Deckard can at last sleep, knowing that the struggle for vitality continues even when it is embodied as "[l]ife which we can no longer distinguish; life carefully buried up to its forehead in the carcass of a dead world" (*DAD* 208–9).

It is this kind of re-inscription of the human creature that moves it towards a particular kind of existence in space-time where neither human creature nor other is of greater significance. As Nietzsche says in *The Will to Power*, "The destruction of ideals, the new desert; new arts by

---

12. This passage is also quoted with reference to cosmicism in chapter 7.

means of which we can endure it, we amphibians" (331; No. 617 [1883–1885]), and Deckard's rest comes because of his ability to adapt and survive in "the new desert." Like Nietzsche's "amphibian," requiring water to survive, but not so much that he cannot rest in the sand, Deckard "stretched out on the bed, dust sifting from his clothes and hair onto the white sheet" (*DAD* 213).

Like Deckard's toad, which "blended in totally with the texture and shade of the ever-present dust" (*DAD* 207), and similarly like Hendricks's lizard in "Second Variety," the human creature survives by casting away its cosmos of water-soaked ease and adapting to "new arts," assimilating the ways and even appearance of others as it moves through the universe. That creature is vitalised not by standing still in passive observation, but by engaging with the universe it inhabits. Furthermore, like Dora in *TEL*, who may have to consume a friendly other in order to survive (289), the human creature must be prepared to do what is necessary; this is how the proving ground is to be approached. When years later Dora and her family are threatened by others, she does what she has to do by shooting one without hesitation and putting a knife to another's throat within seconds (*TEL* 323). This is exactly what Lazarus Long means when he says to her, "[d]on't talk about what you can't do when the chips are down, dear—because you *can*" (*TEL* 289).

What the human creature begins as in both body and emotions is, in cosmicism, never enough to assure that creature's survival. Neocosmicism's proving ground is about a kind of sublimation[13] of that creature inasmuch as heat is applied to refine it, so that it might then become something more than a creature floating in some illusory stasis. The proving ground is about survival based on what in that landscape is becoming—the basic precept of the universe, that is, everything changes—but this is not change for change's sake. The proving ground is about adapting to change and moving towards an unknown future that cannot be imagined, because to imagine it is immediately to consign the future to finitude.

Survival in the universe is not focused around beginnings or end-

---

13. The *OED* defines a sublimate as "a refined or concentrated product" (*OED* 17.37) that is the result of "subject[ing] (a substance) to the action of heat in a vessel so as to convert it into vapour, which is carried off and on cooling is deposited in solid form" (39).

ings, but around the fact that the human creature exists. In the universe where a beginning and end constitute the same event, where neither first nor final cause governs, the human creature is undoubtedly insignificant, but no more so than any other that survives where the horizon reaches up through the vertical and into the darkness. Movement prevents stagnation and adaptation prevents reification.

In his 1941 speech at the World Science Fiction Convention, Heinlein discusses change as the "primary postulate" of science fiction and of the idea that many human creatures "believe that the customs of their tribe are the laws of nature, immutable and unchanging" (156). When the human creature "makes predictions," when it endeavours to ascribe an ordered purpose to the way events unfold, "and they keep failing to come true, time and again," that creature "goes insane, functionally insane" (157–58). In order to survive in the psychotic universe, the human creature in letting go of measures of finitude is better able to move past schizophrenic insanity and madness, and into psychosis.

Psychotic Morality

Although in neocosmicism the universe is no longer carceral, to enter it is to walk knowingly into what might become a trap. Herbert's Duke Leto says to Paul in *Dune* that "'[k]nowing where the trap is—that's the first step in evading it'" (D 47),[14] and as the test of the Bene Gesserit box exemplifies, the human creature's strength is to be found in its capacity to identify and, despite the risk, choose to enter the trap (D 48). It is in harsh conditions that the universe sifts through its inhabitants "to find the humans" (D 16), to select the ones that are something more than machines or animals in the Garden.

Leto Atreides says to Moneo in *GED* that "'[t]he target of the [Butlerian] Jihad was a machine-attitude as much as the machines'" (282), highlighting the root of the human creature's fear in cosmicism: that it might not remain human. The Genesis cosmology's ideological positioning of the human creature as significant in its world, and by extension

---

14. The scene in which this is said by the Duke is also discussed in chapter 8, with reference to the way that he appears to be transformed to something other than human when caught in the trap.

the universe, is in stark opposition to that creature's insignificance under the governance of the cold equations in the universe as machine. When that creature arrives at this seemingly irreconcilable juncture the revelation of its insignificance threatens devolution to something other, and that creature fears its finitude as an insect or contagion. To trap the trapper, however, to overcome cosmicism's engulfment and accept immersion in the psychotic universe of neocosmicism, means facing imminent threat so that in its innate desire for survival the human creature might also engage its vitality.

The "Vitality struggle"[15] has been previously discussed in reference to the Fremen warrior who returns from jihad so transformed by his encounter with an abundance of water that he loses his vitality. While a poignant example of the tyranny of the Garden in cosmicism, this scene is also significant within neocosmicism. This particular Fremen's loss of vitality is readily extrapolated across the Fremen population more generally, and it highlights the necessity for struggle. Rather than simply giving up because the fight against the deluge becomes too hard, or because there is no escape from its consequential decay, the proving ground allows the human creature to commit to jihad; not as a struggle in the name of an external deity or other force, but as a way of life that ensures that creature is continuing to move within the universe and be strengthened by its innate capacity to survive. With its severe lack of water and harsh conditions in which human life must balance with the laws of the cold equations, Dune is exactly the proving ground that the human creature requires. As DiTommaso observes, rather than enforce a map of peace and order upon the chaos, "Dune reintroduced the grand conceptions of personal combat and heroic elitism, the presence of crack forces such as the Sardaukar and the Fremen, and the inclusion of personal weaponry like the kindjal, the slip-tip, the shigawire garrotte, and the maula pistol" ("History" 313). The planet Dune effectively weeds the human creature of its weaknesses, hones it for survival, and in doing so strengthens the species.

Like any human creature that dwells in the wilderness, the Fremen approach life and death as aspects of the same event (DM 148), an ap-

---

15. Lorenzo DiTommaso's idea of the "vitality struggle" is introduced in chapter 8.

proach that is in itself unencumbered by negative emotion. Similarly, the stowaway in Godwin's story "The Cold Equations," when facing imminent death, knows that it is her brother living at "the frontier"—the human creature in the proving ground—that will understand and will "not hate the EDS pilot for doing nothing to prevent her going; he would know there had been nothing the pilot could do . . . though the understanding would not soften the shock and pain when he learned his sister was gone" (110). The great test for the human creature—as it is for the stowaway's brother—is to reconcile its own emotive and empathic qualities with the psychotic universe; and to do this requires coming to terms with the universe's cold moral frame while also avoiding devolution. In his essay discussing the difference between science fiction and fantasy, Darko Suvin acknowledges that it is science fiction in which "cold reason" ("Considering" 227) is more commonly found. He then later writes that "[e]motion is a survival tool, no more sacred than any other: it may be life-furthering or genosuicidal, and I have argued (in 'Cognitive' and 'Haltung') following Brecht and some feminists, that it can only be the former if it is articulated and clarified" (240). What Suvin's argument touches on here is the idea that, irrespective of what kind of universe the human creature considers itself to exist within, more than understanding, that creature must also reconcile its emotive state with that universe without leaving itself vulnerable to destruction. One of the questions with which neocosmicism's proving ground tests the human creature is whether it is possible to survive in the cold equations with emotion and empathy intact.

When faced with this question in Dick's story "Human Is," Lestor Herrick's wife Jill must decide whether to testify that the body of her emotionally abusive husband is taken over by a Rexorian that has removed Lestor's "original psychic content . . . and stored [it] in some sort of suspension" (CS 2.263), or remain silent and allow the Rexorian to continue to inhabit her husband's body. This is a process curiously similar to that of the removal of Henry Wentworth Akeley's brain to a cylinder in Lovecraft's "The Whisperer in Darkness," the purpose of which is to allow Akeley to travel through space (CF 2.519), and the use of Akeley's body by an other for the purpose of communication with the human creature (535). Returning to Dick's story, the Rexorian accomplishes the exchange on his home world and then returns to the human creature's world as a man who loves life and values the company of the human creature that is his wife (CS 2.260, 262, 267). Jill is horrified when she first learns what has happened to her husband, and her testimony of a change in Lestor since returning from Rexor is all that she needs to offer to secure the death of the inhabiting Rexorian, the restoration of Lester, "[a]nd this horrible nightmare you've been living with will be a thing of the past" (CS 2.265). In balancing the equations, however, Jill's silence is a reply that not only accepts what has happened but accepts the revelation of where her nightmare really lies. When faced with the equations' outcome that has seen Lestor Herrick removed from his body, coupled with the redress of emotion within her own life, Jill makes a calculation of her own and accepts that the Rexorian as an other is preferable to the human creature Lester who dismisses emotion as "'[m]erely an opinion'" that "'contains no factual information'" (CS 2.257).

In his essay titled "Science Versus Ideology," Fredric Jameson writes that "[t]he most striking feature of the equation is surely the absence in it of any place for the subject" (287), which, if aligned to the idea of the human creature being the subject, can be read as inscribing that creature's presence in the universe of cold equations as an absence. Indeed, Jameson's words highlight the idea of the insignificance of the human creature, but more than this, once that creature's emotive response to its imminent absence is overcome, Jameson's statement directs attention to an important aspect of equations. This is to say that the cold equations continue to operate irrespective of the human creature. Moreover, just as Jameson says that "the suppression of the shifter or pronoun" seems to signify a shift "to some more complex and elaborate form of thought" rather than regress "from the Symbolic to the Imaginary" (287), the insertion of the *tabula rasa* human creature into the psychotic universe of cold equations is exactly the condition in which that creature is surrounded by, and has access to, progression rather than regression.

Jameson also claims that the next significant "feature of the equation ... is its seeming reversibility" that "distinguish[es] the equation rather sharply from the irreversibility of the verbal sentence" (287–88). This is to say that the cold equations operate congruently and simultaneously in opposing directions, whereas the symbolic ordering of language that generates cosmoses does not. The implications of this idea for the cold equations in neocosmicism are significant, and while only touched on here, signify ground for further enquiry.

In *GED*, Leto makes a similar observation when he considers that "the use of words is so little understood by a civilisation which still believes unquestioningly in a mechanical universe of absolute cause and effect—obviously reducible to one single root-cause and one primary seminal-effect" (285; italics removed). This is the heimlich universe where differences are manifestations of the same totality, and, as Jameson says, "the two sides of the equation are never really the same" (288). The human creature's absent-presence is the "structural peculiarity" (288) that invokes the distance between the subject and the equation—between the human creature and the universe of cold equations—as a distance erased that generates a "lethal proximity."

This is to say that just as a subject that speaks has emotionally invested itself in some way with the language it utters and the cosmos that language has constructed, so too in the erasure of distance is the human creature in the psychotic universe emotionally invested in the cold equations, and it is invested in an outcome that is participatory rather than adversarial. The choice that Jill Herrick makes in "Human Is" is both a response to and founded on the cold equations, and it is a choice that allows her to participate with others in the universe beyond the confines of her cosmos. The equation's reversibility that Jameson speaks of is the facility that triggers this relationship because the cold equations render the human creature entirely insignificant. That creature has become a reinscribed invisible other; the *tabula rasa* that standing at the balance point of reversibility becomes a "Janus, looking simultaneously backward and forward" (*GED* 277).

It is Russell Letson in his discussion of Heinlein's *TEL* who plainly states what the measure for morality becomes in the psychotic universe, when he says that the "engineering point of view . . . of the book . . . offer[s] a rationale for most human activities and a supreme value—species survival—for a universal morality" (200). While the issue of moral purpose in neocosmicism is not necessarily as simple or as proscriptive as this, it is a good foundation on which to build, and highlights a departure from cosmicism's position that the universe lacks moral purpose or direction. When the human creature is no more or less significant than any other in the proving ground, that creature's desire for survival becomes a significant factor in how it survives. While Letson's argument is focused on Heinlein's character Lazarus Long, much of what he discusses in his essay is applicable within the broader context of *neocosmic morality*, where "morality is ultimately founded not on humanism or any other emotional basis" (208), but on survival. As Lazarus Long observes in *TEL*, "stupidity is the only universal capital crime; the sentence is death, there is no appeal, and execution is carried out automatically and without pity" (247), occurring in a universe where the cold equations as "[n]atural laws have no pity" (351).

In MC, when Slayton Ford is considering what to do now that the long-lived members of the Howard Family are discovered, he knows that

> Cultures could not be kept apart forever, and when they did come into contact, the hardier displaced the weaker; that was a natural law.
>
> A permanent and effective quarantine was impossible. That left only one answer—an ugly one. (330)

It seems that not only do "natural laws have no pity," but the human creature's solutions to the effects of such laws are equally lacking in empathy when that creature endeavours to maintain its cosmos and keep the rest of the universe at arm's length; which is precisely how that creature responds to the problem under cosmicism. But as Žižek points out in his afterword to *Revolution at the Gates*, it is easier "to abolish this detour [than] to rethink the Enlightenment project itself" (299). It is this kind of erasure that Slayton Ford is reaching for in Heinlein's novel, and rather than accept the changes before him, Ford makes what could be ascribed a "fascist" decision that "[t]he only point left undecided in his mind was whether to liquidate them all, or simply to sterilize them. Either would be a final solution. But which was the more humane" (MC 330). This is not necessarily to say that the "fascist decision" is either right or wrong, and in this instance it highlights Ford's desire to retreat back into a denial of what he faces by choosing to eradicate it, as cosmicism would suggest he do. More critical here for neocosmicism is that this example highlights the idea that the universe will at times demand that the human creature consciously make what might be called hard decisions.

Beginnings and Endings

When the human creature encounters others impinging upon its cosmos, such encounters shatter that cosmos in a way that makes impossible any return to the illusion that others do not exist. As a preface to the newly disclosed universe, the void becomes a kind of *terra firma* that does not dissolve as the cosmos does when the human creature encounters others. Even though that creature might be disturbed by the meeting, the empty and open terrain of the void remains unchanged and, accordingly, allows a footing to be maintained while adjusting to the darkness that is the universe. As Virilio says in *Grey Ecology*, "to see is not to know,"[16] and the experience of what something is and the human creature's relationship with it precedes the mental abstraction of realising that *it is* what it appears to *be* (69). Adjusting vision occurs in the silent dark where there are no words or ordering that captures the knowledge.

Irrespective of the map in hand, or even if the human creature chooses to follow no map at all, the universe remains one of cold equations, and that creature remains subject to the machinations of those equations that determine beginnings and ends. When endings occur, these can be likened to a process of weeding, and in discussing the progressive eradication of the native population on the planet Felicity in Heinlein's *TEL* (8-9), Letson remarks that regardless of whether it is the human creature or some other on the receiving end, "genocide is not a crime but a condition of existence, nature's way of telling you that you were not a survivor" (209).

To do what is required and do so without emotional conflict is, perhaps, the proving ground's most difficult test, because in order to achieve this is continually to walk the knife-edge of risk where toppling over into becoming something less than what it thus far has been remains possible for the human creature. While arguably one of the easier targets for such an assessment, Paul Atreides is also an excellent example of the difference between the regression of the human creature to an insect or infection in cosmicism's universe and the progression of that creature in neocosmicism to adapt, survive, and keep intact what makes it human.

Julia List argues that Paul Atreides's "transition into manhood and adult responsibilities is marked by a kind of dehumanization," and his "capacity for empathy decreases further as he ages" (36). I suggest that List argues from the bipolaric morality that is inherent within the Gene-

---

16. This is similar to James Kneale's idea of the real being "thrown into relief by the irruption of something impossible," which is discussed in chapter 10.

sis cosmology, and what is overlooked from such a perspective when dealing with characters like Paul Atreides and his son Leto is that the morality of the universe in which they exist is neither confined nor governed by the parameters of cosmological maps. This is not to say that such characters are anarchists doing as they please and bearing no responsibility for their actions—indeed, they take deep responsibility for what they do and recognise the price that they pay—but they do operate from within chaos rather than being externally passive observers of chaos.

List continues her argument with a recognition of the pivotal event in Paul Atreides's life: the jihad. While she makes a negative assessment of this, the jihad signifies Paul's embrace of and suitability for survival within the universe. List writes that "Paul's attempt to avert the holy war he sees in his prescient visions is thwarted by the biological drives of the human 'race consciousness,' which seeks mass violence in order to diversify the gene pool and ensure the survival of the fittest" (38). While this statement acknowledges the human creature's inherent drive for survival, which is the basis of morality in the psychotic universe, the value judgement implied by the phrase "mass violence"—as a negatively connoted event—is rooted in the morality of the Genesis cosmology, which tends to view the survival of all human creatures as imperative. As a consequence, while List infers the value of the proving ground for weeding the human creature, her conclusion remains embedded within the cosmos that supposes Paul's "impotence in the face of death and destruction" (38). List may be correct to assert that seeing the inevitability of the coming jihad is "terrifying to him," but she then fails to acknowledge that when Paul does take the path of jihad he does so not as a human creature resigned to the fight—as he would be in cosmicism—but as a creature making an active choice to take on the "terrible purpose" (D 191) that he would be responsible for within that struggle for survival. By

> thinking with the race consciousness he had first experienced as terrible purpose [Paul finds] that he no longer could hate the Bene Gesserit or the Emperor or even the Harkonnens. They were all caught up in the need of their race to renew its scattered inheritance, to cross and mingle and infuse their bloodline in a great new pooling of genes. And the race knew only one sure way for this—the ancient way, the tried and certain way that rolled over everything in its path: jihad. (D 192)

This is the morality of neocosmicism's universe, and it shapes the universe as if it were a gardener pulling weeds. Furthermore, it is only after this apocalyptic thinking that Paul finds the capacity to mourn his father; to respond emotionally to the events that have brought him into the desert. Jihad may be, as Leto says in CD, "'a kind of mass insanity'" (CD 267), but he also knows, as his father does before him, that jihad is also the necessity that strengthens the human creature, for the alternative only serves to enclose and domesticate that creature.

It is not only the human creature in the universe that is "caught up in the need of their race to renew its scattered inheritance"; for others, the drive for survival compels movement of their own that threatens and even destroys the human creature. When the buggies in Dick's story "Martians Come in Clouds" make it to Earth because they wish to escape their dry and dying planet (CS 2.123-24), they are weeded out by the human creature, and so too are the Rexorians in "Human Is" for their possession of human bodies at the expense of the original inhabitant. In both cases these others are seeking the renewal of their kind, and while they are perhaps seeking less bloody paths than jihad, they are inevitably weeded by the morality that compels all species to strive for survival. While the buggies pose no significant threat to the human creature, inasmuch as they seek to live on the waters where the human cannot survive (CS 2.124), the Rexorians do present a threat and the struggle between human creatures and these others results in the stronger surviving. Just as "Human Is" implies that numerous Rexorians successfully make it through to Terra in human bodies, so it is that the ending of one creature signals a beginning for another. As the human creature is in this universe a re-inscribing *tabula rasa*, the question of which is the legitimate creature and which is the other no longer registers; for all are other.

It is Donald R. Burleson who identifies what List appears to have missed, when he writes that "[i]n the binary opposition into which Lovecraft thematically carves reality—the dichotomy of worth-seeking humankind versus the uncaring cosmos—one discerns that in a sense each pole of the opposition necessarily contains the other" ("On Lovecraft's Themes" 151). Although Lovecraft's work is rightly read under the lens of cosmicism, what I believe is undervalued by theorists and critics alike in his corpus is its capacity to reflect neocosmicism's possible alternatives for the human creature—alternatives available not because the crushing revelation disappears, but because the human creature can make a choice in how it will respond. The universe may be "uncaring," but it is nonetheless the universe in which the human creature seeks its sense of what it is to be human.

So what is it that does the weeding, and where does it come from? While the answer to this is perhaps as varied as the innumerable species that have been written into science fiction and an analysis of all the variants is beyond the scope of this text, there are two significant places from which they come: the antediluvian and the machine.

The machines of Dick's post-atomic landscape in "Second Variety" are efficient killers, and while the character Rudi may assert, "They're not a race. They're mechanical killers" (CS 2.30), the evolving varieties of the claws clearly demonstrates that these machines are adapting (CS 2.19-20, 27-28, 51). They may behave "like a horde of locusts" (CS 2.32), but "'[i]t only takes one of them. Once the first one gets in it admits the others' . . . 'Perfect socialism'" (CS 2.31). Organised and working collectively for survival, the machines are learning how to be worthy adversaries of the human creature in the struggle for species survival. As the character Tasso says, "'You people have always done good work. You build fine things'" (CS 2.50), and in order to survive those "fine things" are becoming something other than what they first were.

Founded within the almost unimaginable scope of space-time, when the human creature is confronted with the apocalypse of the universe, that creature must find some way to cognise the idea that much has risen and fallen before ever it existed, and much will most likely rise and fall after it is gone. To assimilate this revelation is to re-inscribe within the human creature what, in reference to an earlier quotation from Leto Atreides, might be called a "Janus-vision." Rather than antediluvian space-time eliciting crisis and a fear of finitude within the human creature, this complete eradication of significance opens up that creature's opportunity for vitality, inasmuch as the limits of finitude are entirely removed rather than exacerbated.

Neocosmicism asks if it may be possible that the universe is a proving ground for precisely this purpose: to unshackle the human creature from finitude. This implies that the psychotic universe may appear to exact some sort of cruelty in order to be kind; if this is so, the implication arises from this point that despite the human creature's spatial and temporal insignificance and perhaps even because of it, that creature is in some way significant to the universe. Gardeners do not remove weeds for the sake of the removal.

For the human creature to be weeded out by events in the universe is one matter, but to be weeded out by the direct intervention of others becomes a differing order of *equation* altogether. The hallmark of cosmicism embodied within Lovecraft's corpus is the apparent lack of anything even remotely like human emotion and morality being employed in the process of human eradication. Lovecraft's others simply swat the human creature as that creature in turn swats flies. This order of survival may be easily dealt with in cosmicism where the human creature is afforded the opportunity to run into hiding from the universe, but do the actions of these others translate to something accessible in neocosmicism, or are they firmly bound within a way of thinking about them that cannot be moved from the demonic and malevolent? The easy, and supportable, answer to this question is to consign Lovecraft's others to the parameters of cosmicism and be done with it; but the Lovecraftian apocalypse directs attention towards possibilities that are variant to the iconic heimlich conundrum.

In the universe of chaos the one certainty the human creature can have is that nothing is certain. Utterly dwarfed to insignificance by the depth and reach of space-time, that creature is now free to make its own choices, including how it responds to what is beyond its grasp of control. "The Call of Cthulhu" deals with the relationship between the human creature and others in the universe when those others are neither benign nor conquerable. They are "the Great Old Ones who lived ages before there were any men, and who came to the young world out of the sky" (CF 2.37), descending from the dark expanse beyond the reach of the vertical horizon.

When others are transcribed as desirous of the extermination of the human creature, that creature's experience of the void prepares it for accepting that its localised human morality has neither meaning nor power in the universe beyond its locality. In this, the human creature's insignificance is liberating, for when the universe is so vast as to defy that creature's sense of order and plunges into chaos, that creature becomes the void that is bound by nothing other than its own depths and its own desire to survive. For Lovecraft's Great Old Ones, the span of their reign "paled the speculations of theosophists and made man and the world seem recent and transient indeed," and although it would seem that they "all died vast epochs of time before men came ... there were arts which could revive Them" (CF 2.38-39). It is an interesting aspect of the human creature's contact with these others that it seems to be triggered by that creature's deliberate choice of action.

Similarly, while it is the human creature that can revive the Great Old Ones, it is also the human creature that first creates the machines; such as Dick's claws in "Second Variety," and an assortment of androids in stories including "To Serve the Master," "James P. Crow," and *DAD*, or Herbert's "thinking machines," which are eradicated in the Butlerian Jihad. It is worth considering in all this the idea that the human creature is drawn towards others that may threaten it, and then ask to what purpose? Is the human creature masochistic or destructive by nature, or is there something else going on? Is it that the drive for vitality draws that creature to something that in beginning may also herald an end?

Reaching for antediluvian beginnings, for "some terrible Cyclopean vista of dark and dripping stone"[17] ("The Call of Cthulhu," CF 2.26), is a reaching back to what the amnesia of the cosmos has hidden. In "The Call of Cthulhu" and its antecedent "Dagon," once the revelation of the antediluvian reignites an inexplicable memory within the human creature, and despite imminent danger, that creature follows a compulsion to bodily move further into the territory (CF 1.55-57; 2.50-53). In doing so, that creature is vitalised, and it is this symbiotic coupling of movement and vitality that fuels a thirst for contact with the enigmatic source of something unidentifiable. After moving beneath a "sun ... blazing down from a sky which seemed ... almost black in its cloudless cruelty" (CF 1.53), the narrator of "Dagon" is "[a]westruck at this unexpected glimpse into a past beyond the conception of the most daring anthropologist" (CF 1.57). Johansen and his men, in "The Call of Cthulhu," are similarly "awed by the cosmic majesty of this dripping

---

17. This kind of antediluvian architecture characterises many Lovecraftian landscapes and is particularly evocative in "The Shadow out of Time" where Lovecraft writes of Cyclopean architecture (CF 3.378-81), black basalt towers (380, 382, 386), "ruins of great stones in far places and under the sea" (391), and the "vast, dark, windowless ruins from which the Great Race shrank in curious fear" (402). While beyond the limits of this present discussion, architectural manifestations in the landscape are deemed as playing a significant role in neocosmicism.

Babylon of elder daemons" (CF 2.51), while "[t]he very sun of heaven seemed distorted" (CF 2.51). These stories foreshadow the human creature's evolving complicity for engaging with others, irrespective of the potential threat to survival; and this is a complicity that culminates in "The Shadow over Innsmouth" when Robert Olmstead resolves to join with others that he might continue his own becoming in the universe.

Under the perspective of cosmicism, the adversarial forces with which the human creature contends are inescapable because they lie at the foundation of their respective cosmoses. In the background of the universe as machine, the machines wait, and no matter how the human creature turns, it will encounter those machines and the cold equations that drive them. Similarly, the antediluvian terrain and that terrain's inhabiting others, which by the sheer weight of their significant occupancy of space-time render the human creature's reach insignificant, lurk beneath the verdant Garden of the Genesis cosmology. When under neocosmicism the cosmos dissolves to reveal the universe, these others are not eradicated; now that they are unhidden and unleashed, they cannot be negated. In the psychotic universe where beginnings and ends are the same, where there is no longer any distinction between first and final cause nor privilege of one above the other, the human creature's fear of its own finitude as a consequence of the adversary's power dissolves. That creature may still be required to fight for its survival, but it will do so within the context of an emotional shift that allows it to engage in the "vitality struggle" of the proving ground, with the knowledge that it is doing no more or less than any other that it encounters in the universe.

Balanced between beginnings and endings, Janus-faced, the human creature is reaching for both its purpose in being and its possibility to become. Poised between the cold darkness of the universe of inseparable waters and the burning light of the universe of illimitable wilderness, the human creatures engages in a relationship of "lethal proximity" with this spinning heimlich paradox—a relationship in which it will never be the same again, nor from which will it ever wish to retreat into the absolute cessation of vitality that characterises cosmicism's madness and death.

Chapter 12: Chimeras and Cannibals

>You can imagine anything at all. And real life is never what you imagine.
> —Arkady and Boris Strugatsky, *Roadside Picnic*

Everything Changes

When Lovecraft's character Tillinghast in the story "From Beyond" presents a supposition of the universe and asks what is it that the human creature really knows, he does so understanding that such creatures cannot comprehend the "boundlessly complex cosmos," although beings of a "different" kind could.[1] Tillinghast's quest ultimately ends in his death, for like many human creatures, and despite knowing how to "overleap time, space, and dimensions . . . to the bottom of creation" (CF 1.193), he remains incapable of surviving in the universe. In writing about the universe, Lovecraft is writing about the proving ground; but it is important to keep in mind that cosmicism does not figure the universe in such terms. That most of Lovecraft's protagonists do not survive intact is cosmicism's predicted outcome; but more than this, the human collateral damage his texts contain highlights a certain kind of lack in terms of what that creature requires for survival.

Many of Lovecraft's human creatures fall, but not all, and the closing scene of "The Shadow over Innsmouth" makes it clear that a *neocosmic* survival is possible. In writing about this particular story, Donald R. Burleson underscores the localised attainment of human survival wherein the story's protagonist Robert Olmstead "accepts his lot," with a more precarious future for the species in general because "the implications to humankind remain: there are older tenants of the Earth, and a melding of the races leaves no question as to which race has the capacity for dominance and survival" ("On Lovecraft's Themes" 149).

As "The Shadow over Innsmouth" reveals, uncovering the antediluvian foundation is a necessity that propels the human creature towards

---

1. Tillinghast's assertions, actions, and his consequential demise are examined from the perspective of cosmicism in chapter 6.

and indeed beyond the accident of the deluge, because in doing so, that creature obtains a sense of place in the universe relative to foundations. It is the human creature's sense of its foundations, irrespective of how far back those foundations temporally reach, that enables it to maintain the balance between the importance of its individual and embodied locality and its utter insignificance in the universe. In "Lovecraft's Concept of Background," Steven J. Mariconda stresses that even "[t]hough human concerns were of no importance to the universe at large, this need not mean that they were of no value to the individual psyche" (4). For the human creature to navigate within the universe where the prime morality is one of species survival, the application of "the concept of relative values ... tradition in its largest sense" becomes a means by which the human creature can secure "an emotional anchor" (12).[2] Understanding its own space-time position relative to the antediluvian is what triggers the human creature's access to this emotional anchor.

When the human creature is poised at the water's edge and looking towards the antediluvian universe that the deluge buried, that creature is located in the borderland territory of damp decay and mould, of fungi, insects and worms, fish and strange creatures.[3] In "The Call of Cthulhu,"

---

2. For further analysis of the link between Lovecraft's development of cosmicism and his sense of "background" in terms of tradition and antiquarianism, Timothy Evans's essay titled "Tradition and Illusion: Antiquarianism, Tourism and Horror in H. P. Lovecraft" (2004) is an excellent complement to Steven J. Mariconda's essay discussed above.

3. The release of Ridley Scott's *Prometheus* (2012) as the next instalment in the *Alien* saga—a series that can itself be read through the lenses of both cosmicism and neocosmicism—offers a challenging alternate view of the birth of the human creature from the mingling of the altered DNA of others within the waters of the human's planet. When the human creature finds the interplanetary waypoint of these others, that creature enters a realm that is damp and, in disturbing the cargo of that realm, ignites the evolution of both indigenous worms and of itself to become something else again. A Lovecraftian influence upon this film is readily identifiable, as is an arguably more deeply embedded maritime faunal representation of antediluvian proportions; culminating in the human-alien hybrid that is birthed with the appearance of an octopus or squid and rapidly grows to resemble something more often aligned with representations of Lovecraft's Old Ones and particularly of Cthulhu. This film challenges both assump-

the human creature faces images of "a sort of monster ... an octopus, a dragon, and a human caricature" (CF 2.23), an image later encountered adorning "the immense carved door with the now familiar squid-dragon bas-relief" (CF 2.52). In the earlier story "Dagon," the human creature encounters engravings and bas reliefs of "conventionalised aquatic symbols such as fishes, eels, octopi, crustaceans, molluscs, whales and the like," and more significantly the images of creatures "damnably human in general outline despite webbed hands and feet, shockingly wide and flabby lips, glassy, bulging eyes, and other features less pleasant to recall" (CF 1.56–57). For the human creature to attempt a denial of the existence of such others, as it does in cosmicism, is to fail to accept the universe as it is, and in consequence of this denial the human creature itself decays and crumbles in the pervasive water from and for which it is not made. The human creature's observation of an apparently human chimera in "Dagon" is a precursor to an embodied experience in the later story "The Shadow over Innsmouth." By implying the human necessity to accept the antediluvian foundation, "The Shadow over Innsmouth" signifies for neocosmicism that the blending of that creature with the other becomes an accessible transformation that allows for an alternative embodied means by which to survive, for "[t]his was to be my realm, too" (CF 3.230).

It is symptomatic of neocosmicism's inherent paradox that while the human creature may in one instance seek survival in the universe by moving towards engulfment in the deluge of cold and literal ocean depths, it is equally and simultaneously possible that other human creatures will seek survival in deserts where damp-clinging mould and decay pose no threat. "The Shadow over Innsmouth" reveals the human creature's willingness to interact with the antediluvian foundation, and Herbert's *Dune* chronicles map that creature's acceptance of participation with the antediluvian.

---

tions of human origin and assumptions of possible human futures, suggesting that chimeric blending has been present from the very foundation of the human species. Further compounding this is the progression of the story in *Alien: Covenant* (2017), which brings the demise of the human creature's creators through an android's deploy of a catastrophic virus and that android's subsequent experimenting hybridization of human creature and pathogen to create what is to become the more familiar alien "xenomorphs" of the original film series.

After Leto absorbs numerous sandtrout in a symbiotic enshrouding of his human body in *CD* (307–9), the biological parameters of his body develop an increasing discomfort with water as he evolves, writing in his Journals that "[t]he sandtrout skin which impels my metamorphosis has learned the sensitivities of the worm . . . I can feel my ending in it" (*GED* 151). The event that signifies the beginning of Leto's transformation that he might survive also foreshadows his end, but in ending Leto knows that his transformed body has secured the future survival of the vitalised human "because there are no other sandtrout, only the half-dormant creatures of my skin. Without sandtrout to bring this world back to desert, Shai-Hulud will not emerge; the sandworm cannot evolve until the land is parched. I am their only hope" (*GED* 151). In neocosmicism's universe, into which Leto enters with the altered vision of prescience (*DM* 212–13) and re-inscribes himself as a chimera of human and other, the opportunity for vitality is offered to the human creature through the eventual death of its God Emperor and the scattering of the sandtrout from his skin, so that the worms of Dune might once more live and produce the vision-altering spice that extends life and allows the human creature greater reach within the universe (*GED* 444, 452).

It is the sublimating quality of neocosmicism's proving ground that necessitates change and adaptation; and because the biological body is as inseparable from the empathic sentience that it contains as the human creature is inseparable from the universe, that creature's body is also subject to change. Beginnings and endings are intimately connected in the proving ground where mutation and accident are natural events. As Leto says to Moneo Atreides when they are discussing the approaching testing of Moneo's daughter, Siona, "'[y]ou are right to observe that accidents happen even in my universe'" (*GED* 71). Moneo may fear the death of his daughter, but not to test her and not to risk an unforeseen accident is to ask Leto unequivocally to "'delegate authority to a weak administrator'" (*GED* 71).

Lovecraft writes in a letter that "[i]t takes what amounts to a rare *accident* to produce a solar system, & still another rare accident, to produce the stream of biological modifications culminating (so far) on this planet as mankind" (*SL* 4.324), drawing out the idea that the biological fact of being human is entirely an accident in the universe that was waiting to happen. Moreover, other accidents may change or even eradicate that biology, and irrespective of the nature of the accident:

> there will certainly come a time when the mammal will have to go down to subordination as the reptilia went before him ... Probably the period of human supremacy is only the prologue to the whole drama of life on this planet–though of course some cosmic collision is always capable of smashing up the theatre before the prologue is done. (SL 3.43)

In acknowledging that the human creature's chance of survival is no better or worse than that of any other in the universe, Lovecraft also recognises that survival may necessitate an evolutionary change, if indeed that creature can avoid the direct impact of an integral accident such as a "cosmic collision."

In Dick's story "Oh, to Be a Blobel!", the accident comes as warfare of such proportions as to transect planetary boundaries (CS 4.359). It is interesting to note that while the Blobels "probably" came from Proxima, unlike the Proxers in *TSPE* (78), they did not come with an agenda of invasion or controlling the human creature, but in the hope of species survival, and settled on Mars and Saturn's moon Titan accordingly (CS 4.360). The accident of conflict in "Oh, to Be a Blobel!" brings human creatures and Blobels together, and the morality of species survival compels both to develop spies capable of physical transformation to appear as the other, and therein infiltrate their enemy (CS 4.360). For the protagonist of this story, George Munster, the apocalypse that conflict offers comes when, as a human creature on Earth, he inhabits a body that is human some of the time and then "for almost twelve hours out of the day he reverted ... to his old war-time Blobel shape" (CS 4.361). To survive the stress of being a chimeric other, Munster attends the "Veterans of Unnatural Wars Headquarters" in "human form or in Blobel forms; this was one place in which both were accepted" (CS 4.366). For more than a decade after the war, Munster quarrels with his compatriots (CS 4.367, 370); fathers four children—one of whom "looks like it washed up on the beach" (CS 4.367)—to a Blobel that involuntarily reverts to human; and fails at every business venture he tries (CS 4.366, 367). Deciding that "'we must not think about the old days—we have to close our minds to our pasts.' *Nothing but our future*" (CS 4.369) wherein human creatures and Blobels are no longer "natural enemies" (CS 4.366), Munster finds success at last when he develops a business based upon "'[a] Blobel idea'" (CS 4.372) and is bodily re-inscribed as a fully transformed Blobel (CS 4.373).

Cosmicism interprets this story as one in which the human creature surrenders, in the worst kind of way, to the cold equations and abandons all human empathy for wife and family in the pursuit of material success, a pursuit that culminates in Munster's reduction to something less than human. Margaret Lee Zoreda largely supports this perspective in her 1994 essay titled "Bhaktin, Blobels and Philip Dick," and while I do not support all her assertions, her assessment of Munster's final outcome (59–60) and analysis in terms of Mikhail Bakhtin's "concept of *dialogism*" (55) in particular contribute a sound analysis of Dick's story as it is framed within the general parameters of cosmicism.

Neocosmicism, however, allows for the human creature to erase a past where it has been confined and, in this confinement, taught to consider its embodied form as superior and to cherish its biological separation from everything other than itself. This is not a rejection of the antediluvian past, but rather an acceptance; and an acceptance of the human creature's locality within space-time. Blobels have the capacity quite literally to merge and blend and then separate again. Their fluidity allows them to move within the current of the universe, to adapt to events and accidents. Munster's apocalypse is the conclusion he draws that it is this fluidity, this capacity to extend his reach beyond human confines, that will best support his capacity for survival, because he moves with and within the universe rather than in spite of it.

The accident, irrespective of its kind, highlights the insignificant inasmuch as the accident is the apocalypse that, in revealing finitude, reveals the insignificant. According to Virilio, this "opens up a new type of thought: the magnitude of the thin (*minceur*) . . . I am not speaking about death, or the end, but of finitude, an enormous curiosity in the face of finitude" (*Grey Ecology* 43); and it is this curiosity that stirs the human creature to extend its reach and move in the universe. Virilio considers the accident an "integral" event, a distinction he draws between the localisation in the human creature's past of an earthquake or a fire occurring "*somewhere*" and the evolving global sense of the accident as integral that is made possible through the pervasive presence of, and accessibility to, the world via a technology that is typically, and ironically, viewed by the human creature through the tele-objectivity of the screen (48). Comparable to Lovecraft's accident in the universe that the human creature is, the accident as it is framed by Virilio "affects the expanse of the common world" (31), and the accident's ensuing apocalypse is "linked to the grandeur of smallness, linked to the grandeur of humility, to the grandeur of failure" (42), wherein the human creature's insignificance is significant.

The accident is operationally similar to Žižek's removal of the shadow to reveal the substance.[4] When the accident occurs, irrespective of what order of accident it is, such an event initiates the apocalypse; that is, the revelation of the substance. In *TSPE*, when Leo Bulero is in Palmer Eldritch's created universe, he says to the child he knows as Monica, "'You're Palmer, aren't you? I mean, down underneath? Actually?'" Eldritch responds by saying, "'Take the medieval doctrine of substance versus accidents ... My accidents are those of this child, but my substance, as with the wine and the wafer in transubstantiation—'" to which Bulero responds by acknowledging Palmer's implied conclusion (95). It is the accident that triggers a "lethal proximity" by removing the shadow to reveal the substance that is both symbol (or shadow) and substance *at the same time*; just as Eldritch's metaphorical "wine and the wafer" are simultaneously symbol and substance of actual blood and body. The accident turns the possibility to an actuality and demands transformation in the human creature through that creature's participation.

To survive in the universe the human creature must come to terms with the possibility that its transformation may be located not only within itself at an empathic and emotional level, but also at the interface between what it is and the universe; that interface being the biological body. If cosmicism highlights nothing else, it clearly demonstrates that all too often the raw substance of the human creature's biology is not enough to assure its survival. For neocosmicism, after immersion in the void and re-inscription as *tabula rasa*, to survive, the human creature must adapt; and this can also mean the adaptation of its body.

Engaging the Interface

Whether manifest within the deep cold of space or the searing atomic reaction of stars and explosions, neocosmicism's proving ground trans-

---

4. Žižek's concept is noted in chapter 10 and discussed in chapter 11.

forms. When Major Hendricks in Dick's story "Second Variety" leaves the enclosure of his bunker to seek his Russian enemy, he encounters within the blasted landscape a young boy named David who lives in "[t]he ruins" and whose body has adapted to survival in the proving ground with "skin . . . dry and rough; radiation skin"; "looking into the boy's face [Hendricks saw] no expression" (CS 2.21). To the human creature that Hendricks is, David is "strange," but Hendricks also knows that the surviving children were "[q]uiet. Stoic. A strange kind of fatalism gripped them. Nothing came as a surprise. They accepted everything that came along. There was no longer any normal, any natural course of things, moral or physical for them to expect. Custom, habit, all the determining forces of learning were gone; only brute experience remained (CS 2.22–23). As a survivor in the post-atomic proving ground, the human creature Hendricks accepts the accident's moral and physical revisions, and survival equals adaptation.

As the survivor of an accident David is adapted to be something other than he once was, and the visible nature and physical attributes of his body are not what eventually surprise Hendricks. The revelation that shocks is not that the human creature has become an other in the proving ground, but that the adversarial other, in this case a machine commonly referred to as a claw, has adapted to become an *other* other that appears to be human. The true nature of the boy is revealed only after he has been shot by the Russians and "[f]rom the remains of David a metal wheel rolled . . . Parts popped out, rolling away, wheels and springs and rods" (CS 2.26). The human body, and more specifically the surface of that body, becomes an interface between the visible and the invisible. It becomes an interface between the internal, emotional entity and the external background that is the universe of cold equations, and in the case of "Second Variety," it becomes an interface between the machine and the human.

The body that cosmicism designates as a frail and insignificant insect shell of contagion, the body that Merleau-Ponty speaks of as a "third term" in relation to the "figure-background structure" and the "horizon" (115),[5] is in itself a threshold. Unlike the threshold that in cosmicism

---

5. This reference to *Phenomenology of Perception* is discussed in the opening of chapter 8.

the human creature rejects and in neocosmicism must cross, the experience of this particular threshold is one from which the human creature never escapes so long as it lives. As Ingebretsen points out, when the internal and external collide, when the invisible and the visible meet, such "moments of epiphany . . . usually provoke distress and fear," and the human creature's solution to such circumstances is to "divide and separate visible from invisible worlds; to map heaven . . . and thereby to map a human world and to set a firm boundary between the two kingdoms" (156). When the external horizon of a safe and ordered cosmos gives way to the psychotic universe of chaos, it is the interfacing body that carries the internal human creature through that externality, and the local through the universal.

Accidental Cannibals

The external other cannot be ignored, and whether or not that other intends to consume the human creature in some way, that creature is unavoidably re-inscribed by the encounter. The surface of the human creature's interfacing body may or may not signify the exchange, but internally it is caught within the becoming of something other than it previously was; sublimated before and by the universe.

In Lovecraft's "The Shadow out of Time," others arrive unbidden and possess the human creature (CF 3.366), later to dispossess when their purpose is fulfilled (CF 3.372-73). In CD, the twins Leto and Ghanima Atreides actively seek the possession of themselves by their father and mother respectively, so that they might draw on the knowledge of those others for guidance in navigating the universe (66-71). In yet another case, the human creature in Lovecraft's "The Thing on the Doorstep" is possessed by an other for a binding permanence in that other's own bid for survival (CF 3.338-43, 346-49). And in Dick's TSPE, the question is asked: "Who gets sacrificed? . . . which of us gets melted down for Palmer to guzzle? Because that's what we are potentially for him: food to be consumed. It's an oral thing that arrived back from the Prox system, a great mouth, open to receive us" (190). Whether permanent or not, the exchange that penetrates the human interface in neocosmicism leaves that creature irrevocably transformed. Furthermore, it seems that irrespective of whether the possessing other's intention is affirmative or destructive, once having been consumed in some way, the human creature's loss of that possessing other leaves it bereft of a sense of wholeness, a lack that in cosmicism is never subsequently resolved.

Just as the possessing other consumes in its pursuit for survival, so too may the human creature. Ingebretsen asserts that Lovecraft's "themes are the endless return of the body, and thus, the haunting of the soul by its own hungers; by time; by memory" (133). While cosmicism readily categorises the outcome of events related to the hungers of the body, the resolution is not quite so straightforward in neocosmicism. Irrespective of the form taken, neocosmicism is reluctant to classify acts of consumption only from within the more conventional parameters of what is good and right and what is by contrast therefore bad and wrong. Neocosmicism tends to examine not so much the moral question of the act itself, as it does the question of the intent behind the act and its subsequent outcome.

What is an unfulfilled haunting in cosmicism, wherein the human creature is potentially locked within an adversarial standoff with its own body, is a potentially satiable imperative of the body in neocosmicism. Chimeric transformation, which is often accompanied by a visible, external change of or addition to the body's appearance, can be enhanced by cannibalistic transformation. Chimeras and cannibals in their acts of consumption internalise what has been external, and in doing so transform rigid demarcations of boundaries to fluid incongruities that remain in motion. This is a rewriting of the substance of the human creature; it is the blurring of the heimlich familiar with the heimlich unfamiliar until everything and nothing is familiar.

When the "fusing of domains" that cosmological mapping once concealed from the human creature is uncovered, Ingebretsen argues, the apocalypse of the destabilised map speaks directly from the territory of "a sort of miscegenation, that—were it found in any Gothic text— would be read as disgusting, horrible, unspeakable. Gods and virgins, indeed" (158). The removal of the tele-objectivity of the map that has operated as if it were some sort of intercessory between the human creature and the accidents of the universe allows that creature to move freely beyond the map's confines because it can see the territory beneath. Quite simply, the cold equations' sum calculation of "what is," while perhaps more terrifying than the illusion that has been supported by the amnesia of the cosmos, is an apocalypse that allows the human creature direct access to an open terrain wherein it will be compelled to make choices rather than accept its lot within a predetermined and limited confinement.

What Ingebretsen alludes to within the orthodoxy of the human creature's vision of deity, Lovecraft openly confronts in "The Dunwich Horror" when the human creature and the other produce offspring that are simultaneously neither of them and both of them. Miscegenation within cosmicism is an accident characterised by only negative outcomes, always read as producing something that, in being other than human, is also less than human. "The Dunwich Horror" is an excellent example of the lessening of the entity inasmuch as Wilbur Whateley is ultimately not strong enough to pass as human and survive within that creature's cosmological parameters, for he was only "partly human, beyond a doubt, with very manlike hands and head, and the goatish, chinless face had the stamp of the Whateleys upon it. But the torso and lower parts of the body were teratologically fabulous, so that only generous clothing could ever have enabled it to walk on earth unchallenged or uneradicated" (CF 2.435). The description of Wilbur Whateley that follows directly from this passage is detailed, and while too long to include in its entirety here, it is significant that it not only renders a stark image of a human-other chimera, but that it is a distinct blending of the terrestrial human body and "the symmetries of some cosmic geometry unknown to earth or the solar system" (CF 2.435). Just as Wilbur Whateley cannot pass for human, neither can his invisible and enormous twin conceal itself in the terrain, saturated and alien to the human creature though that terrain might be (CF 2.414-17).

Beyond the limits of cosmicism, however, in disrupting the cosmos with the accident of the other that resides within or somehow transforms the bodily space of the human creature, "The Dunwich Horror" points towards more successful consumptions. These blendings pass largely unnoticed by human creatures for generations in stories such as "The Festival," where in secret "people had . . . kept festival in the elder time when festival was forbidden" (CF 1.405), and "The Shadow over Innsmouth," where heredity is often "peculiarly puzzling" with its details being "unfamiliar," and those human creatures who would know having "dropped out of sight," or being "long dead" (CF 3.225). Although not entirely identifiable by the human creature, the chimeric descendants of embodied blending are negated by means of simple avoidance, and Innsmouth is "a town not shewn on common maps" and from which human creatures beyond its borders "'always try to cover up any Innsmouth blood they have in 'em'" (CF 3.161–62).

These stories speak of the human creature's imperative for survival in the proving ground where its biological limits are in some way caught up within the biological influence and intermingling of others. The narrator of "The Festival" returns to the port town of his ancestral kin "who had founded the Yule worship" (CF 1.414) and where "against the rotting wharves the sea pounded; the secretive, immemorial sea out of which the people had come in the elder time" (CF 1.406). Similarly, Robert Olmstead returns to Innsmouth after dreaming of his "grandmother under the sea" (CF 3.229) and resolves to "live with those who had lived since before man ever walked the earth" (CF 3.430). While the narrator in "The Festival" responds with a flight of fear that is typical of the human creature in cosmicism, in "The Shadow over Innsmouth" Olmstead chooses to move towards the antediluvian.

The consumption of the human creature by an other in cosmicism, its disembodiment and dismemberment, is about collecting that creature as if it were an insect in a jar.[6] In neocosmicism, however, rather than collecting insects for observation, disembodiment and dismemberment are about eating insects, they are about consumption for the purpose of assimilating the internal with the external. An interesting case of consumption is that of Dick's returned explorer Palmer Eldritch, who appears to have cannibalised himself. It is Barney Mayerson during his self-imposed exile to Mars who watches a craft land "on the flat desert" and:

> From the ship stepped Palmer Eldritch.
> No one could fail to identify him ... Gray and bony, well over six feet tall, with swinging arms and a peculiarly rapid gait. And his face. It had a ravaged quality, eaten away; as if, Barney conjectured, the fat-layer had been consumed, as if Eldritch at some time or other had fed off himself, devoured perhaps with gusto the superfluous portions of his own body. (TSPE 170)

---

6. This idea is discussed in chapter 7.

12. Chimeras and Cannibals

Like the snake that swallows its own tail in an unbroken circle where its end and beginning are the same, Palmer Eldritch appears to consume for his own sustenance what is bodily "superfluous" to his survival within the universe. Like Herbert's desert Fremen, starved of water and reclaiming it from their own bodies by means of the "stilsuit" that they wear (*D* 33-34), Palmer Eldritch is re-inscribed for survival. The human creature may be consumed by itself or by others, and it may in turn choose to consume others.

It is the embodied internalisation of something that has been external to it that ties the human creature more intimately to its antediluvian foundation. The consumption of the human creature via descent from an act of miscegenation with a "prehistoric white Congolese civilisation" (*CF* 1.171) in Lovecraft's story "Facts concerning the Late Arthur Jermyn and His Family" speaks of a connection with the antediluvian landscape of Africa that is reinforced in another of Lovecraft's stories, "The Picture in the House." Despite the apparently devolved terrain and character that typifies this as a story embedded in the principles of cosmicism, it is significant that within such circumstances cannibalism points towards a strengthening of the human creature and the mastery of some aspect of space-time.

The consumption of the body by either cannibalism or chimeric blending is the merging of something external to the body as an accident of the re-inscription of the human creature. Only through some form of death—and the proving ground often requires a partial death from which the human creature ultimately survives—will that creature have life. The cold equations of the psychotic universe legitimise consumption as an appropriate response of the human creature to certain conditions.

In the Fingers of Machines

A possessive consumption of the human creature by others is not the only conduit through which that creature might enhance its opportunity for survival in the universe. In writing of a blind man's walking stick, Merleau-Ponty highlights at a most basic level the retrofitting of the biological body, and this stick not only "becomes a familiar instrument," it extends the human creature's sense of its location in space-time as "not at the outer skin of the hand, but at the end of the stick" (175-76).

Just as Merleau-Ponty's blind man can see farther into the darkness around him, so too is Crawford Tillighast's mechanical device in Lovecraft's story "From Beyond"[7] an external addition to the biological body that awakens "sleeping senses"; and Tillinghast's machine affects a transition not unlike that of Paul Atreides in *Dune* when he declares that "the sleeper" has been "awakened." As Tillinghast says to his friend, "'The waves from that thing are waking a thousand sleeping senses in us; senses which we inherit from aeons of evolution from the state of detached electrons to the state of organic humanity'" (CF 1.195). The machine is used to reconnect the body with some aspect of the universe that the incarceration of the cosmos and subsequent amnesia once disconnected.

This reconnection with the universe is quite literally an embodied experience for Dick's character Garson Poole in "The Electric Ant." Once Poole understands that the mechanical extension of his body is also contained within that body[8] (CS 5.226-27), and once he finds the spool of tape that is a "reality-supply construct" (CS 5.229), he contemplates what cutting it will mean: "If I cut the tape, he realized, my world would disappear. Reality will continue for others, but not for me. Because my reality, my universe, is coming to me from this miniscule unit" (CS 5.229). The universe for Poole comes from within the machine, and significantly it comes from within his body: "My universe is lying in my fingers, he realized" (CS 5.230). The question this raises is: how far will Poole extend his reach? By re-inscribing the body, the machine can become a necessary component for interfacing the internally emotional creature with the externally cold equations. The body is the conduit through which the universe moves and merges with the human experience. When Dick's machine, which once thought it was a human, cuts the tape writing its reality, the universe ends because the machine ends (CS 5.239). The limits of the body in which the human creature exists determine the extent of that creature's reach.

Similarly, just as the integral accident for Dick's Garson Poole is the cutting of the reality tape, the Butlerian Jihad against thinking machines

---

7. This story has been discussed with reference to the machine and the failure of success in chapter 6.

8. This is another example of the *other* other that is discussed earlier in this chapter with respect to the evolved claws in "Second Variety."

12. Chimeras and Cannibals 277

at the foundation of the *Dune* chronicles is the integral accident that triggers a kind of resetting of the human creature and within which the mentats are developed. The mentat presents an opposition to the idea of the machine as separate from nature and challenges the notion of what constitutes a "natural" human creature.[9] If, as the Bene Gesserit claim "'[t]he *natural* human's an animal without logic'" (D, 149), the mentat is by virtue of this logic immediately designated as unnatural. When in *Dune* Jessica complains to Hawat that "'Your projection of logic on to all affairs is unnatural'" (D 149),[10] she also infers that as a mentat he is no longer human because he disengages his use of emotion. Paul Atreides, however, exemplifies the error of Jessica's view when the mentat in him makes the calculations of his Harkonnen hereditary and his "terrible purpose," and the human in him "mourns" his father (D 190-92). Similarly, Duncan Idaho understands that "his own emotional balance depended now upon retreat into mentat coldness" (CD 278), but later "allowed his grief to spend itself" (CD 281). The emotions of the human in Duncan Idaho may grieve for the loss of the woman he loves, but it is the cold equations of the mentat that secure his survival.

Under the lens of neocosmicism, the mentat is a potent example of the re-inscribed *tabula rasa*, the human that in surviving the void is equipped for the proving ground. The *Dune* chronicles present three kinds of mentat: the human mentat; the ghola mentat of successive Duncan Idahos; and the prescient mentats of Paul and Leto Atreides. Almost exclusively do mentats fall into the first category, and significant within their number are the original human Duncan Idaho, Thufir Hawat (mentat for House Atreides), Piter DeVries (mentat for House Harkonnen), and the Reverend Mother Anteac (a Bene Gesserit trained as a mentat after Emperor Leto has expressly forbidden such training). But it is the mentat that is something other than merely a human mentat that best succeeds in the proving ground of the psychotic universe.

---

9. It is worth noting that Dick's novel *DAD* also explores the question of what constitutes a natural animal in its blurring of the boundaries between biological and electric animals, and the empathic connections made by the human creature with both kinds (6-7, 8-10, 34-37, 210-11).

10. This conversation from *D*, between Jessica Atreides and Thufir Hawat, has also been discussed with respect to the cold equations in chapter 5.

After the death of the original human Duncan Idaho in *D* (215–16), the successive embodiments of Duncan are not only encounters with the mentat, but with a Tleilaxu grown ghola mentat (*DM* 17–18). A chimera of human and other, the other embodied within the ghola comes from the dead flesh of the original human creature regrown in an axolotl tank, and then trained with the machine's capacity for cold logic. Ultimately, it is this kind of Duncan Idaho that best survives in the universe. Duncan Idaho becomes a doubly potent reminder of what the human creature, by virtue of its biology and emotions, is not. It is this distinction, however, this human creature's otherness, that facilitates Idaho's survival in the universe for a cumulatively longer period of space-time than any other human creature. Despite many different iterations of the ghola, Duncan Idaho's survival surpasses even that of Leto as God Emperor because his original birth predates Leto's and he survives beyond Leto's death (*GED* 450).

It is the negation of historic biological limitations that neocosmicism endorses as legitimate possibilities for the human creature within the universe. While the human and other produce the chimera, the human and machine produce the cyborg. This is a significant area of critical study, well beyond the confines of this text,[11] but a brief discussion here will highlight the entry point and the human possibilities of examining the cyborg in neocosmicism.

Thought of as incompatible with the biological and the emotional, the machine is alien to the human body. In discussing the cyborg, Viviane Casimir argues that it "stands also for the discursive space where a crisis occurs ... a crisis in the representation of the 'living' or what it means 'to be alive'" (279).[12] Casimir argues that this "discursive space" is grounded

---

11. Since Donna Haraway's publication in 1985 of her essay "The Cyborg Manifesto," this particular area of critical study has expanded well beyond the borders of her work and often in contradiction to and argument against it. Haraway's text does, however, remain a significant work for further reference, and is well complemented by Chris Gray's text *Cyborg Citizen: Politics in the Posthuman Age* (2001), William Haney's *Cyberculture, Cyborgs and Science Fiction: Consciousness and the Posthuman* (2006), Cary Wolfe's *What Is Posthumanism?* (2010) and Rosi Braidotti's *The Posthuman* (2013).

12. This is also discussed in Chapter 10.

within the body and inspires the same question raised in "The Book of the Machines" of where organism stops and machine begins. In asking this, the human creature is compelled also to ask where the cosmological structure supporting that creature's sense of a God-created biological superiority ceases, and where the cosmological structure supporting the integral presence of the machine and its equations begins. The avenue of enquiry that neocosmicism points towards is the interface of the human body with its capacity for connection between the localised, empathic human creature and the illimitable space-time that is the universe, and as Casimir claims, "since the cyborg destabilizes our sense of ontology and identity, something has happened in the tableau of nature and made a change from What are we? to Who are we? It is a shift from the structural level—machine and organism as information-processing systems—to the functional level—machine and organism having a subjectivity" (285). Whether the shift occurs through the internalisation of the machine or some other externality, neocosmicism suggests that as a consequence of the shift the human creature will be better equipped to participate in a direct relationship with the universe.

Chapter 13: The Romance of the Universe

> Anybody who thinks of the world in terms of what it "ought" to be, rather than what it is, isn't ready for the final examination.
>
> —Robert A. Heinlein, *Tunnel in the Sky*

Significant Insignificance

The sense of insignificance that emerges from the dissolution of the cosmos in the wake of the universe's apocalypse is the juncture at which the human creature is afforded freedom. When captured within a cosmos that endorses an illusory status of omnipresent significance within and to the universe, the human creature's reach is simultaneously limited, and an irreconcilable bipolarity with devastating consequences is created. However, the human creature's knowledge in neocosmicism's universe of its insignificant status beyond the embodied interface liberates that creature, because in being no longer confined within the limits of a cosmos' safety net, that creature is free to explore how far its reach may extend.

David Samuelson points out that with respect to Heinlein's significant focus upon the idea of freedom, exploring its reach is an endeavour open to every human creature and in which not all succeed. For those that do succeed, "freedom, for the most part, [is not] a simple escape," but rather, "a complex issue, involving both power and responsibility and requiring various kinds of trade-offs" (108-9). To withhold the safety net of a cosmos from the human creature is to parallel what Laing refers to in *The Divided Self* as an imposition of "the necessity to make [its] own decision about the person [it] was to become ... [and] only by withholding was it possible to provide a setting in which [that creature] could take this responsibility into [it]self" (64).

Herbert's Leto Atreides cautions Duncan Idaho against "that false sense of freedom from responsibility for your own actions" (*GED* 172), drawing attention to the idea that the human creature should not dupe itself into the belief that confessing ownership of its actions negates all consideration of any others that are also bound up in the *equation* of those actions. Similarly, the Baron Harkonnen says to his nephew in *Dune*, "'[n]ever obliterate a man unthinkingly . . . Always do it for an overriding purpose~and *know your purpose!*' " (D 226). Paul Atreides says to Stilgar, before mounting the attack that ultimately dethrones the Emperor Corrino in *Dune*, that "'the test of a man isn't what you think he'll do. It's what he actually does'" (D 428). Furthermore, Dick's significantly re-inscribed character Bruce-who-was-once-Bob in *SD* is also told that "'[i]t doesn't matter what a person does; it's that he gets so he can do it right and be proud of it'" (1067). The point to be made is that irrespective of what a human creature chooses to do, it is the intent and the calculation behind the action that matters more than the action itself; and this includes the action of eliminating others. Responsibility for choices and actions, moral or otherwise, lies not with an external other, but within the individual human creature, and Paul reminds his mother Jessica that "'[t]here are no innocent any more'" (D 447).

The responsibility of freedom concerns not only what a human creature may do or reveal, but also what it does not do. Lovecraft is particularly sensitive to this idea, and the withholding of revelation is often framed as a means by which to save others. Examples include the decision made by William Dyer and the graduate student Danforth in *At the Mountains of Madness* to dissuade further exploration of Antarctica (CF 3.155-57); and the hope of the narrator Francis Weyland Thurston in "The Call of Cthulhu" that his "executors may put caution before audacity and see that [the manuscript] meets no other eye" (CF 2.55). While such nondisclosures in cosmicism are about saving others from madness or death, inevitable though death might be, neocosmicism tends to frame such choices more as conscious decisions to leave revelation for each individual to arrive at or not, dependent upon their own relationship with the universe beyond cosmos and the choices they make. The universe they experience, may not be the universe as it is experienced by others.

When engulfed by the void, the *tabula rasa* that the human creature becomes is the beginning in the ending from which it must choose. Passive observation from tele-objective safety requires no participation, no imperative for choosing between possibilities, and no responsibility for outcomes. Most, if not all, integral responsibility for outcomes in cosmicism is conferred upon some other agency and commonly shrouded in the image of a deity or an adversary. But in neocosmicism's psychotic universe, which follows immersion in the void—the universe that is the random field of chaos from out of which every choice manifests itself, in which the morality of species survival governs the proving ground, and in which the human creature must also consider its empathic response—participation is necessary and the human creature is directly responsible for the choices it makes.

In "The Returns of Lazarus Long," Russell Letson discusses what he calls a "potential conflict" in Heinlein's *TEL* between the idea of each human creature taking responsibility solely for itself and "the collective biological morality of species survival" (201). The significant aspect of Letson's subsequent discussion from this point, and his use of Damon Knight's notion of "several Heinleins," is the initially simple observation that Heinlein "is willing to posit a universe more mysterious than the ideological materialist will allow" (202). Such a position is not about oscillating between opposing forces, but rather, as Letson describes, "a willingness to accept facts whether they fit a model or not" (203); or as neocosmicism claims, to be comfortable within the paradox of the universe as something other than purely a mechanistic operation of binary pairings in perpetual conflict.

Lazarus Long accepts in *TEL* that "[r]esponsibility *cannot* be shared" (309), and it is Herbert's Leto Atreides who embodies this sentiment to an extreme end of responsibility for the entire human species. As Leto writes in his journals, the "Golden Path . . . is the survival of humankind, nothing more nor less. We who have prescience, we who know the pitfalls in our human futures, this has always been our responsibility (*GED* 14). It is the antediluvian reach of Leto's memory that enhances his prescient capacity for a unique view of the human creature in the universe, and provisions both his freedom to move through the universe and the responsibility that he accepts for his programme of "enforced tranquility" (*GED* 15) that is intended to spark the revitalisation of the human creature. Like Dick's boys Timothy Schein and Fred Chamberlain in "The Days of Perky Pat" (*CS* 4.305-7, 314, 321), Leto may have once held the appearance of a child, but in respect to taking responsibility for survival in the universe he was "never a child," and having taken on the mantle that he does, "must accept responsibility for the decision [he] made" (*CD* 224).

The human creature cannot seek to hide from others in the hope of abnegating its responsibility, as Adam and Eve once attempted in the Genesis cosmology's Eden (Genesis 3:8-10). That creature's sense of significance assembles directly from its choices and their consequences, rather than from a cosmos' morality. The universe remains indifferent, the morality of species survival is intimately bound up with the operation of the cold equations, and the human creature must reconcile its own empathic balance within this. Significant enough to note in two separate papers, Rafeeq McGiveron highlights from Heinlein's novel *Tunnel in the Sky* ("Maybe the Hardest" 184; "He 'Just Plained Liked Guns'" 294), that "'when it gets down to fundamentals, do what you have to do and shed no tears'" (*Tunnel in the Sky* 15). The psychotic universe requires the human creature to suspend its emotions so that it may determine how it responds to the choices laid out by the cold equations; for as Arkady and Boris Strugatsky write in *Roadside Picnic*, when a choice must be made in the proving ground, the human creature does not "get to feel pity" (131).

The cold equations become an anchor of order in the chaos, governing by the stability of calculation rather than the instability of emotion. Having little if any apparent effect upon the equations, the human creature while remaining insignificant in the universe simultaneously draws a sense of significance from an acutely localised and anthropomorphic position. This localisation of significance may very well extend no further than the interface of the body, and neocosmicism suggests that such a limit may also be that creature's most advantageous position with respect to its capacity to survive.

Immersed in the universe that is chaos, the only ground on which the human creature may feel secure—and with no guarantees of maintaining security—is its own body, and ontological security may very well begin, and end, there. Laing claims that it is the ontologically secure human creature that can relate with others (43-44), and if this is so, then the human creature must find a way to stabilise its sense of security within an ordered, albeit limited, body that is immersed within the psychotic universe of chaos. Cosmicism clearly demonstrates that an autonomous separation from everything else, the universe included, is not the means by which to secure an ontological foundation; for as Laing maintains, the human creature can be subject to "feel[ing] more unreal than real ... precariously differentiated from the rest of the world" (43) and indeed the universe. Laing also claims that the human creature "may feel his self as partially divorced from his body" (43), a sensation that neocosmicism suggests can be likened to the experience of tele-objectivity, which creates a sense of distance between the body and the universe.

Paradoxically, it is the "ontological insecurity"[1] that the human creature is subject to in cosmicism that holds the key to that creature establishing ontological security in neocosmicism. Both the key to and cost of survival lie within chaos, and the human creature's challenge is to sustain a sense of ontological security when everything that surrounds its embodiment is chaotically insecure, unpredictable, and forever changing. Laing claims that the ontologically insecure human creature "is preoccupied with preserving rather than gratifying himself" (44). While at its surface this may appear equivalent to the morality of species survival that the proving ground unleashes, therefore suggesting that this is an insecure morality, there are significant differences in play.

It is worth noting that when read through cosmicism's lens, the act of cannibalism wherein the protagonist Delapore partially consumes Captain Norrys in Lovecraft's story "The Rats in the Walls" is an act of madness that Laing's analysis suggests is Delapore preserving himself. Neocosmicism's lens figures Delapore's act more as one of gratification in which he also makes a linguistic connection with an antediluvian memory (*CF* 1.395). Although Delapore returns to the moral parameters of the cosmos after the event, within the experience of the act he is ontologically secure.

Similarly, Captain Franco in Dick's story "Beyond Lies the Wub" maintains a sense of ontological security inasmuch as he gratifies the biological impulse of his body for sustenance, while also believing he will preserve that body from the alternate possibility of the wub-as-other engulfing him. However, as a requisite for enhancing the human creature's capacity to survive, the proving ground demands participation—with others and within the universe. Captain Franco may choose to remain incapable of participating in conversation and therefore relationship with the wub that he regards as a "dirty razorback hog" (*CS* 1.33), but the injury of killing the wub is the accident through which Franco is re-inscribed.

---

1. The concept of "ontological insecurity" is first introduced and discussed in chapter 6.

13. The Romance of the Universe

The wub is, quite literally, internalised by Franco and then continues its previously interrupted discussion of Greek myth (CS 1.33).

Laing's "relatedness with others [that] is potentially gratifying" (44) occurs, I suggest, not because the human creature derives its ontological security from maintaining a sense of embodied and objectified separateness from others and from "[t]he whole physiognomy of [its] world" (43), but rather from its relationship with others, and more significantly with the universe, that develops as a consequence of letting go of the imperative to remain an impervious and unalterable human island.

As a requirement for the human creature to move beyond the illusion of tele-objectivity-as-reality and into the universe, engulfment is a sublimation and submission to the consumption of chaos. According to Laing, "[t]o be understood correctly is to be engulfed, to be enclosed, swallowed up, drowned, eaten up, smothered, stifled in or by another person's supposed all-embracing comprehension" (46) and, indeed, by that of the universe. To be engulfed by the universe is the unequivocal necessity of being engulfed by chaos. It is in the chaos that the human creature becomes something other than it first was, and it is in the chaos that the human creature can reconcile its internal, albeit arbitrary, sense of order within the universe and do so without *cosmic* incarceration.

Chaos

In chapter 8 I argue that "it is the ordered universe rather than the chaotic that entraps." As the condition that precedes and underpins all else, chaos is the foundation of the universe. Zukav writes in *The Dancing Wu Li Masters* that "particle physics is a picture of chaos beneath the order" and acknowledges that chaos is also often viewed as a fundamental component of the universe's overlying, visible landscape (216-17).

If chaos is a universal foundation, then the need for "the human creature to reconcile itself as an ordered, biological being adrift within the chaos" is also grounded within this foundation. In discussing the use of science within science fiction texts in *Science Fiction: History, Science, Vision*, Robert Scholes and Eric Rabkin write that "[e]ntropy is disorder, randomness, chaos. The Second Law of Thermodynamics says that all real phenomena operate with less than perfect efficiency. This means that some of the input energy in any machine or process is wasted as heat or noise. This wasted energy is not organised into work but is random" (136). At this stage of its development, neocosmicism presumes that the universe is a "real phenomen[on]" from which "some of the input energy ... is wasted as heat or noise." The warmth and noise that are categorised by Scholes and Rabkin as components of the "disorder" and indeed the chaos of the universe are also significant elements of the human creature's biology. Just as heat is attracted to cold, the human creature is drawn to the universe by its interaction with the cold equations that operate as a form of order in the chaos. It is the cold equations that connect the human creature's apparent need for biological and empathic order with the chaos surrounding and indeed penetrating that creature.

This is congruent with Zukav's description of "a set of conservation laws" that exist above the chaos and "do not specify what must happen, as ordinary laws of physics do, rather they specify what can*not* happen. They are permissive laws. At the subatomic level, absolutely everything that is not forbidden by the conservation laws actually happens" (216). Zukav describes these laws as stating that irrespective of the event, the "quantity of something" involved does not change, and that with respect to energy—what a subatomic particle is—"the total amount of energy in the universe always has been and always will be the same" (176). This principle is significant for neocosmicism, translating into the idea that the cold equations reconcile the human creature's apparent requirement for order with the chaotic foundation of the universe. Like the laws of conservation that frame a certain degree of order within the disorder, the cold equations unify the external and visible with the internal and invisible through the interface of biological order. Although referred to as something "awful," this is exactly how the undercover narcotics agent Donna describes herself in SD, saying that "'I am warm on the outside, what people see ... but inside I am cold all the time.'"[2] While the form that order assumes may change, as indeed may the interfacing body of the human creature, the essential substance that is embodied within or by the reordered, indeed re-inscribed, form need suffer neither diminishment nor destruction. The cold equations reconcile the human creature's accidental "impermanence and insignificance" (SL 1.302) with the psychotic universe.

---

2. This is referred to in chapter 5.

13. The Romance of the Universe

Paul Atreides says in *DM* that "'[l]aw filters chaos and what drips through? Serenity? Law—our highest ideal and our basest nature. Don't look too closely at the law . . . You'll find the serenity, which is just another word for death'" (168). Similarly, in *CD*, Paul's son Leto claims during his captivity and testing at Jacurutu that "[e]very question, every problem doesn't have a single correct answer. One must permit diversity. A monolith is unstable" (256); and thousands of years later, the idea that it is the chaos beneath the order that vitalises, echoes in Leto's reflection that "[t]he primate thinks and, by thinking, survives. Beneath his thinking is a thing which came with his cells. It is the current of human concern for the species. Sometimes, they cover it up, wall it off and hide it behind thick barriers . . . there is a cellular awareness" (*GED* 284). Whether expressed as a "cellular awareness" or the energy of subatomic particles, it is this underlying foundation that facilitates the human creature's movement within neocosmicism's universe as that creature reaches behind and ahead of itself for an anchorage of significance within the chaos. The recovery of memory from the amnesia of the cosmos is a recovery of an awareness that terrifies the human creature in cosmicism, and yet strengthens the territory beneath its feet in the ever-changing currents of neocosmicism's universe.

Acting as if it were some kind of memory in the machine, the paradoxical random-pattern of chaos that cannot be confined, pervades the universe like the buried spring in Freud's examination of heimlich in "The Uncanny" (419). Chaos as a natural state may be unfamiliar; it may have been buried and forgotten; but when it emerges, when the human creature remembers that chaos is and always has been, it becomes the utterly unstable-stability that in its ubiquitous presence renders the universe "familiar . . . comfortable, homely" (419): paradoxically heimlich.

Reconciling with chaos is the means by which the human creature, in recovering antediluvian memory, is better suited to seeing in the darkness that is characteristically the universe. When that creature develops cosmoses that rely on the order of the symbolic, as these do in cosmicism, it is afforded a sense of ontological security that only lasts while the universe remains hidden from view. Within the limiting field of vision that is consequential of the governance of the light space of the sun, the Genesis cosmology's accident of the Deluge, inasmuch as it covers over the existence of antediluvian others and reinforces human centricity, provides a universe in which the human creature feels significant. However, when some other event reveals the universe as machine wherein deity is absent and the human creature is subject to the cold equations that render it utterly insignificant; when the universe as machine threatens that creature's sense of ontological stability; the accidents that lead to apocalypse become inextricably entwined with survival. It is the recovery of the human creature's connection to the antediluvian that furnishes that creature with an understanding of the necessity for its participation within the chaotic tides of the universe.

Within the overarching frame of Lovecraft's philosophy of cosmicism, Steven J. Mariconda identifies the primacy of paradox as a mean through which to "provide [a] solution" to the human creature's sense of personal significance in a universe where it is insignificant, by means of the "pragmatic adoption of relative values" ("Background" 4). It is the grounding of the human creature's sense of connection with its past that Mariconda claims then provides security in a universe where human survival is of no significance one way or the other; and the greater the temporal depth of that reach, the stronger the point of anchorage. In quoting from Lovecraft's letters where he writes of "merg[ing] oneself with the whole historic stream and be[ing] wholly emancipated from the transient and the ephemeral" (SL 3.220), Mariconda identifies that "[t]his acute realization of background . . . is what Lovecraft labelled 'continuity'" (9); and neocosmicism labels as the recovery of memory.

Such recovery is not about a return to the comfort of the Genesis cosmology's prelapsarian Garden of Eden, but rather it is about a recovery of the antediluvian universe in which Eden is contextually only one comparably insignificant event within an infinite variety. As the character Galahad in TEL acknowledges when reflecting on "his mother's wisdom in pushing him from the nest" (Letson 214), "if she hadn't cut the cord, I would have hung around, an overgrown infant" (TEL 408). This is also reflected in the case of Dick's story "The Days of Perky Pat," wherein the materially rich but experientially immature Perky Pat doll is held onto by the flukers while they are horrified by the maturity of the Connie Companion doll who has grown up and left infancy behind (CS 4.320). It is also in this story of Dick's that the children Timothy and Fred are more capable than their own parents (CS 4.304–6, 314, 321), and, like the cloned twins of Lazarus Long in TEL, more than capable of self-sufficient survival in the proving ground (373, 402–3).

What these examples suggest is the idea that the proving ground of human survival is in and of itself an antediluvian territory; in short, synonymous with the psychotic universe of chaos. Recovering the antediluvian is about the human creature leaving the inherent conflict of interaction with cosmos that Laing phrases as "the polarity . . . between complete isolation or complete merging of identity" (56), and engaging with reconciling empathic and biological manifestations with the cold machine. Furthermore, neocosmicism's universe requires the human creature to then reconcile these re-inscripted polaric fields with the accidents that deliver unforeseen and future chaos, and with which that creature will engage in order to survive.

The accident fuels the vision wherein the invisible becomes as tangible as the visible.[3] Like Nathaniel Wingate Peaslee in Lovecraft's "The Shadow out of Time" (CF 3.418, 420–21, 424, 427, 432, 435, 439, 441, 444–45, 447, 451), the human creature can extend the capabilities of its embodiment via a machine as simple as a torch, and in doing so it is accepting that its biological parameters are not enough to guide it through the dark. Something more is needed for the human creature to attain a sense of "be[ing] important and significant *to someone else*" (Laing 57), or more precisely to something other than itself, because like the patient of Laing's case study, the human creature cannot "be [it]self, by [it]self, and so c[an] not really be [it]self at all" (61).

Engulfed within the universe, the human creature reaches beyond the restrictive notion of pairs of irreconcilable opposites, beyond the dictates of "on" and "off," and into what might be called an ontological field. Ontological security, neocosmicism claims, is grounded in chaos and psychosis. The secure foundation on which the human creature stands in neocosmicism is not the enclosure of a cosmos, but rather the ever-shifting background of chaos.

The universe moves in curvatures and currents; vortexes of coexistence. The "vertical littoral" (Virilio, *Open Sky* 1) of the horizon draws the human creature's gaze upwards and reveals that the antediluvian depths above and beyond its terrestrially grounded body are also eternally touch-

---

3. This idea is discussed with reference to Roger Luckhurst's cultural historical analysis, and Paul Virilio's idea of the accident in Chapter 11.

ing and resonant with that body. It is the dark universe and not the sunlit cosmos towards which the human creature extends its reach. "Ontological insecurity" is rooted in the realm of blinding light that deletes all other views existing beyond that light. Ontological security is spawned within the experience of the dark that for so long has been the fearful other space beyond the reach of the sun, and the heimlich paradox of the universe that embraces the human creature is renewed.

The Voice of the Other in the Dark

In chapter 8, the human creature is described as "[l]ooking into the mirror . . . [to] a reflection that is not quite right . . . a universe that is not the universe at all." Engaging with the psychotic universe entails a kind of reversal of the reflection; an act not of looking into the mirror, but of moving through the mirror. This is not about resurrecting what lies behind, nor is it what the French psychoanalyst Christiane Olivier refers to as "that other moment which by putting an end to the duality first discovered [in the mirror stage], would restore the primary unity" (91), that is, the "pre-Oedipal history with the mother" (92). Reversing the mirror in neocosmicism is about acknowledging the antediluvian past of the universe and entering into a *future* relationship with it. A parallel imaging of this idea is presented in the film *The Cell* (2000). In the hope of finding the latest victim of a serial killer before she is killed, and after several unsuccessful attempts to find the information by transferring, quite literally from her own body and into the now-catatonic killer's, the psychiatrist decides to "reverse the feed" and bring the external other into her mind and therefore her body in which that mind is housed. This idea of "reversing the feed," or reversing the mirror, is about internalising what has been previously approached as completely external. In neocosmicism, there is no return to an Eden of childhood because the mirror reflects only what faces it; and what faces the mirror in the psychotic universe is the re-inscribed human creature.

For the Bene Gesserit of Herbert's *Dune* chronicles, looking into the mirror aligns with looking into the place they fear, because the future they see will not be limited to the cosmos of their design. Re-inscribed, Paul Atreides is the challenge to the Bene Gesserit cosmos they have hoped to control, and he challenges the Reverend Mother Mohiam to "'[t]ry looking into that place where you dare not look! You'll find me there staring out at you'" (*D* 452). In response, the Reverend Mother reminds Paul that she once declared him human after testing him with the box,[4] and also suggests that he should be mindful of that declaration and its hidden implication of remaining within a limited human reach that the Bene Gesserit can then control. Despite the Bene Gesserit goal that is achieved in Paul of a male Bene Gesserit that can look where they cannot (*D* 452), as something other than he was when born and transformed by the proving ground, Paul affirms that he will neither be bound by their order nor limited by their sense of what it is to be human (*D* 453). He is no longer deceived by the image they have held up to him.

In discussing the Lacanian idea of "the Other of the Other" (Žižek, *Looking Awry* 81), attention is drawn in psychoanalytic terms to a kind of layered differentiation that parallels neocosmicism's premise that the order of cosmos is simultaneously underpinned by the chaos of universe as well as overlain by visibly manifest chaos in the proving ground. In claiming that "the psychotic subject's distrust of the big Other" is a kind of "paranoia" that is sustained by a "subject, who holds and manipulates the threads of the deception proper to the symbolic order" (81), Žižek sustains the idea within cosmicism of the human creature's sense of the other as an adversary. In neocosmicism, however, when the human creature is re-inscribed by the void as something other than it was in the cosmos—no matter which cosmos—rather than support the human creature's sense of entrapment, cosmicism's adversarial "Other of the Other" becomes the human creature's manifest position inasmuch as it is no longer confined by the illusion of cosmos.

This is not to say that the human creature becomes the thing it fears, but that this creature, in no longer being deceived by the cosmos, realigns its sense of familiarity in the universe with a field of chaos rather than a progression of order. In an analysis of Dan Simmons's novel *The Rise of Endymion*, science fiction critic and author John Clute writes similarly that "[t]he evil twin of the past becomes the twin in the mirror, a nanosecond or an aeon out in front of us, begging for life" ("On the Cusp of Far" 163). The "dark glass" of the mirror becomes the invisibil-

---

4. This episode is discussed in chapters 7, 8, and 11.

ity through which the universe is seen and through which the human creature can move. As Herbert's Leto Atreides writes in his journals:

> The realization of what I am occurs in the timeless awareness which does not accumulate nor discard, which does not stimulate nor delude. I create a field without self or centre, a field where even death becomes only analogy. I desire no results. I merely permit this field which has no goals nor desires, no perfections nor even visions of achievements. In that field, omnipresent primal awareness is all. It is the light which pours through the windows of my universe. (GED 329)

The merging of the human creature with the universe is the event wherein that creature's insignificance becomes significant. Donald R. Burleson writes, in reference to the human creature's sense of the universe as indifferent, that this position can only be held by "a consciousness that has had loftier expectations, so that in a paradoxical way, humans subvert themselves to contribute to their own insignificance; on the cosmic canvas, the human face is missing precisely because it is present—it paints its own absence" ("On Lovecraft's Themes" 151). SD's Donna is similarly "[n]owhere. Because she was not there in the first place" (1083). As Burleson suggests, it is precisely because the human creature is insignificant and therefore absent that it actually acquires presence. The human creature is provisioned with a different way of sensing the universe; with an enhancement of its capacity to participate in a relationship of meaningful exchange with the universe. In reference to the underlying purpose of Lacanian psychoanalysis, Fredric Jameson writes similarly of the capacity to hear the "voice of the Other" as the endgame of the human creature's "psychic life [that] has been structured by a search and a longing for a reply from" that voice ("Science" 299). While Jameson is referring specifically to that voice as a "parental authority," the principle of this idea remains applicable in neocosmicism with respect to the human hearing—more specifically registering—and therefore participating with, others; indeed, with the universe.

Life in Psychosis

In the short fragment titled "Azathoth," Lovecraft writes that "the dream-haunted skies swelled down to the lonely watcher's window to merge with the close air of his room and make him part of their fabulous wonder" (CF 1.337). The titular character experiences the rapture of apocalypse, the revelation that he is no longer alone and isolated from all others but is embraced and enfolded within and by the universe. In the essay "A Last Defence against the Dark: Folklore, Horror, and the Uses of Tradition in the Works of H. P. Lovecraft," Timothy Evans writes convincingly of the human creature's sense of connection with the past as a means by which to facilitate a sense of stability in the present when surrounded by the chaotic and ever-shifting nature "of a timeless and infinite cosmos" (128). Evans claims that "[s]etting is so crucial in most of [Lovecraft's] stories that it cannot be separated from character. Lovecraft saw place, or groundedness, as the center of his own identity and the basis for any true art or civilization" (118).[5] This is to say in the first instance that the character of the human creature is inseparable from the setting, that is, the universe; and in the second instance, to imply that the setting is of such a nature that it is in itself a character. Moreover, given the space-time reach of the universe to its background of chaos that infinitely precedes the advent of the human creature, it is potentially the first character.

Neocosmicism's universe becomes an entity, the substance of which is expressed in the varying forms of its infinite landscapes. It becomes a living landscape. In writing about E. A. Poe's story "The Fall of the House of Usher," St. Armand claims that "[t]he atmosphere which the narrator feels is emanating from the landscape of Usher makes that landscape not only a simple configuration of natural objects but, rather a true Self, an Ego, a thing that is alive and which breathes,[a landscape that is] conscious and alive" ("Poe's Landscape" 37). In the introduction to *The Cambridge Companion to Science Fiction*, Farah Mendlesohn writes "that sf is a discussion" (James and Mendlesohn 2) with a structure that often compels "the reader to look out of the corner of his/her eye at the

---

5. Prior to this publication in the *Journal of Folklore Research* in 2005, Evans published his essay "Tradition and Illusion: Antiquarianism, Tourism and Horror in H. P. Lovecraft," in *Extrapolation*, writing that: "Setting is so crucial in most of his stories that it cannot be separated from character, and it was from his travels that Lovecraft picked up the details of setting. Lovecraft saw place, or groundedness, as the center of his own identity, and as the basis for any true art or civilization" (190).

context of the adventure, mystery or romance" (4–5). This romance, Mendlesohn later clarifies, is "the romance of the universe [wherein] sf protagonists fall in love with the macrocosm. Where mainstream fiction writes of the intricacies of inter-human relationships, the discourse of sf is about our relationship to the world and the universe" (9).

Related to Mendlesohn's idea of relationship, St. Armand's essay also explores a significant point made by the German psychologist Kurt Koffka in his text *Principles of Gestalt Psychology* (1935), writing that Koffka "argues that our emotions are not purely subjective responses but, rather, belong to parts of the environmental field as well as to our Ego" (32). What St. Armand then skilfully argues, using Poe's story as example in conjunction with commentary from the weird fiction author Arthur Machen,[6] is the idea that the sense of emotion that can be "'attribute[d] to a particular landscape is really and efficiently in the landscape and not merely in ourselves'" (33). What is pertinent to neocosmicism here is the inference that the relationship that develops between the human creature and the universe is not one in which that creature observes an inanimate and ordered cosmos-masquerading-as-universe from some external position; rather, it is a relationship of direct experience with the universe that is made possible by an empathic connection.

The notion of the universe and its interstellar contents as some kind of living character is also noted by the science fiction critic Susan Stratton, who refers to Herbert's "two heroes: the planet Dune (Arrakis) and the young Paul Atreides" (307). Rather than anthropomorphise the planet, Stratton acknowledges it as a hero in its own right. Dune is a proving ground that responds to the human creature; it is an entity that, in being taken to the brink of destruction by that creature's terraforming, is nearly lost to that creature and the Fremen decay like lovers abandoned (*GED* 52–54, 81–82). Paul Atreides reflects in *DM* that "putting on a stilsuit, he put on the desert. The suit with all its apparatus for reclaiming his body's moisture guided him through in subtle ways, fixed his movements in a desert pattern. He became wild Fremen" (24), and

---

6. A literary contemporary, Lovecraft writes that "Machen is a Titan—perhaps the greatest living author—and I must read everything of his" (*SL* 1.234); and there exists a reasonable body of evidence to suggest that Machen's work was a significant inspiration for Lovecraft (Joshi and Schultz 161–62).

13. The Romance of the Universe

Jessica Atreides says to a young Farad'n Corrino in *CD* that "'[l]ife is a mask through which the universe expresses itself'" (286). Both human creature and planet, and ultimately the universe, are linked in a mutually binding relationship.

In elements too numerous to examine in detail here, the planet Dune is comparable to the Zone of Arkady and Boris Strugatsky's novel *Roadside Picnic*, and both of these positions in the universe reflect similar qualities as Poe's landscape that is possessed of "a true self" (St. Armand, "Poe's Landscape" 37). The Zone is referred to as "the bitch" (Strugatsky and Strugatsky 36, 81), a landscape with nuances of character (perhaps even personality) and seemingly responsive to the human creature; the Zone embraces and releases that creature at will (28, 41-42, 137-38). Similarly, for Paul Atreides in *DM*, the revelation is that "[y]ou do not take from this universe . . . It grants what it will" (108), and irrespective of his efforts "[t]he universe opposed him at every step. It eluded his grasp, conceived countless disguises to delude him. That universe would never agree with any shape he gave it" (146).

As if playing a game of hide-and-seek with the human creature, the universe is more than a painted backdrop to some strange *cosmic* theatre; it is a participant in its own game. Lovecraft may deny the existence of a divine presence in the universe, but he seems to endorse the idea of the universe as being in possession of qualities that are resonant beyond hollow objects[7] in space-time, writing:

> I like to view the universe as an isolated cosmic intelligence outside time and space—to sympathise not only with man, but with forces opposed to man, or forces which have nothing to do with man, and do not realise that he exists. When Kleiner showed me the sky-line of New York I told him that man is like the coral insect—designed to build vast, beautiful, mineral things for the moon to delight in after he is dead. (SL 1.172)

The romance of the universe involves the relationship not of human individuals with others or with a deified other, but with the universe. It is about the foundation of chaos and a relationship out of which all other relationships are defined. The human creature in relating with antediluvian others and participating with the raw substance of what the universe

---

7. The idea of the hollow object is presented in chapter 6.

is; by retrieving its memory of and therefore knowing these connections; by reaching out for them; is what allows that creature to sustain its vitality and move freely. The universe is a breathing, moving chaos, and the human creature breathes with it.

The "haunted universe of shadow and veiled truths" discussed in chapter 8, wherein "the human creature senses a haunting of the space in which it exists," is a negatively connoted position in cosmicism that reduces "the human creature to a vulnerable object." Ingebretsen's claim for Lovecraft's corpus of "the endless return of the body" (133), discussed in chapter 12, relates to themes that serve to alienate that creature from the content beneath the shadows of the universe. However, it is within Ingebretsen's statement that he also seeds the idea that the "effacement" of the human creature, its reduction to insignificance as a direct "consequence of ill-fated love," as opposed to its reinscription as *tabula rasa*, is what neocosmicism frames as that creature's missed opportunity for relationship with the universe because it neither acknowledges nor sees the romance. When the human creature voluntarily opens itself up to the effacing experience of the void, that creature's sense of its embodiment in the universe is transformed—and paradoxically so—by the same event that serves in differing circumstances to eliminate it.

The map is no longer needed; the relationship is direct. There is no other that intercedes on behalf of the human creature; that creature speaks directly to and is responsible for its own self in the universe. For the human creature, autonomous survival is not about being as an object separate from all others but about sensing the perpetual flux of any given position. The human creature is both an autonomous entity and an integrated element within the universe.

In *The Courage to Be*, German theologian Paul Tillich discusses the idea of the "God above the God of theism" and that entity's connection with what Tillich calls "the courage to be" (180). Tillich writes of this other as "present, although hidden, in every divine-human encounter," and as an other presence, it "makes us a part of that which is not also a part but is the ground of the whole" (180-81). Irrespective of whether a "God of theism" (Genesis cosmology), a deity that does not exist (universe as machine), or a deity from beyond the limits of the illimitable universe (Lovecraft's "Outside"), what stands "above" any of these in neocosmicism is the universe itself. The universe is the pulsing background from which the human creature derives its sense of significant-insignificance in the chaos; the chaos that is the foundation of, and simultaneously *is*, the universe.

Neocosmicism is pointing towards the idea that in the void's reinscription of the human creature, that creature's vision of and therefore relationship with something that has at times been mistakenly elevated to some other domain beyond its reach is also re-inscribed. This is not quite the same, however, as interpreting Tillich in a manner after Watts in *The Book* when he writes that Tillich's "'Ultimate Ground of Being'" as a "decontaminated term for 'God'" translates directly to being "*you . . . you're IT*" (18). As an element of neocosmicism, the concept of how deity is figured and relates within the universe is still very much in development. The issue at this point is about neither the elevation of the human creature nor the devaluation of any particular deity; rather, in acknowledging chaos as integral to the universe, it is about the human creature's developmental progression of survival and relationship to all others when immersed within heimlich paradox. As Schrödinger writes in *My View of the World*, "this life of yours which you are living is not merely a piece of the entire existence, but is in a certain sense the whole; only this whole is not so constituted that it can be surveyed in one single glance" (22). Or as Leto Atreides muses in *GED*, "'humans see first one part and then another. Delusions can be called accidents of the senses'" (253).

The Paradox

Timothy Evans writes that "[a] profound dualism—nostalgia and terror, beauty and disgust—runs through Lovecraft's attitude toward New England, toward tradition, and toward his own heritage, and it also permeates his stories" ("Last Defense" 119). More than presenting dualisms, I suggest that through the lens of neocosmicism what Lovecraft is actually presenting, what lies concealed behind the interpretive framework of adversarial oppositions in cosmicism, is the revelation of the ubiquitous paradox on which the universe is *founded* and against which the human creature has mistakenly shielded itself, believing that if it can make one side of the equation go away the other will be a stable terrain on which to place its feet.

It *is* and *is not*. The universe is the indivisible-division, the heimlich field of the unfamiliar-familiar, the *void* that is full where beginnings and endings are the same event. "In the end," Žižek writes, "we are thrown back to the beginning" (*Looking Awry* 81), and neocosmicism affirms that in ending, everything is beginning. The idea that everything will end is linked to the idea of first and final causes, which for neocosmicism are the same event; to be different implies finitude. For a materialist cosmos such as the universe as machine, because there is no external cause inasmuch as the machine is "perpetual," self-contained and mindless (*SL* 5.195), there is neither purpose nor first cause, and therefore no final cause. For a vitalist cosmos such as the Genesis cosmology an external cause, framed as a creating deity, exists and confers both purpose and first cause, with these implying also a final cause.

Neocosmicism's psychotic universe unveils the heimlich attribute of cause and purpose. What cosmicism refers to as the "outside" is simply the territory beyond the parameters of the cosmos; in neocosmicism, everything is universe. Everything will end because there is no outside, there is no external cause, and the psychotic universe is materialist by virtue of this. However, because neocosmicism's universe is also a proving ground in which the human creature can be vitalised, the universe has purpose, and in having purpose implies cause. Neocosmicism's universe is a universe of *vitalised materialism*.

The "gap . . . is abolished [in a] collapse of 'fiction' . . . and 'reality'" (Žižek, *Looking Awry* 81)—of cosmos and universe—and all that remains is the universe of chaos. Chaos is a manifest first cause, and it is the void. Neocosmicism's apocalypse is that the void manifests the human creature as a creature of chaos. The void empties the full, makes a *tabula rasa* of the human creature, so that it might be re-inscribed by chaos and re-connected with the first state of the universe. The void that is interpreted as a negative irruption of stoppage in cosmicism is all that the universe is in neocosmicism. As a young Leto says to his grandmother, Jessica Atreides, "'the entire universe with all of its time is within me . . . Whether one walks rapidly through the sietch or slowly, one traverses the sietch. And that passage of time is experienced internally'" (*CD* 95). The horizon that demarcates the content of the cosmos from all else outside that cosmos, the horizon that Virilio refers to as the "very first littoral" that separates the "void from the full" (*Open Sky* 1), is the horizon that separates the hollow object of cosmos not from empty space, but from the universe that is full. The universe is a *tabula rasa* field that both causes and is its own cause, that re-inscribes and is re-inscribed by the human creature.

The psychotic universe and the human creature are symbiotically connected. The vitalising of that creature in the proving ground is a vitalism that is without cause—first or final—without beginning or ending, because these apparent opposing poles are inscribed upon the same heimlich coin. Neither one overshadows the other. The void is the universe, and the human creature encounters the universe only when it chooses to enter the void.

When the Earth was created, according to the Genesis cosmology, so too were the heavens, the space beyond the Earth. That cosmology declares the Earth and not the heavens to have been created as empty, and indeed, as David Bohm writes, "what we call empty space contains an immense background of energy, and that matter as we know it is a small 'quantized' wavelike excitation on top of this background, rather like a tiny ripple on a vast sea" (242). Paul Atreides beholds the universe in *DM* as "a rolling sea from which no rock lifted above the chaos. No place at all from which to survey turmoil" (67). Rather than inspire Paul to seek separation from that "turmoil," however, the knowledge of the absence of stable territory leaves him "preferring the role here of a Time-fish swimming not where he willed, but where the currents carried him" (*DM* 129-30). According to Watts, "[s]pace is the *relationship* between bodies" (27), and it is Zukav's "unceasing dance of annihilation and creation" (241). From the writhing, non-linear ocean of chaos is the universe centrifugally thrown, as if from a whirlpool, a vortex; and the human creature swims in the antediluvian currents of the living, breathing, psychotic universe. The human creature that is a re-inscribed other, is the human creature romanced by the universe.

Bibliography

A. Books

Abraham, Lyndy. A *Dictionary of Alchemical Imagery*. Cambridge: Cambridge University Press, 1998.

Abrash, Merritt. "Sparring with the Universe: Heroism and Futility in Philip K. Dick's Protagonists." *Extrapolation* 27 (1986): 116-22.

Aldiss, Brian W., and David Wingrove. *Trillion Year Spree: The History of Science Fiction*. Rev. ed. London: Victor Gollancz, 1986.

Anton, Uwe, ed. *Welcome to Reality: The Nightmares of Philip K. Dick*. Cambridge, MA: Broken Mirror Press, 1991.

Asimov, Isaac. *I, Robot*. London: Panther Books, 1950.

Asma, Stephen T. *On Monsters: An Unnatural History of Our Worst Fears*. New York: Oxford University Press, 2009.

Bakhtin, Mikhail. *Rabelais and His World*. 1941. Tr. Helene Iswolsky. Bloomington: Indiana University Press, 1984.

Barron, Neil, ed. *Horror Literature: A Reader's Guide*. New York: Garland, 1990.

Baudrillard, Jean. 1981 "Simulacra and Simulations." In J. Rivkin and M. Ryan, ed. *Literary Theory: An Anthology*. 2nd ed. Malden, MA: Blackwell, 2004. 365-77.

———. *Simulations*. Tr. Paul Foss, Paul Patton, and Philip Beitchman. New York: Semiotext(e), 1983.

———. "Two Essays: 1. Simulacra and Science Fiction 2. Ballard's *Crash*." Tr. Arthur B. Evans. *Science-Fiction Studies* 18 (1991): 309-20.

Bealer, Tracy. 2011. "'The Innsmouth Look': H. P. Lovecraft's Ambivalent Modernism." *Journal of Philosophy* 6 (2011): 44-50.

Berkeley, George. *Three Dialogues Between Hylas and Philonous*. 1713. New York: Liberal Arts Press, 1954.

Bible. *The NIV Study Bible: New International Version*. Ed. Kenneth Barker. Grand Rapids, MI: Zondervan, 1985.

Blackmore, Tim. 1995. "Talking with Strangers: Interrogating the Many Texts That Became Heinlein's *Stranger in a Stranger Land*." *Extrapolation* 36 (1995): 136-50.

Blavatsky, Helena P. *The Secret Doctrine: The Synthesis of Science, Religion and Philosophy*. 1888. Pasadena, CA: Theosophical University Press, 1963. 2 vols.

Bloch, Robert. "Heritage of Horror." In H. P. Lovecraft. *The Best of H. P. Lovecraft: Bloodcurdling Tales of Horror and the Macabre*. New York: Random House, 1982. 1-14.

Bloom, Harold, and Lionel Trilling, ed. *Romantic Poetry and Prose*. Volume 4. New York: Oxford University Press, 1973.

Bohm, David. *Wholeness and the Implicate Order*. London: Routledge, 1980.

Braidotti, Rosi. *The Posthuman*. Cambridge: Polity, 2013.

Brantlinger, Patrick. "The Gothic Origins of Science Fiction." *NOVEL: A Forum on Fiction* 14 (1980): 30-43.

Bree, Germaine. *Camus and Sartre: Crisis and Commitment*. New York: Dell, 1972.

Bretnor, Reginald, ed. *The Craft of Science Fiction*. New York: Harper & Row, 1976.

Broderick, Damien, ed. *Earth Is But a Star: Excursions through Science Fiction to the Far Future*. Perth, Australia: University of Western Australia Press, 2001.

Brooke, Roger. *Jung and Phenomenology*. London: Routledge, 1991.

Bukatman, Scott. *Terminal Identity: The Virtual Subject in Postmodern Science Fiction*. Durham, NC: Duke University Press, 1993.

Burleson, Donald R. 1981. "H. P. Lovecraft: The Hawthorne Influence." *Extrapolation* 22 (1981): 262-69.

———. "Lovecraft's 'The Colour out of Space.'" *Explicator* 52 (1993): 48-50.

———. "On Lovecraft's Themes: Touching the Glass." In David E. Schultz and S. T. Joshi, ed. *An Epicure in the Terrible: A Centennial Anthology of Essays in Honor of H. P. Lovecraft*. 1991. New York: Hippocampus Press, 2011. 139-52.

Burton, Robert. *The Anatomy of Melancholy*. 1621. London: J. M. Dent & Sons, 1932.

Butler, Andrew M. "Legit-Dick." *Science-Fiction Studies* 35 (2008): 485-91.

———. *Philip K. Dick*. Rev. ed. Harpenden, UK: Pocket Essentials, 2007.

Butler, Samuel. *Erewhon*. 1872. London: Penguin, 1970.

Calvin, Ritch. "The French Dick: Villiers de l'Isle-Adam, Philip K. Dick and the Android." *Extrapolation* 48 (2007): 340-63.

Campbell, Joseph. *The Inner Reaches of Outer Space: Metaphor as Myth and as Religion*. 1986. Novato, CA: New World Library, 2002.

———. *The Masks of God*. London, UK: Souvenir Press, 1962-68. 4 vols. (vol. 1: 2nd ed. 1969).

———, and Bill Moyers. *The Power of Myth*. New York, NY: Doubleday, 1988.

Campbell, Laura E. "Dickian Time in *The Man in the High Castle*." *Extrapolation* 33 (1992): 190-201.

Camus, Albert. *The Myth of Sisyphus*. 1955. London: Penguin, 2000.

Cannon, Peter. *The Chronology out of Time: Dates in the Fiction of H. P. Lovecraft*. West Warwick, RI: Necronomicon Press, 1986.

Capra, Fritjof. *The Tao of Physics*. 2nd ed. London: Fontana Paperbacks, 1983.

Carter, Cassie. "The Metacolonization of Dick's *The Man in the High Castle*: Mimicry, Parasitism, and Americanism in the PSA." *Science-Fiction Studies* 22 (1995): 333-42.

Carter, Lin. *H. P. Lovecraft: A Look Behind the Cthulhu Mythos*. New York: Ballantine, 1972.

Casimir, Viviane. "Data and Dick's Deckard: Cyborg as Problematic Signifier." *Extrapolation* 38 (1997): 278-91.

Certeau, Michel de. *The Practice of Everyday Life*. Tr. Steven Rendall. Berkeley: University of California Press, 1984.

Chalker, Jack L. *The New H. P. Lovecraft Bibliography*. Baltimore, MD: Anthem Press, 1962.

Chambers, Robert W. *The King in Yellow*. 1895. Rockville, MD: Wildside Press, 2005.

Chambers, William, and Robert Chambers, ed. 1904. *Chambers's Encyclopaedia: A Dictionary of Universal Knowledge*. London: William & Robert Chambers, 1904.

Clareson, Thomas D., ed. *Voices for the Future: Essays on Major Science Fiction Writers.* Bowling Green, OH: Bowling Green University Popular Press, 1976.

Clarke, Arthur C. "The Nine Billion Names of God." 1953. In Robert Silverberg, ed. *A Century of Science Fiction 1950–1959: The Greatest Stories of the Decade.* New York: MJF Books, 1996. 114–21.

Clements, Nicholaus. "Lovecraft's 'The Haunter of the Dark.'" *Explicator* 57 (1999): 98–100.

Clute, John. "On the Cusp of Far." In Damien Broderick, ed. *Earth Is But a Star: Excursions through Science Fiction to the Far Future.* Perth, Australia: University of Western Australia Press, 2001. 151–63.

———. "Truth Is Consequence." In Andrew Milner, Simon Sellars, and Verity Burgmann, ed. *Changing the Climate: Utopia, Dystopia and Catastrophe.* Melbourne, Australia: Arena, 2011. 124–40.

Colavito, Jason. *Knowing Fear: Science Knowledge and the Development of the Horror Genre.* Jefferson, NC: McFarland, 2008.

Coleman, J. A. *The Dictionary of Mythology: An A–Z of Themes, Legends and Heroes.* London: Arcturus, 2007.

Collins, Andrew. *From the Ashes of Angels: The Forbidden Legacy of a Fallen Race.* London: Signet, 1997.

Connors, Scott. "Lovecraft's 'The Picture in the House.'" *Explicator* 59 (2001): 140–42.

Cooper, J. C., ed. *Brewer's Book of Myth and Legend.* Oxford: Helicon, 1992.

Cornford, Francis M. *Plato's Cosmology: The Timaeus of Plato Translated with a Running Commentary.* London: Routledge & Kegan Paul, 1937.

Crispin, Edmund. ed. *Best SF Three: Science Fiction Stories.* London: Faber & Faber, 1958.

Dalley, Stephanie, ed. *Myths from Mesopotamia: Creation, the Flood, Gilgamesh and Others,* Rev. ed. Oxford: Oxford University Press, 2000.

Dantec, Maurice G. *Babylon Babies.* Tr. Noura Wedell. New York: Semiotext(e), 2005.

Darwin, Charles. *The Origin of Species by Means of Natural Selection; or, The Preservation of Favoured Races in the Struggle for Life.* 1859. New York: Random House, 1936.

Delany, Samuel R. *The Jewel-Hinged Jaw: Notes on the Language of Science Fiction.* Elizabethtown, NY: Dragon Press, 1977.

Derleth, August. 1952. "Contemporary Science-Fiction." *English Journal* 41 (1952): 1-8.

———. "H. P. Lovecraft and His Work." In H. P. Lovecraft. *The Dunwich Horror and Others*. Sauk City, WI: Arkham House, 1963. ix-xx.

———. "H. P. Lovecraft's Novels." In H. P. Lovecraft. *At the Mountains of Madness and Other Novels*. Sauk City, WI: Arkham House, 1964. ix-xi.

Descartes, René. *Discourse on the Method of Rightly Conducting the Reason, and Seeking Truth in the Sciences*. 1637. Project Gutenberg. www.gutenberg.org/files/59/59-h/59-h.htm#part4.

Dick, Philip K. *The Collected Stories*. London: Orion, 1987. 5 vols.

———. *Do Androids Dream of Electric Sheep?* 1968. London: Orion, 2007.

———. *Five Novels of the 1960s and 70s: Martian Time Slip; Dr. Bloodmoney; Now Wait for Last Year; Flow My Tears, the Policeman Said; A Scanner Darkly*. New York: Library of America, 2008.

———. *The Shifting Realities of Philip K. Dick: Selected Literary and Philosophical Writings*. Ed. Lawrence Sutin. New York: Vintage, 1995.

———. *The Three Stigmata of Palmer Eldritch*. 1964. London: Orion, 2007.

DiTommaso, Lorenzo. "The Articulation of Imperial Decadence and Decline in Epic Science Fiction." *Extrapolation* 48 (2007): 267-91.

———. "Gnosticism and Dualism in the Early Fiction of Philip K. Dick." *Science-Fiction Studies* 28 (2001): 49-65.

———. "History and Historical Effect in Frank Herbert's *Dune*." *Science-Fiction Studies* 19 (1992): 311-25.

———. "A Logos or Two Concerning the Logoz of Umberto Rossi and Philip K. Dick's *Time out of Joint*." *Extrapolation* 39 (1998): 287-98.

———. "Redemption in Philip K. Dick's *The Man in the High Castle*." *Science-Fiction Studies* 26 (1999): 91-119.

Dunsany, Lord. *The Gods of Pegāna*. 1905. In *Time and the Gods*. London: Millennium, 2000. 531-84.

———. *Time and the Gods*. London: Millennium, 2000.

Eagleton, Terry. *Literary Theory: An Introduction*. Oxford: Basil Blackwell, 1983.

———. "Literature and Politics Now." *Critical Quarterly* 20 (1978): 65-69.

Easterbrook, Neil. "Dianoia/Paranoia: Dick's Double 'Imposter.'" In Samuel J. Umland, ed. *Philip K. Dick: Contemporary Critical Essays*. Westport, CT: Greenwood Press, 1995. 19-41.

Einstein, Albert. *The Meaning of Relativity.* 1922. Tr. Edwin Plimpton Adams, Ernst G. Straus, and Sonja Bargmann. 6th rev. ed. London: Routledge, 2003.

———. *Relativity: The Special and the General Theory.* 1916. Tr. Robert W. Lawson. 15th ed. London: Routledge, 1954.

Ellis, Bret Easton. *American Psycho.* London: Picador, 1991.

Ergang, Robert. *Europe: From the Renaissance to Waterloo.* 3rd ed. Lexington, KY: D. C. Heath, 1967.

Erisman, Fred. "Robert Heinlein, the Scribner Juveniles, and Cultural Literacy." *Extrapolation* 32 (1991): 45-53.

———. "Robert A. Heinlein's Primers of Politics." *Extrapolation* 38 (1997): 94-101.

Eshbach, Lloyd Arthur, ed. *Of Worlds Beyond: The Science of Science Fiction Writing.* Chicago: Advent Publishers, 1964.

Evans, Timothy H. "A Last Defense Against the Dark: Folklore, Horror, and the Uses of Tradition in the Works of H. P. Lovecraft." *Journal of Folklore Research* 42 (2005): 99-135.

———. "Tradition and Illusion: Antiquarianism, Tourism and Horror in H. P. Lovecraft." *Extrapolation* 45 (2004): 176-95.

Faivre, Antoine. *The Eternal Hermes: From Greek God to Alchemical Magus.* Tr. Joscelyn Godwin. Grand Rapids, MI: Phanes Press, 1995.

Farnell, David. "Unlikely Utopians: Ecotopian Dreaming in H. P. Lovecraft's 'The Shadow over Innsmouth' and Octavia Butler's *Lilith's Brood.*" In Andrew Milner, Simon Sellars, and Verity Burgmann, ed. *Changing the Climate: Utopia, Dystopia and Catastrophe.* Melbourne, Australia: Arena Publications, 2011. 141-56.

Ferber, Michael. *The Poetry of William Blake.* London: Penguin, 1991.

Finocchiaro, Maurice A., ed. *The Essential Galileo.* Indianapolis, IN: Hackett, 2008.

Foucault, Michel. *Discipline and Punish: The Birth of the Prison.* 1975. Tr. Alan Sheridan. London: Penguin, 1977.

———. *Madness and Civilisation: A History of Insanity in the Age of Reason.* 1961. Tr. Richard Howard. London: Routledge, 1967.

Freud, Sigmund. "Group Psychology and the Analysis of the Ego." 1921. In Julie Rivkin and Michael Ryan, ed. *Literary Theory: An Anthology.* Malden, MA: Blackwell, 2004. 438-40.

———. *The Interpretation of Dreams.* 1900. Tr. A. A. Brill. Ware, UK: Wordsworth Editions, 1997.

———. *Three Essays on the Theory of Sexuality.* 1962. Tr. James. Strachey. New York: Basic Books, 1975.

———. *Totem and Taboo: Some Points of Agreement Between the Mental Lives of Savages and Neurotics.* 1913. Tr. James Strachey. London: Routledge, 1950.

———. "The Uncanny." 1919. In Julie Rivkin and Michael Ryan, ed. *Literary Theory: An Anthology.* 2nd ed. Malden, MA: Blackwell, 2004. 418-30.

Frost, Andrew. "The Colour of Nothing: Contemporary Video Art, SF and the Postmodern Sublime." Paper presented at Changing the Climate: The Fourth Australian Conference on Utopia, Dystopia and Science Fiction. Melbourne, Australia: Monash University 2010.

Galilei, Galileo. *Dialogue concerning the Two Chief World Systems.* 1632. Tr. Stillman Drake. 2nd ed. Berkeley: University of California Press, 1967.

Galvan, Jill. "Entering the Posthuman Collective in Philip K. Dick's *Do Androids Dream of Electric Sheep?*" *Science-Fiction Studies* 24 (1997): 413-29.

George, David. E. R. "Quantum Theatre–Potential Theatre: A New Paradigm?" *New Theatre Quarterly* 5 (1989): 171-79.

Gillespie, Bruce, ed. *Philip K. Dick: Electric Shepherd.* Melbourne, Australia: Norstrilia Press, 1975.

Gillis, Ryan. "Dick on the Human: From Wubs to Bounty Hunters to Bishops." *Extrapolation* 39 (1998): 264-71.

Godwin, Tom. "The Cold Equations." 1954. In Edmund Crispin. ed. *Best SF Three: Science Fiction Stories.* London: Faber & Faber, 1958. 93-118.

Golden, Kenneth L. "*Stranger in a Strange Land* as Modern Myth: Robert A. Heinlein and Carl Jung." *Extrapolation* 27 (1986): 295-303.

Goodman, Martin. *The Roman World 44 BC–AD 180.* London: Routledge, 1997.

Goodrick, Edward W., and John R. Kohlenberger, ed. *The NIV Exhaustive Concordance.* Grand Rapids, MI: Zondervan, 1990.

Gray, Chris Hables. *Cyborg Citizen: Politics in the Posthuman Age.* New York: Routledge, 2001.

———, ed. *The Cyborg Handbook.* New York: Routledge, 1995.

Grazier, Kevin R., ed. *The Science of Dune*. Dallas, TX: Benbella, 2008.

Grebowicz, Margaret, ed. *SciFi in the Mind's Eye: Reading Science through Science Fiction*. Chicago: Open Court, 2007.

Greenham, Ellen. J. "Vision and Desire: Jim Morrison's Mythography Beyond the Death of God." Unpublished Research, Edith Cowan University, Perth, Australia, 2008.

Gribbin, John. *In Search of the Multiverse*. London: Allen Lane, 2009.

Halperin, Paul, and Michael. Labossiere. "Mind out of Time: Identity, Perception, and the Fourth Dimension in H. P. Lovecraft's 'The Shadow out of Time' and 'The Dreams in the Witch House.'" *Extrapolation* 50 (2009): 512-33.

Hamilton, Edith. *Mythology*. New York: Warner, 1969.

Hammond, J. R. *An H. G. Wells Companion*. London: Macmillan, 1979.

Haney, William S. *Cyberculture, Cyborgs and Science Fiction: Consciousness and the Posthuman*. New York: Rodopi, 2006.

Haraway, Donna. "A Cyborg Manifesto: Science, Technology, and Socialist-Feminism in the Late Twentieth Century." *Socialist Review* (1985): 28-37.

Hayles, N. Katherine. *How We Became Posthuman: Virtual Bodies in Cybernetics, Literature, and Information*. Chicago: University of Chicago Press, 1999.

Hegel, Georg Wilhelm Friedrich. *Science of Logic*. 1816. Tr. A. V. Miller. London: George Allen & Unwin, 1969.

Heinlein, Robert A. *Expanded Universe*. 1980. New York: Baen, 2003.

———. *The Fantasies of Robert A. Heinlein*. New York: Tor, 1999.

———. "Guest of Honor Speech at the Third World Science Fiction Convention Denver, 1941." In Yoji Kondo, ed. *Requiem: Collected Works and Tributes to the Grand Master*. New York: Tor, 1992. 153-67.

———. "Guest of Honor Speech at the XIXth World Science Fiction Convention, Seattle, 1961: The Future Revisited." In Yoji Kondo, ed. *Requiem: New Collected Works by Robert A. Heinlein and Tributes to the Grand Master*. New York: Tor, 1992. 168-97.

———. "Guest of Honor Speech at the XXXIVth World Science Fiction Convention." 1976. In Yoji Kondo, ed. *Requiem: New Collected Works by Robert A. Heinlein and Tributes to the Grand Master*. New York: Tor, 1992. 205-13.

———. *The Moon Is a Harsh Mistress.* 1966. London: New English Library, 1979.

———. "On the Writing of Speculative Fiction." 1947. In Lloyd Arthur Eshbach, ed. *Of Worlds Beyond: The Science of Science Fiction Writing.* Chicago: Advent Publishers, 1964. 11-19.

———. *Requiem: New Collected Works by Robert A. Heinlein and Tributes to the Grand Master.* Ed. Yoji Kondo. New York: Tor, 1992.

———. *Rocketship Galileo.* London: New English Library, 1947.

———. *Starship Troopers.* London: New English Library, 1959.

———. *Stranger in a Strange Land.* 1961. New York: Berkley, 2003.

———. "This I Believe: A Credo for 2089 and Beyond." *The Humanist* 49 (1989): 16.

———. *Time Enough for Love.* New York: Ace, 1973.

———. *2 × Robert A. Heinlein: Revolt in 2100 and Methuselah's Children.* New York: Baen, 1999.

———. *Tunnel in the Sky.* London: Pan, 1955.

Heisenberg, Werner Karl. *Physics and Philosophy: The Revolution in Modern Science.* London: Allen & Unwin, 1958.

Herbert, Brian, and Kevin J. Anderson. *Legends of Dune I: The Butlerian Jihad.* London: Hodder & Stoughton, 2002.

Herbert, Frank. 1954. *Chapterhouse Dune.* London: New English Library, 1985.

———. *Children of Dune.* London: New English Library, 1976.

———. *Dune.* 1965. London: New English Library, 1978.

———. *Dune Messiah.* 1969. London: New English Library, 1979.

———. *God Emperor of Dune.* London: New English Library, 1981.

———. *Heretics of Dune.* London: New English Library, 1984.

———. "Men on Other Planets." In Reginald Bretnor, ed. *The Craft of Science Fiction.* New York: Harper & Row, 1976. 121-35.

———. "Pack Rat Planet." *Astounding Science-Fiction* 54 (December 1954): 121-42.

———; Herbert, Brian; and Anderson, Kevin J. *The Road to Dune.* London: Hodder & Stoughton, 2005.

Hodgson, William Hope. *The House on the Borderland.* 1908. London: Penguin, 2008.

Holliday, Valerie. "Masculinity in the Novels of Philip K. Dick." *Extrapolation* 47 (2006): 280-95.
Houellebecq, Michel. *H. P. Lovecraft: Against the World, Against Life.* Tr. Dorna Khazeni. London: Gollancz, 2005.
Huang, Betsy. "Premodern Orientalist Science Fictions." *MELUS* 33 (2008): 23-43.
Ingebretsen, Edward J. *Maps of Heaven, Maps of Hell: Religious Terror as Memory from the Puritans to Stephen King.* Armonk, NY: M. E. Sharpe, 1996.
Istvan, Csicsery-Ronay, Jr. "Science Fiction and the Thaw." *Science-Fiction Studies* 31 (2004): 337-344.
Jackson, Pamela Renee. "The World Philip K. Dick Made." Ph.D. thesis: University of California, Berkeley, 1999.
James, Edward. 2003. "Utopias and Anti-Utopias." In Edward James and Farah Mendlesohn, ed. *The Cambridge Companion to Science Fiction.* Cambridge: Cambridge University Press, 2003. 219-29.
James, Edward, and Farah Mendlesohn, ed. *The Cambridge Companion to Science Fiction.* Cambridge: Cambridge University Press, 2003.
Jameson, Fredric. *Archaeologies of the Future: The Desire Called Utopia and Other Science Fictions.* London: Verso, 2007.
———. "Science Versus Ideology." *Humanities in Society* 6 (1983): 283-302.
———. *Signatures of the Visible.* London: Routledge, 1992.
Janicker, Rebecca. "New England Narratives: Space and Place in the Fiction of H. P. Lovecraft." *Extrapolation* 48 (2007): 56-72.
Joshi, S. T. *The Evolution of the Weird Tale.* New York: Hippocampus Press, 2004.
———. *H. P. Lovecraft: The Decline of the West.* 1990. Berkeley Heights, NJ: Wildside Press, 2000.
———. *Lovecraft's Library: A Catalogue.* 2nd ed. New York: Hippocampus Press, 2002.
———. "On Rottensteiner on Lovecraft in SFS #56." *Science-Fiction Studies* 19 (1992): 437-39.
———. *Primal Sources: Essays on H. P. Lovecraft.* New York: Hippocampus Press, 2003.
———. *A Subtler Magick: The Writings and Philosophy of H.P. Lovecraft.* San Bernardino, CA: Borgo Press, 1996.

———, and Marc A. Michaud, ed. *H. P. Lovecraft in "The Eyrie."* West Warwick, RI: Necronomicon Press, 1979.

———, and David E. Schultz. *An H. P. Lovecraft Encyclopedia.* 2001. New York: Hippocampus Press, 2004.

Jung, C. G. *The Archetypes and the Collective Unconscious.* 1959. Tr. R. F. C. Hull. 2nd ed. Princeton, NJ: Princeton University Press, 1968.

———. *Critiques of Psychoanalysis.* Tr. R. F. C. Hull. Princeton, NJ: Princeton University Press, 1975.

———. *Four Archetypes: Mother, Rebirth, Spirit, Trickster.* 1953. 2nd ed. London: Routledge, 2001.

———. *The Portable Jung.* Ed. Joseph Campbell. New York: Penguin, 1976.

King, Stephen. *Danse Macabre.* London: Warner, 1981.

———. *On Writing: A Memoir of the Craft.* London: Hodder & Stoughton, 2000.

Kiyoko, Magome. "The Player Piano and Musico-Cybernetic Science Fiction between the 1950s and the 1980s: Kurt Vonnegut and Philip K. Dick." *Extrapolation* 45 (2004): 370-87.

Kluger, Daniel. "Fables of Desire." *Science-Fiction Studies* 31 (2004): 415-17.

Kneale, James. "From Beyond: H. P. Lovecraft and the Place of Horror." *Cultural Geographies* 13 (Issue 1, 2006): 106-26.

Kocsis, Sacha.; Braverman, Boris; Ravets, Sylvain; Stevens, Martin J.; Mirin, Richard P.; Shalm, L. Krister., et al. "Observing the Average Trajectories of Single Photons in a Two-Slit Interferometer." *Science* 332 (2011): 1170-73.

Korzybski, Alfred. *Manhood of Humanity: The Science and Art of Human Engineering.* 1921. Gloucester, UK: Dodo Press, 2008.

———. *Science and Sanity: An Introduction to Non-Aristotelian Systems and General Semantics.* 1933. 4th ed. Lakeville, MN: International Non-Aristotelian Library Publishing Co., 1958.

Krabbenhoft, Kenneth. "Uses of Madness in Cervantes and Philip K. Dick." *Science-Fiction Studies* 27 (2000): 216-33.

Kristeva, Julia. *Powers of Horror: An Essay on Abjection.* 1980. New York: Columbia University Press, 1982.

Krutch, Joseph Wood. *The Modern Temper: A Study and a Confession.* 1929. New York: Harcourt, Brace & World, 1956.

Kucera, Paul Q. "Listening to Ourselves: Herbert's *Dune*, 'the Voice' and Performing the Absolute." *Extrapolation* 42 (2001): 232-45.

Lacan, Jacques. *Écrits: A Selection*. 1966. Tr. A. Sheridan. London: Routledge, 1977.

———. "The Mirror Stage as Formative of the Function of the I as Revealed in the Psychoanalytic Experience." 1949. In Julie Rivkin and Michael Ryan, ed. *Literary Theory: An Anthology*. 2nd ed. Malden. MA: Blackwell, 2004. 441-46.

Laing, R. D. *The Divided Self*. New York: Pantheon, 1960.

Lee, Gwen, and Doris Elaine Sauter, ed. *What If Our World Is Their Heaven? The Final Conversations of Philip K. Dick*. London: Duckworth., 2006.

Lee, Penny. *The Whorf Theory Complex: A Critical Reconstruction*. Amsterdam: John Benjamins Publishing Co., 1996.

Leiber, Fritz; Bloch, Robert; Russell, Samuel D.; Cox, Arthur Jean; and Sapiro, Leland. *H. P. Lovecraft: A Symposium*. 1963. Folcroft, PA: Folcroft Library Editions, 1972.

Letson, Russell. 1978. "The Returns of Lazarus Long." In Joseph D. Olander and Martin Harry Greenberg, ed. *Robert A. Heinlein*. Edinburgh: Paul Harris Publishing, 1978. 194-221.

List, Julia. 2009. "'Call Me a Protestant': Liberal Christianity, Individualism, and the Messiah in *Stranger in a Strange Land*, *Dune*, and *Lord of Light*." *Science-Fiction Studies* 36 (2009): 21-47.

Lovecraft, H. P. *The Ancient Track: The Complete Poetical Works of H. P. Lovecraft*. Ed. S. T. Joshi. San Francisco: Night Shade, 2001.

———. *The Annotated Supernatural Horror in Literature*. 2000. 2nd ed. Ed. S. T. Joshi. New York: Hippocampus Press, 2012.

———. *At the Mountains of Madness and Other Novels*. Sauk City, WI: Arkham House, 1964.

———. *The Best of H. P. Lovecraft: Bloodcurdling Tales of Horror and the Macabre*. New York: Random House, 1982.

———. *Collected Essays*. Ed. S. T. Joshi. New York: Hippocampus Press, 2004-06. 5 vols.

———. *Collected Fiction: A Variorum Edition*. Ed. S. T. Joshi. New York: Hippocampus Press, 2015-17. 4 vols.

———. *The Dunwich Horror and Others*. Sauk City, WI: Arkham House, 1963.

———. *Selected Letters 1911-1937*. Ed. August Derleth, Donald Wandrei, and James Turner. Sauk City, WI: Arkham House, 1965-76.

Lovett-Graff, Bennett. "Shadows over Lovecraft: Reactionary Fantasy and Immigrant Eugenics." *Extrapolation* 38 (1997): 175-92.

Lowell, Mark. "Lovecraft's CTHULHU MYTHOS." *Explicator* 63 (2004): 47-50.

Luckhurst, Roger. "Border Policing: Postmodernism and Science Fiction." *Science-Fiction Studies* 18 (1991): 358-66.

———. *Science Fiction*. Cambridge: Polity Press, 2005.

Lyell, Charles. *Principles of Geology: Being an Attempt to Explain the Former Changes of the Earth's Surface, by Reference to Causes now in Operation*. 1830-33. Lehre, Germany: J. Cramer Publishing, 1970. 3 vols.

McAuliffe, Jane Dammen, ed. *Encyclopaedia of the Qur'an*. Leiden, Netherlands: Koninklijke Brill, 2003.

McCarthy, Cormac. *The Road*. 2006. London: Picador, 2009.

Macdonald, Gina. "Frank Herbert." In Jay. P. Pederson, ed. *St. James Guide to Science Fiction Writers*. 4th ed. New York: St. James Press, 1996. 432-36.

McGiveron, Rafeeq O. "From Free Love to the Free-Fire Zone: Heinlein's Mars, 1939-1987." *Extrapolation* 42 (2001): 137-49.

———. "He 'Just Plain Liked Guns': Robert A. Heinlein and the 'Older Orthodoxy' of an Armed Citizenry." *Extrapolation* 45 (2004): 389-407.

———. "'Maybe the Hardest Job of All—Particularly When You Have No Talent for It': Heinlein's Fictional Parents, 1939-1987." *Extrapolation* 44 (2003): 169-200.

McGuirk, Carol. "Nowhere Man: Towards a Poetics of Post-Utopian Characterization." *Science-Fiction Studies* 21 (1994): 141-54.

Machen, Arthur. *Tales of Horror and the Supernatural*. Volume 2. Frogmore, UK: Panther, 1964.

McNelly, Willis E. *The Dune Encyclopedia*. New York: Berkley, 1984.

Malmgren, Carl. "Meta-SF: The Examples of Dick, LeGuin, and Russ." *Extrapolation* 43 (2002): 22-35.

Mariconda, Steven J. "Lovecraft's Concept of Background." *Lovecraft Studies* No. 12 (Spring 1986): 3-12.

———. "Lovecraft's Cosmic Imagery." In David E. Schultz and S. T. Joshi, ed. *An Epicure in the Terrible: A Centennial Anthology of Essays in*

Honor of H. P. Lovecraft. 1991. New York: Hippocampus Press, 2011. 196-207.

Marinis, Marco de, and Paul Dwyer. "Dramaturgy of the Spectator." *Drama Review* 31 (1987): 100-114.

Maxwell, Anne. "Eugenics and the Classical Ideal of Beauty in Philip K. Dick's 'The Golden Man.'" *Science-Fiction Studies* 36 (2009): 87-100.

Mendlesohn, Farah. "Introduction: Reading Science Fiction." In Edward James and Farah Mendlesohn, ed. *The Cambridge Companion to Science Fiction.* Cambridge: Cambridge University Press. 2003. 1-12.

Merleau-Ponty, Maurice. *Phenomenology of Perception.* 1954. Tr. C. Smith. London: Routledge, 1958.

Milner, Andrew; Sellars, Simon; and Burgmann, Verity, ed. *Changing the Climate: Utopia, Dystopia and Catastrophe.* Melbourne, Australia: Arena, 2011.

Mulcahy, Kevin. "The Prince on Arrakis: Frank Herbert's Dialogue with Machiavelli." *Extrapolation* 37 (1996): 22-36.

Nelson, Victoria. "H. P. Lovecraft and the Great Heresies." *Raritan* 15 (1996): 92-121.

Nickelsburg, George W. E., and James C. VanderKam, ed. *1 Enoch: A New Translation Based on the Hermeneia Commentary.* Minneapolis, MN: Augsburg Fortress, 2004.

Nietzsche, Friedrich. *The Birth of Tragedy and The Case of Wagner.* Tr. Walter Kaufmann. New York: Vintage, 1967.

———. *The Gay Science: with a Prelude in Rhymes and an Appendix of Songs.* 1887. Tr. Walter Kaufmann. New York: Vintage, 1974.

———. *The Portable Nietzsche.* Ed. Walter Kaufmann. London: Penguin, 1954.

———. *The Will to Power.* Tr. Walter Kaufmann and R. J. Hollingdale. New York: Vintage, 1968.

Nisan, Noam, and Schimon Schocken. *The Elements of Computing Systems: Building a Modern Computer from First Principles.* Cambridge, MA: MIT Press, 2005.

Olander, Joseph D., and Martin Harry. Greenberg, ed. *Robert A. Heinlein.* Edinburgh: Paul Harris, 1978.

Olivier, Christiane. *Jocasta's Children: The Imprint of the Mother.* Tr. George Craig. London: Routledge, 1989.

Onions, C. T., ed. *The Oxford Dictionary of Etymology.* Oxford: Oxford University Press, 1969.

O'Reilly, Tim, ed. *The Maker of Dune: Insights of a Master of Science Fiction.* New York: Berkley, 1987.

Orwell, George. "Good Bad Books." 1945. In *The Collected Essays, Journalism and Letters of George Orwell.* Ed. Sonia Orwell and Ian Angus. Harmondsworth, UK: Penguin, 1968. 4.37–41.

Orwell, Sonia, and Ian Angus, ed. *The Collected Essays, Journalism and Letters of George Orwell.* Harmondsworth, UK: Penguin, 1968.

Palmer, Christopher. "Critique and Fantasy in Two Novels by Philip K. Dick." *Extrapolation* 32 (1991): 222–34.

———. *Philip K. Dick: Exhilaration and Terror of the Postmodern.* Liverpool: Liverpool University Press, 2003.

———. "Postmodernism and the Birth of the Author in Philip K. Dick's *Valis*." *Science-Fiction Studies* 18 (1991): 330–42.

Palumbo, Donald. *Chaos Theory, Asimov's Foundations and Robots, and Herbert's Dune: The Fractal Aesthetic of Epic Science Fiction.* Westport, CT: Greenwood Press, 2002.

———. "The Monomyth as Fractal Pattern in Frank Herbert's *Dune* Novels." *Science-Fiction Studies* 25 (1998): 433–58.

Panshin, Alexi. *Heinlein in Dimension: A Critical Analysis.* Chicago: Advent Publishers, 1968.

Parkerson, Ronny W. "Semantics, General Semantics, and Ecology in Frank Herbert's *Dune*." *et Cetera* 55 (1998): 317–28.

Parrett, Aaron. 2003. "Tripping Down the Totalitarian Path with PKD." *Science-Fiction Studies* 30 (2003): 513–14.

Pederson, Jay P., ed. *St. James Guide to Science Fiction Writers.* 4th ed. New York: St. James Press, 1996.

Piazza, L.; Lummen, T. T. A.; Quinonez, E.; Murooka, Y.; Reed, B. W.; Barwick, B., et al. "Simultaneous Observation of the Quantization and the Interference Pattern of a Plasmonic Near-Field." *Nature Communications* 6 (2015): 6407.

Pirsig, Robert M. *Zen and the Art of Motorcycle Maintenance: An Inquiry into Values.* London: Vintage, 1974.

Plank, Robert. 1978. "Omnipotent Cannibals in *Stranger in a Strange Land*." In Joseph D. Olander and Martin Harry. Greenberg, ed. *Robert A. Heinlein.* Edinburgh: Paul Harris, 1978. 83–106.

Potin, Yves. "Four Levels of Reality in Philip K. Dick's *Time out of Joint*." *Extrapolation* 39 (1998): 148–65.

Price, Cynthia. "A Heinlein Child Pays Homage to the Master." *et Cetera* 64 (2007): 349–53.

Price, Robert M. "H. P. Lovecraft: Prophet of Humanism." *Humanist* 61 (2001): 26–29.

Reno, Shaun. "The Zuni Indian Tribe: A Model for *Stranger in a Strange Land*'s Martian Culture." *Extrapolation* 36 (1995): 151–58.

Rickman, Gregg, ed. *The Science Fiction Film Reader*. New York: Limelight Editions, 2004.

Rivkin, Julie and Michael Ryan, ed. *Literary Theory: An Anthology*. 2nd ed. Malden, MA: Blackwell, 2004.

Robb, Brian J. *Counterfeit Worlds: Philip K. Dick on Film*. London: Titan, 2006.

Roberts, Ian F. "Olympia's Daughters: E. T. A. Hoffmann and Philip K. Dick." *Science-Fiction Studies* 37 (2010): 150–53.

Rosa, Jorge Martins. "A Misreading Gone Too Far? Baudrillard Meets Philip K. Dick." *Science-Fiction Studies* 35 (2008): 60–71.

Rose, Lois, and Stephen Rose. *The Shattered Ring: Science Fiction and the Quest for Meaning*. Richmond, VA: John Knox Press, 1970.

Rose, Mark. *Alien Encounter: Anatomy of Science Fiction*. Cambridge, MA: Harvard University Press, 1981.

Rossi, Umberto. "Fourfold Symmetry: The Interplay of Fictional Levels in Five More or Less Prestigious Novels by Philip K. Dick." *Extrapolation* 43 (2002): 398–419.

———. "The Game of the Rat: A. E. Van Vogt's 800-Word Rule and P. K. Dick's The Game-Players of Titan." *Science-Fiction Studies* 31 (2004): 207–26.

Rottensteiner, Franz. "In Response to S. T. Joshi." *Science-Fiction Studies* 19 (1992): 439.

———. "Lovecraft as Philosopher." *Science-Fiction Studies* 19 (1992): 117–21.

Russell, Bertrand. *History of Western Philosophy*. London: Routledge, 1946.

Russell, D. A., and M. Winterbottom, ed. *Classical Literary Criticism*. Oxford: Oxford University Press, 1989.

Sagan, Carl. *Cosmos*. New York: Ballantine, 1980.

St. Armand, Barton Levi. "Poe's Landscape of the Soul: Association Theory and 'The Fall of the House of Usher.'" *Modern Language Studies* 7 (1977): 32-41.

———. *The Roots of Horror in the Fiction of H. P. Lovecraft*. Elizabethtown, NY: Dragon Press, 1977.

Samuelson, David N. "The Frontier Worlds of Robert A. Heinlein." In Thomas D. Clareson, ed. *Voices for the Future: Essays on Major Science Fiction Writers*. Bowling Green, OH: Bowling Green University Popular Press, 1976. 104-52.

Santillana, Georgio. de. *The Origins of Scientific Thought: From Anaximander to Proclus 600 B.C. to 300 A.D.* Chicago: University of Chicago Press, 1961.

Sartre, Jean-Paul. *Being and Nothingness*. Tr. H. E. Barnes. New York: Simon & Schuster, 1956.

Scholes, Robert, and Eric S. Rabkin. *Science Fiction: History, Science, Vision*. New York: Oxford University Press, 1977.

Schrödinger, Erwin. *My View of the World*. Cambridge: Cambridge University Press, 1964.

Schultz, David E. "From Microcosm to Macrocosm: The Growth of Lovecraft's Cosmic Vision." In David E. Schultz and S. T. Joshi, ed. *An Epicure in the Terrible: A Centennial Anthology of Essays in Honor of H. P. Lovecraft*. 1991. New York: Hippocampus Press, 2011. 208-29.

———, and S. T. Joshi, ed. *An Epicure in the Terrible: A Centennial Anthology of Essays in Honor of H. P. Lovecraft*. 1991. New York: Hippocampus Press, 2011.

Schweitzer, Darrell. *The Dream Quest of H. P. Lovecraft*. San Bernadino, CA: Borgo Press, 1978.

———. *Pathways to Elfland: The Writings of Lord Dunsany*. Philadelphia: Owlswick Press, 1989.

———, ed. *Discovering H. P. Lovecraft*. Holicong, PA: Wildside Press, 2001.

Selden, Raman; Widdowson, Peter; and Brooker, Peter. *A Reader's Guide to Contemporary Literary Theory*. 4th ed. London: Prentice Hall, 1997.

Seligmann, Kurt. *The History of Magic*. 1948. New York: Pantheon, 1997.

Shippey, Tom. "On Which Planet?" *Times Literary Supplement* (2 October 2009): 21-22.

Shreffler, Philip A. *The H. P. Lovecraft Companion.* Westport, CT: Greenwood Press, 1977.

Silverberg, Robert, ed. *A Century of Science Fiction 1950–1959: The Greatest Stories of the Decade.* New York: MJF Books, 1996.

Simpson, J. A., and E. S. C. Weiner, ed. *The Oxford English Dictionary.* 2nd. ed. Oxford: Oxford University Press, 1989.

Sims, Christopher A. "The Dangers of Individualisation and the Human Relationship to Technology in Philip K. Dick's *Do Androids Dream of Electric Sheep?*" *Science-Fiction Studies* 36 (2009): 67–86.

Slusser, George. *The Classic Years of Robert A. Heinlein.* 1977. Rockville, MD: Wildside Press, 2006.

———. "Heinlein's Fallen Futures." *Extrapolation* 36 (1995): 96–112.

———. *Robert A. Heinlein Stranger in His Own Land.* 2nd ed. San Bernadino, CA: Borgo Press, 1977.

———. "Robert Heinlein." In Jay P. Pederson, ed. *St. James Guide to Science Fiction Writers.* 4th ed. New York: St. James Press, 1996. 426–30.

Smith, Nicholas; Allhoff, Fritz; and Vaidya, Anand Jayprakash, ed. *Ancient Philosophy: Essential Readings with Commentary.* Malden, MA: Blackwell, 2008.

Sondergard, Sid. "Mapping the Lovecraft Idiolect: Iterative Structures and Autosemiotization as Reading Strategies." *American Journal of Semiotics* 18 (2002): 87–107.

Stableford, Brian. *The A–Z Guide of Science Fiction Literature.* Lanham, MD: Scarecrow Press, 2005.

Sterling, Bruce. *Crystal Express.* Sauk City, WI: Arkham House, 1989.

———. "Swarm." In *Crystal Express.* Sauk City, WI: Arkham House, 1989. 3–26.

Stratton, Susan. "The Messiah and the Greens: The Shape of Environmental Action in *Dune* and *Pacific Edge.*" *Extrapolation* 42 (2001): 303–16.

Strugatsky, Arkady, and Boris Strugatsky. *Roadside Picnic.* 1971. London, UK: Orion, 2007.

Stuckenbruck, Loren T., ed. *The Book of Giants from Qumran: Text, Translation and Commentary.* Tübingen, Germany: Mohr Siebeck, 1997.

Stypczynski, Brent. "No Roads Lead to Rome: Alternate History and Secondary Worlds." *Extrapolation* 46 (2005): 453–68.

Sutin, Lawrence. *Divine Invasions: A Life of Philip K. Dick.* New York: Citadel Press, 1989.

Suvin, Darko. "Considering the Sense of 'Fantasy' or 'Fantastic Fiction': An Effusion." *Extrapolation* 41 (2000): 209-47.

———. "Goodbye and Hello: Differentiating Within the Later P. K. Dick." *Extrapolation* 43 (2002): 368-97.

———. "On the Poetics of the Science Fiction Genre." *College English* 34 (1972): 372-82.

Szonyi, Gyorgy E. *John Dee's Occultism: Magical Exaltation through Powerful Signs.* Albany: State University of New York Press, 2004.

Tepper, Sheri S. *Sideshow.* London: Harper Collins, 1992.

Tillich, Paul. *The Courage to Be.* London: Fontana, 1952.

Tolley, Michael J. 1980. "Beyond the Enigma: Dick's Questors." In Michael J. Tolley and Kirpal Singh, ed. *The Stellar Gauge: Essays on Science Fiction.* Melbourne, Australia: Norstrilla Press, 1980. 199-237.

Michael J. Tolley, Michael J. and Kirpal Singh, ed. *The Stellar Gauge: Essays on Science Fiction.* Melbourne, Australia: Norstrilla Press, 1980.

Turner, Victor. *Dramas, Fields, and Metaphors: Symbolic Action in Human Society.* Ithaca, NY: Cornell University Press, 1974.

———. *From Ritual to Theatre: The Human Seriousness of Play.* New York: PAJ Publications, 1982.

Tyree, J. M. "Lovecraft at the Automat." *New England Review* 29 (2008): 137-50.

Umland, Samuel J., ed. *Philip K. Dick: Contemporary Critical Interpretations.* Westport, CT: Greenwood Press, 1995.

Valle, Ronald. S., and Rolf von Eckartsberg, ed. *The Metaphors of Consciousness.* 1981. New York: Plenum Press, 1989.

VanderMeer, Jeff. "Precious Ambergris." *Locus* 49 (2002): 76-78.

Virilio, Paul. *Grey Ecology.* Tr. Drew. Burk. New York: Atropos Press, 2009.

———. *Open Sky.* 1997. Tr. Julie. Rose. London: Verso, 2008.

Walters, F. Scott. "The Final Trilogy of Philip K. Dick." *Extrapolation* 38 (1997): 222-35.

Watson, Nelle, and Paul E. Schellinger, ed. *Twentieth-Century Science Fiction Writers.* 3rd ed. Chicago: St. James Press, 1991.

Watts, Alan. *The Book: On the Taboo Against Knowing Who You Are*. 1966. New York: Vintage, 1989.

Waugh, Robert H. "Landscapes, Selves and Others in Lovecraft." In David E. Schultz and S. T. Joshi, ed. *An Epicure in the Terrible: A Centennial Anthology of Essays in Honor of H. P. Lovecraft*. 1991. New York: Hippocampus Press, 2011. 230-55.

Weber, Renee. "Reflections of David Bohm's Holomovement: A Physicist's Model of Cosmos and Consciousness." In Ronald S. Valle and Rolf Von Eckartsberg, ed. *The Metaphors of Consciousness*. New York: Plenum Press, 1981. 121-40.

Wegner, Phillip E. "Jameson's Modernisms; or, the Desire Called Utopia." *Diacritics* 37 (2007): 3-20.

Weiskel, Thomas. *The Romantic Sublime*. Baltimore: Johns Hopkins University Press, 1976.

Wells, H. G. *The Sleeper Awakes*. 1899. London: Penguin, 2005.

———. *The War of the Worlds*. 1898. In *The Time Machine: Complete and Unabridged*. London: William Heinemann, 1983. 9-195.

Westermann, Claus. *Genesis 1-11: A Commentary*. 1974. Tr. J. J. Scullion. London: SPCK, 1984.

Will, Bradley. "H. P. Lovecraft and the Semiotic Kantian Sublime." *Extrapolation* 43 (2002): 7-21.

Williams, Donna Glee. "The Moons of LeGuin and Heinlein." *Science-Fiction Studies* 21 (1994): 164-72.

Wolfe, Cary. *What Is Posthumanism?* Minneapolis: University of Minnesota Press, 2010.

Wright, D. E. "General Semantics as Source Material in the Works of Robert A. Heinlein." *et Cetera* 68 (2011): 92-109.

Wynne-Davies, Marion, ed. *Bloomsbury Guide to English Literature*. London: Bloomsbury, 1992.

Yates, Frances. *Giordano Bruno and the Hermetic Tradition*. 1964. London: Routledge, 2002.

Yeats, W. B. *Poems of W. B. Yeats: A New Selection*. Ed. A. Norman Jeffares. London: Macmillan, 1984.

Zeender, Marie-Noelle. "The 'Moi-peau' of Leto II in Herbert's Atreides Saga." *Science-Fiction Studies* 22 (1995): 226-33.

Žižek, Slavoj. "Afterword: Lenin's Choice." In Slavoj Zizek, ed. *Revolution at the Gates: A Selection of Writings from February to October 1917*. New York: Verso, 2002.

———. *Looking Awry: An Introduction to Jacques Lacan through Popular Culture*. Cambridge, MA: MIT Press, 1991.

———. "Notes on a Debate 'From Within the People.'" *Criticism* 46 (2004): 661–66.

———, ed. *Revolution at the Gates: A Selection of Writings from February to October 1917*. New York: Verso, 2002.

Zoreda, M. L. "Bakhtin, Blobels and Philip Dick." *Journal of Popular Culture* 28 (1994): 55–61.

Zukav, Gary. *The Dancing Wu Li Masters*. 1979. New York: Perennial Classics, 2001.

B. Films, Television Shows, and Computer Games

Alien. 20th Century Fox, 1979.
Alien: Covenant. 20th Century Fox, 2017.
Blade Runner. Warner Brothers, 1982.
The Book of Eli. Sony Pictures, 2010.
The Cell. Roadshow, 2000.
Children of Men. Universal, 2006.
The Chronicles of Riddick. Universal, 2004.
Contagion. Warner Brothers, 2011.
Dark City: Director's Cut. Reel, 1998.
Dawn of the Planet of the Apes. Twentieth Century Fox, 2014.
The Day After Tomorrow. 20th Century Fox, 2004.
Daybreakers. Lionsgate, 2009.
Dune. Warner Brothers, 2021.
Elysium. TriStar, 2013.
Event Horizon. Paramount, 1997.
Foundation. Skydance Television, 2021.
Gladiator. Columbia Tristar, 2000.

Hellraiser. New World Pictures, 1987.
The Hero's Journey: The World of Joseph Campbell. Acacia, 1987.
The History Boys. 20th Century Fox, 2006.
I Am Legend. Warner Brothers, 2007.
In the Mouth of Madness. Roadshow, 1994.
Interstellar. Paramount, 2014.
Joseph Campbell and the Power of Myth. Mystic Fire Video, 1988.
Knowing. Icon, 2009.
Life. Columbia Pictures, 2017.
Lovecraft: Fear of the Unknown, 2008.
Mad Max: Fury Road. Roadshow, 2015.
The Man in the High Castle. Amazon Prime, 2015-19.
Mass Effect. Bioware, 2007.
Mass Effect 2. Bioware, 2010.
Mass Effect 3. Bioware, 2012.
The Matrix. Warner Brothers, 1999.
Matrix Reloaded. Warner Brothers, 2003.
Matrix Revolutions. Warner Brothers, 2003.
The Mothman Prophesies. Columbia Tristar, 2002.
El Orphanato. Roadshow, 2007.
Predestination. Pinnacle Films, 2014.
Prometheus. 20th Century Fox, 2012.
Resident Evil. Screen Gems, 2002.
Resident Evil: Apocalypse. Screen Gems, 2004.
Resident Evil: Extinction. Screen Gems, 2007.
Resident Evil: Afterlife. Screen Gems, 2010.
Resident Evil: Retribution. Screen Gems, 2012.
Resident Evil: The Final Chapter. Screen Gems, 2016.
Rise of the Planet of the Apes. 20th Century Fox, 2011.
The Road. Icon, 2009.
Screamers. Columbia TriStar, 1995.
Snowpiercer. CJ Entertainment, 2013.
Stalker. Shock, 1979.
Star Trek: First Contact. Paramount, 1996.

Star Trek: The Next Generation. Paramount, 1987-94.
Star Trek: Voyager. Paramount, 1995-2001.
Starship Troopers. Columbia Tri Star.
Sunshine. 20th Century Fox, 2007.
The Terminator. MGM, 1984.
Terminator 2: Judgment Day. Columbia Tristar, 1991.
Terminator 3: Rise of the Machines. Columbia Tristar, 2003.
Terminator Genisys. Paramount, 2015.
Terminator Salvation. Sony Pictures, 2009.
THX1138. Warner Brothers, 1971.
28 Days Later. 20th Century Fox, 2002.
28 Weeks Later. 20th Century Fox, 2007.
2012. Columbia Pictures, 2009.
What the Bleep!? Down the Rabbit Hole. Hopscotch Entertainment, 2006.
World War Z. Paramount, 2013.
The X Files. Twentieth Century Fox, 1993-2002.

Index

A–Z Guide of Science Fiction Literature, The (Stableford) 137, 226
Abraham, Lyndy 41
Absolute Benefactor ("Faith of Our Fathers") 63, 150-51, 155-56, 222-23
accident 21, 69, 172, 206-7, 220, 266-73, 275-77, 284, 288-89, 289n3, 297; of the deluge 264, 87; human as 163, 201, 206, 266, 269, 286
"Afterword: Lenin's Choice" (Žižek) 196, 255
alien 48, 62, 73, 81, 82, 90, 103, 122, 135, 203, 221, 233, 273, 278; as outsider 63, 79, 100
alien universe 79-86, 99, 111-12, 119, 183, 188
Alien (film) 264-65n3
Alien: Covenant (film) 264n3
Allhoff, Fritz 40n1, 53
"All You Zombies" (Heinlein) 16
amnesiac 89, 117, 197, 217
amnesia of the cosmos. See cosmos
Anaximander 40-41, 53, 109
Ancient Philosophy (Smith et al.) 40n1, 53
Ancient Track, The (Lovecraft) 86
Anderson, Kevin J. 146n9
android 37-38, 85, 98, 102, 131, 138-41, 143-44, 248, 261, 265n3; Nexus-6, 62, 140
Annotated Supernatural Horror in Literature, The (Lovecraft) 72, 75, 76, 77, 151

Anteac, Reverend Mother (*GED*) 46, 277
antediluvian 35, 56, 59-61, 61n7, 103, 111n5, 121, 123n8, 150 178, 216, 223, 231-32, 237, 239, 259-65, 268, 274-75, 287-90, 299; landscape, 35, 56, 60, 174, 219n4, 223, 261n17, 263-64, 275; mind/memory, 282, 287; others, 103, 163, 179, 220, 264n3, 287, 295; territory, 164, 202, 262, 289. See also Cyclopean
apocalypse 109, 122, 124, 128-29, 155, 170-76, 185-86, 195, 201, 202, 208, 214, 218, 220, 228, 233-34, 243-48, 259-60, 267-69, 272-73, 280, 288, 293, 298
Arctor, Bob (*SD*) 64-65, 100, 111, 112, 116-17, 119-20, 158, 159-60, 161, 188-89, 215-16, 281; as Fred, 100, 111, 116, 119-20, 160, 161, 188, 216; as Bruce, 111, 116-17, 160, 216, 281
Aristarchus 90
Arrakeen 162, 166n20, 167
Arrakis 135, 166n20, 167, 175, 184, 189, 294
ash 48, 89, 138, 178, 234, 241, 245-46, 248. See also ash
Asma, Stephen T. 88, 89, 132, 217
astronomy, ancient 40, 41, 177
Atreides, Alia 146; *DM*: 45, 84, 113-14, 119, 128, 219; *CD*: 84, 149-50, 187
Atreides, Ghanima 146; *CE*: 114, 183, 187, 221, 247-48, 271

325

Atreides, House 166n20, 277
Atreides, Lady Jessica: *D*: 93-95, 132-33, 162, 212, 218-20, 233, 277, 277n10, 281; *CD*: 247, 295, 298
Atreides, Duke Leto (*D*) 99, 184, 250, 250n14
Atreides, Leto II 14, 91-92, 146, 257, 259, 277; *DM*: 134; *CD*: 130, 145n8, 150, 160, 162, 167, 187, 210-11, 213, 214, 233, 246, 247, 258, 266, 271, 282, 287, 298; *GED*: 105, 145n8, 160-62, 166n20, 231, 239-41, 250, 254, 266, 277-78, 280, 282, 292, 297
Atreides, Moneo (*GED*) 240, 250, 266, 280
Atreides, Paul 14, 256-57, 294; *D*: 53, 80, 83, 87, 91-92, 99, 116, 132, 145-46, 161-62, 181-84, 209, 211, 212, 216, 218, 219-220, 227-28, 230, 231-33, 235-36, 246-47, 250, 257-58, 276, 281, 290-91; *DM*: 114, 116, 120, 135, 147, 148, 175-76, 231-34, 239, 241, 277, 287, 294-95, 299; *CD*: 130, 150, 221, 237, 237n4, 247
At the Mountains of Madness (Lovecraft) 9, 102, 111n5, 166n20, 225, 226, 230, 281
Azathoth (Lovecraft) 212, 212n1, 292-93

Babylon 39, 49, 58n4, 59n6, 123n8, 154, 203, 262
background 47, 81n2, 87, 111n5, 118, 120, 163, 169-70, 172, 191, 197n1, 211, 262, 264, 264n2, 270, 288, 289, 293, 296-97, 299
Bakhtin, Mikhail 208, 268
"Bakhtin, Blobels and Philip Dick" (Zoreda) 268
Baty, Roy and Irmgard (*DAD*) 98
Baudrillard, Jean 51n4, 180
Being and Nothingness (Sartre) 63, 64, 152, 202
Bene Gesserit 46, 83, 99, 135, 145-48, 160-61, 218, 220, 227-28, 231-32, 236, 239-40, 250, 257, 277, 290-91; testing box, 132, 183, 235-36, 250, 291, 291n4
Berkeley, George 129
"Beyond Lies the Wub" (Dick) 284-85
"Beyond the Wall of Sleep" (Lovecraft) 84
birth 102, 116, 134, 139, 185, 199, 208, 264n3, 278
black 56, 118, 154, 183, 222, 225; in landscape, 38, 59, 81, 90, 127, 155, 170, 176, 219, 223-24, 226, 261, 261n17; in space, 96, 107, 228-29; and white 50, 55, 66, 109-10, 110n4, 177, 238, 243
Blade Runner (film) 15
Blake, William 87n6
Bloom, Harold 87n6
Bloomsbury Guide to English Literature (Wynne-Davies) 137
Bohm, David 45, 299
Book of Eli, The (film) 124
Book of Enoch 58n4
Book of Giants from Qumran, The (Stuckenbruck) 58n4
"Book of the Machines, The" (Butler) 136-49, 158, 279
Book, The (Watts) 32-34, 37, 40, 44, 50, 55, 66, 86n5, 97, 108, 109-10, 110n4, 119, 125, 142n5, 163, 163n17, 199, 199n3, 238, 243, 297, 299
box 127, 174; of the Bene Gesserit, 132, 183, 235-36, 250, 291; of carceral universe, 222; Einstein's, 184; empathy, 120-21; *Hellraiser* puzzle, 132
Braidotti, Rosi 278n11
Bruno, Geordano 42
Bulero, Leo (*TSPE*) 37, 119, 151, 177-78, 236, 269
Burleson, Donald R. 77, 102, 151n10, 156, 186, 258, 263, 292
Butlerian Jihad 131-32, 131n1, 145-50, 145n8, 146n9, 250, 261, 276. *See also* jihad

"'Call Me a Protestant'" (List) 99, 198, 256

Index

"Call of Cthulhu, The" (Lovecraft) 42, 56, 60-61, 61n8, 73, 77, 84, 95, 102, 107, 166n20, 174, 219-20, 219n4, 240, 260-61, 264-65, 281
Cambridge Companion to Science Fiction, The (James-Mendlesohn) 10-11, 38, 137, 293-94
Campbell, John W. 10, 11
Campbell, Joseph 39-40, 55n2, 58n4, 62, 63, 79, 106n1, 123n8, 157n14
Capra, Fritjof 42, 46, 63, 199, 243
carceral universe 33, 33n1, 184-85, 187, 210, 221n5, 222, 233, 250
Carter, Lin 9, 10
Casimir, Viviane 221-222, 278-279
Cell, The (film) 290
Certeau, Michel de 34
chaos 21, 24, 32-33, 39, 53, 107-10, 118-19, 128, 133, 145, 149, 155-57, 157n14, 173-74, 185-86, 198-99, 204, 208, 219, 221, 225, 233, 235, 237, 239, 245, 251, 257, 260, 282-89, 291, 293, 295-99; as background, 289, 293; as kaleidoscopic, 109, 115, 126; universe of, 25, 32, 60, 72, 108, 113, 115, 119, 155, 171, 175, 179, 198, 222, 234, 248, 260, 271, 283, 285, 289, 291, 296-97; waters of, 175-76, 210, 234, 299
Chapterhouse Dune (Herbert) 48, 102
Chien, Tung ("Faith of Our Fathers") 63, 80-81, 83, 126-27, 150-51, 152, 155-56, 166, 222-23
Children of Dune (Herbert) 32, 53, 84, 113, 114, 121n6, 130, 145n8, 147, 149-50, 160, 162, 166n20, 167, 175, 183, 187, 189, 210-11, 213, 214, 221, 233, 235, 237, 246-48, 258, 266, 271, 277, 282, 287, 295, 298
Children of Men (film) 123
chimera 134, 265, 265n3, 266-67, 272-75, 278
Chronicles of Riddick, The (film) 86n4
Clute, John 80n1, 291
Colavito, Jason 10, 11, 13, 90, 170, 217

cold equations 21, 73, 92-104, 109, 125, 130-31, 140, 145, 159, 165, 171, 198, 200-206, 217, 220, 223, 229, 235, 241, 253-55, 272, 275, 283; and emotion, 94-95, 98-100, 205-6, 233, 235, 239, 252, 254, 268, 277, 277n10; and insignificance, 100; and the machine, 25, 99, 107, 109, 124, 140, 145, 171 247, 251, 262, 288; say "no," 93, 122, 122n7; of "on" and "off," 172; as order, 233, 239, 283, 286; and the proving ground, 217, 251; and romance of the universe, 205-6
"Cold Equations, The" (Godwin) 21, 38, 92-93, 95, 101-3, 238, 252
Coleman, J. A. 45
"Colour out of Space, The" (Lovecraft) 9, 77, 96, 102, 106, 166n20, 178
Collins, Andrew 46
"Considering the Sense of 'Fantasy' or 'Fantastic Fiction': An Effusion" (Suvin) 101, 252
consumption 103, 158, 167, 178, 207, 222, 249, 271-75, 284-85
contagion 72, 88, 156, 161-62, 165, 167, 206, 251, 270
Contagion (film) 124
Copernicus, Nicolaus 42, 79, 90, 106n1
Cornford, Francis M. 177
Corrino, Farad'n (CD) 113, 295
Corrino, House 237n4
Corrino, Princess Irulan (D) 31, 83, 87
Corrino, Shaddam IV, Padishah Emperor (D) 181-82, 257, 281
cosmic 7, 42, 45, 59n6, 87, 88, 91, 95, 108, 112, 128, 133-35, 142, 152, 156-57, 180, 261, 267, 273, 285, 292; definition of, 69-70; existence, 42, 69, 110; fear/horror/terror, 72, 75, 76, 88, 217, 224, 224n9; indifference, 13, 101, intelligence, 69, 151, 204-5, 295; in Lovecraft's philosophy, 7, 42, 72, 73, 75-76, 133, 156, 164
cosmicism: and the antediluvian, 56, 262, 264n3; and contagion, 156-57, 167, 264-65, 264n3, 270; as

critical framework, 11–13, 18, 24, 25, 69–78, 79–80, 132, 168, 195–97, 200–204; and darkness, 86–91; and deity, 152–57, 281–82; and emotion, 75, 99, 236–37, 236n3, 249, 255, 268; and engulfment, 129, 155, 172, 176–78, 190–91, 214, 217–20, 270–75; and fear, 75–77, 91, 148, 189, 208, 219, 225, 250, 257, 274, 291; and insignificance, 76, 80, 88, 105, 111, 116–17, 124, 103, 135–36, 142–43, 148, 155–59, 163, 208, 237, 245n10, 255, 288, 296; in Lovecraft's philosophy, 7–8, 12, 69, 71–78, 79, 81n2, 153, 191, 221, 259–60, 264n2, 297; and madness, 77, 99–100, 142, 158, 208, 214–15, 281, 284, 287; principles of, 18–19, 21–22, 151–53, 221–22, 228, 269; and the map, 33, 97, 106, 117–19, 225–26, 229–30; universe in, 42, 72–73, 79, 92, 100–101, 108–10, 124–25, 163–64, 186, 188, 206, 210, 236, 243, 247, 263, 283, 298

cosmism 69–70

cosmos 18–19, 21, 22, 23, 24, 25, 31–38, 45–52, 63, 65–66, 69–70, 81, 117–18, 122, 131, 217–219, 233–34, 242–43, 254, 258, 262, 290–92, 298; absent or dissolved, 60–61, 108, 117, 150, 156, 172, 173, 177–80, 213, 220–21, 242, 262; amnesia of 21, 49, 60, 84, 86–89, 105, 108, 112–13, 123, 126–29, 148, 158–59, 165, 170, 172, 179, 200, 202–9, 211, 237, 261, 273, 276, 287; as confinement, 115–16, 138–40, 158, 176–77, 182, 201, 210, 225–27, 231, 255–56, 276, 289; of light, 47, 55–57, 61, 83–84, 109, 112–13, 118–19, 121, 125–28, 135, 161, 170–73, 179, 190–91, 196–97, 205, 207, 228, 231, 239–40, 290; ordered 45, 53–54, 57, 60, 103–10, 113, 145, 149, 155, 171–72, 175, 199, 220, 228, 233, 235, 280; postdiluvian, 58, 81–82; as tele-objective, 145, 158–62, 182, 188, 218

Cosmos (Sagan) 87–90, 122, 152

Courage to Be, The (Tillich) 296–97

"Critique and Fantasy in Two Novels by Philip K. Dick" (Palmer) 160

Cthulhu 13, 95, 157, 174, 264n3

Cthulhu Mythos 226

Cyberculture, Cyborgs and Science Fiction (Haney) 278n11

Cyborg Citizen (Gray) 278n11

"Cyborg Manifesto, A" (Haraway) 278n11

Cyclopean 61n7, 224, 261, 261n17. *See also* antediluvian

"Dagon" (Lovecraft) 60–61, 78, 81 102, 130, 157, 166n20, 219, 219n4, 261, 265

Dalley, Stephanie 45, 54n1, 58n4

Dancing Wu Li Masters, The (Zukav) 33, 49, 50–51, 53, 63, 105, 107, 109, 184–85, 199, 215n3, 285, 286, 299

Danse Macabre (King) 98

dark (darkness) 86–91, 94, 97, 106–9, 117, 123, 135, 182, 188–91, 209, 210–15, 230–33, 276, 289, 291; of Creation, 43–44, 46; and fear, 76, 87, 89, 91, 125, 128, 183, 191; and landscape, 35–36, 49, 61, 129, 130, 155, 165, 168, 174, 219, 225–28, 261, 261n17; as ontological background, 118, 126, 170–71, 191, 197–98, 197n1, 197n2, 227, 233; of universe, 38, 46–47, 86–91, 96, 112, 119, 161, 172, 183, 213–14, 218, 243, 250, 256, 260, 262, 287, 290

Dark City: Director's Cut (film) 182n2

Darwin, Charles 64, 136, 137, 207

"Data and Dick's Deckard" (Casimir) 221–22, 278–79

Dawn of the Planet of the Apes (film) 124

Day After Tomorrow, The (film) 123

"Day Mr. Computer Fell Out of His Tree, The" (Dick) 180–81, 182

Index 329

"Days of Perky Pat, The" (Dick) 37, 48, 103-4, 124n10, 211, 240-41, 244, 247, 282, 288
Daybreakers (film) 124
death 47, 83, 84, 91, 96, 98, 99, 103, 110-11, 114, 116, 122n7, 132-33, 137, 145, 158, 163, 166n20, 174-75, 181-83, 185, 188-90, 202, 209, 212, 214, 218, 221, 229, 237n4, 247, 251-53, 255, 257, 263, 266, 268, 275, 278, 287, 292 ; god as, 155-56; of God, 64; and madness, 7, 19, 23, 24, 76-77, 84, 100, 103, 183, 190, 208, 210, 215-16, 225, 233, 262, 281
decay 35, 61, 86, 129, 133, 153-55, 167-68, 177-78, 182, 234, 248, 251, 264-65, 294, 288. See also mould
Deckard, Rick (*DAD*) 37-38, 51, 62, 80, 84-85, 87, 140-41, 143-44, 248-49
deity 14, 22, 24, 41, 46, 55, 62-66, 69, 72, 75, 77, 81, 89, 105, 151-57, 173, 198, 204-5, 221, 251, 273, 282, 288, 296-98
Deluge (Noachian) 22, 54-57, 58, 60, 123n8, 174, 175, 201, 219, 231, 287
deluge 54, 56n3, 165, 168, 174-76, 178, 179, 189, 216, 219-20, 219n4, 221, 222, 225, 228, 233, 251, 265; as accident, 264, 87; of threshold, 202, 209, 220, 231-32. See also flood
Derleth, August 163n16
Descartes, René 143
desert 48, 82, 134, 162, 167, 169-70, 175-76, 213, 214, 221, 233, 241, 246-49, 258, 266, 274-75, 294
devolution 144, 148-50, 161, 168, 176, 217, 245, 251, 252, 275. See also evolution
Dialogue concerning the Two Chief World Systems (Galilei) 43
Dick, Philip K. 7, 10, 13, 14-16, 143, 179-80, 244
Dictionary of Alchemical Imagery, A (Abraham) 41

Dictionary of Mythology, The (Coleman) 45
Discipline and Punish (Foucault) 184-85
Discourse on Method (Descartes) 143
DiTommaso, Lorenzo 148, 233, 251n15
Divided Self, The (Laing) 280, 283-84, 285, 289
Do Androids Dream of Electric Sheep? (Dick) 15, 48, 51, 62, 80, 84-88, 97-99, 102, 120, 124n9, 124n10, 131, 140-41, 143-44, 178, 244, 248-49, 261, 277n9; and Voigt-Kampff, 37, 51, 98, 132, 236, 236n3
Dramas, Fields, and Metaphors (Turner) 55n2
Dream Quest of H. P. Lovecraft, The (Schweitzer) 10, 76
"Dreams in the Witch House, The" (Lovecraft) 108
dry land 46, 47-48, 55, 56-57, 165-66, 165n20, 211, 220, 258
Dune (Herbert) 31, 53, 81, 83, 87, 91, 93, 99, 110, 116, 120, 121n6, 132, 133, 135, 145-46, 162, 166n20, 182-84, 209, 211, 212, 216-18, 220, 227-28, 230, 232-33, 235, 243, 246, 247, 250, 257, 275, 277, 281, 291
Dune (film) 17
Dune chronicles 17, 45, 114, 124n10, 132n1, 145, 146, 150, 166n20, 176, 181, 227, 247, 265, 277, 290
Dune Encyclopedia, The (McNelly) 45, 93, 132n1, 146n9, 181, 227, 237n4
Dune Messiah (Herbert) 45, 62, 113, 114, 116, 119, 120, 121n6, 128, 134-35, 145n8, 147-49, 166n20, 175-76, 219, 231-32, 234, 239-40, 241, 251, 266, 278, 287, 294-95, 299
Dunsany, Lord 156-57
"Dunwich Horror, The" (Lovecraft) 35, 96, 127n11, 134, 151, 157, 166n20, 167-68, 169, 273

dust 37, 48, 56, 71, 73, 80, 104, 134, 140, 142, 163, 178-79, 211, 234, 240-49. *See also* ash

Eagleton, Terry 11
Earth (planet) 31-32, 37-38, 47-48, 56, 60, 65, 85, 89-91, 96-106, 106n1, 109, 122, 124-25, 124n10, 133-36, 139, 151, 155, 157, 164, 165, 174, 177, 181, 1977n1, 211-13, 258, 263, 267; in Genesis, 43-46, 54-55, 54n1, 57, 299
Écrits: A Selection (Lacan) 188
Eden 46, 82, 87, 95, 104, 128, 129, 174, 182, 201, 210, 211, 217, 247, 262, 283, 288, 290
Einstein, Albert 31, 105, 106, 184-86
Eldritch, Palmer (*TSPE*) 37, 113-14, 151, 178-79, 236, 236n2, 269, 271, 274-75
"Electric Ant, The" (Dick) 129, 172-73, 229, 276
Elements of Computing Systems, The (Nisan & Schocken) 40
Elysium (film) 124
embodiment 21, 48, 49, 62, 79, 93, 170-79, 181, 183, 187-89, 198, 208, 212, 225-26, 229-31, 247-48, 260, 264-65, 268, 274-76, 278, 280, 284-86, 296
empathy 85, 97-100, 115-16, 120-21, 128, 140, 153, 203, 252, 255-56, 268-69, 282; and cold equations, 203-4, 206-7, 279, 283, 286, 289; empathic connection, 116, 143-44, 183, 188, 200, 247, 253, 266, 277n9, 294; and empathy box, 120-21; and Voigt-Kampf, 37-38
Encyclopaedia of the Qur'an (McAuliffe) 145n8
engulfment 19, 22, 23, 25, 84, 119, 129, 173-74, 177, 190, 195-96, 209, 216, 217-18, 233, 240, 251, 285; and deluge, 167, 174, 177, 216, 219, 219n4, 221, 222, 231-32, 265; of madness or death, 84; at threshold, 110, 128, 195; at the void, 208, 214, 225, 233

"Entering the Posthuman Collective in Philip K. Dick's *Do Androids Dream of Electric Sheep?*" (Galvan) 51
Epic of Creation, The 45, 53n1, 58n4
equations 39, 95, 104, 122-23, 126, 149, 162, 163, 186, 228, 253-54, 260, 279, 281, 297. *See also* cold equations
Erewhon (Butler) 136-37, 146
Ergang, Robert 42-43
Erisman, Fred 161
estrangement 47-49, 57, 62, 63, 77, 81, 85n3, 87, 89, 93, 100-101, 116, 125, 140-41, 175, 183, 186, 190-91, 203-4, 206, 236
Europe: From the Renaissance to Waterloo (Ergang) 42-43
Evans, Timothy H. 35, 71, 264n2, 293, 293n5, 297
"Evening Star" (Lovecraft) 86, 89, 91
Event Horizon (film) 89, 132
evolution 13, 137, 139, 149-50, 165, 196, 207-8, 234, 241-42, 267, 276; hidden foundation of, 207; of machine, 131, 137, 141, 144, 148; and *Prometheus*, 264n3; of universe, 72, 157, 160. *See also* devolution
eye (eyes) 60, 61n7, 81, 83, 86-87, 113-15, 121, 126, 168, 174, 176, 178-79, 184, 216, 223, 232, 240, 265, 281

Fabin, Jerry (*SD*) 158, 159, 161, 173
"Facts concerning the Late Arthur Jermyn and His Family" (Lovecraft) 275
"Faith of Our Fathers" (Dick) 63, 80, 81, 83, 107-8, 126-27, 150-51, 152, 155-56, 165n20, 166-67, 222-23
Fantasies of Robert A. Heinlein, The (Heinlein) 173, 180, 187
Farnell, David 223n7
Fedaykin 235, 237n4
"Festival, The" (Lovecraft) 154, 166n20, 273, 274
fight 55, 65-66, 110, 110n4, 115, 119, 122, 126, 130, 141, 149, 184,

Index 331

198, 200, 202, 220, 236, 245-46, 251, 257, 262
finitude 121-26, 142, 168, 199, 203, 208, 212, 218, 222, 226, 249-50, 251, 259, 262, 268, 298
flood 54, 56, 56n3, 123n8, 165, 175, 176, 177; flash 189. *See also* deluge
Ford, Slayton (MC) 82, 84, 184, 255
Foucault, Michel 184-85
foundation 19, 22, 39, 44, 49, 63, 77, 94, 97, 101, 103, 118, 134-35, 141, 145, 165, 167, 172, 176-77, 183, 189, 202, 217, 228, 231, 239, 247, 263-65, 275-77, 287; chaos as, 25, 53, 198, 285-86, 289, 295-97; cosmological, 22, 41-42, 115, 117, 118, 153, 180, 185, 262; ontological, 231-32, 283
Fremen 132-33, 165n20n, 167, 175-76, 189, 232, 233, 237n4, 241, 245, 247-48, 251, 275, 294
Freud, Sigmund 36, 57, 64, 89, 106, 129, 140n4, 239, 239n7, 287
From the Ashes of Angels (Collins) 46
"From Beyond" (Lovecraft) 62, 78, 84, 106, 111-12, 111n5, 114, 125-28, 226, 263, 276
"From Beyond: H. P. Lovecraft and the Place of Horror" (Kneale) 233-34
"From Microcosm to Macrocosm: The Growth of Lovecraft's Cosmic Vision" (Schultz) 76-77, 163-64, 191, 195
From Ritual to Theatre: The Human Seriousness of Play (Turner) 55n2
"Frontier Worlds of Robert A. Heinlein, The" (Samuelson) 239, 280
Frost, Robert 118, 152n12, 180
Fugate, Roni (*TSPE*) 178

Galilei, Galileo 43, 112
Galvan, Jill 51
game 55, 104, 109-11, 110n4, 126, 200, 243, 295
garden 83, 103, 127, 129, 160, 167, 182, 220, 250, 251, 258, 260. *See also* Eden

Gay Science, The (Nietzsche) 64, 153
Genesis (Book of) 22, 43-44, 46-47, 49, 54, 55, 57-58, 95, 123n8, 140, 164, 169, 175, 283
Genesis 1-11: A Commentary (Westermann) 43-44
Genesis Cosmology 18, 22, 43-49, 53-58, 53n1, 59-60, 62, 63, 64, 75, 77-78, 82, 84, 86, 95, 101, 105, 107, 109, 115, 123, 123n8, 125, 129, 131, 140, 149-51, 153, 164-66, 174, 175, 180, 182, 198, 203, 205, 210, 215, 219n4, 227, 250, 257, 262, 283, 287, 288, 296, 298, 299
ghola 113, 147-48, 232, 277-78
Giordano Bruno 42
God 43-58, 60, 63-64, 75, 78, 81, 85, 89, 95, 106n1, 107, 129, 140, 150-55, 172, 175, 177, 201, 203-05, 210, 279, 296-97; as death, 155-56; death of, 64
God Emperor 91, 160, 239, 266, 278. *See also* Atreides, Leto II
God Emperor of Dune (Herbert) 46, 91-92, 105, 145n8, 150, 160-61, 166n20, 167, 231, 237, 239, 240, 241, 250, 254, 266, 278, 280, 282, 287, 292, 294, 297
gods 17, 44, 45, 54n1, 127, 145n8, 149, 151-52, 156n14, 169, 177, 184n4, 200, 213, 272
Gods of Pegāna, The (Dunsany) 156n14
Godwin, Tom 21, 38, 92-93, 95, 101-3, 238, 252
"Golden Man, The" (Dick) 132, 236
Golden Path 150, 233, 282
Goodrick, Edward W. 59
Gray, Chris 278n11
great creatures of the sea 46, 56-59
Great Old Ones 56, 59-61, 102, 169, 226, 260-61, 264n3
Greenham, Ellen J. 187
grey 59, 175-80, 127n11, 181, 212, 222, 241, 243, 248, 274
Grey Ecology (Virilio) 24, 32, 81, 115, 123, 125, 144n7, 244, 256, 268-69, 289n3

Gribbin, John 47, 66, 78, 157, 228, 243
"Guest of Honor Speech at the Third World Science Fiction Convention Denver, 1941" (Heinlein) 80, 79-80, 250
"Guest of Honor Speech at the XIXth World Science Fiction Convention, Seattle, 1961: The Future Revisited" (Heinlein) 93, 95, 223

H. P. Lovecraft: A Look Behind the Cthulhu Mythos (Carter) 9, 10
H. P. Lovecraft: A Symposium (Leiber et.al.) 9, 163
H. P. Lovecraft: Against the World, Against Life (Houellebecq) 11-12, 74, 76, 93, 163, 168, 195, 238
"H. P. Lovecraft: The Hawthorne Influence" (Burleson) 151n10
"H. P. Lovecraft and the Semiotic Kantian Sublime" (Will) 58, 58n5, 183, 225
The H. P. Lovecraft Companion, The (Shreffler) 71
H. P. Lovecraft Encyclopedia, An (Joshi-Schultz) 61n8, 96n8, 154n13, 212n1, 219n4, 224, 294n6
H. P. Lovecraft in "The Eyrie" (Joshi-Michaud) 73, 171
Halleck, Gurney (D) 211
Hamilton, Edith 58n4
Haney, William S. 278n11
Haraway, Donna 278n11
Harkonnen, House 83, 161, 212, 277
Harkonnen, Feyd-Rautha (D) 243
Harkonnen, Vladimir, Baron (D) 110, 149, 162, 184, 241, 243, 257, 281
"Haunter of the Dark, The" (Lovecraft) 77, 96, 96n8, 102, 153-55, 166n20, 228-29
Hawat, Thufir (D) 93, 95, 110, 216, 277, 277n10
Hawthorne, Anne (TSPE) 65, 113
Hawthorne, Donna (SD) 99, 286, 292
Hawthorne, Nathaniel 77, 151, 151n10

heimlich 23, 25, 36, 66, 89, 108, 171, 189-90, 197n1, 198, 201, 202-03, 219, 224, 262, 272, 297-98; in "The Uncanny" 36, 57, 287; universe 231, 254, 287, 290, 297-98,
heimlich coin 66, 122, 150, 199-200, 238, 299
heimlich conundrum 23, 84, 116, 123, 134, 167, 190, 195, 197, 208, 214, 218, 224, 260
Heinlein, Robert A. 7, 13, 14, 16, 40, 79, 79n1, 93, 95, 161, 201, 202, 223, 239, 250, 282
Heinlein in Dimension: A Critical Analysis (Panshin) 239
Heisenberg, Werner Karl 111
"He 'Just Plain Liked Guns': Robert A. Heinlein and the 'Older Orthodoxy' of an Armed Citizenry" (McGiveron) 283
Hellraiser (film) 132
Hendricks, Major ("Second Variety") 241-42, 246-47, 249, 270
Herbert, Brian 146n9
Herbert, Frank 7, 13, 14, 16-17, 45, 48, 131, 146-47
Heretics of Dune (Herbert) 102
Herrick, Jill ("Human Is") 252-53, 254
Herrick, Lestor ("Human Is") 165, 189, 252-53
"History and Historical Effect in Frank Herbert's *Dune*" (DiTommaso) 148, 233
History of Magic, The (Seligmann) 39, 41
History of Western Philosophy (Russell) 41, 41n2, 53, 109
Holliday, Valerie 134, 244
Honoured Matres 102
"Horror at Red Hook, The" (Lovecraft) 166
Horror Literature: A Reader's Guide (Barron) 226
Houellebecq, Michel 11-12, 74, 76, 93, 163, 168, 195, 238
Howard Family (MC) 91, 121-22, 165n20, 181, 213-14, 255

"Human Is" (Dick) 165, 189, 252-53, 254, 258
"Hypnos" (Lovecraft) 124

I Am Legend (film) 123
Idaho, Duncan: D: 83, 277-78; DM: 113-14, 119, 121, 147, 232, 234; CD: 113-14, 149-50, 277; GED: 241, 278, 280
Ingebretsen, Edward J. 71, 75, 116, 118, 129, 152n11, 153, 169, 171, 172, 180, 184, 186-87, 197n2, 211, 221, 228, 230, 271, 272-73, 296
Inner Reaches of Outer Space, The (Campbell) 63, 106n1, 123n8, 157n14
In Search of the Multiverse (Gribbin) 47, 66, 78, 157, 228, 243
insect 40, 74, 157, 158, 159, 160-65, 162n15, 164nn18-19, 167, 173, 251, 256, 264, 270, 274, 295
insignificance 21, 23, 32, 69, 72-77, 91, 92, 96-97, 100, 105, 116, 121, 123, 126, 141, 148, 152-53, 156-65, 168, 170, 190, 199-201, 204-6, 210, 217, 222, 233-34, 237, 240-43, 245n10, 250-54, 260, 262, 264, 268-70, 280, 283, 286, 288, 292, 296
interface 269-71, 279, 280, 283, 286
Interstellar (film) 124
"In the Walls of Eryx" (Lovecraft-Sterling) 82, 94-95
"Introduction: Reading Science Fiction" (Mendlesohn) 38, 293, 294
invisible 18, 24, 71, 82, 94, 108, 110, 112-17, 126-28, 170, 172, 173, 201, 212, 218-19, 227, 232-34, 243-44, 246, 254, 270-71, 273, 286, 289, 291-92
Isidore, John (DAD) 86-88, 97-98, 120-21

Jameson, Fredric 253-54, 292
"James P. Crow" (Dick) 131, 139, 245, 261
jihad 116, 120, 135, 145n8, 166n20, 175-76, 233, 239, 251, 257-58. See also Butlerian Jihad

Jocasta's Children (Olivier) 290
Johnson, Captain ("Strange Eden") 82
"Jon's World" (Dick) 48, 124n10, 131, 138, 218, 223, 245
Joshi, S. T. 9, 10, 13, 61n8, 71, 73, 96n8, 154n13, 171, 212n1, 219n4, 224, 294n6
Jupiter (planet) 43

kaleidoscope 72, 106, 109, 115, 126, 118, 177, 200
King, Stephen 75, 93, 98, 214
kipple 178, 248
Kneale, James 233-34, 256n16
Knowing (film) 124
Knowing Fear (Colavito) 10, 11, 13, 90, 170, 217
Kocsis, Sacha 199
Kohlenberger, John R. 59
Korzybski, Alfred 79, 79n1, 202
Krutch, Joseph Wood 79, 81, 81n2, 126, 197
Kucera, Paul Q. 227-28
Kynes, Liet (D) 162, 246

Lacan, Jacques 128, 130, 187-88, 189, 231, 291, 292
Laing, R. D 118, 197n2, 280, 283-84, 285, 289
landscape 14, 21, 23, 33-38, 39, 43, 45-46, 47, 48, 53, 55, 58, 58n4, 64-65, 82, 86-87, 90-91, 100-103, 109, 125, 132, 136, 154, 156, 163, 165, 176, 203, 211-12, 217, 240-41, 247, 249, 261n17, 285, 293-95; antediluvian, 35, 56-60, 219n4, 275; crumbling or decaying, 35-36, 167, 177, 248; hidden or shadowed, 33, 56-57, 106, 171-72, 230; machines within, 136, 139, 140, 181, 241-42, 259, 270; mapped, 34, 52, 138; saturated, 35, 58-59, 61, 219-21, 233
"Last Defense against the Dark, A" (Evans) 35, 293, 297
"Landscapes, Selves and Others in Lovecraft" (Waugh) 171
Lee, Tanya. *See* Tanya

Legends of Dune I: The Butlerian Jihad (Herbert-Anderson) 146n9
Leiber, Fritz 9, 10, 163, 168
lethal proximity 170, 209, 234, 242, 247, 254, 262, 269
Leto II (GED) 14, 91-92, 105, 130, 134, 145n8, 146, 150, 160, 162, 166n20, 167, 187, 210-14, 231, 233, 237, 239-41, 246-47, 250, 254, 257-58, 259, 266, 271, 277-78, 280, 282, 287, 292, 297, 298
Leto, Duke (D) 99, 184, 250, 250n14
Letson, Russell 134, 217, 254, 256, 282, 288
leviathan 58n4, 59-60, 165, 212, 220. *See also* monster
Libby, Andrew Jackson (MC) 45, 107, 122-23, 159, 185-86
Life (film) 124
light: of cosmos 36, 83, 86, 109, 112, 117-18, 127, 161, 170-73, 178, 179, 182, 190, 196-97, 205, 209, 215, 231, 232, 287, 290; of Creation, 43-47, 49, 215; in landscape, 36, 86-92, 96, 104, 114, 117, 125, 158, 172, 174, 183, 190-91, 228, 234, 290; language of, 90, 91, 227, 231; in physics, 199; of sun, 47, 86-89, 103, 115, 118, 158, 167, 172, 182, 189, 191, 197n1, 214, 243, 287; twilight, 38, 59, 89, 170-71, 212; of universe, 46, 49, 86, 91, 92, 109, 115, 128, 134, 151, 165, 170, 197, 199, 209, 214, 218, 229, 262, 292; and the void, 225, 227, 230; and warmth, 47, 91, 172, 196, 225, 228
light space 86, 89-91, 161, 165, 170, 173, 183, 189-90, 197, 209, 214, 218, 287
List, Julia 99, 198, 256-57, 258
"Listening to Ourselves" (Kucera) 227-28
logic 22, 31, 53, 83, 93-94, 98, 137, 173, 277, 278
Long, Lazarus (MC, TEL) 14-15, 51, 82, 107, 122, 159, 160-61, 165n20, 181-82, 184-86, 213, 217, 232, 249, 254-55, 282, 288-89

Looking Awry (Žižek) 130, 131, 132, 153, 170, 202, 209, 227, 230, 235, 239, 242-43, 291, 298
Lovecraft, H. P. 7, 9-13, 21, 22, 48n3, 69, 71n2, 77, 82, 118, 132, 195, 224n7, 234, 258, 264, 264n2, 288, 293, 293n5, 294n6; on accident and insignificance, 69, 73, 74-75, 130, 133, 163, 200-201, 206, 266-67, 286; on everything ending, 74, 125, 133, 208; on fear, 72, 75-76, 191, 224n9; on deity, 69, 152-53, 152n12, 204-5, 221, 221n6; and Hawthorne, 77, 151-52, 151n10; on the human, 69, 71, 73-74, 76, 130, 133, 156-57, 163, 168, 171, 183, 200, 203-4, 206-7, 266-67; on the universe, 42, 70-73, 76, 92, 109, 125, 133, 151-52, 157, 171, 183, 186, 199, 201-5, 221, 221n6, 266, 295, 297-98
"Lovecraft's Concept of Background" (Mariconda) 81n2, 264, 264n2, 288
Luckhurst, Roger 10, 12, 244, 244n9, 289n3
Luft, Luba (DAD) 51, 62
"Lurking Fear, The" (Lovecraft) 78, 166n20, 174-75
Lyell, Charles 63-64

McAuliffe, Jane Dammen 145n8
McCarthy, Cormac 74n3, 124
McGiveron, Rafeeq O. 201, 283
Machen, Arthur 72, 101, 294, 294n6
machine 24, 31-32, 41-42, 66, 112-15, 125-26, 127n11, 139, 139n3, 142, 156, 172, 180-81, 229, 238, 244-45, 250, 259, 276-77, 285; and emotion/empathy, 63, 72-73, 85, 98, 131, 146n9, 278-79, 289; evolution of, 129, 131, 136-37, 138, 140-41, 144-50, 146n9, 241, 244-47, 259, 270; human in the, 158-63; language of, 40, 107; testing, 98-99, 132, 183, 235-37, 250, 291; thinking, 131-32, 139, 142-43, 142n6 145-50, 147n9, 261, 276. *See also* universe as machine

McNelly, Willis E. 45, 93, 132n1, 146n9, 181, 227, 237n4
Mad Max: Fury Road (film) 124
Man in the High Castle, The (TV show) 15
map 18, 23, 24, 25, 32-38, 40, 44, 50-53, 57-66, 73, 77, 82-86, 87, 97, 99-100, 103, 107, 109, 112, 117-19, 123, 129, 131, 138, 148, 155, 165-66, 172, 174, 180, 182n2, 183, 186, 197-200, 211, 223-26, 230-35, 251, 256, 271-72, 296. See also cosmos
Maps of Heaven, Maps of Hell (Ingebretsen) 71, 75, 116, 118, 129, 152n12, 153, 169, 171, 172, 180, 184, 186-87, 197n2, 211, 221, 228, 230, 271, 272-73, 296
Mariconda, Steven J. 81n2, 264, 264n2, 288
"Martians Come in Clouds" (Dick) 48, 102, 124n9, 165n20, 179, 258
"Masculinity in the Novels of Philip K. Dick" (Holliday) 134, 244
Masks of God, The (Campbell): 39, 40, 58n4, 62, 79
mathematician 42-43, 77, 143
Matrix, The (film) 139n3, 162, 182n2
Maturin, Charles Robert 75
"'Maybe the Hardest Job of All—Particularly When You Have No Talent for It'" (McGiveron) 201, 283
Mayerson, Barney (*TSPE*) 83, 113, 114-15, 119, 177, 274
Meaning of Relativity, The (Einstein) 31, 106
mechanism 25, 32, 39, 40, 42, 63, 72-74, 83, 106, 108, 120, 140, 160, 200, 221; as indifferent, 21, 69, 72-73, 92, 109, 111-13, 116, 131, 173, 180, 186, 243
Melmoth the Wanderer (Maturin) 75
Mendlesohn, Farah 38, 293-94
mentat 93, 99, 110, 147-50, 241, 277-78
Mercer, Wilbur (*DAD*) 84-85, 120
Merleau-Ponty, Maurice 117, 118, 169-70, 172, 211, 270, 275-76

"Messiah and the Greens, The" (Stratton) 294
Methuselah's Children (Heinlein) 45, 47, 51, 54, 82, 84, 91, 103, 107, 121-22, 124n9, 142, 159, 163, 165n20, 184-86, 213-14, 217, 255
Michaud, Marc A. 73, 171
"Mirror Stage as Formative of the Function of the I as Revealed in the Psychoanalytic Experience, The" (Lacan) 128, 187-88
Modern Temper, The (Krutch) 79, 81, 81n2, 126, 197
Mohiam, Reverend Mother (*D*) 145-47, 183, 227-28, 235, 290-91
monster 57, 59, 59n6, 88, 165, 191, 265. See also leviathan
moon 40, 46-47, 135, 219, 267, 295
"Moon-Bog, The" (Lovecraft) 78, 166n20
Mothman Prophesies, The (film) 157
Muad'Dib 146; *D*: 31, 83, 145n8; *DM*: 135, 149
mould 36, 56, 154, 163, 168, 177, 264, 265. See also decay
Munster, George ("Oh, to Be a Blobel!") 267-68
music 80, 108; of the spheres, 80-81, 107, 152; untuning, 80, 108
"Music of Erich Zann, The" (Lovecraft) 35, 171
Mythology (Hamilton) 58n4
Myths from Mesopotamia (Dalley) 45, 54n1, 58n4
My View of the World (Schrodinger) 297

NIV Exhaustive Concordance, The (Goodrick-Kohlenberger) 59
NIV Study Bible, The 57-58
Necronomicon (Lovecraft) 151n10, 154, 169
necosmicism: and the antediluvian, 56, 202, 216, 220, 223-24, 231-32, 239, 261-62, 263-65, 268, 274-75, 282, 287-91; and chaos, 198-99, 204, 210, 219, 221-22, 225, 234-37, 257, 271, 283-91,

295-99; and consumption, 207, 272-75, 284-85; and the cosmos, 99, 196, 199-201, 206-7, 210, 215, 220, 289; as critical framework, 7-8, 18-19, 23-24, 25, 32, 195-210, 221, 228, 237, 253, 297-98; and deity, 204-5, 251, 296-97; and emotion, 203-6, 244, 278-79; and engulfment, 195-96, 208-9, 214, 216-19, 221, 225, 231, 233, 240, 285; and the horizon, 197-98, 202, 209, 211-15, 220-24, 231-33, 249-50, 260, 270-71, 289-90, 298-99; and human insignificance, 200-201, 206-7, 259-60, 280, 283; and lethal proximity, 209, 234; and ontological stability, 197, 202, 264n3, 283-85, 288-91; and proving ground, 201, 209, 217, 222, 237, 239-41, 243, 249, 252, 259-60, 266, 281, 298; and psychosis, 250-51, 282, 289, 293-94, 298; and reinscription, 207, 256-59, 264-69, 264n3, 270-71, 275, 278-79, 290-91, 296-97; universe in, 73, 99, 195-96, 198-200, 201, 202, 205, 208, 210, 215-16, 222, 234, 236-37, 243-44, 247, 250-51, 254-55, 258-59, 268, 279, 280, 282-87, 289, 292, 294, 296-98; and the void, 216, 229-30, 247, 269, 282-83, 291, 297-98; and weeding, 204, 206-7, 220, 256, 257, 259
"Nemesis" (Lovecraft) 96n8
Newton, Sir Isaac 42, 43, 80, 105
Nickelsburg, George W. E. 58n4
Nietzsche, Friedrich 64, 214, 237, 248-49
Nisan, Noam 40
numbers 39-42, 69, 92-93; and mathematical cosmology, 123n8; and mathematics, 39-40, 41n2; numeric language, 122, 186; sheer weight of, 161

"Observing the Average Trajectories of Single Photons in a Two-Slit Interferometer" (Kocsis et al.) 199

ocean 25, 45-46, 53, 59, 72, 79, 90-91, 130, 135, 142, 152, 165-66, 179, 199, 211, 215, 219-20, 223, 225-26, 241, 265, 299
off (and on) 33-34, 36, 40, 50, 86n5, 88, 97, 107-8, 109-10, 118, 142n5, 147, 17 73, 180, 190, 238, 289
"Oh, to Be a Blobel!" (Dick) 128n12, 267-68
Old Ones. *See* Great Old Ones
Olivier, Christiane 290
Onions, C. T. 31, 56n3
"On Lovecraft's Themes: Touching the Glass" (Burleson) 77, 102, 156, 186, 258, 263, 292
On Monsters (Asma) 88, 89, 132, 217
"On the Cusp of Far" (Clute) 291
"On Which Planet?" (Shippey) 178, 180
Open Sky (Virilio) 169-70, 211, 213, 289, 298
Origin of Species, The (Darwin) 64, 207
Origins of Scientific Thought (Santillana) 41
Orwell, George 11
"Other Gods, The" (Lovecraft) 213
"Outsider, The" (Lovecraft) 36, 38, 166n20, 186-87, 189
Oxford Dictionary of Etymology, The (Onions) 31, 56n3
Oxford English Dictionary, The (Simpson-Weiner) 31-32, 39, 41, 53, 54, 56, 61n7, 69-70, 81, 85, 211, 218, 225, 229, 249n13

Palmer, Christopher 160
Panshin, Alexi 239
Pathways to Elfland (Schweitzer) 157, 157n14
Peaslee, Nathaniel Wingate ("The Shadow out of Time") 84, 88, 89-90, 92, 94, 102-3, 112-13, 117, 170, 226, 229, 238, 289
Phenomenology of Perception (Merleau-Ponty) 117, 118, 169-70, 172, 211, 270, 275-76
physicist 43, 45, 46, 49, 111, 185, 228

physics 13, 14, 32, 53, 107, 109, 199, 221, 224n9, 285-86. *See also* quantum physics
Physics and Philosophy (Heisenberg) 111
Piazza, L. 199
"Pickman's Model" (Lovecraft) 34-35, 36, 52, 84, 166n20
"Picture in the House, The" (Lovecraft) 166n20, 275
Pirsig, Robert M. 85n3
"plans within plans" 120-21, 121n6
Plato 177
Plato's Cosmology (Cornford) 177
Poe, Edgar Allan 71, 75, 293, 295
Poems of W. B. Yeats: A New Selection (Yeats) 65
"Poe's Landscape of the Soul" (St. Armand) 224n9, 293-94, 295
"Polaris" (Lovecraft) 39, 81
Poole, Garson ("The Electric Ant") 129, 172-73, 229-30, 276
Portable Nietzsche, The (Nietzsche) 64
postdiluvian 56-60, 174, 232
Posthuman, The (Braidotti) 278n11
postmodern 35, 51n4
Practice of Everyday Life, The (Certeau) 34
Predestination (film) 16
Principles of Geology (Lyell) 63-64
Pris (*DAD*) 97-98
prison 181, 184, 187, 200, 210, 217
Prometheus (film) 264n3
proving ground 24, 25, 201, 204, 207, 210, 217, 233, 236, 239-42, 245-54, 257, 259, 262, 263, 266, 269-70, 274-75, 277, 282, 283-84, 289, 291, 294, 298, 299
psychic 165, 186, 252, 292
psychoanalyst (analysis) 36, 64, 128, 130, 290-91, 292
psychosis 181, 188, 215-16, 250, 289; life in, 292
psychotic 181, 235, 242, 291
psychotic universe 24, 25, 202, 207-8, 235-62, 271, 275, 277, 282-83, 286, 289-90, 298-99

quantum physics 8, 14, 32, 33, 45, 78, 79, 109, 199, 215n3, 224n9

Rabelais and His World (Bakhtin) 208
Rabkin, Eric S. 137, 285, 286
rainbow 55, 175, 176-77, 218, 232
"Rats in the Wall, The" (Lovecraft) 77, 166n20, 284
reinscribe 23, 207, 230, 232, 254, 296
Resident Evil (films 1-6) 124
"Returns of Lazarus Long, The" (Letson) 134, 217, 254, 256, 282, 288
revelation 23, 36, 65, 84, 108, 112-15, 121-27, 139, 140, 152, 154-56, 158, 163-66, 172-73, 176, 180, 183, 185, 190, 196-97, 209, 214, 220, 223, 226, 230-34, 241, 251, 253, 259, 261, 269-70, 281, 293, 295, 297. *See also* apocalypse
Revelation, Book of 55
Revolution at the Gates (Žižek) 196, 198, 255
Rexor ("Human Is") 165, 189, 253
Rexorians ("Human Is") 165, 189, 152-53, 258
Rise of the Planet of the Apes (film) 124
Road, The (McCarthy) 74n3, 124
Road, The (film) 124
Roadside Picnic (Strugatsky-Strugatsky) 263, 283, 295
"Robert Heinlein, the Scribner Juveniles, and Cultural Literacy" (Erisman) 161
romance of the universe 24, 205, 293-96
Romantic Poetry and Prose (Bloom-Trilling) 87n6
Roots of Horror in the Fiction of H. P. Lovecraft, The (St. Armand) 224n9
Rosen, Rachael (*DAD*) 37, 98-99, 143
Russ, Joanna 118, 190
Russell, Bertrand 41, 41n2, 53, 109

Sagan, Carl 87-90, 122, 152
St. Armand, Barton Levi 224n9, 293-94, 295
Salusa Secundus. *See* Secundus
Samuelson, David N. 239, 280
sand 162, 176, 179, 233, 241, 249

sandtrout, 266
sandworm 212, 220, 233, 266; Shai-Hulud, 266
Santillana, Georgio de 41
Sardaukar 83, 181-82, 237n4, 251
Sartre, Jean-Paul 64, 152, 202
Saturn (planet) 267
Scanner Darkly, A (Dick) 64-65, 79, 99-100, 111-12, 116-17, 119-20, 158-60, 173, 188-89, 215-16, 281, 286
shadow 47, 56, 57, 63, 85, 107, 112, 114, 125, 170-72, 177, 179, 217, 225, 230, 232, 237, 243, 247, 296 removal of, 230, 233-34, 239, 242, 247, 269
Schein, Timothy ("The Days of Perky Pat") 240-41, 247, 282, 288
Schellinger, Paul E. 190
schizophrenic 85, 98, 100, 103, 118-19, 183, 250; landscape, 86, 97; universe, 24, 79-104, 85, 107, 117
Schocken, Schimon 40
Scholes, Robert 137, 285, 286
Schrödinger, Erwin 297
Schultz, David E. 61n8, 76-77, 96n8, 154n13, 163-64, 191, 195, 212n1, 219n4, 224, 294n6
Schweitzer, Darrell 10, 76, 157, 157n14
Science Fiction (Luckhurst) 10, 12, 244, 244n9, 289n3
Science Fiction: History, Science, Vision (Scholes-Rabkin) 137, 285, 286
"Science versus Ideology" (Jameson) 253-54, 292
Screamers (film) 16, 246
sea 35, 56, 59-60, 136, 154, 166n20, 175-77, 215, 224, 261n17, 274; creatures of, 46, 56-59, 59n6, 164; universe as, 73, 75, 156, 234, 299. *See also* ocean
"Second Variety" (Dick) 16, 48, 124n10, 131, 132, 138, 144-45, 178, 241-42, 244, 246-47, 249, 259, 261, 270, 276n8
Secundus 181-82
Selected Letters (Lovecraft) 42, 69-75, 109, 125, 130, 133, 152, 156, 157, 163, 195, 199, 200, 201-8, 221, 221n6, 266-67, 286, 288, 294n6, 295, 298
Seligmann, Kurt 39, 41
"Shadow out of Time, The" (Lovecraft) 9, 48, 84, 88-89, 92, 94, 102-3, 112-13, 117, 135-36, 142, 163, 166n20, 170, 226, 237-38, 241, 261n17, 271-72, 289
"Shadow over Innsmouth, The" (Lovecraft) 35, 102, 154, 154n13, 166-67, 218, 219n4, 223-24, 262, 263-65, 273-74
Shippey, Tom 178, 180
Shreffler, Philip A. 71
silence 33, 44, 50, 59, 69, 86-92, 86n5, 97, 107-8, 116-17, 127, 133, 179, 173, 179, 197, 226-28, 233, 235, 246, 252-53, 256
"Simulacra and Simulations" (Baudrillard) 51n4
"Simultaneous Observation of the Quantization and the Interference Pattern of a Plasmonic Near-Field" (Piazza et al.) 199
Simpson, J. A. 31-32, 39, 41, 53, 54, 56, 61n7, 69-70, 81, 85, 211, 218, 225, 229, 249n13
Simulations (Baudrillard) 51n4
skin 237, 266, 270, 275
Smith, Nicholas 40n1, 41n1, 53
Snowpiercer (film) 124
spice 80, 114, 266
spiceblow 235
Stableford, Brian 137, 226
star (stars) 14, 40, 42, 46-47, 56, 60, 65, 71, 74, 76, 81, 86, 88, 89, 90-91, 107, 115, 116, 122, 135, 141, 152n12, 156, 199-200, 208, 219, 228, 243-44, 269
Starship Troopers (Heinlein) 16
Starship Troopers (film) 16
Star Trek (TV show) 141
Star Trek: First Contact (film) 141
Star Trek: The Next Generation (film) 141
Star Trek: Voyager (film) 141
Stilgar: D: 233, 281; CD: 167, 175, 189

"Strange Eden" (Dick) 82
Stranger in a Strange Land (Heinlein) 16, 198
Stratton, Susan 294
Strugatsky, Arkady and Boris 263, 283, 295
Stuckenbruck, Loren T. 58n4
Subtler Magick, A (Joshi) 9, 10, 71
Sumer 39, 40, 41, 45, 53, 53n1, 58n4
sun 40, 46-47, 60-61, 74, 86-91, 96, 99, 103, 106n1, 109, 115, 118, 134, 156, 158, 164-65, 167, 170-82, 189, 197n1, 207, 208, 214, 218, 228, 239, 243, 261-62, 287, 290
Sunshine (film) 123, 197n1
supernatural 76, 93, 101
Suvin, Darko 101, 252
swarm 34, 54, 155, 159, 161, 162, 162n15

tabula rasa 229-31, 242, 253, 254, 258, 269, 277, 281, 296, 298-99
Tanya ("Faith of Our Fathers") 80-81, 108, 152, 166, 167, 222-23
Tao of Physics, The (Capra) 42, 46, 63, 199, 243
Tasso ("Second Variety") 242, 259
tele-objectivity 24, 115-16, 117, 126, 131, 140, 143, 145, 149, 151, 158-62, 177, 182, 188, 190, 198, 200-201, 203, 218, 222, 227, 235, 268, 272, 281, 284-85
"Temple, The" (Lovecraft) 61, 77, 166n20, 218, 223-24
Terminator, The (film) 142n6, 246
Terminator 2: Judgment Day (film) 142n6
Terminator Salvation (film) 143n6, 246
territory 7, 18, 23, 24, 25, 33-38, 45, 49-52, 53, 57, 62, 65-66, 79, 81-89, 97-100, 103, 107, 109-10, 118-19, 126, 128-29, 131, 138-39, 148, 155, 163-68, 171-74, 182, 186, 197-202, 199n3, 211-12, 215, 219, 225, 230-31, 233-34, 241, 248, 261, 264, 272-73, 287, 289, 298-99. *See also* universe
test 24, 25, 98, 133, 145n8, 147, 201, 210, 216, 236-37, 240, 252, 256, 266, 281, 287; testing box, 99, 132, 183, 235-36, 250, 291, 291n4, 250; of science, 74, 207; Voigt-Kampff, 37-38, 51, 98 132, 236, 236n3
"They" (Heinlein) 173, 180, 187
"Thing on the Doorstep, The" (Lovecraft) 78, 229, 271
thinking machine. *See* machine
Three Dialogues Between Hylas and Philonous (Berkeley) 129
Three Stigmata of Palmer Eldritch, The (Dick) 37, 48, 63, 65, 83, 102-4, 108, 113-15, 119, 124n9, 151, 177-79, 190, 211, 236, 236n2, 267, 269, 271, 274-75
threshold 24-25, 55-64, 55n2, 77, 85, 89, 112, 114, 116, 119, 125-29, 142-43, 155, 165, 168, 169-91, 195-96, 197, 202, 210-20, 225-26, 231, 236, 247, 270-71
Thus Spoke Zarathustra (Nietzsche) 64
Tillich, Paul 296-97
time-binding 79-80, 80n1, 159, 202
Time Enough for Love (Heinlein) 40, 51, 107, 121, 160-61, 162-63, 165n20, 181, 182, 185, 217-18, 226, 232, 249, 254-56, 282, 288-89
Titan (moon) 267
Tleilaxu 113, 121, 147, 148, 175, 232, 278
"To Serve the Master" (Dick) 48, 124n10, 131, 137-39, 143, 244-46, 261
"Tradition and Illusion" (Evans) 71, 264n2, 293n5
trap 94, 135, 172-73, 182-84, 187, 189, 246, 247, 250-51; universe as, 129, 153, 180-91, 250
Trilling, Lionel 87n6
"Trouble with Bubbles, The" (Dick) 97-98, 124-25
"Truth Is Consequence" (Clute) 80n1
Tunnel in the Sky (Heinlein) 280, 283
Turner, Victor 55n2
Twentieth-Century Science Fiction Writers (Watson-Schellinger) 190
28 Days Later (film) 123

28 Weeks Later (film) 124
2012 (film) 124
"Two Essays" (Baudrillard) 180

"Uncanny, The" (Freud) 36, 57, 89, 106, 129, 140n4, 239n7, 287
universe: as alien, 79–86, 99, 111–12, 119, 183, 188; as carceral, 33, 184–85, 187, 210, 221n5, 222, 233, 250; as chaos, 25, 32, 60, 72, 108, 113, 115, 119, 155, 171, 175, 179, 198, 222, 234, 248, 260, 271, 283, 285, 289, 291, 296–98; as dark, 38, 46–47, 86–91, 96, 112, 119, 161, 172, 183, 213–14, 218, 243, 250, 256, 260, 262, 287, 290; as engulfing, 19, 99, 119, 174, 176, 195–96, 214, 217, 221, 251, 285, 289; evolution of, 72, 157, 160; as heimlich, 231, 254, 287, 290, 297–98; as indifferent, 13, 41, 77, 94–96, 100–101, 107, 111, 116, 119, 131, 151n10, 156, 188, 190, 198, 200–204, 222, 235, 237, 283, 292; as kaleidoscopic, 72, 106, 109, 115, 200; as psychotic, 24, 25, 202, 207–8, 235–62, 271, 275, 277, 282–83, 286, 289–90, 298–99; as schizophrenic, 24, 79–104, 85, 107, 117; as trap, 129, 153, 180–91, 250. *See also* territory
universe as machine 18, 25, 31, 39–43, 53, 62, 66, 77, 79, 83, 84, 92, 105, 107–8, 120, 123–24, 131–32, 141–42, 150, 155, 171, 180, 182, 198, 203, 227, 251, 262, 288, 298
"Unlikely Utopians" (Farnell) 223n7
"Unnamable, The" (Lovecraft) 77

Vaidya, Anand Jayprakash 40n1, 53
VanderKam, James C. 58n4
Venus (planet) 94
Virilio, Paul 24, 32, 81, 115, 123, 125, 144n7, 169–70, 211, 213, 244, 256, 268–69, 289, 289n3, 298
vision 36, 38, 63, 89, 106, 107, 113–14, 121n6, 126–28, 129, 134–35, 157, 161–62, 175–76, 179, 183, 190, 195, 204–5, 212–16, 218, 221–22, 230–31, 232, 246, 256–57, 259, 266, 273, 287, 289, 293–94, 297. *See also* eye
"Vision and Desire" (Greenham) 187
vitalised 19, 25, 237, 240, 249, 261, 266, 298
vitalised materialism 25, 298
vitality 90, 143, 173, 233, 245, 248, 259, 261, 266, 296
vitality struggle 175, 182, 233, 245, 251, 251n15, 262
voice 44, 87, 120, 128, 164n19, 227–28, 290, 292
void 25, 53, 69, 90, 97, 118–19, 121, 128, 155, 183, 186, 188, 190, 195, 198, 208–9, 211, 214–16, 218–19, 223, 225–33, 236, 243, 247, 256, 260, 269, 277, 281–82, 291, 296–99
Voigt-Kampf 37, 51, 98, 132, 236, 236n3

War of the Worlds, The (Wells) 162n15
water 35–36, 41–50, 53–61, 95, 106, 110, 129, 134–35, 162–68, 174–78, 182, 189, 191, 210, 216, 220–24, 231–33, 241, 245, 247, 249–66, 264n3, 275
Watts, Alan 32–34, 37, 40, 44, 50, 55, 66, 86n5, 97, 108, 109–10, 119, 125, 142n5, 163, 199, 238, 243, 297, 299
Waugh, Robert H. 171
weeding 204, 207–8, 210, 220, 239, 241, 251, 256–60; weeds, 137, 260
Weiner, E. S. C. 31–32, 39, 41, 53, 54, 56, 61n7, 69–70, 81, 85, 211, 218, 225, 229, 249n13
Wells, H. G. 162n15
Westermann, Claus 43–44
What Is Posthumanism? (Wolfe) 278n11
"Whisperer in Darkness, The" (Lovecraft) 52, 57, 77, 88–89, 96, 105, 142, 164–65, 166n20, 167–68, 237–38, 246n11, 252
white 50, 55, 66, 109–10, 110n4, 177, 243, 249; of Earth, 152; and

heimlich coin, 238; in *Dune*, 243; in Lovecraft, 91, 154, 225, 275
"White Ship, The" (Lovecraft) 59
Wholeness and the Implicate Order (Bohm) 45, 299
Will, Bradley 58, 58n5, 183, 225
Will to Power, The (Nietzsche) 64, 214, 217, 237, 248-49
Wolfe, Cary 278n11
womb 44-46, 187
World War Z (film) 124
worm 35, 167, 264, 264n3, 266
Wynne-Davies, Marion 137

X Files, The (TV show) 207-8

Yeats, W. B. 65

Zen and the Art of Motorcycle Maintenance (Pirsig) 85n3
Žižek, Slavoj 130, 131, 132, 153, 170, 196, 198, 202, 209, 227, 230, 235, 239, 242, 243n8, 255, 286, 291, 298
Zoreda, M. L. 268
Zukav, Gary 33, 49, 50-51, 53, 63, 105, 107, 109, 184-85, 199, 215n3, 285, 286, 299

www.ingramcontent.com/pod-product-compliance
Lightning Source LLC
Chambersburg PA
CBHW060108170426
43198CB00010B/820